UNTOLD STORIES
&
UNKNOWN SAINTS

MICHAEL WELLS

Abiding Life Press

© 2008 by Michael Wells
Published by Abiding Life Press
A division of Abiding Life Ministries International
P.O. Box 620998, Littleton, CO 80162

Printed in the United States of America

Library of Congress Cataloging-in-Publication Data
Wells, Michael, 1952-
Untold Stories & Unknown Saints/Michael Wells
p. cm.
ISBN 0-9670843-7-7
1. Christian Life—1960—2. Presence of God. I. Title.
    BV4501.2.W41818   1993   93-31241
    BV4501.2.W4182   1991   90-49987 CIP
    248.4—dc20

Scripture quotations are from the New American Standard Bible, © the Lockman Foundation 1960, 1962, 1963, 1968, 1971, 1972, 1973, 1975, 1977. New International Version®. NIV®. Copyright© 1973, 1978, 1984, 1985 by International Bible Society. Used by permission of Zondervan Publishing House. All rights reserved.

Untold Stories
&
Unknown Saints

To the GOD of the unknown saints,
those who are known intimately by HIM.

CONTENTS

Preface

"And opening his mouth, Peter said: 'I most certainly understand now that God is not one to show partiality, but in every nation the man who fears Him and does what is right, is welcome to Him'"—Acts 10:34, 35.

Over the past two decades I have had the privilege of traveling to many countries around the world to spend time encouraging Christians through teaching and preaching. At the same time, there have been very many Christians in these countries who have more than encouraged me in my walk with Christ and my faith. These believers have touched me deeply with their accounts of ways the Lord has interjected a powerful work, a timely message, or significant meaning into their lives. Their stories are in some ways inconsequential in impact, because these believers may well never leave their own village or city; their sphere of influence is relatively negligible; and the believers know that their stories are not spectacular, but are the doing of a spectacular God. Some of the stories are very short, nearly just a thought, and some involve years and years of the Lord's persevering love to change a life. However, when taken together, no matter how small a work the Lord did or how grandiose, the stories teem with Holy-Spirit goodness that lights up the reader's mind and heart with praise and thanksgiving for all He does, for

i

never neglecting even the least of all believers, for giving strength to witness to His might and beauty despite the danger involved, and for revealing His glory in ways never anticipated, but which give cause for great joy. Of necessity, some of the experiences must be narrated from the point of view of my involvement as I traveled, and some of my thoughts and teachings remain intact in the accounts, but for the most part, I am truly only the messenger as I relate these true tales I have heard from many over the years. You, the reader, will never know the names of the believers, and for the safety of those who live in hostile regions, I have kept the location of their homes very vague or nondescript. Nevertheless, I hope we can all rejoice together with them in heaven, when these works and so many countless more will be revealed to all.

During my travels I encountered firsthand reports of the sin of atrocities committed toward people by warring soldiers or government heads, and while these are interesting in reminding us of the sober realities of man's inhumanity toward his fellow man and Satan's hideous nature, I only rarely included long and gross descriptions of those in this book in order not to distract the reader from his focus on Christ.

John said that were all of the sayings and doings of Jesus on earth written down, all of the books in the world could not contain them. If we multiply what Jesus has directly accomplished through the activity of His Holy Spirit since that time, we must ponder an unfathomable body of material. As you read, I hope you will consider that all of the saints mentioned are a mere fraction of those this one man has met in a relatively short time of his life. Just imagine all of the mighty and countless things the Lord does every single day that the earth is allowed to continue spinning on its axis!

Those of you who are familiar with my materials will recognize that many bits of wisdom out of the mouth of these believers have found their way into the truths of God that I teach. My position on knowledge dispensed has not changed over the years. I always encourage people to take our material, copy it, and use it. If they use any of my illustrations in a presentation, I do not want them to say, "Mike says it," but just say it. After all, God is the source of every inspirational, beneficial speck of knowledge man has. If He gives revelation to a believer through teaching, the revelation itself equips the listener (or reader) to claim the information as his own; the Lord has made it a part of the recipient. One man told me that he felt wrong in preaching another's material. Well, I do not, and neither do I lay claim to being original in what I say. I hope it is not original. This brings an interesting question (a question beyond the fact that there is nothing new under the sun, as well as the fact that Paul himself was not laying claim to being original). If a man preached an innovative sermon and the Holy Spirit touched people in power, was it original? If a man preached another's sermon and the power of the Spirit moved, does the sermon make the Spirit move, or does the Spirit give power to the words? Which is greater, the words or the Spirit? Therefore, I would rather preach another's sermon and see the Spirit move than voice a so-called original sermon and see no such movement. The Spirit is the real issue, and He is the source of words no matter which man uttered them. If you hear something that ministers to you, pass it along, trusting the Spirit to minister to others.

Many years ago the Lord spoke to me, saying, "You are losing your citizenship!" I knew what He meant. I could not function properly in this international ministry as an American; I had to see myself as belonging to the Kingdom of God and to the believers with whom I would minister in over a hundred countries. That is not to say that I do not love America. I just will not allow myself to be sidetracked into a discussion of America's foreign policy. Most of us in America have no clue as to exactly what that policy is or what drives it, and we probably would not even agree with it were we to find out. That admission does not readily excuse me from countless discussions I have had with citizens of other countries, even though I attempt to avoid such debates; however, often the topic of America's shortcomings is of paramount interest to others. I try to remember that government's job is to make us proud and defensive of our own country. You will find in the text of the book that at times I candidly discuss problems I see in America or in other countries, so I am obviously not immune to musing over such topics. I will not seem "culturally relevant" or "politically correct" to some readers, but I am not seeking to engender further discussion on any of the topics, but merely further pondering.

One purpose of this book, it seems to me, is furthering the personification of the notion of a "foreigner" that can arise after many years of hearing or reading reports from around the world. I think of the word "them" in the "us and them" mentality. For instance, what if I were to ask an American,

Western European, Australian, or South American what the Russians are like? The answer might come all too quickly: "They are vicious, stupid, tactless people." But I think of my Russian translator; he would lay down his life for me. He loves the Lord. What are men from India like? "They are arrogant, aggressive, manipulating businessmen, hard to trust." But I think of my gentle, loving teacher and the time we were falsely accused of being spies; he helped me despite the great personal cost officials extracted from him. What are the Africans like? "They steal, do not tell the truth, and have a high rate of AIDS due to immorality." But I think of one pastor's big smile and of how despite the great needs in his church, when the people heard my mother was dying, the whole place erupted in prayer for me; and I remember how they reached deeply into their own poverty and gave me five hundred dollars just to bless me. The list goes on and on. I am happy that God does not see us as "them." We are individuals, and He deals with each one, not ashamed to cast His lot with any of us. I, too, want to deal with each one as an individual, and if I maintain the attitude of the "one," I will not be led astray by the generalization of "them." A Latvian proverb says that a short post buried in the road will tip the whole wagon. The wagon of prejudice or hatred can be tipped by one post in the form of a person who understands how to abide in God's love and moves away from seeing "them" as each "one." In an overseas airport I met a New Yorker who quite comically explained all that he knew of the world according to him. He said, "Listen, we must bomb every country where the people wear their laundry on their heads." I just thought how I would like to take that man to Iran and have him stay with the believers there or even with a workingman, the man whose worries are the same as his. After one week, he would no longer feel that way. It is very easy to lose focus on sharing the possibility of "Christ in you, the hope of glory." The reader will encounter bouts of my own loss of focus in this book when I am overcome with despondency over "the world according to Mike."

Another point to this book involves fertilizing the mind and spirit with knowledge of believers far and wide to facilitate a growing awareness and discernment of the Body, because the family of God comprises many folks who do not look like us or live like we do. One man said that the proof of God was the wondrous working of the thumb, its location and how it operates. God puts each one of us together physically. The more a person understands his body, the greater can be his revelation into THE Body. We have an unpresentable member in the physical body, which in our estimation is considered unseemly and rarely discussed. However, not only is its function ordained by God, but amazingly, He assigned to this member the perpetuation of His ongoing creation. Are we correct when we assess what is seemly and unseemly? God puts more abundant honor on the members that in worldly terms seemed to lack it. One day we discover that we are the less honorable members. "I thought it was you, and I find out it was I!" When a young man falls in love and presents a photo of his sweetheart, what does it show? The face, of course! He does not show an x-ray of the kidneys: "These are the lovely kidneys of my girlfriend." However, were her kidneys not working, the young lady would not be presentable. The point is to see more and more that what we do is an end result of the Lord's work through others. For instance, look at how many things had to come together for me to speak at one prison. I had to meet the interpreter who invited me, and the

Lord had to give him a love for the message. The interpreter needed to know the old man who is the key chaplain in the prison. The old man needed to work for years with the prisons for them to allow an American in to speak. The facilitator had to know both men AND be at a place where he would take a risk on someone he did not know. We all had to have jobs and the finances that allowed us to be together at the exact time, but even all of that is for nothing but for the fact that a prison guard heard the old man preaching and became excited about the old man and his God. It is the guard that ultimately got the clearance to get us in. Someone had to have invented the airplane, cars, e-mail, and more to get us here. I must stop for I am going mad! Do you see why I believe I am the less honorable member? The Scripture says to "grieve not the Holy Spirit." Falling out with those on whom I am so dependent is just wrong. When we fall out with another member of the Body, one for whom Jesus shed his blood, that grieves the Spirit. There is no forgiveness for an unforgiving heart; when we see its seriousness we will break and cry. Forgiveness is serious; judgment begins with the house of God. When Judgment begins, where will God start? With us, with our judgments wherein we believed we were right and others were wrong. Every time we judge a person, we are guilty of lacking forgiveness, yet the Church blindly goes on its way.

I was listening to a former astronaut talking about his bravery and all that he had accomplished. He was a hero! I wondered to myself how he could see himself as such a great hero when it was a monkey sent up before him! It has been proven that a monkey could do his job! Could he not see that it was not what he did but the efforts of a multitude of other people that put him there and brought him back safely? Then God spoke to me, saying, "Michael, you are My monkey! I worked through so many people to set you in the place you are. It is not you, it is Me." I could see it. The believers organizing my speaking engagements did all the work, prayed with the people, shared with them, gave of their life, and I only went to stand on their work, His work through them. I am only God's monkey! Again I was reminded that without the supporters who go to work each day, pray for Betty and me, hold us up, and encourage and love us, I would not be here. I do not mind being a monkey, but the fact is that I am God's monkey.

I wrote the following while on one of my early trips: "I was handed the two-page schedule of speaking for the duration of my time here, and I knew without a doubt that this trip would be like all of my trips: that though this island is known for giant butterflies, caves the size of cathedrals, and miniature owls, I would not be seeing them. I knew that the greatness of the oppression and opposition that I had experienced for months prior to my departure would not equal the far greater blessings that would come from the time here. I am once again surrounded by people with thick accents, of various colors, and in assorted dress. I am surrounded by the family of God that is so diverse, so beautiful, so welcoming, and so much like all other believers in every other place. I surely love this great family to which we all belong . . . At the front of the church the young women dance with fluid hand and body movements in white silk dresses with gold-embroidered vests. The damp air of a jungle climate envelops the room. For one brief moment I have the feeling of isolation, and yet there is a deeper, overriding feeling that I am with my family, not strangers. I actually am comfortable here in the Body of Christ. There is the assurance that I am connected to something with deep roots. I could be in a meeting nearly two thousand years ago and it would be the same as this room, filled with people just like these, with the same struggles at work, in relationships, and with illness. And the same message that touched those first believers touches us. There is no insecurity; all is secure in Christ."

In every trip report from which this book was compiled, I thanked the supporters of Abiding Life Ministries International several times, and while those words of gratitude did not find their way into this book, it goes without saying that the discoveries during my travels were completely, unalterably dependent upon the care and generosity of the support team the Lord supplied to send me out. Without Him I would be nothing; without them I would go nowhere! I thank each one who has sent donations to the ministry.

I once was asked a simple question: What did I want from others? I want to see that they had the revelation of Christ in them, the understanding that He is the positive in all their negatives, the desire to go forward with the song of ascent, the witness of the truth to others, the view that the Sermon on the Mount is the exact expression of their lives, and the hope and joy to live like sparrows and flowers, believing that they have a God. When I see that in believers, my heart sings, and this is the revelation of my selfishness, for when someone sees Him and witnesses to the TRUTH in his spirit, it brings an equal explosion in my spirit; when I see a heart sing, my heart sings, and it drives me forward.

I will exhaust myself to travel over mountains, oceans, and deserts to see such things. I had to learn by experience the meaning of the parable of the four soils: Some seed fell "along" the pathway, some fell "on" stony ground; some "among" thorns; and some fell "into" good soil. I have had to learn to put up with the "along," the "on," and the "among" while waiting for the "into." Three out of the four efforts to get a harvest would be lost; 75% of all my efforts produce nothing. However, the 25% produces much more than we imagine, thirtyfold, sixtyfold, and a hundredfold. Those are large returns: 3,000 percent, 6,000 percent, and 10,000 percent. Exaggerated? No, fact!

A wise friend told me of an old man that would keep all his fingers in the same position while he strummed the guitar. One day a passerby stopped to watch him play and commented, "I notice that you keep your fingers in one place while you strum the guitar, while others move their fingers up and down the neck of the guitar. Why?" The old man replied, "They are all looking for the note that I have found." I like to say that I am a one-string guitar, so every time I speak, people hear the same message: "There is nothing the nearness of Jesus will not cure." I hope the reader will find the thread of that truth throughout this book.

Introduction

The following accounts took place over a fifteen-year period of travel, so from one paragraph to the next, a different time in the cultural context may be presented. Some accounts of dreadful conditions in countries will no longer be true due to the ongoing process of globalization. Some descriptions of my airport experiences will be read incredulously by those who had no experience with the freedoms encountered in airports and flights before September 11, 2001. Just remember as you read that each paragraph is self-contained as a relating of a time and a place independent from paragraphs around it; it has its own story to tell that stands alone and does not impact other paragraphs. It has been lifted from one of the many trip reports I wrote for the Abiding Life Ministries International Support Team and is describing the unfolding of the event as I lived it. In that sense, this book could be treated much as a daily devotional is perused, in that one paragraph at a time could be viewed without the need to recall the information read previously.

The reader may note some repetition in this book caused by my similar reaction to events transpiring over the fifteen-year period.

CHAPTER 1

Poor in this World, Rich in Faith

"In a great ordeal of affliction their abundance of joy and their deep poverty overflowed in the wealth of their liberality. For I testify that according to their ability, and beyond their ability, they gave of their own accord, begging us with much urging for the favor of participation in the support of the saints, and this, not as we had expected, but they first gave themselves to the Lord and to us by the will of God. So we urged Titus that as he had previously made a beginning, so he would also complete in you this gracious work as well" (II Corinthians 8:2-6).

Before I speak of the blessings of God in regard to the poor or discuss how much the "rich" should be giving, I want to discuss a few practical aspects of poverty in light of God's sovereignty. First, I do not think that the poor are properly taught about their condition. The Bible indicates that the poor are blessed, that God is to meet needs, and that there are reasons prosperity is withheld, such as the faith training of God or sin. Too often believers in the developing world have things out of order and simply become beggars. I do not see the need for God's people to be beggars.

Second, in places of poverty there is often a problem with the leadership's living in nice homes, having servants, and driving Mercedes Benz automobiles, all the while accusing Christians in other lands of having too much and being materialistic. It is difficult to reconcile all of this.

Third, I do not see world compassion as a valid reason for giving or tool to be used for manipulation. I have been thinking about how intervention in another's life shifts the responsibility for that life. When we intervene to stop a country's infighting, since it is not their choice to cease the conflict, we will be bound for years to keep the peace. Once the intervention stops, the warring continues until the parties choose to stop. God did not intervene in Israel until they chose to move into His kingdom; once they did, everything changed. My point is that there should be choice before intervention. When it comes to our flesh life, we want God to intervene and take it away. However, if He comes and delivers us by intervention, He is now responsible to come every time we are in trouble. Therefore, His formula is that we choose not to walk in the flesh. Once we make that choice, He will then intervene and deliver. At that point we are just realizing what is freely given in His kingdom. Until we choose, we live in our kingdom, and the only way we will learn its frailty and the fact that it is not the Way is to rule it. Do not ask Him to improve it when His business is tearing it down. We want God to intervene in governments that are antichrist, but if He were to do that, there would only be a temporary fix. The kingdom is not His and will return to its former state the instant His participation ends. A wicked government must come to the end of itself, choose to turn to Him, and then

He will certainly intervene. We must be cautious about harping on donating, as the world does, on the strength of the characteristic of world compassion. We do not know which groups have given up on the world and their own resources to trust Christ for His provision. Therefore, we must rely on the peace of God to lead in where His resources are to be sent.

Fourth, I see the wisdom in Christ's sending the disciples out without any extras. Why did He tell them to take nothing with them? For the very reason that we are seeing that taking extras (books, supplies, medical supplies, and money) can get in the way of presenting the Gospel. "Silver and gold have I none" pretty much puts an end to the concept that a believer is compelled to take aid along on a missionary journey. Sundar Singh pleaded with God to take away the gift of healing, for to the extent that people were coming to him for something other than Jesus, it got in the way of presenting Him. This is a great danger, one about which we cannot be too cautious, for when all that is offered is Jesus, the only associations made are with people who truly want only Jesus. I know I have made mistakes in this regard when I was being abused and used by church leaders requiring money or other favors, but I went along with it for the opportunity to preach to those who would not get anything out of my being there except Christ. I can have a relationship with a believer who only sees me as a potential donor, but I cannot have fellowship with him. For instance, a certain pastor, like all of us, could stand to expand his faith in the area of God's provision. His denomination comprises 700 churches with many thousands of members, all with the participation of none but poor people. I do not know of a single place in the world where this has happened among rich people. In the present time, the pastor seeks monetary donations from the West, which makes me ask if all were rich in his country, would they be Christian? Is he seeking something that will ultimately lure people out of the Kingdom and exclude others from entering in?

Some pastors were telling me about losing their congregations over beans. One of the churches in town had organized some relief aid in the form of beans; anyone who attended the church service was given beans. Many pastors went to church that night to discover that their congregation had gone missing to the church that offered beans! It is well and good to say that we are only to present the Gospel, and if food is given, the people will only come for the food. Jesus did say, "The poor you always have with you!" It is true that Jesus noticed He was only being followed because He fed the people. However, the reality of seeing starving, naked, and sick people is much different from discussing the problem in a seminary classroom. I do not believe in guilt manipulation, for to the extent that good is the enemy of the best, human compassion is the enemy of Christ. Therefore, here is my approach. I will listen to Him, give where He directs me, and not give where He does not lead. A few of our support team members give funds to be distributed as I see needs along the way. This is a heavy responsibility, for I realize that if I took the combined incomes of everyone I know, we really could not make a lasting change in any country. I must listen to every appeal, pray for the people, keep preaching Christ, and give as He has given to me (but only where

He tells me). Once my friend, Sam Jones, asked me how I felt about all the requests for handouts. I explained that if I wanted more money, I could find extra work, even if it were at the local convenience store. However, in some countries, if people wanted even daily bread, they had no way of getting it. They saw me as hope, and I did not despise them for it. He just said, "Good." However, from a ministry standpoint, I believe that believers should not live on other people's faith. In other words, if I have the faith to give donations to someone who asks, he should have had the faith to ask God and not ask me! It is a marvelous thing when people are getting on in the joy of Jesus and do not even know how miserably impoverished their lives are until they are told so.

In one place in Africa I was told that the basic diet is rice and beans, with meat once a week. I keep having shifts in the way I see things. These people are not forsaken. I want, under His leading, to give, and give liberally, as to reflect the liberality of ALMI's support family that has allowed much to be given to people over the years. The funds at ALMI are multiplied, multiplied, and multiplied to the point that Betty and I are amazed at what so few are able to do. However, I am more convinced than ever that the main objective is presenting Jesus. It seems that those who present anything else find it simpler to explain what they do. I listened to a missionary share about the unsanitary conditions in a hospital. "They have to use surgical gloves more than once." There were gasps from the congregation, and true enough, it is shocking, but is not the state of going to hell more shocking? Missing abundant life is shocking! Living in want and not knowing one can live like a sparrow is shocking! In short, missing Jesus is the most shocking thing that can occur. Jesus can fix all the problems in the world, yet I heard nothing from the missionary about Him. Well, amen. Pray for me that I will not budge, that I will keep focus, and that Christ be lifted up.

Once one has been surrounded by poverty, the initial shock slowly over the years deadens, except that the faces of poverty on friends will haunt him for years. I stop and look at the narrow streets, mounds of garbage, burning piles of trash, the diesel smoke, the heat, the noise pollution, the yelling, and the constant flood of people going past. It is admittedly difficult to exist in these conditions.

Asia

In Asia one morning we got up early for a rugged Jeep trip to the interior. It was worth the bouncing and juggling along. On the road was a five-gallon yellow plastic container sitting on a pile of bricks; we were told that was the sign for black-market gasoline. We stopped and a slight woman with a child came with a pitcher, put an army hat in a funnel, and poured the petrol into the Jeep. We continued on. The destination was a leper colony started by the church. The pastor believes that the Gospel comprises not just teaching and preaching but action, and he therefore has started several programs that meet the physical needs of others. The village is made up of those cured of leprosy and those with deformities or physical disabilities, about forty families who were gathered from several areas and brought to the property. The village is typical, consisting of simple structures on stilts to protect from flooding during the monsoon season; there are wells and open sewage. Shacks were built and gardening skills given, along with the sense of community and worth that come from working. I arrived in the middle of a one-week Bible school held for the residents. We had wonderful meetings, all of us under bamboo poles covered with vegetation, and judging by the response, a real move of the Lord occurred. I spoke on how our outer condition can affect our inner man, and I emphasized the need for a new inner man, Christ's life. Afterwards we ate the meal the villagers had prepared in appreciation. (I remembered the missionary prayer, "Father, whatever it is, please kill it!") The women had spent considerable time making dried chili with beans and pumpkin soup to pour over rice. There were also nice little omelets made from duck eggs. We all sat on the floor as the men waved large branches over us to both cool us and drive away the flies. I kept complimenting the food, and the ladies just beamed and kept bringing it. We were then escorted to the village road with smiles, hugs, and words of appreciation. It was a wonderful time of ministry.

We hopped into a Range Rover and headed off to inspect a plantation. It is beautiful in the jungle, and I welcome its heavy air compared to that in the dry Rocky Mountains. We find a small hill from which several thousand acres can be inspected. There is a tower to climb, and we watch as the afternoon showers move in. After the descent we go to a small hut that is a temporary office. Workers are checking in and preparing to listen to me speak tonight. I was the first white man they had ever seen. It is interesting how they have been acquired. The manager had to take a boat to a village in a neighboring country, an activity that is not very safe. Once there, an "agent" brings the men whom he has recruited. Each man signs a two-, three-, or four-year contract, and none will see their families for the entire length of this service. They will get between $50-$100 per month, which is much more than they were getting unemployed in their home village. As the meeting began, I did not have a message to share. Then it came to me. "You may think that I have nothing in common with you. I do. I, too, have spent many nights in bed wondering and worrying about my family." I had everyone's attention. I went on to talk about the importance of the peace of God, having God, and knowing God watches out for those we love. It was all done through an interpreter, and yet the men were riveted. The Lord really moved and drew men to Himself. The rain was pounding so loudly on the roof that finally the interpreter and I were yelling. When we finished, all fifty of the workers got in a single line. I assumed that they were going to shake my hand. I was surprised to discover that they each came forward, took my hand, knelt on the ground, and kissed my hand. I prayed for each one. I knew that all this attention was not for me. As so many have pointed out, the donkey that carried Jesus never thought the parade and palm leaves were for him. I knew they wanted to show some appreciation to God, and kissing my hand was something tangible they could do. Later one of the managers asked me, "What did you think of their kissing your hand?" I said, "I think things need to change at my home!" We all got a good laugh.

Couples have been invited from the surrounding areas for a three-day marriage conference; a little over 200 have come, some having walked for days. We had organized food for their meals. It is quite an experience to have a marriage conference in the middle of nowhere. The conference begins and there is a real receptivity. The host always does a great job interpreting, but I remember that this message is one of witnessing to what God has already prepared in the believers, and if God is not speaking in the hearts, the best interpreter in the world will not help. As I look out in the audience the men are on one side and the women are seated on the other, as is their custom. No one is wearing shoes. We finish this first day like most days, tired and yet refreshed in our spirits. At lunch the second day we discuss many things; the pastors are happy with the conference. Then I am taken alone to the toilet by the pastor, who wants to know if I would be willing to pay for two toilets to be built there. I did not see a problem but said he would have to talk to my host, the minister who always prepares for my visits to this country. It is better for me if I work through one central man who understands the needs and the culture. When asked, my host agreed, and we gave $100 for the two toilets to be built. In just awhile, my traveling companion came up to me and said, "The pastor just took me to the toilet and asked if I would help build two more." This is exactly why we go through my host, who then looked at us and said, "Brothers, money is not everything, and though some have Jesus, they do not see how rich they are." I was happy to hear him say that. Some people view us as those who bring a message that will set them free; to others, such as this pastor that wanted the toilets, we are seen only as a means for getting money. It never really bothers me, because I was sent not for the pastors but to the poor, who would normally never have an opportunity to attend a marriage conference or work out anything in their lives. Day three of the conference will end early, since the people have traveled a long distance to get here, and we do not want them walking home in the dark with the rebel soldiers going about enforcing curfews. Therefore, we have decided to finish before lunch, feed them, and let them get on their way. As the service ends, a large number come forward for prayer. Many of the women are barren and want children. There are also many who are sick. The crowd becomes so large that I ask all of them to sit down. Then I explain that there is one mediator between man and God, and that mediator is not Mike, it is Jesus. I will stand by all of them, but they must pray to Jesus and ask Him themselves, that He personally can answer them. The believers are satisfied with this and we pray. After that it is a mad rush, for we, too, must complete our journey before nightfall's curfew.

Were a home characterized by the four walls that surround it, this is not much of a home. The whole place is probably twelve by twenty feet. I am staying in the "school office," which is separated from the rest of the room by a curtain. A bed has been made for me, and there is a place for my bags, though truly there is not enough room to swing a cat. Next to me reside the three children. The oldest, a son, is a student of computers; his maturity belies his twenty years of age. His father has great trust in him, and the son moves quickly and effectively from task to task, always talking to God. He reminds me of the father in the Broadway production, "Fiddler on the Roof." "Yes, Jesus! Thank You, Jesus! Oh, please protect us, Jesus! Help me, Jesus. Oh, praise Jesus." Then there is the middle child, a daughter, eighteen years old. She was asked to participate in the school fashion show and won, but after it was discovered that she was a Christian, the award was taken from her and given to a Muslim girl. She is studying engineering. Finally, there is the younger daughter, who has another year and a half of high school, and then she will be off to university. The mother of these children is filling this place with joy. She emerges with her parrot on her shoulder. It, like every other dweller of the house, wants to kiss her continually. Grandma is also with us. She has diabetes, blindness, and senility; little did I know how interesting that would make things in the wee hours of every morning. The children's mastery of the English language is impeccable, unlike their mother, who struggles, but we can communicate. I have only been here minutes and the whole family is sitting on my bed asking questions. Here, as in many places, I am called "Uncle." "Uncle, do you like it here?" "Uncle, what do you think of this country?" "Uncle, what do you like to eat?" The kitchen is simply a gas stove at one end of the room; a rope is strung from one end of the room to the other for the purpose of hanging up everyone's clothing. I was shown the facilities located under the stairwell; there was a proper toilet along with a ceramic hole in the ground that was directly under the shower. This would all prove to be a minor challenge when taking a shower. My host had wanted me to stay in one of the hotels in town, but his wife had said, "No! Bring him here, and if what we have is not comfortable, then you will take him to town." It does not look like I will be going to town. I could not see the point, given my standard policy that if I cannot live as do the people to whom I minister, then I should not be going. Anyway, what is not to like? This brings me to a different definition of a home. If home is what is happening between the four walls, then this place is a mansion, one of the greatest homes in which I have ever stayed.

We arise early for the day's journey. We will be going to one of the slave colonies. Many of the Christians are slaves to the Muslims, and it comes about in this way. A poor Christian goes to the Muslim master, who may own a brick factory, a rice paddy, a sugarcane farm, or a mill. The Christian says that he needs a job. The master pays him for ten years in advance. He pays him a fraction of what his work is worth, but getting the money all at once makes it seem like a lot. The Christian, never before having such resources at his disposal, immediately buys a one-burner stove, shoes for the kids, and a bicycle. At that he is out of money. He returns to the master, explains his plight, and is paid for ten more years of work; again he quickly spends the money. Within two years the Christian has sold his whole life to the master. He next sells his wife and, finally, his kids. This is how generations are placed in bondage. Where I am headed for the day, the master has agreed that I can have two hours with the slaves. It is Sunday, and my host and I have decided to buy rice as soon as we get there and feed the people. We draw near the compound in which the slaves live; the "village" is walled and rounded at the top, tan in color, with each house connected to the other; ladders allow access to the roof, where it is possible to move from one house to the other. The pueblo is made of brick and then covered by hand with a mixture of clay and manure. The road worsens as we approach and enter by the gate. In the courtyard the rice will be cooked, but it must first be purchased. Since we have so little time with the slaves, we want the meal cooked before we call them for the meeting. Inside the compound are cows, ducks, and children, all of whom are busy moving the manure, bringing grass to the cows, or mixing clay. Everyone works. Women by hand are mixing the cow manure with straw and making what would appear to be bowling balls that will be dried and sold to the methane factory. The younger ones must start working at age two. Everyone must get up and be in the field or factory around 4:00 a.m. and work until sunset. There are NO days off, ever, and though the people work long days, after work they still need to prepare their own dinners, tend their small garden plots or fields, and feed the livestock. The master does not provide any food, so everyone must continue to work at home once the workday is finished. When the people arrive for the meeting, I see that this is the perfect group for me. They are not allowed an education. Actually, how could they find the time? Therefore, none of them can read. We begin with music. I never before saw such a mishmash of objects used as musical instruments. One is a piece of iron bar eight feet long and bent in the middle so the ends nearly touch; a steel ring is placed over one end of the bar and banged against the other end. It produces a high-pitched sound. There are also things as simple as a spoon being hit on a cup. Nothing looked like an instrument, but everything made a sound called music, and we were singing. Beautiful. Next, I explained that there are two books that teach us about Jesus, the Bible and the book of life. Today we were using the book of life, for every created thing preaches Jesus. I began to look around the pueblo, pointing to a chicken here, a horse there, a well, and so on. I asked, "What does this teach you about Jesus?" Between the illustrations I would tell a story and ask the same question. I wanted them to see that even while working all day long, they could still have a lift in their spirits by looking to Jesus. At the end of the meeting many came forward for prayer. Most of the young women were vexed because they could not conceive. It was obvious why: malnourishment. Next, the food was served, to everyone's delight. I was seated with one of the leaders of the colony and given hot rice and raw sugar. Outside some of the men were smoking a strange-looking pipe, a large bowl on a stand with a hose and mouthpiece coming out of the bottom of the bowl. A small bit of tobacco about the size of half of a golf ball was first placed in the bowl, followed by a heaping pile of cow manure, which was lit, and the men sucked on the hose to draw the heat of the manure over the tobacco. There was a lot more manure being smoked than tobacco! I bypassed this customary social activity. It was a full day and hard for me to leave. I sat and talked to several of the people. They were happy in Christ. I thought that these slaves fared better than the poor in the city, even though few will escape this place. It is possible to go to the master and ask the cost to buy a family's freedom, but what would they do with such freedom? Some actually escape, only to be hunted down and killed. This is their lot. Can they see Jesus in it? Well, I would rather be a Christian slave in a Muslim country than a free Muslim. Also, these people can worship freely. I suppose it all depends on what man wants, comfort or the revelation of Christ. Everyone waved and hugged us as we left.

Today is a special day at the school, and I wanted in on it. This place has no playground or materials, and yet these students will test out in the top 10% of students in this country. Christian schools may be the greatest tool of evangelism in these types of places. Though Christians are only allowed to live in the poor section of town, Muslims recognize that the Christian- or Catholic-run schools are the best, with their higher test scores, and therefore, many of the rich Muslims send their children to Christian schools. In the past the government had nationalized all Christian-owned property. The present Prime Minister attended a Christian school and is amiable toward the believers; he actually returned all of their property to them. This building's main floor is brick with a concrete covering. The school is accessed through the same green gate that lets us into the room that is called the pastor's house. Go straight and one comes face to face with a little old pudgy widow selling fried peas, seeds, candies, and more. She used to come around the school in a depressed state and begging. The pastor's wife said to her, "Come and set up a food table for the children. You can make a little money and you will be happy being around the children all day long." It turned out to be true. Venture past her to find the first classroom on the left, typical of all the other eight classrooms; there are only benches to sit on, a window fashioned by knocking a hole out of the wall and shared with the classroom next door, rough floors, a small chalkboard with a crack down the middle, no paper, no books, and maybe one picture on the wall. Go further and find the main "hall" with a small platform. Go up the stairs and find six more classrooms. Take another flight of stairs to land on the roof, but these folks have a vision for making it a third floor. The salary of a teacher is $50 per month, but most of the time the teachers do not get paid. Today the students are receiving their test scores from the government; it will be my job (and pleasure) to hand out the test scores and any special certificates to them. Each child comes forward and gives me a hug. Many take the opportunity to practice a little English. I hear, "What is your name? How are you? I am happy to meet you," and so on. Great fun. Next I call the teachers forward and just happened to have with me a pen for each of them. I thank them for the job that they are doing. They are a wonderful group of teachers and so loving with the children. After the students are dismissed, I send the pastor's son to get some money for me. I want enough five-rupee notes to give one to all 150 students and twenty rupees for each teacher. I want the students to spend the money during their break at the snack table of the widow outside. When the son appears with a brick of bills, he accompanies me to every classroom, where I do some magic tricks and then give every child his or her rupees. I do not think the old woman had ever done that much business. At the end of an hour she motioned for me to come over and get my free peas.

In the morning we are off to the leprosy colony. Many lepers pass, put their palms together, and give the greeting of believers, "Jesus is Lord." Various people without hands, feet, noses, or ears stop to tell me that they remember the conference from last year. As we move along we see the fruit of past work, such as purchasing chicks and cages for the people to be able to make a living. The payoff from that investment continues; the people are still raising chickens and selling them a bit cheaper than elsewhere, so many from the surrounding regions come to purchase them. Some are raising pigs and others have opened shops, though a shop opened by a leper generally only attracts customers that are also lepers. We enter an old building to discover a woman with no hands that has just been robbed of her two chickens and fifteen kilograms of rice that was provided by the church. The local gang took it all. Of course, she cannot put a lock on her door; she has no way of turning the key. Entering her room I notice one light bulb, two rope beds, and a few pieces of clothing hanging on a string. In the corner is the typical mud stove. Outside, a crowd has gathered. We go up the narrow stairs to another similar room and another old woman who is a recipient of the rice program. On up, looking into the third floor, I can see straight through to the sky above; one more earthquake and this place is done. Back outside we walk through the entire lepers' complex; some are taking baths, women are drying grain, and men are building very small houses with foundations of bricks and interiors filled with dirt; old broken bricks will be placed in the dirt and tamped down to create a base floor, which will then be covered with a mixture of dung and dirt. We meet several people along the way that have been given strict instructions by the pastor to stay home and rest from their assorted infections. My father is handing out bubblegum as we go along, giving the people great pleasure. There are no toys for the children of the village, so they make their own; the most interesting is a piece of sugarcane bent in

17

the shape of a triangle and held together with a reed; in the center is a piece of rubber cut out of an old tire. The whole "toy" looks a bit like the front part of a wheelbarrow, and the child pushes it along. It does not look like much or do much, but it is a delight to the children. Moving along we come to a most shocking sight. Lying on a mat is an old man that only has stumps for feet; his body is eaten with infection, he is staring straight ahead, and he is nothing more than a fly feast. The flies are sucking the liquid from his eyes, yet he does not even blink. His relative yells to tell him that there are visitors. At that, he attempts to move about. This minor movement reveals a foot that is a chunk of raw meat. The flies also cover this part of his body. He is wearing a diaper, and his legs are no larger than a woman's wrists. Honestly, if he were an animal on a farm, he would be shot and put out of his misery. Immediately I tell the pastor to call an ambulance. He informs me that he would be a minimum of three months in the hospital at nearly $100 per month. I explained that I did not care how much it cost as long as he was cared for in the hospital. He assured me that the elders of the church would be informed and the man would be taken. It is difficult even to write about it and remember the man's state and the smell of death. Obviously, many people just let their family members go ahead and die rather than seek unaffordable treatment for them. There have, however, been improvements here at this Christian enclave! At the bottom of the terraced rice fields, we see the church that replaced the primitive conditions of preaching under a stable with the goat urine dripping from the ceiling! Those days are over. The lepers have a proper building, and they so enjoy it. I remember standing on the land and praying that we could buy it. Now, three years later, there is a church building on the land with two finished stories and a third on the way. There is also a place for an infirmary. Three travel-weary companions, American brothers in Christ, have just arrived to complete the finish work on the third floor of the church at the leper colony.

Pacific Nations

What can I say of "Uncle," a name gained during years of ministry to youth? He is a gentle, quiet, but powerful old man, respected by all. He is on his way to eighty, but for the last twenty years the Lord has awakened him at four a.m. just to talk to Him, and the prayer times often end with tears running down his cheeks. He told me of a missionary couple that said they could not stay in the village because they were not raised that way; the woman said, "My father always provided the best for us." "Uncle" responded, "Jesus' Father provided heaven, glory, and a throne for Him, yet He left it all to visit my village!"

The first night of one conference I spoke on the will of God, and how I am not as smart as God, so I would not know what I or others need; therefore, the Lord has commanded me to pray, "Thy will be done." I had walked to the conference with a fellow who had been very quiet, and after I said this, I noticed he began to smile. After the meeting he told me how that very day he had been denied reentry into another country, making it impossible to return to his job. He realized that he merely needed to say, "Thy will be done," and peace would come. Anxiety is the measure of the distance between a believer and God.

Any treasure hunter would be delighted to find on this island, on a grass mat, an old man with only one defining characteristic, a big smile. Within him is Christ, the treasure God has put in an earthen vessel. I used to think in terms of my material possessions compared to what others in the developing countries do not own, but I no longer do. If Christ is in a man, then how could outer adornment add to that? "Father, I want more and more to know what it means to have Christ in me, the hope of glory."

One mother of six was, as every mother knows, exhausted, yet she had been under guilt and condemnation for years because she just could not seem to work a consistent quiet time into her busy day of caring for the children! I shared with her that Jesus is the God of the everyday, not the someday. He was not raised in a castle but lived in workaday surroundings. We tend to think He should have spent more of His first thirty years engaged in preaching, witnessing, spending time in the synagogues, and keeping more people from hell. Instead, He worked an eighteen-hour shift, took care of a widowed mother, stayed in a small, boring village, and helped take care of His brothers and sisters. In the everyday He fellowshipped with God, grew in God, was pleasing to God, ministered to others, and was at peace. Now the everyday God lives in us. We do not wait for the great "someday" when we shall have time for Him, for we can find Him as we work. We pray without ceasing in our tasks; we do not have to set aside a time. She began to weep! "I am so happy that He is my everyday God."

I do not know where this tiny island nation would be without our tax dollars at work supporting it; the latest "gift" was $128 million, which goes for who knows what. U.S. currency is used here, and English is the language that unites the various indigenous peoples. Though it is not U.S. soil, it is considered to be, all of which is a bit confusing, but amen; we, like the other missionaries, have come to share Christ, not sort out the flesh of man in politics. Our friends are here for the long term to see the people trained and to make building relationships the top priority; they do love the people. It is past midnight, and they have other guests, but they made the time to come and pick us up from the airport. The man is quite the mechanic. He drives a 1985-'87 Jeep. Why the age spread? It is an '85-'87 because four different wrecked Jeeps were put together to make the one! Some of the things he has done to fashion the vehicle are nearly genius. The ignition switch kept falling out of the steering column; since it is impossible to get parts here, he went to the marina, purchased an ignition switch for a boat, and mounted it in the cigarette-lighter opening. It looks odd to put the key in the cigarette lighter to get started, but, hey! It works! There is also a light switch off of a boat for his headlights. All in all, he fits in here. Being this resourceful is a must in such a place. Speaking of light switches, rain here pours instantly and immediately stops, like throwing a light switch on and off; the annual accumulation is just over 400 inches of rain, making it the second wettest place of which I have heard. These islands are also filled with superstition, witchcraft, and spirits, something with which every missionary must come to grips. Our friends have only been here nine months but have risen to the challenge. They live in a simple little house on the church property with no hot water, clothes

21

needing to be dried in a room with a dehumidifier, and very expensive electricity. These islanders do not have a concept of personal property and therefore come through the yard and pick whatever they want. Our friend diplomatically says, "We take care of the trees. I am not asking for much. I would just like to get one lime once in awhile!" Children come and stare in the windows to watch the foreign people work and cook. Actually, there is not much to do here, and if I lived here, I would probably find myself watching the missionaries work, also. This place is rough going for a missionary, and with each day this couple gains more of my respect. This is not going to be an easy place. However, with the call will come the provision, and I am looking forward to seeing how God's plan will unfold through this family. The man said, "We are training the pastors in the intellectual pursuits, but we want something to give them that has to do with LIFE." Amen.

Eurasia

I believe that to suppress femininity or masculinity is a wicked thing. For years in the former Soviet "Republics" women had to dress nearly like men; and when it came to purchasing shoes, no matter what size someone wore, he or she would buy the shoes that were available, in hopes that later they could be traded for the right size with someone else who had also bought the wrong size for himself. Clothes were made cheaply with no consideration to style. I can remember my daughter at a very young age dressing up and looking beautiful; that just was not possible here. Now that the wall has been torn down, femininity has been blooming. The women may only own one outfit and wear it seven days a week, but it is made up entirely of designer clothing. Everyone in the shops and office places looks unique and neat as a pin. It is really odd, but pleasant, to walk through a market, city street, or shop and see all the men and women dressed as though they are off to church. Of course, my elderly friend, who spent years confined in Siberia, has her own unique perspective on this and told me, "No one has ever died from craving." By the way, for the more fortunate, a typical home here is a two-room apartment in a twenty-story high-rise, very poorly built. Inside the door in a short hallway are two bunks for the kids, a kitchen with a small table, and a bedroom that doubles as a living room. That is all, just two rooms, not two bedrooms. This is considered big enough to house a family of five.

I sensed that the Lord wanted me a take a walk and listen. As I walked, He said, "Why do you hang on to any of your self life?" I thought long and hard to find the answer, and then said, "Because I think I can find in it some enjoyment." Just then an old woman appeared, walking with a cane and dragging a bag and purse. I passed her but then was quickened to stop; I turned, and she was fearful of my taking notice of her, because of my suit (organized crime members in this country dress that way) and our being on a lonely stretch of road. I reached in my pocket, opened her hand, and placed on it some money. She immediately broke down, began to weep, and explained something in her language. She sounded hopeless, something about having to go and having nothing. She cried so much that I reached forward to hold her as she wept. I only said, "Jesus." I walked away, crying myself, and the Lord spoke,

"Do the things you hold on to give you that much joy?" I turned to look once more at the old woman, but she was gone. All night I could smell on my clothes the distinct odor of a homeless person, but this time the aroma carried with it a sweet memory. Nothing compares to God's little surprises. I did not bless her, but she had blessed me.

At the last minute I was informed that I would be the speaker at the morning service. My topic was on Jesus and His beauty. At the end of the service an old man came forward, unannounced and weeping. He handed me a bundle of flowers and said, "I have no food, but thank you, thank you!" One day, not far off, you may be in a similar position, for the return of Christ is near; it is one day closer than yesterday. Remember then that there is nothing His nearness will not cure. Like this man, when you see Jesus you will give even though you have nothing. We need not fear; just as God has taken care of this man, He will fend for you.

I want to describe a wonderful ministry site; last year we attempted to stay there, but it was freezing and the hot water for the city was not yet turned on (regardless of weather conditions, it is turned on in mid-October and turned off mid-April). This year the weather is warmer and we will be staying there. Any believer would absolutely love this place! There will be no baths for the coming week; the water is freezing. I went in to wash my hair and started screaming from the cold water. We will be sleeping on old divans, and the mosquitoes at this place in the far north can drill right through us. No, the accommodations are not what the believer would love, but the people. The director is a single woman in her early sixties, full of life and love.

Her associate is in her seventies and has the deep glow in her beautiful countenance that only comes from a woman of God who has spent time in His presence. There are two volunteers: the wife of a starving artist and a woman abandoned by her husband and raising eight children; she sorts the donated clothes from Sweden. Together this ministry team comprises four fragile women of God with mighty hearts. All have the gift of serving and hospitality, and there is not a bad cook in the bunch! They were really excited about an occurrence during the previous week, when one man came with a miserable toothache; they prayed and he was healed. Another came with a leg that would no longer function. They prayed, and he was healed. "See how good God is!" was their adulation.

We had just enough time to visit the farm of a well-known inner-city mission. A group of visiting Swedes had told the director that she needed a place outside of town to rest and get away from the constant onslaught of people coming for help. They bought her a small farmhouse for $900 U.S. The woman and her cohorts immediately got busy painting, knocking out walls, and putting in pews to make a church! I had to laugh! "You were supposed to be coming here to rest!" We all got on our knees to ask a blessing on the new church. Many had prayed for years that there would be a church in this area. The past Sunday the first worship service had been held; the people were ecstatic. We spent a few minutes filling the car's trunk with apples from the surrounding trees. Nothing here is wasted.

One of the elderly ladies pointed to an old train station in a field and said, "That is where my family departed for

Siberia." She then proceeded to tell me her story. I will retell it, but not to stir pity or compassion, but to bring about praise in our God, for in the worst of situations, there is nothing that His nearness does not cure. She was ten and her brother thirteen when the Russians came. First their father was taken to fight in the Russian army on the frontlines. He was never heard from again. It is said that the Russians would take young boys to the frontlines so they would have something to eat. Years later many frozen soldiers' bodies were appearing at sea. She, her brother, and mother were taken at night for the one-month trip to Siberia, though it was never clear why. If the Russians wanted to kill them, why not do it quickly in their home? I know this: Evil does not have a plan apart from indifferent destruction. Once arriving, they were given a daily ration of a mere 300 grams of bread. She and her brother spent four years in Siberia. In order to perpetuate and justify all abuse, the Eskimo locals had been told that these people's nationality had caused the war. The Americans often sent supplies, but they never made it to these people. The mother became very sick, so the girl and her brother gave her their bread and said they had already eaten with the neighbors. Her brother would take the crumbs from the bread and set up a small bird trap to capture the hummingbird-sized "snowflake" birds. Once plucked, they were no bigger than a finger, but on a lucky day they were supper. Besides being expected to help in the mines, they lived on a river and were forced to help fish. However, they were never given any fish to eat themselves. On the rare occasion that they were allowed to have the salt that was scraped from the flesh of the preserved fish, the children boiled and drank it. They got no nutrition from it, but the salt made their stomachs swell and left them feeling as if they had just had a large meal. After a few months the mother died. The girl's brother was able to scrounge a few boards and make a coffin. The two of them performed the funeral. Once it was discovered that their mother had died, both were sent to a local orphanage. To their surprise, the home was given a few coats lined inside and out with rabbit fur. If they cut the lining out, they could make two coats out of one. Everyone had to be very careful at night, because the bears were notorious for regularly killing cattle and, on occasion, people. Shoes were made from sacks tied at the ankles with rope. She looked at me and said, "You can go visit any place in your dreams. Once I visited Colorado in my dreams. Can I come and visit you sometime in my dream?" I responded, "Oh, yes, you can visit anytime you want! But when you come in your dream, remember to bring your pots and pans, for I like your cooking!" After we had a good laugh, I asked, "How did you survive?" "Jesus, only Jesus! He kept us! In that place my brother and I developed a wonderful sense of humor and joy!" Yes, Jesus keeps us. The sun shining on a dead tree rots it, but on a live tree, the same sun gives life. The Son had shone on this old woman who was alive in Him, and she had grown. The day may come when we will be in just such a place. The Son will shine, and we will grow, too. I like this woman and the promise her life represents.

We were greeted at the house in which we would be staying by a short, blonde woman who was reminiscent of Mrs. Claus. She and her husband definitely have the gift of hospitality; long ago they married with the resolve to feed anyone who came into their house seeking food. There have been hundreds of guests in this house that comprises only two rooms. Later in the evening we all went off to sleep. In the middle of the night, I made my way to the toilet/shower/kitchen room. I shone my light on the small divan that earlier had served as seating for dinner. There was the older couple, sandwiched on the couch, somehow sleeping. As I said, they have the gift of hospitality. In the morning we (including other visitors) had a breakfast of bread, sausage, cheese, and porridge (oatmeal). I have never before seen anyone put ketchup on oatmeal, but it is not bad. We leave for a village more than an hour away. I have made it a priority to do meetings in places where others cannot or will not, and it is not uncommon for meetings in these out-of-the-way villages to attract more people than those in the city, because they are such a rarity. We drive past a village that for 600 years has been conquered, possessed, and dispossessed by many different peoples. It is famous for its sausages and a large Jewish synagogue. There are no longer any Jewish folks in this place, but a very elderly man remembers Germans marching the rich and powerful Jews past his village on their way to Poland to be killed. He said the occurrence struck him in two ways: that great men were being reduced to weak men, and that it was an incomprehensible fact that with so few German soldiers marching them, the Jews did not simply overpower them and flee. I have noticed that when a people who have suffered see themselves as victims, it becomes their identity and they never can move on. It causes their suffering of the past to continue to dictate life in the present. In contrast, those who seem to believe, "If

God is for us, then who can be against us," get busy and move on. I admire that.

One man was thinking seriously about moving to the U.S. "for a better life." Two of his friends had offered to pay the expenses of passage for his whole family. The man went to his father and told him, and the older man opened the Bible and read, "If you have food and clothing, with these things be content." The man looked at his father and said, "I will stay here and minister to my people!" He did eventually visit the U.S. His impression was that in the U.S. we have many things, but it is not worth the life of hurry and working from sunup to sundown.

When the Soviet occupiers left, all property was to be returned to its original owners. It is a bit of a mess to work out, but it is getting done. Many of the Russians remain on here from the long years of the Soviet occupation; they do not belong here, but neither do they have a place in Russia. I do feel sorry for them. As we walked along, I noticed a lonely old woman, barely walking and poorly clothed. I had it in my spirit to give her some money. We walked over and discovered she was Russian and only spoke Russian. I wanted to give her a book, but she would not have been able to read it. Instead I opened her hand and placed the money in it. She looked completely bewildered and said, "Why?" Our answer, "Only Jesus; it is from Jesus." She took my interpreter friend's hand and kissed it while gently bowing. He repeated, "It is not me; it is from Jesus." There is often a sinking feeling when the pastor of a multi-million-dollar building says, "If one person gets saved, it is worth it." That is how he justifies his kingdom. On the other hand, I have to say that it would not surprise me to discover that God would have us here for that one woman. He does seek the one. That is our God and His heart.

We headed off in what is the poorest region of the country. We arrived at the Catholic school to find a room full of women listening to a tape and singing along. I was not sure in what direction the Lord would have me go when I spoke to the women, but as we were sorting out the overhead to use during the lecture, He spoke, and I went with the topic of the love of God. The people were so responsive, with several ladies testifying that God had prepared them for that message. Ministry is useless if not witnessing to the place where the Lord is working in the hearts. The woman that leads the group has a beautiful countenance and, I was told by the pastor, over the years has been given an authority from above. If she agrees with a teacher, he can teach in this poor place; if she does not, he will not come. She is a delightful, glowing lady in her sixties, and she said, "We are the poorest place in all of our country, but God has made us rich. He sends us people that would normally only go to the huge capital city. See how He loves us in this place? There is much witchcraft, but God is greater and keeps encouraging us. We are under His eye!" She just beamed that God was remembering them. He remembers us all; however, her heart is attuned to it in thanksgiving. An English teacher here has been disfellowshipped for teaching Jesus only in the church. She is really excited and in love with Him, which has cost her dearly in this small community.

We have arrived in a small village. The people here have a saying that those from the city never come to visit them. The young man laboring here to pastor the church was also put in charge of putting together the only year-round Christian camp in the country. The last time I saw it, it consisted of no more than an old dilapidated building. Since then, the floors have been replaced, there is a kitchen, and beds for fifty students have been installed. This year they hosted ten different camps. The government will not allow them to cook, so they cut a deal with the school, about a ten-minute walk down the road, to feed the students when they are there. It saves a lot of time and effort, and the pastor's time can more fully be given to teaching. Probably eighty percent of the students that come to the camp have no church background. This brother is doing all of this on the support of an American sister church. He is not paid much, and I am wondering how long he will be able to stay here. The house and building are out in the woods. The wind is howling, and snow is beginning to form in the air. We have a nice Russian meal; his wife is a great cook. We are housed in a room in the attic heated by a wonderful little heater; it looks like a couple of 55-gallon drums that have been welded together and lined with porcelain and bricks. A very small door exists for opening and putting in a few sticks. Once the bricks are hot, heat radiates through the night.

India

The hawk is a mystery to me. Several times in my life I have stopped to look at a hawk overhead, but I cannot understand his world, so I look back down at the world that I do understand. I stopped at a "quarry," which actually was a woman in her fifties with a pile of granite and a hammer. Her job was to break the granite into pieces the size of crackers; upon completing a bushel basketful, the woman receives one rupee, thirty paise (four cents). She has to work on holidays, because, like other workers, she is paid at the end of the day, buys food, and returns to her family. She just looked up at me for an instant and immediately turned her attention to her world. I asked how many years she had been sitting there, and she said thirty years.

There are many donkeys. I was wondering what they were about. I was told to notice that the donkeys all had cuts in their ears. The village people cut the ear, take the blood, mix it with milk, and then give it to their children to drink. The belief is that if the children drink the milk, their descendants will not stutter. I noticed small handmade tents at the side of the road, homes of the diggers, which are bands of people, not unlike gypsies, that contract with local governments to dig the trenches for utilities. Everyone in the family, from grandpa to the youngest child, is involved in digging from sunup to sundown. No need for the children to attend school; their lifetime vocation is already determined. They will be diggers like the generations before them. I look at my own state, the state of my children, and our opportunities, and it is easy to feel guilty. However, I am mindful of two things: one, the believer is not to be motivated by guilt, but compassion. Second, if we have an easier life, we are enjoying the fruits of those who have gone before us. A country built on faith in Jesus naturally (He is in the natural) goes much better.

Reportedly there are enough millionaires in India to equal a full third of the American population. Again, as in all governments, the wealthy and "powerful" have exactly the kind of country they want and do not place much of an emphasis on delivering people from poverty. A boom in the middle class trickled down to the poor, and there is such a contrast from when I first started traveling here in the 1980's. I never thought I would see such things as many new cars, refurbished hotels, and public advancements, along with very few starving people. However, this wealth and general improvement has not brought revival; a rise in income has not produced a rise in conversions. Jesus said, "Blessed are the poor." Generally speaking, we do not see the impoverished as blessed, but cursed, though it is very wrong to assume that poor people are unhappy people.

We are at a boys' school that would normally have over 1,000 students. However, it is between semesters and there are only seven boys who are receiving additional coaching. They are great fun. The dorm parent asks to talk to me. He is a great blessing to me because he shares so many things. He was a Brahman, one of the elite of Hinduism, a god, an idol-worshipper. He was taught that there were many ways to God, and yet he began to wonder, "Do I have the right way?" It was this questioning as the Holy Spirit drew him that brought him to Jesus. Once he confessed his faith, he was banned from coming to his house, a ban that he, of course, honored. After sixteen years, his father died without reconciliation. He is now tolerated and allowed to visit his house but not stay. He really does not care. He has found Jesus. Luke 18:29, 30, "And He said to them, 'Truly I say to you, there is no one who has left house or wife or brothers or parents or children, for the sake of the kingdom of God, who shall not receive many times as much at this time and in the age to come, eternal life.'" Leaving behind those we once considered to be "ours" is, then, another type of poverty that gives rich rewards.

I met one man God is using to spark revival in ten separate Hindu villages. A revival is so important among the Hindus; it is not something that we can bring, but we can be available as the Holy Spirit begins to move. It is important that the whole village be converted. If there are only a few converts, they will be persecuted and attempts made on their lives. I have heard many stories from people who convert, and when they tell their parents, the parents recruit other villagers to kill their own children. This man is having an average of one family convert a day. Two of the new converts have even given land for a church. He was sharing, not asking, but said in passing, "There is no water in those villages, and therefore we cannot baptize. I will wait until we have the money to hire a bus to bring all the converts to the city for baptism." Baptism is very important because it signifies a complete break from their old life (just like the Bible teaches), in this case, Hinduism. One of the ALMI friends had given me some money to use for special needs. I gave the man the bus money.

One of the pastors tells me of his work among the Hindus. He is seeing many from the middle and lower castes coming to Christ; this year they even celebrated Christmas in his village, with one Hindu dressed up to give candies to the children. When asked why, the man said, "There are many gods in India, but I discovered that there is really one God, and that one God is Jesus, the Savior of the world!" The brother told me that such things would not have been seen in India a few years ago. He believes there will be a revival among the Hindus, and I have thought that same thing for many years. Hindus, when not enraged by pride or political outlook, are religious, and many are honestly seeking peace. Jesus gives the only true peace.

We meet up with a fellow who had been in real estate in New York City for thirty years. He made some money and moved to Florida, where he did a couple of interesting things. One is that he, along with a group of other expatriate Indians in the U.S., started a seminary in India that is now the largest in that country. He explained that they were wondering where to get the funds to start, when one man from the board of directors was sitting in an airport, and he and the man next to him were reading the same book. The American and the Indian conversed, and the board member began to share his vision for the seminary. In the end, the American paid half a million dollars to construct the first building. The group did not have to look for funds, the funds came to them, and so far, that is the story of the seminary. There are five buildings constructed and only two more needed in order to finish the complex. The seminary pays the students to continue on and earn a Ph.D. with the requirement that they return to teach. The pay is quite good, and the seminary has just finished constructing a twenty-unit housing complex for the teachers, each with three to four bedrooms. Then the fellow tells me about the Indians' purchase of a church building in Florida. There was a student in Michigan that was going to Florida for grad school. Before he left, the Lord told him that he would be working with Indians. He had never even met one. Upon arriving in Florida, he was headed to church and stopped at a doughnut shop; there he saw an Indian reading a Bible. They started to talk, and the

Indian invited him to church. During the service, the grad student gave a testimony as to what he had been told, and he believed that he was to stay in that small church. During the service there was talk about getting a new building. The next day, the student called this fellow and said that he knew a realtor that could help. The realtor immediately found a church that was planning to move and sell their building. They had received an offer for $2.6 million, and the land was expected to go for ten times that, because it would be developed into a housing community. This fellow offered one and a half million dollars. The realtor said that was impossible, for they already had the higher offer, but my new friend said, "Go to the church and tell them it is not right to see the property go for condos. It is God's building and must remain God's building." The realtor reluctantly went to the church board meeting and relayed the message. The pastor of this Baptist Church spoke up, saying, "Yes, I believe that to be true. It must remain God's building. We should take the offer." They did, and the Indians had a church on five acres for one point five million dollars. They did not have the money to pay for it, since their old house church was worth a mere five hundred thousand. This fellow wanted one point five million. The Christian realtor came to him and said, "I will buy it for the amount you want and do something with it." Once again, funds came to this Christian fellow; he did not have to go looking.

Africa

We met a wonderful seven-year-old boy who plays drums for a church of nearly five thousand. He cannot hear and needs an operation that would cost fourteen hundred dollars, something unattainable for his family. He has never quite sorted out the pastor's name and thinks it is "Praise the Lord," so in a muffled way he says, "Hi, Praise the Lord!"

A young man the age of sixteen became a believer; he told his father with excitement, and his father's response was, "I will no longer feed or clothe you. Let the God of the Christians provide for you." The young man believed that God would provide. His clothes became threadbare, and he began to lose weight. One day a group of Christian boys he knew at his school secretly contributed different articles of clothing, put them together, and made a new set of clothes; they also put together a few food staples. When the boy walked into his father's home in all new clothes and with a food sack, the father angrily said, "Where did you get the clothes?" He said with great joy and excitement, "The God of the Christians!" Psalm 37:25 says, "I was a young man and now I am old, yet I have never seen the righteous forsaken or their children begging bread."

A necessity for one particular Bible college is that the professors live in town, because to date the school has not had the facilities to accommodate them. Each professor will spend around three hours to get there and up to five hours to return, an eight-hour day of just moving from bus to taxi to bus. The school has as its goal to reach the pastors of the very large denomination that is considered by many to be a cult, and without question it incorporates much magic. However, the principal at the school sees it more as a problem of ignorance than disobedience, and his assessment has been proven, for when he brings some of the pastors to the school and trains them in Biblical foundations (in a two-year or four-year course), it is just amazing to see the men return to their churches and preach the pure Gospel. In a few short years a real miracle has occurred within this school. A two-story classroom and library, new duplexes for the professors, and a hostel for the men and women attending school have been constructed. The biggest surprise is the securing of electricity! I appreciate the principal, who is not teaching to put anything into the people but to reveal what God has put in them already, the riches of Christ Jesus. He said to me, "I contributed nothing. I mean it; I contributed nothing to this building. I prayed in unbelief for it. That is all. God did it all. I contributed nothing." Of course, that is true about every one of us; we all contributed nothing to what we have, what we are, or where He has brought us. There was no way that the principal was taking any Glory (I capitalize the G in Glory, for God is Glory, and apart from Him there is none).

We visit the site for a small station church; the congregation is led by an ex-military officer. In the compound lie all the bricks needed to build the place. The government has not granted permission, for they will await a bribe. This is an excellent location, and the government would like to sell the property again. One man had a shipping container delivered to the site; inside was a crazy man who claimed that the land under the container was his and he therefore had a foothold on the property! Can you imagine? It took months to get the man off of the property. We pray, look around, and depart. The believers know that waiting builds faith; therefore, they do not borrow money for a building. Rather, they start with the foundation and wait. Sometimes it will take ten years, but in the end there is a building, along with built faith!

When an offering is taken, often there are three baskets: one for evangelism, one for the church, and one for helping others. In many ways rural people are cash poor and yet live better than those in the city. Typically an offering consists mainly of coins, but perhaps a woman will come up and very gently place an egg in the offering; a small boy might come and give two ears of corn. They give what they have! Always the New Testament comes alive for me as I watch these people.

One of the pastors told me his story. The day he became a Christian, he was cast out of his family. His mother had already been removed for being a believer. His father wanted to kill him. A pastor took him, provided for him, and trained him. The pastor's wife was the only one who could find work, so she provided for the entire family for some time as a seamstress.

A meal was served by the villagers after I had spoken over the course of several days. Adults were served first, then the pastors, then the children, who had waited patiently under one of the few large trees that exist in the compound (most trees have been cut for wood, which is having its effect on the environment). Each child was given a bowl of rice and was quite happy; it was funny to see their stomachs so swollen after the dinner. At the conclusion of the very last service, I was honored by being taken 100 feet from the front door of the church, where the men had dug a small hole, filled it with water, and mixed the dirt back in. "Brother," the men said to me, "plant us a tree! The children will keep it irrigated with water from the spring. We will remember that you planted this tree; as it grows, so do we." I was handed a small shoot, tender and weak. During the course of the teaching over the previous few days, I had repeatedly said, "As a believer, you are not a weed becoming a tree, you are a tree, regardless of your stage of development." As I planted the tree, I reflected on how this small symbol of their life in Christ would be so important. They had already told me that war would destroy the people; tribes had cut off people's lips, hands, and feet. "Leaders" who wanted control of politics in the country incited these tribes. "The people must understand that we all lose when there is a war. Only a select few will benefit." I agree that men who want glory at any cost stir up these wars, each of which sets a country back for decades or, in reality, centuries. They are just recovering from the last vicious dictator, and that has taken twenty years. Wicked profiteering goes on; a small generator that would sell in the U.S. for $300 costs $3,000 here, $2,700 of which is tax. Those residing in the poor areas need a generator the most, yet they are heavily taxed to enrich the corrupt leaders. If a leader is going to hell, I suppose twenty-seven hundred dollars is not enough to gain for the price of his soul.

In countries where the economy is wrecked and basics have been ravaged by war, the foreigner is seen only as someone from whom to get something, anything. Those of us who have not experienced life in such a place do not really understand that kind of desperation. I have on occasion worked three jobs at once when I needed extra cash. In these places, a person who needs extra money simply goes without; there is absolutely nothing to do to get the money. At a church fifty miles from the capital, pastors cannot get people who are naked to come to church. They do not own a stitch of clothing; they have lost everything. Unfortunately, the believers fall into the trap with everyone else of, in essence, saying, "Dear foreigner, give us this day our daily bread." I am with some pastors who are fine fellows with great hearts! The fellow who organized the meetings directs over fifty different churches that serve the poor people in the bush. I am seen as the potential "pot at the end of the rainbow." That is amazing given that I do not have money! The Lord sees fit to send me the airfare and enough for expenses, if I watch it carefully. The last two days have been a hassle as constantly I was being asked for money, for invitations to the U.S., and for every form of material aid. I ask myself and my supporters, "Is it worth it?" The constant pressure of people wanting things rather than Christ, $100 cab rides, being ripped off, bad food, no water, being away from home, and being used? Are those things worth it? To me they are! Why? I remember working so hard to be a Christian, depressed from failures, living in condemnation, never feeling acceptable; and then came the revelation that Jesus did it all, that there was nothing His nearness would not cure, that I was acceptable because of Him, and I could enter into true rest. I do not believe that God brought me to these leaders who see me as a dollar sign; He brought me to the weak. I have to go through the leaders to get to the people who are the priority. I put up with all the other stuff just to have the opportunity to share what has gotten hold of me, Jesus. Any time I was stuck in the car or in a meeting with the leaders, I had to check my spirit so I would not react negatively to the greed. However, when we stopped at a church where a congregation had gathered to meet the speaker (me), I got out of the car as the drumming, shouting, and dancing began. The crowd parted so that men could lead me by the arm to the platform. Two fellows with makeshift drums began to beat them, while two sisters with gourds wrapped in seashells began to wave. The hall filled with prayer. This is the Africa I enjoy. There is speaking interrupted with dancing and shouting, then more speaking. Finally, it is my turn. "There is nothing the nearness of Jesus will not overcome! I will prove it to you." I shared the difference life makes when Jesus is our focus. I talked about our relationship with God, based in grace; how we feel about ourselves, and why; and what God has for us in marriage. These were all things they had not heard about previously. I could see that the Holy Spirit was tugging at their hearts, witnessing to the Christ that is in them. They laughed and laughed, listening to every word. As I spoke, I could hear the Lord whispering so quietly and gently to my spirit like a breeze: "This is why you are here." I could sense His voice forcing out thoughts of the airport, the crowds, and all the discomfort. He was to me the Comforter. I finished to shouts of joy. A short trip to my room incited more requests for money, but I was at peace.

We arrive at the next church, called Mike's Church, because when I visited it last year, I took the money that was given to me from offerings at other churches and gave it by way of encouragement to the man who is trying to start this church. He has been there many years under intense opposition. When he saw me, he came running and nearly jumped in my arms. We hugged and laughed. He then showed us around; I was happy to see that the foundation had been laid. A traveling companion made a peculiar request: "Ask them to count the money that we just received from the last church where we spoke." I explained that it would take a long time to count so many bills, and though it looked like piles of money, it was not worth a great deal. My companion insisted that it be counted. The men counted it, and there was the equivalent of $175. The companion asked, "How many churches are there in this town?" "Twelve." The men were still looking puzzled until the companion said, "I will give to this church twelve times the amount of the offering we received earlier!" The man building this church really could not believe it and was so excited that he fell to the ground, lifted his arms in the air, and began to shout with joyful praises to God. All the other men were so taken by it that they, too, began to shout. It was beautiful, just beautiful. He would not stop shouting. We were all smiling with great joy ourselves. Finally, when he arose, we held hands and prayed. He whispered to me, "Michael, I will continue to build the church." One thing so different about the church buildings in this denomination is that they are constructed in the poorest section of the towns; then the people are invited to come. This work is only suited for those with the highest level of faith.

One pastor told us a bit about growing up. There was always the potential of having three meals a day; however, sometimes the table was set and he was not allowed to eat. Why? His grandmother wanted to teach him to be content with what he had, for there would be many times in his life when people had a full table (material gain) and he would not. She felt it important for him to learn to be content with what he had; if not full, content. The lesson has served him well; there is not a materialistic bone in his contented body. He works twenty hours a day, often missing meals, having few resources, and yet he is content. In the public schools when he grew up, the Catholics and Anglican students were separated into two different groups and given Bible teaching. All other students, this future pastor included, were sent outside, where there was no teaching.

It is a great experience to be around a different race when there is not a lot of emotional baggage or preconceived ideas, when they are Christians, we are Christians, we have mutual respect, and that settles it. The only time I even have to think of race is when I get a glimpse of my reflection while walking with the pastor and notice how pale and unattractive I look. We arrive to see the choir waiting in a long line to receive us. As we approach the end of the choir line, the local pastors await us, and they all begin to sing. I do not have the words to describe the voice of the choir; it is truly celestial. The procession to the front of the church begins; we follow the singing men and women of God. They move to the choir section and we go to the front. The big church is packed. The pastor introduces us to the members, and after some preaching, the choir sings two songs. Honestly, it is as though a person could close his eyes and go missing in the presence of God. It is a lulling sound of humming, chanting, and gentle singing. Then the director begins to sing the song of this denomination's history; how at its inception, the founder received from the Lord the revelation that the people must always worship in joy, clapping their hands and dancing, for joyful dancing before the Lord is one of the best remedies for the sorrows of a poor person. He sang how they were mocked and persecuted for their clapping and dancing, then goes on to tell of the wonderful works of God in bringing many blessings in provision, in building, and in evangelism. The people shout out their approval and praise. How many churches have that kind of joy about their histories? Many only have a history of conflicts upon conflicts, divisions upon divisions, and that is nothing to sing about. Next the offering starts, and that will take the greater part of the service. People in poverty must be involved in giving, and it must be done with joy. Different sections of the church take turns dancing to the front. One lady brings a live chicken and lays it at the altar, another leads in a goat, a small boy donates a gallon of orange juice, and others bring such things as a crate of eggs, motor oil, envelopes with cash, coins, bread, and more. Everyone has something to give, and this is only the beginning; the process is repeated three times. We dedicate the money to God and pray for those who cannot give that God will be with them, increase them, and allow them to enter into the joy of giving. The choir sings again. It is customary for anyone who enjoys the singing to go throw money at the choir. Many did, and I really wanted to but was not carrying any. In the end the pastor stood and said, "I am giving 1,000 [local currency] to the choir." I tugged on his arm, "And I am giving 5,000 local currency ($40 U.S.), because I have not heard anything so beautiful." There is great clapping and rejoicing over a small thing like $40 U.S.! Wonderful! I have seen it announced in church in other places that the budget

45

of one million dollars was met for the year, and hardly a sound issued forth. I like being in a place where the little things count. It makes life more real to me, and taken as a whole, the little things seem to make life bigger.

In the morning we travel for over an hour to get to a church whose pastor is a beautiful and faithful man. Whatever is said to him, the response is the same, "Thank you so much." He is very humble and has pastorates in many places, the membership of the congregation in his district totaling 24,000. The road we are traveling on is badly rutted; built some thirty years ago, it is rarely used because it was in a place of ambush. Water runs under the road, causing the craters around which we must weave. It is slow going. Along the way we pass many round mud huts with grass roofs. The fields are green from the rain, and in the distance we can see the odd butte. Last year there was much starvation here and people were stealing each other's corn. Naturally, that caused many problems. Today is Sunday and the people are just milling around and walking everywhere, not doing anything in particular. We pass a large "market," a series of small brick shacks that sell different things. The product depth is not there. One shop just has a shelf with maybe twelve bottles of pop, another has a few matches, and still another sells some rice. Behind these shacks are the elephant-grass shacks where vegetables are sold. As we pass into the mission station, we go past the first church, its floor made of dung and clay. The benches are made of a few bricks stacked up with more dung and clay on them. Believers here were not allowed to have churches for years, so the government was told that all the benches were for the old men to sleep on. We arrive at the church that is holding the meeting, and it is packed. The building is only partially constructed, but the super structure is done right. All that is standing are the large metal beams and a metal roof. There is a huge pile of bricks that the members have made themselves. The hiccup is the cement, for which the government will gouge the people with taxes of $8 U.S. per bag, too much for a group of starving believers. It is obvious that the people have been waiting for us for a long time; they are sitting on the dirt or on small bricks. God gave me a message and stories for these people, and I stood up to speak. It was a great time watching the men and women smiling as I told, according to my custom and style, many stories to illustrate the living Jesus. When the message concluded, gifts were collected. I really do not know how many people are here, hundreds I imagine. However, they are so poor that the collection is taken by passing a hymnbook. The few coins and notes available are placed on the book. The books, maybe five, are brought to the front of the church, where the money is counted and a report given on how much came from each district. I see a U.S. note in the pile and know my father is somewhere near. I look in the back and see him filming and moving among the people; they are really why he comes. He can no longer hear well and yet is always in the middle of something. I might find him in doing the dishes, visiting among the children, helping a carpenter, and more. Lastly came a communion service, which takes place only every three months, for they have difficulty finding the bread, and acquiring wine is an impossibility. What they do is soak raisins in water, drain it, and call it wine. The music is as beautiful as ever on this continent.

47

One student has a serious problem about which he must talk to me personally. How many times have I heard this line over and over again? Because of my teaching on marriage and how it so impacted him, he says, we need to talk. His wife has been angry with him for the last three years because he does not make enough money as a pastor. He only needs $34.78 per month and the marriage could come back together. "Can you imagine? All I need is $34.78 for me to have a happy marriage!" I asked him, "Brother, if you have had no money for three years, how have you lived? God has given you some money, has He not?" He nods. "Well, you now have a history with God. God does provide. The Lord's Prayer does not have us looking to others for our daily bread, but looking to Him. You have an opportunity to trust God and not man. Do not waste it by turning to man." It was as though he never heard or thought of such a thing. As mentioned before, it is interesting that I can have one hundred people ask for money and I will not have peace to give, and then all of a sudden God will put it on my heart to give to someone that may not even be asking.

We finish the day and head off to one of the poorer districts in the city. We find an old building that has a smattering of white paint on its walls, a suitable screen for showing the movie, "The Passion of the Christ." We do not have extension cords, so the men are busy taking bits of wire, splicing them together, and putting the open connection under rocks. I go to look where they are plugging in the 220V, and they are just shoving the bare wire into the holes. Wow. Then they hooked the bare wires onto the end of my extension cord; amazingly, it worked. By this time a crowd of nearly 400 people had gathered to see what was happening. I fired up the projector, we hooked up the sound, and people went running to tell their friends and family. I shut it down to move the table farther out into the road, which was not a problem at this point; with such a large crowd congregating, no one was going to attempt to drive past us. There were close to 2,000 people watching the movie. At the conclusion, there was really very little to say. The people had laughed when Judas hung himself, but no one was laughing at the end. The pastor merely said, "It was for our sins that Jesus Christ died; let us repent and pray." All of the people prayed at once.

My pastor friend appeared early in my room and began to explain, "How can you share the Gospel with people who have no food, no training for a job, and children that they cannot send to school? Why, I went to one village where the people were starving, and yet I had no means to feed them. I just told them to sit and listen to the words of Jesus, give their lives to Him, and trust Him to provide. As I was leaving the village, a truck full of grain came in that no one knew was coming. The next time I came, the people said, 'Tell us about Jesus.'" He then proceeded to give me an annual budget he wanted met for food, job training, and an orphanage. I looked at him and said, "Brother, do you hear yourself? People will not listen until you feed them? That is not true, for those people listened to you without being fed, and the Lord fed them. The Lord's Prayer says, 'Father, give us our daily bread.' It does not say, 'Pastor, give us our daily bread.' I was in India during a famine. In one day I saw thousands of starving people. I do not have the resources to meet that need,

49

so should I just leave the country? No, I should preach Christ. I have spent time in Africa with a man who saw the people starving, so he got enough rice to feed the fifty in front of his house. Word spread, and the next day there were 500; he bought rice to feed them, but the next day there were 3,000, and he bought every bit of rice in the village to feed them. The next day there was no rice, and people wanted to destroy his home for not feeding them." At that he laughed and said, "Yes, brother, I have seen such a thing, too." I urged him to let others do the social work that is being emphasized from every corner and to get on preaching the Gospel. He then told me that we had to do something because the Muslims were coming into the country building schools and giving free scholarships, and people were turning to them. This kind of thinking comes from those that see Christianity as a competing religion. It is not a religion, so how can it compete with a religion? Man does not compete with a dog, does he? Man is completely different. Likewise, we are not wooing people with food and education to convert them to our club so we will be the most popular folks in the country. If the only way people will come to Christ is for food, then I do not care if they come. Jesus fed the multitude, and the multitude rejected Him. Peter said, "Silver and gold have I none, but such as I have give I to thee." There is a very strong side benefit to the Gospel, which is that we become others-minded; however, no person will ever truly be others-minded until he discovers and receives the living Jesus. The pastor then told me that he had to rebuke the village pastors, for when he told them I was coming—and they were quite surprised, because they had not heard of a visiting speaker moving outside of the capital city—the pastors said, "What will he give us if we let him come?" My pastor friend went off on them, saying, "The man of God is coming, and you ask what will he give us? He will give you Jesus! Do you want more? He is not charging you to come, and yet you want to know what he will leave you?" The pastor shamed them, and I will be going and leaving nothing but Jesus. Sometimes it is difficult to stick to my conviction of "determining to know nothing among you save Christ, and Him crucified."

Latin America and Caribbean

One afternoon between meetings some of the brothers dropped me off at the home belonging to one of them. I decided to take a nap, so I was taken to the attic and shown a hammock. This home is in a very nice, but unsafe, neighborhood, so every home is behind a fifteen-foot wall with razor wire or electric fencing at the top. While looking out of the upper window, I saw a tent that piqued my interest, for it was in a vacant lot and its size was nearly a thousand square feet. Do not picture a neat tent from the nearby sporting goods store; it was actually several pieces of plastic stretched over metal supports and not all that attractive. I asked what it was and found out it was the home of gypsies. Amazing. Though they own a house in the wealthy neighborhood, they refuse to live in it, prefer to rent it out, and like to live in the tent, where they will stay for one to two months before moving on. Gypsies, I am told, are frightening; they are fortune tellers and thieves, and little else is known about them. I ask why they can live in a tent, without benefit of the security fences, and not have their goods stolen. The answer was, "Anyone would be crazy to enter the tent of a gypsy." I become more and more interested in these gypsies. "Let's take some of the books and go down there. I want to meet the gypsies." No one was the least bit excited at this proposal, but because I am a guest, they agreed to go with me. We entered the camp, to the surprise of the gypsies. I told them that I am an author from the United States and gave them a book. They could see my photo on the back cover. The tent is empty with the exception of mattresses and boxes at the far end. Next I make a request. "I know nothing about the gypsies. Can I talk to you?" To our surprise they get very excited, bring us chairs, and invite us to stay. They give us lots of information. When the children are born, they sleep with the fathers. As they grow older, they sleep with the grandfathers. The marriages are stable, with very few divorces. None of them can stand to stay in one place, for they soon become restless and must move on, and they love traveling. Since their children are in any one school for only a few weeks, the women are fearful for their education. I wonder if sometime in the distant past, God spoke to the forefathers of the gypsies, saying, "You will never settle and will not rest in any place." Their language has never been written down. There are gypsies all over the world, even, they tell me, in the U.S. I asked, "Why is it that nearly everyone in Brazil has a large wall around his home to avoid the thieves, and yet you have no such protection?" A woman responded, "We trust Jesus. We pray to Jesus, and we trust Him to protect us!" She could tell we were surprised, so she pointed to a small carving of Jesus that was hung on one of the tent posts. "Jesus!" She then explained to us that there are a group of evangelical gypsies that travel the world leading other gypsies to Jesus. They are at every major gathering. I was invited to come to a wedding over the weekend where these evangelists would be. Unfortunately, I was going to be leaving, or I would have gone. I asked if I gave them a case of books, could they get them in the hands of the evangelical leaders? "No problem!" It was a really nice time. As we left, one of the gypsy ladies, with a tear in her eye, said, "No one comes to visit us. We were blessed by your visit!" How true it is that when we judge, we judge wrongly.

A man who often visits homes in the poorest areas of town gave an example of the concept of hospitality among the poor of this country. One old man ushered him to a small cabinet and opened the door to reveal one bag each of rice and beans. The old man had no staples in his house except those two bags, and yet he stood proudly displaying them, for to him it was proof that life is not hopeless, that life has not dealt him a bad hand, and that tomorrow may get better.

A young man from a developing country was completing Bible college in the U.S. What he heard there shocked him. Some of the students would apply for work at various churches and wait to see what the salary was going to be before they committed to a church. The young man could not understand the call of God in such a situation. "How can money determine where a man serves Jesus?"

So many of the children here come up to me and just keep saying, "We love you!" This is my second service here, and again the interpreter and I flow together as I speak and he interprets. There are several here who are working beyond the point of exhaustion; since I have been there/ done that, I know the look. We talk, as usual, about the simplicity of letting Christ work through us, about how all we need is in Him who dwells in us, and our choice is where to go, taking Him to the place where He needs to work, for God is still in the business of putting flesh and bone on His message. I like this pastor and his wife. They are dancing during the song service. Soon people are jumping up all around us dancing, and then they form a train and start going around the room. If these are poor people, I cannot sort out what they lack, for there is no shortage of love, kindness, gentleness, humility, faith, and joy. Is there really anything beyond those that amounts to much?

Pastors have come from all over this region. Many have walked a good bit of distance and taken public transportation the rest of the way. One village pastor could walk only during low tide along the oceanfront. Through the period of high tide, he would climb a tree and wait. Another fellow lives deep in the jungle. Someone had given him a radio transmitter, so every morning in his jungle home he turns it on and says, "Good morning, world! I would like to talk about Jesus." Then he gives devotions and turns it off. He was asked if anyone could hear his broadcast, and he said that he did not believe so. He was then asked, "Why do you do it?" He paused, "Well, it is my world, the world Jesus gave me, the audience He has allotted to me, and I want to share Him." Would that we all were that happy with the bit of the world Jesus has given us. Beautiful. Some of the men could not read and/ or did not have Scripture translated in their tongue, so I

was disturbed when the introductory speaker asked them
to hold the Bible to their hearts and commit to reading it
more. Those with no Bible just put the conference program
to their chest. Right after that the meeting was given to
me. I shocked the pastors by telling them this meeting
was not going to be about reading and witnessing more.
It was going to be about God using their situation to
reveal Christ. I then told them I have had many failures in
ministry, so they should take a short break and go rest, and
if they did not want to bother to come back for meetings
with a speaker who was such a failure, no one would blame
them. After the break, the place was packed, and for the
entire week we had to extend the sessions over what had
been planned. The atmosphere was filled with the Holy
Spirit, where life in Christ makes sense, one's past failures
are in perspective, and there is hope. The eldest stood up
at the end and said, "We are wrong! It has been easier to
teach law and curses than to preach Jesus! I feel like Peter
when he said, 'What must I do to be saved?'" As always, I
know there was no contribution on my part. It was Jesus
at work, and it was the fullness of time for these men. At
the beginning of the week they had been beaten down by
comparisons and false definitions of success, but now they
were alive with excitement. At every break, small groups of
men were huddled together praying for one another. One
man said, "The day of the great man is over. We must be
like Jesus and work in our villages." My interpreter is an
American wife and mother who has lived here for some
time, and she is doing a wonderful job. In fact, I knew I
would be saying some challenging and hard things to the
men; therefore, I was happy to find a woman doing the

55

interpreting. Women can say the same hard statement that a man says, and yet it sounds so much softer and palatable. One thing that was interesting to me was the discussion on marriage. When I talked about women respecting their husbands, I realized that their cultural definition of *respect* included the notion that a woman was never to question a husband's decision. I made it clear that respect is not a rug under which men sweep all issues, but rather a place in which a woman stands before she asks the question. In the end, they chewed that truth and swallowed! In many places around the world, the revelation of a couple's oneness has yet to come. At the end of our week together, I heard the men shout over and over again, "Glorious Deos!"

This pastor is well respected in the ghetto area and has built a church and a community center. We stopped by the school he instituted for the inner-city children. The classrooms are small and filled with smiling faces. Each preschool child is issued a uniform and taught both English and the native tongue. This group cannot wait to tell me the names of colors in English. In turn, I do some magic tricks and tell them some stories. Next, we stop by the computer room, for the pastor has been given several old tower machines. He fixed half of them and sold them to afford the parts to fix the other half. The kids love working on the computers. The pastor always has something happening. When he gets broken computers, he prays over how to fix them, sells them, and buys something such as soccer balls for the school. He has a good vision for church buildings and wants to see them used every day of the week.

CHAPTER 2

Blessed Are Those Who Mourn

India

On my first trip here, my initial submerging into such wonderfully diverse surroundings, every sense is overwhelmed, and I am in culture shock much of the time. I arrive in the midst of a famine and a push by the Russians to make India their communistic "friend." Every move is monitored in a very uncomfortable manner. The first thing that I notice as I left the airport is the odor of ammonia coming from the masses using the streets as toilets. The second thing is the beggars and "baggage handlers" that insist on touching my bags as I carried them and then asking for a tip. The third thing is the taxi drivers' charging me a "skin tax" for riding with them (white people are discriminated against, so the meter is always declared to be broken). Because of the famine, at every corner there seem to be malnourished children with bloated stomachs using their last bit of energy to lunge forward, grab my leg, and beg for food. My teacher, who is there to pick me up, quickly informs me that I do not have enough resources to help the children, and if I do decide to give to one child,

57

the mob of others will attack for what they can get.
Remember, I am from Kansas, from a farming community.
As a child I was told, "Eat everything on your plate, for
there are kids in Africa and India that have nothing to eat."
This reminder haunts me, and everything in me says,
"Give, give, give!" Yet the reality has hit me that I do not
have enough to give; this must be God's job, for the Lord's
Prayer was, "Father, give us this day our daily bread," not,
"Dear Mike, give us our daily bread." I met up with another
Indian teacher, an Achin (Indian for teacher) who remains
quite optimistic amid all of the suffering around us. We are
to travel together for what will prove to be a difficult two
months as I live with the poor, the lower caste, and the
outcast. When we take a train (that still uses a steam
engine), I must travel with the very poor. A first-class ticket
is one dollar and a third-class ticket is fifty cents; the Achin
insists that we only go in third class, where I find myself in
stuffed compartments, sleeping on luggage racks or even
on the roof of the coach. At night, we stay in the most
modest of accommodations; at one point I fell asleep on
the dirt floor of a home. In the morning I awoke to find
that ants were building an extension of their anthill on the
side of my face, which was completely red from their
irritating bites. There was no bottled water, and in this heat
I quickly dehydrate. I am constantly looking for fresh
coconut juice, because it is impossible to be poisoned by
the liquid. I decided to throw my banana peel to a group
of baboons, without realizing that if the people were
starving, so were the monkeys. They instantly attacked the
car (at this time in India the 1948 Ambassador continued
to be produced without any changes. If the door handles

fell off of the 1948 Ambassador, they fell off the 1986 version) to the point that it soon looks as though we have a fur-lined car. We take off with the driver cursing me, and as we gain speed, the monkeys fall off, one by one. Next, I was given the schedule. For the next two months, my brother and I will be leaving Delhi daily, arriving at the airport at 3 a.m. for departure to a city, speaking all day, and returning by midnight. The schedule is consistent. I speak at a camp in the morning, a university, seminary, or Bible school during the day, and a church at night. Then I return to Delhi for a very few hours of sleep. It is grueling. Everything is outside of the box for a Westerner. People defecate on the street and at the beach. Toilet paper is unheard of, but the food, when we are successful at fighting off the rats that are worshipped, is a cornucopia of flavors. The believers are such a blessing. Actually, I must go beyond stating that, for they break my heart. My brother and I were with one couple that very much wanted us at their home for dinner. The family had no food. Therefore, they called the relatives and collected what they could. We arrived to boiled chicken bones with the broth poured over rice. In a family of twelve, we were the only two people to eat there that night. I remember that when I see any East Indian in my country. We pressed on, from one day to the next. Each night the Achin, who was 100% Indian and 100% Christian, would come to my bed, kneel, read a Scripture, and pray for me. One day we arose, and as I was getting into an Ambassador to go to a conference at a convent, I paused to look at the biggest raven that I had ever seen. Before I could enter the car, the raven dumped on me; it felt like an entire cup of excrement hit my head.

As it ran down my face and I was wiping it off, the Achin pronounced this a blessing from God! I asked, "How?" He said, "Everything that comes from heaven is a blessing from God!" Well, amen. I spoke that day with a white streak in my hair. We took an afternoon rest, and there was no water in the convent for cleaning up. I awoke in one hour, got up, looked in the mirror, and discovered two giant cockroaches in my hair eating the residue of the bird dung. I wrestled with being in India, and one day my teacher said, "Michael, you will leave India, but India will never leave you." Never were truer words spoken. This man was a blessing to me, and since at its inception Christianity was an Eastern Religion, not Western, he confirmed many things. In those months I went from caste to caste, from homeless person to homeless person, and from one type of inhumanity to another, and all the while, the communists were following. It was wonderful to drink tea from the same cup as a peasant, to sleep where the poorest of the poor sleep, and to travel as an Indian. I must admit that I love India. In the book of Esther we are told that the King of Israel married the queen of India. Did you know that the Hindu temple is exactly fashioned like the Old Testament temple? Amen. At the end of two months, I was totally, unequivocally exhausted; I cannot explain what that is like other than to say that the world, the body, the soul, and the spirit shut down. Only the heart that invites Him remains. I was spent! I flew my final trip out of Delhi and arrived in the city. I did a morning camp meeting and then a general meeting for seminary students and residents of the community. By this time, I barely knew my name. I was asked to come to a private room to meet with one of the locals. I sat down, and there before me was a dark-skinned Indian woman looking at the ground. She spoke first: "I am dark skinned, I have a limp when I walk, and my parents have told me from birth that I am a curse from God. They will never be able to arrange a marriage for me, and I am a burden to them. Therefore, I stay hidden in a closet during the day, and by night I very quietly do the housework so no one will have to see me. When everyone has left the house, I go to the market for the family. If a light-skinned Indian enters the market, I wait until he leaves. Every day I pray for death." At that moment the Lord spoke clearly to me, "I have had you here for the last two months for this meeting. I have sent you to India for this one young woman. She is the reason that you are here." In one way, that information broke me. Yet, I thought, "Lord, I am completely spent! Why did you not send me directly here?" Since then I have learned that there are wheels within wheels when it comes to His plan and His workings. I began to share Christ with her. I asked, "If you are so worthless, why would God send me 12,000 miles just for you?" We talked everything through, and in the end, she wanted Jesus. We prayed, and I called in the principal of the seminary to tell him what had happened and that she wanted baptism. It is known throughout the Hindu world that baptism completely cuts a person off from his previous culture. The pastor pulled me aside and said, "If I baptize her and she is not genuine, I will go to prison." I assured him that it was genuine and that she was to be baptized. To this he agreed. I explained to her what it meant to be born again and to be a child of the Most High God. She was never to hide or shy away from others.

She, by revelation, could receive what I was saying. After two months of "terrible conditions," I was prepared to go home with the knowledge that it was all God, and it was all beautiful.

As I was leaving our hotel, the lady behind the desk asked if I were a priest. I told her I was a pastor. She then requested that I pray for her daughter and said, "She died. I want you to pray that God would let her into heaven." I explained why children go to heaven and that heaven was not the issue, but today "Mother" would be the issue. Later, when we were able to spend some time talking, she told me that her daughter was hit in front of the house by an auto rickshaw that drug her for seventy feet. She raced to her daughter and carried her to the local doctor, who told her through his own tears that the daughter had already died. At that, she carried the little girl's body to the hospital, all the way crying out, "Jesus, do not let me down and let my daughter die!" (She is a nominal Catholic.) She then told me of her non-Christian in-laws who hated her and had always pronounced curses on her and her daughter, wishing that they would die. She said they did not come to the funeral and were happy to hear of the death. She and her eleven-year-old son had determined to commit suicide. However, when she saw me and heard what I was doing, she decided to talk to me. We talked about many things: mourning, pain, comfort, and mainly Jesus; as we kept speaking of Jesus, her countenance lifted. I asked if she noticed she was feeling better. "Yes! But I do not know why!" I explained the power Jesus has, and she was so open, so ready to move toward Jesus for the first time. As always, there is nothing His nearness will not cure!

I met with a thirty-something couple that had been in ministry for ten years. "We are in the same boat. Both of us are at the end of our ropes. We cannot go on. The Christian life is too difficult. During the past ten days the revelation has come to us: Jesus is our life! But how do we abide? We see the need; we see He can live through us, if only we will abide, but we do not know how to achieve the life of abiding!" I could hardly wait for them to stop talking so I could give them the good news. "How do you abide? When I tell you, you will see that abiding is a God thing, something He does. You abide by simply acknowledging that you are abiding. Abiding is faith. Anything other than acknowledging you are abiding is unbelief. You are abiding! He is the Gardener Who placed you on the Vine. He did the work. Can you just get up in the morning and say, 'Lord, thank You that I abide'?" There was such release on their faces. I continued, "You did not make the revelation of Christ as your life happen. He made it happen. He did it when you were not even asking for it. It is not of you. It is all Him. Now that you knowingly want to move forward, how much more will He do?" This couple had truly been broken by the circumstances in ministry, they were seeing that power could come from their weakness, and they were really excited.

A pastor here was born twice dead; not only was he born dead in trespasses and sin, but born dead in a stillbirth. After a few hours of mourning, his family placed him in rags in the trash. The house servant secretly went and got his body, took a hot iron, and ironed the umbilical cord that hung from him. As she did that, he came to life. She then took the baby back to his mother, alive! This pastor is in charge of a variety of Christian ministries and works. He is a Doer yet has the softness for the hurting that can only come from the Spirit of God. His home is a beehive of activity. His wife, retired chief of staff at the local hospital, is a jewel. Unfortunately, she suffered a stroke two years ago, has diabetes, and needs a knee replacement. This time I find that the man also has brought his parents home to live with him. They are delightful. His mother tells me the greatest changes in India since she was a child are transportation (they always used to walk for miles) and communication.

We take a break and a woman comes to me with a prayer request. I believe that her husband has died. She was working in a hostel in India with her five-year-old daughter. After a month or so the owner threw her out and kept the daughter as his slave. He refuses to release her. The woman is poor and can do nothing. She has a beautiful heart and is working with several other poor people to preach Jesus. She has two older sons that also struggle. She simply wanted prayer that the daughter would be released. I told her that I would share that with my supporters and we would be praying. I believe that Jesus, who is the glue of the universe, holding the man together, will begin to withdraw and the man will come apart. He will know that it is because of the evil that he has done and will release the girl.

During the lunch break I am told of a woman in attendance; in her youth she was unable to conceive, so she made a promise to a Hindu god that if she bore a son, she would sacrifice the child to the river god when the child reached the age of seven. Such things are common occurrences among the practice of Hinduism, and much of New Age thought is merely old-age Hinduism in different clothing. At any rate, she did conceive, and when the boy reached the age of seven, she took him to the bridge over the river, walked to the middle, fought off his clinging attempts to save himself, and threw him over the bridge. As would be expected, afterward the woman went completely off beam with torment, grief, and guilt, but through that, she came in contact with the Church and gave her life to Jesus. There was a definite change in her countenance.

We notice that the priest is missing his index finger and ask him what happened. When he was very young, his cousin gave him a firecracker with a short fuse. Firecrackers in India are the size of a pack of cigarettes and equal to a portion of a stick of dynamite. The firecracker blew his finger and part of the thumb off. There was only one hospital in the area, a cancer hospital. He was taken there and spent many days recuperating. Doctors wanted to amputate his hand, and he refused. He simply said, "Let God heal me. If not, the infection will kill me." He thought that losing his finger was the worst thing that could happen to anyone. However, being in the cancer hospital, he could see that there were many things much worse and that he could be grateful.

Pacific Nations

I had planned an afternoon off when a fellow came up after a session and said, "My life is all in knots, but as I listened to you, the knots came untied one by one, and now I feel free." I knew I was to spend the day with him, and it was a great time. When he was young, his drunken father would beat him with a stick if he missed one of his multiplication tables. We talked about transferring the concept of an earthly father to the Heavenly Father. The light turned on; he could see that secretly in his heart he was waiting for God to hit him. We turned to I Corinthians 13 to find the true character of God, and he was really excited. We went walking later, and he said, "My spirit is jumping."

One husband was involved in multiple affairs; because of his wife's insecure childhood, she wanted to keep her family together at any cost. For that reason, she did not say anything about the affairs, parties, and alcohol; for sixteen years she had feared taking a stand. After our session, she went and told her husband he could bring no more sin into the house. She told him she was not angry, but that Christ held him and the family together, and the sin was a dissolving agent that was making him and the entire family come apart. She reported to me the next day that he came back, repented, and said, "I will be with you in church Sunday and want to become involved."

I saw a friend, and when I asked about his family, he reported there had been trauma; his young daughter had started hearing condemning voices and could no longer think. She had been put on heavy medication. I asked if my associate and I could see her, and when we arrived, she could only tell us what the voices were saying. We have seen God do some marvelous things with people who were in this state. It is said that the average person has around fifty problems, including things they would change in family, job, and themselves. With five billion people, that would mean that mankind could potentially have 250 billion problems. How long would we have to study to have answers for every conceivable problem? Therefore, we go to God for answers. "If any of you lacks wisdom he should ask God, who gives generously to all without finding fault, and it will be given to him" (James 1:5). We asked God. This girl was very sensitive, a feeler. At an early age she was ridiculed for being too outgoing, so she began to withdraw, lying in her bed beating herself up with verbal assaults. "I am so stupid, so defective, so stubborn." Her daily verbal bashings became too much, so she transferred the "I" to "you," for it was better to hear from someone else that she was stupid than to hear it from herself. When she developed a crush on a boy who was not interested in her, it was too much; she disconnected mind from will and emotions, and the assaults started in earnest, intensifying until they were all she could hear. They kept her from thinking about the identity she should have perceived, that she was a fun and outgoing person. It was a bit like having a puppet on her hand that kept talking and undeniably making noise, but it was her noise. The only way to stop it from talking would be to make the hand busy with something else. Therefore, for the next two weeks she will be writing as many as 500 times 33 verses that have to do with being accepted and secure in Christ and significant to Him.

We stopped to visit with a lovely elderly couple and a single woman who stayed with them. They could not attend the meetings because he was recently released from the hospital with severe diabetes (one leg is gone and the other does not function). His wife has Parkinson's, and the single woman is raising four children after being abandoned by her husband. They all asked, "Why?" I asked if they had prayed to know the revelation of Christ in them; they had. Next I explained that we want to know that Christ can rise to our level of need when we are sick, but we do not ever want to be sick. We want the revelation that He can meet every need that man, the world, or the government promises to meet, and yet we never want to be abandoned by man or the world's systems. How can that be? "Has Christ met you in your sickness and loneliness?" "Oh, yes!" was the reply. We continued to share from that perspective and had a great prayer time of thankfulness! Jesus always meets us at our level of need.

A man told me his story: His brother with epilepsy went swimming and drowned, after which this man went out into his boat, picked up the anchor, and as he threw it out of the boat cried out to God, "Just as I throw this anchor out of the boat, I am throwing God out of my life. I want nothing more to do with You!" Several years later when his life had deteriorated, he was out in the boat in a storm. As boats do, it turned toward the anchor. God spoke to him: "I am your Anchor! Just as the boat turns toward the anchor in the storm, you must turn to Me in your storm!" The love of God broke through, the man returned to faith in Christ, and now he loves God because He first loved him. Beautiful.

After the church service the pastor's wife took us back to our hotel and told us a bit of their story, a series of little miracles. They met in the military, she became a believer, they married, and he was called to missions. She was slower coming along to see that call. Their children were often sick, and their eldest son got a type of staph infection that made his skin look like he was a burn victim. If he were touched, his skin would come off in his mother's hand. It has taken years to get over it, but in all of this the boy is coming to a deeper and deeper understanding of who Jesus is. Beautiful. Their house and automobile were destroyed in the hurricane, yet she agreed that there were things to be learned in suffering that could not be found out any other way.

Eurasia

The interpreter and I were asked to provide a counseling session with a woman who was involved in the occult, whose husband had committed suicide, and who herself had attempted suicide. She was sent to a psych hospital, where she was told that her problems were psychological, not chemical, and so she needed to work out her own life; then she was dismissed. She was undone and coming apart at age 37. Her new boyfriend had dropped her off at a building that housed a Christian ministry and told her he was leaving her. We began to work through her history, how she felt, why she felt that way, and the various attempts she had made to change. Then I began to share Christ; I told her she had a life that lost and needed a life that wins. Jesus has the life that wins. Then I explained our crucifixion with Christ, and she said, "Of course." I asked, "Do you understand what I am saying?" "Yes!" "Why do you understand what I am saying to you?" "I do not know!" "Well, think for a minute. Does getting a new life through the crucifixion of the old life make any sense to you?" "Yes." I explained that the only way she could hear this is if God had already been speaking it to her, so I was not teaching her but witnessing to the work of Christ in her life. I had not told her anything new. She could not believe that, but I continued, "I did not tell you things you did not know; I told you things you have always known, but in different words." God had been speaking it to her. I asked if she would like to believe in Jesus. I explained, "You confess Christ as life and Savior, then . . ." and she did not let me finish. Instead, she immediately said, "I believe in Jesus; I will ask Him into my life." Her countenance lifted, she smiled, and she was a different person. It is wonderful how God's network brings about so much, how the interpreter got to develop a ministry in this country, how I was able to travel here, how the woman had gone through a multitude of problems to arrive here, and how we all got together in the fullness of time! All things reveal the Glory of God. There are many questions that we cannot answer, but it is true that God plans wonderful things.

Another woman had prayed for years that God would send help for her problem of having an alcoholic husband. As we talked and I went through her history, she revealed feelings of worthlessness deriving from her upbringing with a physically and verbally abusive father. I asked, "How does a worthless person help an alcoholic? An abusive man— your father—indicated that you were worthless, and now you hope a different abusive man will communicate to you that it is not so. However, abusive people will never—they cannot—undo our feelings of worthlessness." We turned our attention to Christ, and how as a branch is grafted to receive the life of the vine, so she could receive Christ as her life, and Christ's life is sufficient. There is nothing His nearness will not cure. Her fleshly husband, heretofore an expert at bringing her down, would feel pressure from living with a wife who lives in the Spirit, and she would be set free to tell the truth in love. She smiled as the light of God's truth came on for her.

A big, jolly fellow who loved to tell a lot of stories related his past; he had endured a troubled childhood and had no parents. He spent from age seventeen to twenty-five in the prison system, and during that time a   girl began to write him and share the Lord. It was through her testimony that he gave his life to Jesus. I asked what had happened to the girl and whether they had stayed in touch. He introduced me to the "girl," who had become his wife; they had five children. Presently he is the director for a local youth ministry.

I am ushered in with the interpreter to do a radio interview concerning those with disabilities. The woman that hosts the show is blind. All of the questions concern suffering. She is confused herself. Some tell her that being blind is a blessing, and others say that it is a curse. The wickedest thing is when she is told that if she had more faith, she could see again. Of course, those who say such things will always have an opportunity to put their own message into practice. Later on, off the air and in a training session, I asked the blind woman from the radio program to give us her history. It is vexing. She was a real Feeler and Doer and reminded me so much of my daughter; both ladies love and enjoy being around people so much. (As a small girl, my daughter was always fixing anniversary dinners for Betty and me. The food was at times shocking, but the presentation was fun.) I could see how much this woman loved people and needed them. However, as she described her history, I could see that people had only brought her pain. She was sick as a small child, and her mother called her a "write off" because she was in the hospital so often. At school she had no friends once it was discovered that she was Jewish. She felt dismissed, defective, unlovable, and insecure. Then in her last year of medical school she went blind, an event that proved to her that all the aforementioned had to be true. Even God had rejected her. At that point she was a setup for all of the spiritual abuse that she suffered from those who confirmed her fear that she was unacceptable to God. We had a great session, but understanding the history is much easier than explaining the answer. We looked at her history bit by bit and pulled things together. She understood her self-life and the solution—a funeral—and next, what it meant to deny the old feelings. It was a shock to her to realize that the reason she hated feeling defective was that she was not defective. If Christ is in her and His life is her life, then how can she wear the clothes of a defective person and not struggle? Next we looked at daily living. She was taping the whole thing and I was able to witness to what was happening, by His Spirit, in her. Finally, we talked about power in weakness.

Alcoholism is just shocking. I have heard it said that there is a certain state in India where every home has at least one heroin addict. In this place it is alcoholism; I do not think there is a family that has gone unscathed by the problem, and many at the conference have been affected. These people have been drunk for so long that being sober seems odd to them; drunkenness is their reality. Drink all night, sleep most of the day, and start drinking again.

72

The result of all of this is explained simply by saying that someone is "sick." The mayor of the city is drunk half of every day, so he cannot receive the populace through appointments because he is "sick," or rather, stumbling, passing-out drunk. It is sad. Then if someone were to sober up after twenty to fifty years of drinking, he is so emotionally stunted that the residual problems kick in: verbal abuse, pouting, controlling, and temper tantrums. Come quickly, Lord Jesus! There is a really neat farmer doing mission work here. He told me that he got a job cutting wood for an old woman. It took him all morning. The drunks kept coming by, telling him better ways to accomplish the work and complaining about unemployment. In the end, the old woman paid him $20! Doctors only make $90 per month. He protested, telling her that she was paying him too much. She said she was just happy to get the job done; she had been looking for a couple of months for someone that could chop her wood and could not find anyone. Most who could work are drunk. Two young women just beautiful in countenance are here at the meetings, and both are victims of an alcoholic father. I just think of how much he is missing out on. The wife is completely downcast, having thrown in the towel. Emotionally she is done, but every day he is there playing the same old game. I marvel at her life, that she can say that Jesus is all that matters and she is, moment by moment, able to rise above it. What I marvel at more is God, who desires that no one perish. The patient longsuffering of God is a wonderful thing in which to bask and yet not take too lightly. Everyone who knows this drunken husband/father is sick of him. Everyone, that is, but Jesus! One young lady is at the university with unbelieving roommates who harass her daily concerning her faith. She was telling me of the multitude of questions that they had for her. Some were really good. One wanted to know the difference between her and a Jehovah's Witness, because, "You both befriended me, you both offered to teach me English using the Bible, and then you both tried to get me into your church. It looks like you both have a little different teaching, but both of you have the same motive. I do not think either of you are a true friend!" Like I said, they were good questions. However, I have a habit of answering only half of someone's questions. In fairness, they must then answer mine and defend their system. Somehow the world believes that their questions reveal their great minds, but the world is always upside down. Answers reveal intelligence; the most ignorant person alive can ask a question! I insist that inquirers give me answers to my questions. How does a chemical store a memory? In evolution, which calf developed the ability to nurse? Can it be proven there is no Master Planner to the universe? Is it a certainty that a person can do whatever he wants so long as it does not hurt another? If a person does not serve God, he deifies self; how can it be shown that self is helping? A Mormon came to my door and wanted to put me on the defensive by asking if I were a Christian, and then he wanted to start the normal accusations. I said that I did not come to his door to ask questions, he had come to mine, and so I wanted my questions answered. Why were they polygamists? Why were they bigots? Why are women considered less deserving than men? Why did the Mormons slaughter the innocent in Utah? What could be read from the book of Mormon that would make me convert? Why does so much incest, immorality, and divorce exist among the Mormons? I enjoyed being the foolish one that only asks questions!

Asia

I spent an afternoon with a couple from the church. Occasionally in my travels I get frustrated when I talk about Jesus and there are no follow-up remarks, just a moving on to "the real business at hand." The feeling communicated is, "Yes, yes, we all believe in Jesus, but we all have a busy schedule! We are only serving as host to you because some authority figure over us requested us to do so." In those times I must remember what the Lord said to me years ago: "I will send you for the one, the Divine One God and the one person who specially needs Me at the time." We sat down to eat, and assuming that the leadership was not terribly interested in what I was doing, I briefly told them the message of abiding. The man (a real Doer; he learned Chinese in four months and now preaches in it) looked at his wife, then back to me, and said, "Keep talking. We have both been praying, 'Lord, we cannot go on. We have no joy. We only exist.'" It turned into a four-hour lunch! We walked on the beach, and the man looked at me and said, "Why am I so critical and angry?" I responded, "Very simply, you hate yourself, you are sick of yourself, you cannot change, and your hatred has flooded out to others." He began to weep and said, "It is true!" He was working so hard to be a Christian that the hard work had covered up Jesus, Who makes the Christian life naturally possible. I gave him the exercise of holding up his hands and pretending that he was holding his problems. The arms became heavier and heavier until he could not hold them up. I told him to give the problems up, release them to God, and rest in God. Man has a God because man is deficient and dependent. With teary eyes he said with surprise, "I have peace! I have not felt peace for so many years." This couple did not book "the ambulance" or know that it was coming, but God did. For the rest of the afternoon they would not stop asking questions. We covered many topics, from marriage to ministry. He kept saying, "I want this training," but my point to him was that he has it. The training was to come to the end of his abilities and belief system so he could accept what he had always had in Christ. A few days afterward he sat on the front row, correcting his wife as she interpreted. Later in the evening he said that she was very unaffectionate; she should lie on his chest and hold him. I said, "Right! After you have told her she is stupid?" They looked at me and said, "How did you know he says that?" I went on to describe in detail what he (and every other compulsive Doer) does. It was great fun with a lot of laughs. I could see them soften toward one another.

At the end of a service many came forward, as is the custom here, for the pastor or visiting speaker to pray for them. I generally pray for one thing, the revelation of Christ, for those who have that and see Him also see that He meets every need. However, this day there was a long line of women with the same problem, husbands who had left them for younger women. The husbands generally did not want divorces; in fact, they continued to come home either at night or during the day; it is just that they want two women. If just once in any culture I could see the practice of having two wives or a wife and a mistress work out beneficially, I might not be so negative. I finally turned to the pastor and requested that all the women stay while we go over some basic teaching about how to live in that situation. I went an extra hour, but no one was fidgeting or otherwise looking like they wanted to go home; these poor women wanted hope. In that type of situation they have no marriage in any practical sense. The reality of that is resisted because they still believe that a mate can meet spiritual needs (love, acceptance, assurance, security, commitment, and affirmation). However, if those needs are met in Christ, then when legitimate marital needs (communication, companionship, fellowship, and physical) are not met, it is easier to cope. I had to make all of this very specific, after which it was beautiful to see a room full of weeping women slowly begin to smile and even laugh. Why were they smiling? There is nothing the nearness of Jesus will not cure!

In 1950 there were basically no Christians in this country; today there are 500,000, despite the fact that the preaching of the Gospel, open meetings, witnessing, and conversion are strictly prohibited by the Hindu government. There has been much persecution, and the Church has grown without buildings, formal education, programs, or gimmicks. The pastor who works with us said several things that immediately bound me to him. He was offered a job by a large ministry that wanted to expand its kingdom in his country. He refused, because he is called by God to minister to lepers. As a child, he was the youngest of three brothers and two sisters. His Hindu parents were very superstitious; they consulted, through divination, the devil spirit. (This is a little different side to Hinduism, one that is hidden by those in the West that come here to explore mystical matters.) The devil spirit told them that one of their children would die. The smallest son knew, being the youngest and always in poor health, that he would be the one child that died. At age twelve he ran away from home and made his way to the city. As a street child he went looking for a job, but every potential employer that met him thought he was too frail to make any kind of worker. Finally, one old woman told him to go to a church meeting and pray. He went to the meeting, and one of the families at the church hired him. They also found a place for him in a Christian orphanage, where in time he gave his life to Jesus. He was able to complete school. God then called him to work with all the leper families that he had seen abused and moved from place to place. For instance, he had noticed one family that was thrown out of their house. They moved to a straw shack, but it was burnt. Finally, they were chased to the edge of town. The Hindus do not tolerate lepers and believe that they have been cursed by a god. He began to preach to the afflicted and help them as he could. In the end, he found living space for 400 families. There was one husband and wife in which he was particularly interested; well, he was not just interested in them, because they also had a daughter. In time she became his wife. It is so impressive that he did not just go into the community, minister, and leave. He married someone from within the community, something not heard of. Since his conversion, his brothers have come to Christ, and one is a pastor. His parents are now attending church. This son that was marked to die actually became the source of life to his family. He lost his old life, and in so doing became a child of God. He reminds me of Joseph: Others meant it for evil, but God made it for good.

We got to go visit a leper colony by walking two to three miles through an ancient city that had narrow streets, women everywhere hand-spinning wool, old temples, goat heads covered with brass hung on walls, men sitting in small circles talking, and children playing. One man who lives here had apparently died and was taken to the river to be cremated. As the fire touched his feet, he came to and demonstrated that he was still alive. Here it is decreed that once a man is taken to the river to be burned, he can never return to his village, for he is dead. Therefore, he asked to be allowed to leave by another way and settle in this city. All people here are his relatives. As mentioned, everything here is very ancient, and we walk along rough marble roads until we reach the outskirts of the city. What we see next is a beautiful valley below filled with terraced fields many hundreds of years old; the white road winds through the valley, and in the far distance we can see the leper village. The lepers have one of the most beautiful views in the world! Few venture near their place, either, so it is relatively quiet. We stumble along, passing the odd goat or basket of vegetables balanced on the head of a woman, from whom we often get a toothless, "Namastay," the Hindu greeting. Finally, we reach the valley floor, and a large footbridge spans the last part of the valley. We bounce along, while watching our steps, for there are many gaps between the sticks through which a person could fall to his death. We reach the village of the lepers. Walking past many fingerless and toeless people, we make our way to the center of the compound and enter a Spartan, yet comfortable, but cold, two-room apartment. The buildings are in a long row and are actually much better than those in which we find many of the people in the city living. Soon the resident enters, a short man with the handsome look typical of his countrymen, the blending of the attractiveness of two very large neighboring nations. The man tells me that he is the captain of the compound; government officials allow him to be in charge and never come to check on the place. Privately he was told, "You are a Christian, and thus, trustworthy!" His father had been a mean man, so he could not wait to leave home. Twelve days after he was born, he was placed next to a new fire. His mother left, the fire spread, and soon it had nearly burnt his feet off. He then contracted leprosy. The interesting thing about leprosy is that it does not cause pain. However, after it is cured, there is the constant pain from the damaged extremities. I gain insight into the colony. There is a pecking order and heaps of infighting, reminding me of a prison hierarchy. The government gives a ration of rice to each person. So far there is a small building for a church of sixty converts. One problem is that when someone is to be baptized, he has to be taken deep into the mountains to thwart detection and the resulting trouble from Hindu authorities. It is interesting that Hindus seem to have a better grasp of baptism than do Western Christians; Hindus recognize that it is the complete cutting off of the old and becoming something completely new. I ask if he gets depressed. "When I feel despondency coming, I draw near to God, and it leaves." I ask what he thinks of suffering, of getting leprosy. "God has taught me many things through it, and I have no regrets. I came here 27 years ago, married, and had a daughter, for whom I prayed that she would get an education, have a good life, and marry a believer. God answered me. How could I complain?" Amen! His wife appears and shuffles past us, emerging several minutes later balancing a tray of hot tea on hands with no fingers. We each take a cup of really nice tea with cloves. She smiles but withdraws to the back room to drink her tea. I am told of a plan. Imagine how difficult it is to find something that people without fingers, feet, and facial features can do for support; but twenty families could be given materials to build chicken coops, fifty chicks each, and the feed needed. They would be able to sell the eggs and the chickens and become self-supportive. I am shown the room currently used for church services. To get in, we go past two goats and enter a low-ceilinged room in the back of a barn. There is a pulpit, and I am told that up to eighty people have been in there. That is amazing, since there is not enough room to swing a cat, so to speak! I walk by an old woman whose Christian countenance shines through her featureless face. She has nothing but palms for hands and no legs; she is cutting plants to make natural remedies. There are no medications of any kind available for these people. I tell her if I get sick, I will be coming to see her. This is met with great laughter. By the time we leave, a crowd has gathered, and the people are quite joyful about the foreigners that have come. We take the long walk back down the marble path, surveying the mountains all around us.

Another year we traveled to the leper colony for a church service where my son and I will be the speakers. We beat along on the mountain road, stopping periodically to push the car up the incline. Arriving, we remember why we so appreciate this place. The lepers have all come together and are giving us the Christian greeting, holding their hands in a praying position and saying, "Jay-me-she" (greetings in the name of Jesus). Of course, there is not a person in the group with a whole hand; fingers, feet, ears, and noses are all missing. The colony is by a river, and all around us, through the faint mist, we see the terraced fields, beyond which are the great mountains. There was no mistake in the government's placing the lepers in such a beautiful area. Wells must be dug and water hauled by hand, because the river is very polluted from the carpet factories that dump chemicals and dyes directly into the water. A cow drinking from this river would die within a few hours. However, the terraced land next to the river is watered from the springs above and makes an ideal place for growing rice, wheat, and flax. The colony's hope is to buy this piece of land next to the river, for it would allow the lepers to grow some crops and become more self-sufficient, but this is not the main reason for acquiring the land. According to law, the land, or greenbelt, that lies between the river and this property can be used at the discretion of the landowner. The Hindus cremate and the Christians have a conviction to refuse to cremate in order to provide proper burial. Hindus will not permit any of their land to be used for this purpose. Purchasing the land would provide a place in the greenbelt for Christian burials. I asked, "Just how many people would you be able to bury here?" The response, "Endless." How so? Well, it seems that every year the river floods. The farmland, after the crops are taken, would be used for raising pigs. During the floods the pigs would be moved into the leper colony. Those floods would wash downstream the remains of the bodies that had been buried, and when the water receded, there would be no bodies left in the greenbelt, hence freeing up all of the space. The issue is that they all want to have a burial in protest to their Hindu roots, but they know that after burial the corpses do not need to remain buried, for their spirits are with God. Well, amen. Many women pass by the village carrying hay used as goat feed in baskets on their backs with a single strap that passes across the forehead. Others, the very poor, have collected a sturdy weed for heating and fuel. The walls along the roads are covered with brown circles the size of large plates. It is cow dung, shaped and stuck to the walls for drying, after which it will be used as fuel for cooking and heating. The church meets below a room where goats are kept. As is customary here, before entering the "church" (or any home), one has to take off his shoes, which leaves him—in this case, us—standing in the goat droppings. Inside, the ceiling is covered with small pieces of cardboard and plastic in an only partially successful attempt to keep the droppings and urine from coming down through the ceiling. Everyone sits on the floor. The order of service is very similar to that in the West. There are several songs, prayers (where everyone prays out loud at once), and then the sermon. I preach first on the purpose of suffering, using the example of Michael Francis, the Indian leper that blessed so many but only came to Christ because of his leprosy. My son talked about the folly of looking to man for acceptance and approval. We had a beautiful time, and the people were often laughing. It makes my heart sing to see joy on the faces of what some would consider untouchables.

Day three of the seminar begins with my pressing the point concerning the love of God. If only we knew the love of God, we could all sleep so well. In His love, God only permits what He could prevent. At that a man understood the message, got up on his knees, raised up his palms, and shouted, "I have no fingers, I have no toes, I am a leper, and I thank God! If I had not become a leper, I would never have become a Christian. I would have remained a Hindu. I would rather go to heaven with no fingers and no toes than go to hell with fingers and toes." Revelation! A prayer answered as truth made the journey from head to heart.

Two fellows from the base of a mountain have come the farthest, having spent the previous day walking and busing to get here. They are really neat fellows. Often when I am with such great—yet so humble—men, I have to fight off the feelings of inferiority, which are another expression of pride. One fellow was sick and dying at age twelve; his father and brother, Hindu witchdoctors, could not help. He ventured to the capital city, where he was told of Jesus and believed. He was immediately healed. In the last twelve years, he has started over twenty churches with a combined membership of 2,000. Recently, the rebel soldiers kidnapped, interrogated and "trained" him for three days before releasing him. They later returned, and one took out his gun to shoot him. However, at that exact moment an army helicopter appeared, which caused the men to flee. Again they returned and this time wanted all the dollars that he had. He explained his occupation and that he did not have dollars. For reasons known only to

God, the men believed him. He is married and has three children; everyone in the family but his father and brother has come to Christ. His partner is equally interesting, having started over twenty churches that have amassed a membership of 2,100. His family practiced the dark arts, divination, and more. He, too, became quite ill, was told of Jesus, and believed. The rebel soldiers had a "shoot-on-sight" order on him that caused him to flee to the capital city for three months, where for now he is working safely. These two believers wear a look in their faces and bodies that I have seen many places in the world, the look of the frontier, a weathered, wind-burned look. They dress simply, pack lightly, and move quickly. They are intense men, and yet soft in another way. The lifestyle of a frontier evangelist must add a minimum of ten to fifteen years to the appearance of a man's age. I can see faintly what Paul meant when he said, "I complete the suffering of Christ in my body."

One girl here has a great story. Her father was an alcoholic and would often abuse her. He hit her so hard in the eye with his elbow that it blinded her and destroyed the nerves and skin around the eye. In this part of the world, any physical defect means that no marriage can be arranged. The father eventually threw the girl out on the street, where she lived until the pastor found her. She believed in Christ and went to her aunt to tell her the good news. The aunt believed and invited the girl to live with her. Next, the girl told her mother, grandmother, sister, and brother about Jesus. They all believed. At this the father became very angry, and when the pastor would visit the family to pray with them and share with them, the father would leave angrily, until finally one day he told the pastor never to come again. The pastor did not listen! At last, when the pastor was performing a funeral service, the father was in attendance and afterward went to the pastor, asking if he, too, could believe in Jesus. There is a lot of undoing that comes with Christ's doing, and indeed, much changed with the man, yet he still could not stay away from alcohol. The pastor discovered that if he arrived at the man's house when the man was drunk, the man would hide under the bed for shame. The pastor at length went to him, explained that the man was to hide no longer, and assured him that he would continue to disciple him. Again, God does not cause all things, but He certainly causes all things to work together for the good. Consistently, things make us that were meant to break us. Now the girl works in the church and is receiving a salary, not much, but something.

The pastor tells us of another woman that went to the river and sacrificed her son to the river god. She was beating her head on the rock erected to the god until it was bloody and she lost consciousness. A converted Hindu Sadhu saw her, and after she divulged what had happened, she said to him, "If only I had that one minute back." The Sadhu said, "The true God is giving you that one minute to believe in His Son, Jesus Christ." She did and is now pressing on.

Latin America or Caribbean

A true story about a chief in the Amazon region was related to me by one of the support people involved in helping with the tribe. It seems that when any tribesperson got depressed and wanted to commit suicide, he went to a particular place to eat a poisonous plant. (Of course, this sharply contrasts with the tale of anthropologists, who believe everyone in the Amazon led an idyllic life until the missionaries came!) The daughter of the chief fell into depression, found the plant, ate it, and died. The chief, in turn, became so despondent that he decided to kill himself, but when he went to the exact place, picked the plant, and started to place it in his mouth, Jesus appeared to him. An amazing thing is that Jesus appeared wearing the feathers and paint of the tribe; He appeared as a warrior. The chief believed in Jesus, and now the tribe is Christian. Is it not amazing that Jesus still comes down to us, to our level of understanding? Why, then, are we being taught to climb up a ladder to find Him? He comes down. It is the Glory of God.

A certain ministry group is committed to seeing Jesus restore marriages. There is one miracle after another as divorce proceedings are cancelled. One participant had met with his city's local judge, who had said that in his entire career, he had never seen a divorce stopped. The fellow presented the program and offered to begin to visit with the people before a divorce was finalized. The judge was so impressed he decided that no marriage would be performed in the city unless the couple had completed the ministry's course, and no divorce would be granted until the course was completed. Out of sixty divorces on the books, with many of the couples having been separated for five or more years, forty-five have been canceled. These believers are fighting for families; they see it as a battle and call each other warriors. There are many, many testimonies to what God has done. One man who attended the small-group meetings was an atheist only interested in helping his marriage. When it came to the section on prayer, he listened but would not pray. One week, as he was performing a surgery, things began to go wrong. He did not know what to do, but remembered the teaching on prayer. He stopped and prayed, and instantly the solution came to him! He came to the group meeting the next week proclaiming that he was a believer in God and prayer! The ministry is a large production supported through the donations of the members, who give an average of twenty cents each per week; that, in turn, is multiplied by the hand of God, and the ministry thrives. I love this ministry because it is built upon the "lesser man," those with simple lives, few resources, and sometimes, the inability to read. They simply followed the program, allowed Jesus to work in their marriages, were restored to Him and to their mates, and now have become pastors. Amazing! Is not Jesus good?

I ask for a volunteer so I can take a history in front of the group, which always seems to put flesh and bone to the teaching. This volunteer has suffered at the hands of many psychologists. As a child, when he had a fever, his father told him to stop shaking and being sick. When the boy could not stop shaking, he was beaten. The fellow is a Feeler-Thinker, and therefore likes security, hates the unknown, wants information, desires to please, avoids complex relationships, stalls under pressure, and, as a result of all the rejection, is extremely insecure. The solution for him was to get a life! Christ's life! Jesus is not only our Savior from sin, but also our Savior from insecurity. To explain how a teaching can save a man would take volumes, and the man, of course, would remain unsaved. However, we are not saying a teaching will save someone. We are saying that Jesus saves. Jesus is alive, Jesus is a person, and Jesus will walk anyone and everyone through insecurity. ALMI conferences are hard to explain, because we are not introducing people to a teaching, but to a Person who is alive and will help them. This man was seeing Jesus and was being helped, not by my words, but by Jesus' words that were affecting him. It was a great session.

Friends invite me to go with them to pray for a recovering pastor who had TB and was in a coma; the doctors openly gave him no hope. However, as is the habit of this church, the people prayed. He can now walk, even though his feet are quite sore. One of his relatives there said, "I am sick in the mind!" I asked a few questions, looked at his medication, and invited him back to the house for a counseling session. The fellow knew English quite well, and that made the session move right along. There were so many obvious reasons for his behavior. He was a real Thinker whose father had abandoned him, mother had beaten him, godmother had verbally abused him, and adoptive father had told him that he was defective. He could not handle the thoughts, so he was obsessing and trying to think positively, which was no longer working. He asked the question, "Is not positive thinking good?" I responded that it was not good for him, since he was using it as a coping mechanism, an idol to bury his feelings. I explained that he was too spiritual to get drunk, so he thought positively and obsessed; both were attempts to accomplish the same thing: escaping negative feelings. He got it. We worked through so many issues, and he was really tracking with me. At one point he looked at the diagram and just looked to the ground. I asked what was wrong. Looking at me he said, "I see clearly everything. I see why I am the way I am. I see that letting Jesus be my life is the answer. But how would I have known these things if you had not come to me?" I could see clearly that this time he was the one for whom God had sent me.

Africa

A woman calls out to me. Her husband is not a Christian, and she says she cannot serve God with an unbelieving husband. He could not pay his poll tax of 30,000 shillings ($180) for three years, and the authorities put him in jail. She wants him to stay there. I explained that no person keeps a believer from serving God. If that were true, then the person that keeps the Christian from God would actually be greater than God. She must learn that God is God. If one person can keep her from God, and she gets away from that person, Satan will send another to control her; if she gains freedom from the one person, she will have to gain release from the next person. Once she learns she is free always to serve God, then let the peace of God rule in her heart for all other decisions. I have known many people who feel the same way, and I understand her frustration, but she must see God in it. There is a lesson for her.

One of the sisters has just returned from a funeral. She said that any time she leaves, the professor says to her, "I do not like it when you leave; you are always getting into trouble, and so many of the angels leave this school to go along with you to watch over you." Nothing is easily done here, not even getting to a funeral. The only funeral that is easy to get to is one's own. She had to travel in an open-bed truck for hours, and upon reaching a bridge that is weak and could break, she told the driver to hesitate. He simply responded, "Why? We have heard that the angels go with you!" At that she said, "Amen," and they went on. Several times the truck got stuck, but she finally arrived at the home of the funeral, where a crazy woman who wanted food had thrown stones at the beehives by the house until everyone there had to be evacuated for more than three hours. The story went on, but it was just an average day in the life of these missionaries.

At one Bible school in which I was speaking, where most of our meals consisted of an unpleasant dried fish put in water with rice, I was told that we were going to a restaurant one night, and the orders were even taken in the morning; we could have beef, pork, or chicken. I thought everyone was having a big joke at my expense. To my surprise, I found all of us walking down the paths and dirt streets to a small kitchen that had a lean-to attached. There was a table set for all of us. Next, a Portuguese fellow started bringing out huge plates of barbequed pork and chicken. It is the first time that I have ever had the owner of a restaurant serve the food and then pray for all of us before we ate; it was just wonderful. He even sat and had dinner with us. He had come from Portugal in 1965 to fight in the colonial wars. When it came time to leave, he missed the ship, and the record of his coming had disappeared. His passport was onboard. That meant that he could not get home, because he had no proof of citizenship. He was stuck in Africa. In the end, he married a local Catholic woman and went into business. Even when the civil war broke out, he never tried to flee. He has been shot in the foot, hand, and wrist, but all the bullets passed through; he has been ambushed 118 times and once had a rocket fired at his Land Rover. He and the fellow next to him were able to jump out before it blew up. I asked why he stayed. "I like the people and I like it here; plus, I had no way of ever getting the money to leave if I wanted to." Then he smiles and points upward, saying, "With Jesus everything is fine." The pastor took up a course of friendship evangelism with him as soon as they met. Each week they studied all of Matthew, and his heart turned to Jesus. He is still in the Catholic Church but comes to the studies at the school, since he likes hearing about Jesus. He is really a jolly and kind fellow. He has posters in the restaurant that show the narrow path and the wide path. He likes to talk to the men that come there to eat and drink, so the diner is quite a ministry in itself. Look at all the people God touches and works through!

We were talking about the different approaches to death here. This family's gardener and his wife lost their first set of twins, their next daughter, and their last child; the gardener's wife will probably lose her life to the dreaded disease, AIDS. Their crops were stolen at harvest time. Here someone cannot simply call for the police but must go and get them. The police rounded up the boys who stole the food, put them in jail, and beat one of them to death. Since the boys were from his village, the gardener thought that the punishment was a bit harsh, but he had to pay a bribe to get the charges dropped to prevent anyone else from dying. The lady of the house has just returned from the funeral of her housekeeper's baby. She was telling us that she had lain in bed with the woman and the deceased baby for 24 hours, while many others surrounded the bed and all cried. The Africans have a much better system of mourning, I think, than do we; the people wail and scream for a few days with friends, which really helps to get the sad feelings expressed. Also, when someone dies, the closest survivor is never left alone; a niece, nephew, or grandchild will come to live with the relative, which means he or she will not experience the depth of loneliness that we do in the West. All of this is to say that death is more a commonly experienced part of life here. Also, relationships are paramount in Africa. The missionaries were telling us of starting each morning with a half-hour of prayer, followed by a half-hour of hand shaking, and another half-hour of saying good-bye in the parking lot. He had suggested that government officials do the same, and that does not seem to be a bad idea. This couple is doing their bit to help, and it is a joy to see people of faith in positions of authority.

I was in an African country last year when, at the national conference, the pastor was asked to take a particular ministry position. He had worked as director at the Bible school for ten years, and things were finally humming along. Then, one night in a Bible study, he heard the call of God to go to Europe. No man would have ever persuaded this man to leave Africa and the Bible school. He had yet to mention the call to anyone when, at the national conference, he was asked in front of the crowd to take the post offered him. This was not the setting that he had chosen to tell those he loved that he would be leaving. He stood there silently, and the tears began to stream down his cheeks. Few people have seen this man cry. He said, "I cannot take the position!" The room grew quiet enough to have heard a pin drop. No one understood until he explained that God had called him away and he must go. When the people saw how much this decision pained him they were moved, and not one objection to his going was heard. The country to which he will be heading is the kind of place that Jesus must have been talking about when He gave the parable of the lost coin.

I enjoy the morning with the associate pastor. He and the pastor make a wonderful team of two believers who complete and do not compete. He has had quite a journey and has seen the Lord in all of it. His wife died after two years in a coma. She left him with four children. He said that after she passed on, he was a different and new man who did not fear death, but could see that death had been crushed by Christ. "I wish I had a different word for death." He was then called into military service and was sent as a chaplain to armed forces stationed all over the world. It is such a blessing to see someone like him, who likes working with a few and who actually enjoys visiting with people stuck in a hospital. He said, "This may sound odd, but I get a sense of excitement and anticipation when I visit the hospital, for at that time even the greatest of men are stripped naked and left with nothing of their worldly accumulation to support the deceptions of life. In those moments, we have a great opportunity to witness to the truth of Jesus."

CHAPTER 3

Forgiving The Transgressions of Man

Pacific Islands

One man approached who said that he was an American and knew we were, too, because Americans are the only tourists that mingle with the locals. He told of how the American soldiers from World War II were sorely missed after they left. Soldiers from nearby countries had lived in compounds with walls and would not let any of the islanders in, but the Americans had no walls and welcomed everyone. The Americans were always friendly, and when they got paid, they would give their money and chocolates away. He said that had made him want to go to America. He told me his testimony. In 1971 he left his wife and four children and went to the U.S. with only $50. On the plane had been a crippled man whom this man had carried in and carried through customs. All the other islanders were deported from Hawaii because they only had $100, but this man said he was the crippled man's relative and was allowed in. He worked for six months, and then immigration began to look for him. He stopped sending money home and became a drunk. An American woman offered to marry him and get him citizenship. He got married, and his American wife threatened that if he left her, she would turn him into INS as a polygamist. He stayed with her until 1991, when the woman died. He went back to his island to find his wife. She told him, "After you left and stopped communicating, I found Jesus. I have had peace since that day. I do not care what you have done; I forgive you!" He could not believe it! He knew Jesus was real, and he gave his life to Christ. He said that Jesus has never failed him or left him. The problem was that Satan kept coming to him reminding him of his past. I had a great time sharing with him about the mercy and compassion of God.

I spoke with a girl whose father had beaten her. She believed that if he would tell her he was sorry, all her feelings of being worthless and unlovable would go away. I explained that the damage had been done and it was deception to think if he asked for forgiveness the feelings would go. Next, we talked about our crucifixion with Christ. He crucified the worthless and unlovable person. However, she was refusing to bury it, and instead kept the mummy (the old crucified self) in a drawer, each day taking it out and speaking to it thus, "Maybe today Father will ask for forgiveness, and you will come alive to help me." She began to weep, saying, "I see it." I further explained that she must bless the one who cursed her, for it was his rejection that led her to Christ. Many tribes in Africa mark themselves with scars, which I do not personally find offensive. However, when the wounds are not kept clean enough, they become infected before healing, and the resulting scars are unsightly. I thought how other people will always wound us in our soul, but by God's grace they can be clean wounds that leave beneficial scars. A wound that is infected with bitterness leaves an ugly scar. "Heavenly Father, never let our wounds be infected with pride, justification, anger, or resentment, please."

A certain woman was raped and then disfigured with a knife. She was asked, "Why are you not angry with the man?" She responded, "He has already taken my outer beauty. If I am angry, he will also be able to steal my inner beauty!" Wonderful! She had grasped a beautiful truth.

I met a very interesting fellow who moved to this island after his wife divorced him. Being very antiauthority, he built his house without a permit. The council fined him for it. He took it to court, defended his position, and won. He based his argument on a Magna Carte clause, which states that a government is not to hinder the expansion of personal property. Well, back to the story. His son was divorced and was in prison for selling drugs, so the son's ex-wife came to care for this man when he became ill. They fell in love and moved in with each other; this is all typical for this island, so no one thought much about it. With the passing of time they had a child. A local Christian began to share with the man, and one day, to the surprise of all, he gave his life to Christ. Soon his girlfriend/ex-daughter-in-law/mother of his daughter gave her life to Christ, also. It all sounds confusing. However, "if any man [or woman] be in Christ, he is a new creature; the old things passed away; behold, new things have come" (2 Corinthians 5:17). Christians instructed the man to marry the mother of his children, so they had a Christian wedding. Prior to this time, he had been dubbed a "Rat Bag" by the pastors and had gone unnoticed for many years; but when he had a Christian wedding, they deemed it their Christian duty to turn him into the authorities as having had an illegal wedding. It seems a law that had not been exercised for nearly 100 years stated that it is illegal to marry a daughter. In the end, the man was put in jail and the marriage annulled. When he came out of court, he met the pastor who had initiated the court proceedings. The man has a speech impediment so said to the pastor and his wife, "I don't know why you do that to me. But I forgive you and I love you." The pastor's wife looked at him and began to sob. Later, all three pastors complicit in the proceedings came to the man privately and repented of what they had done to him. They agreed that the man and his wife were both new people in Christ. As an aside, the man holds the highest medal that can be given by the British government, because he was in a famous battle during the Korean War. A thousand British soldiers protecting a hill were swamped by a multitude of Chinese soldiers to the extent that they stood back-to-back to fight. He was in a machine-gun placement and never stopped shooting, for the Chinese were like ants coming; no matter how many he killed, they kept coming. In the end 992 British soldiers were killed. He and seven others surrendered, and just as the Chinese were getting ready to shoot them, American troops appeared. The Chinese, though more numerous than the Americans, were filled with fear and fled. He was taken to London and given a medal and a woolen patch with symbols on the front and the back to represent that they had stood back-to-back to fight. He said that as he stood there receiving the honor, he was in shock. The medal meant nothing. In fact, he said that it was better to be killed than to kill so many people. He ended by saying, "There is a big difference between looking down a gun and having a gun pointed at you."

A young couple arrived one afternoon from a distant city. They had been married for two years, and he had fallen, again, into homosexuality. We worked through the issues, and he could really see the source, the reason, the attraction, the condemnation, and the way out, which is the Way, Jesus. They were both so excited, and then I dropped the bomb. "If I let you leave now, I would have a great victory story, but in a few months or years you will once again be disappointed." They both looked puzzled. I explained that the abiding life is moment-by-moment; the flesh never leaves but is only subdued by the Spirit of Jesus, and none of us abide perfectly. I was not giving him an excuse, but I wanted him to understand that the struggle was only gone because his eyes were on Jesus. I looked at her and said, "If you cannot cope with another one of his failures, you had better consider now what you want to do." He was relieved; she was disappointed. She wanted the whole issue to go away forever. I quickly asked a few questions and zeroed in on her own fleshly behavior: anger, anxiety, and worry. Next I said, "I want you to promise me that you will never again walk in the flesh; you will never be anxious, worried, or angry. If you do any of those things again, I want you to agree that he can leave you." She admitted that she could not promise such a thing. The follow-up was obvious: "If you cannot promise never to walk in the deeds of the flesh again, why do you want him to promise?" She got the point, the issue was settled, and they have decided to continue on in Jesus. If one fails, the other will stop and pick him up. Amen!

My friend, an elderly gentleman, mentions that the younger generation does not have discipline and explains to us what happened when he was young if he or any of his classmates came late to class. The principal would take them outside and make them pick 100 thorn weeds in five minutes. A thorn weed has two big thorns at the bottom and is impossible to pick without using both hands. The principal had to see the roots on each weed counted out by the student on the table. To anyone who refused the punishment, the principal would pick a thorn weed himself and wrap it around the pupil's head from the crown to the chin. My friend was only late once. If he did anything wrong in school, he had to put his hand on the table for the knuckles to be rapped with the handle of a dust broom. If he moved his hand, the top of the head was hit. Once the teacher beat him with the buckle side of the belt. At that my friend quit school for one term, refusing to return. "I still hate that man!" I ask, "Is he alive?" "Oh, no, but I still hate him. He would see me later in the streets and greet me. I would only stare, and the man knew he had created a problem for himself." Most of the islands have villages on the outskirts, but there are no roads that connect them; they are linked by boat. My friend's father was a pastor, and it fell on the son and his siblings to row the father to the different churches for services. The son would beg not to but was beaten if he did not. The oars are huge, the boats heavy, and often they were filled with people. I am beginning to see where my friend gets his strong sense of discipline.

Village life here is based on a hierarchical family structure. The elder brother can require something of a younger brother, and wives must speak to other family members through their husbands. One woman had three young children. One day while she was in town, her elder brother-in-law came to her husband and demanded that the youngest, a baby girl, be given to him and his wife, since they were unable to have children. The husband, bound by mores and tradition, gave the child. The mother returned to discover that her baby had been taken, and she had no recourse for bringing the baby back home. We spent the morning talking about Moses' mother and how she, a young mother today, could be like that Biblical mother. She would only be seeing her child occasionally, but in those few moments she could speak lasting truth and love into the child's heart. This grieving mother's countenance grew light as she was encouraged and found the peace of God that is not hindered by any situation. Wonderful.

Europe

I stopped at a bank to exchange some money; unfortunately, the teller did not like Americans and refused to wait on me. Every time a fellow countryman came in, he would ask me to step out of line so he could help the local. At last there were no other clients in the bank, so he took my passport and proceeded to go on break. While he was gone, I came up with a plan. I would ask the man what time he gets off work, and then I would promise to meet him in the alley next to the bank and beat him. There I stood, author, lecturer, and director of ALMI, plotting how to beat a man. As I stood there, I became more and more uncomfortable, until the Holy Spirit broke through with a revelation of Christ and, hence, a new plan. When the teller returned, I said, "I want to apologize. I have done something to offend you. I am just a lost American, traveling through and needing currency. I did not mean to do anything to irritate you." The man stared at me, and then with teary eyes he said, "It is not you; it is me." I had purchased my freedom in Christ with the currency of pride. Self had given way to a life that loves enemies, a life which dwells in me.

A pastor of a huge church in Europe was a third generation African forced out of his country because his family is white. Now he and his father return as often as possible to help their people and have started so many programs. It is a very typical African story: The country there is very rich, but not a penny goes to its citizens due to corruption among the leaders. However, the government officials actually help this pastor in his mission because of his status and citizenship. He has a school for 6,000 children, and the congregation in Europe pays for it. He has aid programs and even a reading program that teaches the illiterate (80% of the people) to read through studying the Scriptures; this is done with international aid that is earmarked for "reading." This fellow does not fight systems that are pitted against him, he uses them, and all the while he has a huge smile. For instance, church buildings are not tolerated in the immense, cathedral-dotted European city he now calls home, because for one hour a week they make too much noise. The church he pastors, therefore, rents as their meeting place an abandoned building in an industrial area of town.

The best part of the day is the quality time that the pastor and I have together. He has been hurt, just as have many pastors. This past year he has resigned his position at the church and just taken time out. What can happen to a pastor at the hands of believers is shocking. I remember one pastor's telling me that he came home to find his wife huddled in the corner crying. She looked up at him and said, "All I ever wanted to do was love the people!" This pastor and I go through the basic material on a personal level and look for God in the hurts, past and present. He has the revelation of it. This is an ambulance ministry; it cannot be scheduled like a haircut. The Lord must bring people together at the right time and place in His plan. It is not my doing; I do not have any illusions that it is. I am only the flesh and blood He puts on His witness to the work He is doing in someone. People witness to me, I to them, and it is all God. My time with this pastor was all of God, and I enjoyed talking to him. We ate pita bread filled with pork, and I drew diagrams on the back of placemats.

Eurasia

A magazine editor whose company had printed one of my books had taken notice of the information contained therein, and later when he heard I was in his country doing a seminar, he came to interview me for his magazine. As the discourse came to an end, he wanted to know what was my closing message for the article. I immediately told him, "Suffering equals life," for so many in the countries of the former Soviet Union believe that life equals suffering. Suffering is God's greatest evangelistic tool. He beamed,

"That is how I came to Christ, through suffering," and he told me of his deliverance from Satan. At a young age he had stuttered, so his parents took him to a sorcerer. The speech problem left, but fear entered his heart. He began to drink, and at an early age joined the Navy. He went to India and became a drug addict, so he was pronounced unfit and sent to Moscow to work with prison labor. Two men were in charge, one a homosexual, and the other a masochist; both demanded favors. At 33 he went to the far north with a new motto: "All people are enemies, so cheat your neighbors before they cheat you." In the north he had more troubles, one time nearly burning to death and more than once almost drowning. Next he was forced to take the Russian "cure" for alcohol and drugs, a treatment that did more damage to the cause, until in the end, he was pronounced incorrigible. Here at the bottom, with no hope and ready to die, Christ came to him and revealed Himself. The man met Christ though he had not been looking for Him, or so he thought; he later discovered that his mother had become a believer and the church she attended had been in constant intercession for him. I was so encouraged by this man's love and softness toward me, a man who had once said that all people are enemies. It is interesting that Adam in his sinless state walked with God, yet because he was sinless, God's glory was not overwhelming and must have even become somewhat commonplace, for Adam traded it for a piece of fruit. Everything being relative, God's glory is revealed in contrast. If God sent His Son for the sinless, we would think very little of His love, but since He sent His Son for sinners, we note the vast expanse between His glory and sinners and begin to comprehend how great His love is. The problem with self-righteousness is that it tries to cover up its contrast with God's love and minimize His glory. Because he had fallen to such depths, this brother knew the difference between himself and God. Man only has around seventy years on the planet, so Satan is allowed to do things that will more quickly reveal our weakness, lack of glory, and sin. Satan's work creates a contrast as we continue to fail, allowing us to see the glory of God, desire it, and turn to it.

There is a difference between soulish people (those who live without the influence of Christ's Holy Spirit on mind, will, and emotions) and those who live in a soulless state. Much of what we see around us here is soulless, and to me that is much sadder. Our battle is not against flesh and blood but spirits and principalities. I am not surprised at some of the demonic attacks I have experienced in places such as this, with their histories of having one group oppressing the other until neither has anything, and then both wondering what it was all about. I know what it was all about: Satan. I have mentioned before that if we understood why Satan would destroy a marriage, we would be much more afraid of him. He will destroy it for nothing! No reason! He is indifferent. After all is lost, people often just look around in wonderment at what happened. At the time it made so much sense to be angry, to protect self, and to pay back insult for insult. Having depleted everything, they stand back and wonder what it was all about. I have seen this spirit in Africa, and now I see it here, where men fought over the flower until it was pulled apart. "Why?" That was the question asked in Africa, and it could be asked here. My father had asked me, "What is the deal with the art?" I explained, "Years of refinement went into making a picture, statue, or painting that could communicate nothing. The art is about nothing. It was dangerous to communicate something with which the authorities might take issue." Communism was about nothing; it inspired nothing, it is the spirit of nothing, and it lingers. The thumbprint of the enemy is always indifference. A boy gets a girl pregnant, and upon that discovery, he does not want to hear from her again. Why? He was doing it all for nothing in complete indifference. The spirit of indifference is growing in its power.

I keep sharing the purpose of suffering with these people who have suffered so much over the years. God brings situations not to show what we can do, but to prove what we cannot accomplish. He is to be all that we are not, but we must first know what we are not before He can be all to us. Moses spent forty years being trained to be a god, forty years finding out that was not true, and the last forty years having God be to him all that he was not. God told him to go and speak, and he said, "I cannot." God's answer was, "I AM. Tell them I AM sent you." It did not matter what Moses could or could not do, for I AM sent him. All that he admitted he could not do, God was to him and did through him.

Everyone seems to have a doctrine of prosperity but not of suffering. In Matthew 27:43, the crowd was clamoring that if Jesus were God's son, "let God deliver Him now!" But the Father did not deliver Him from the cross, He did something better: He brought life out of death. I was talking about owning a problem before being able to disown it. I set a pen on the table and said, "I want to give it to the pastor, but I cannot do so until I pick it up. I must own to disown!" That analogy was well understood and received; the next was not. I asked, "What would you say if I said, 'I hate the Russians! All Russians should die and go to hell, and I hope no Russians ever get saved'?" Typically, as in other former Soviet satellites, people nodded their heads in agreement with such sentiments! I told them about the congregations in the last country I was in agreeing with me, as well, and we all had a good laugh. The point is to own the problem by admitting we cannot love, inviting Him to be our love, and recognizing that when we do love, it will not stem from our compassion but from the very love of God.

Along these same lines, I met with a friend who, when I was here before, was a member of the thriving local police force. Since then a criminal/Mafia-type purchased a large section of the wharf for nearly three billion dollars and required the local police department to be dismantled, for he did not want a group of patriots interfering with his plots and plans. The city council that benefitted greatly from the purchase agreed and commenced a smear campaign in order to justify getting rid of the police department heads and personnel; my friend had suffered greatly due to all of that. At a salary of only one hundred and fifty dollars a month, only a patriot would have ever had the job to begin with. He said, "I must have been stupid." However, the worst part was that his friends from the legalistic church to which he had belonged had all rejected him. He had not heard from them except by way of discovering that many wanted him removed from the church. I had a good bit of time with him and his wife and talked about not letting an enemy live rent-free in one's head and the necessity of loving an enemy.

I was privileged to stop at a fellow's home for dinner, and as he said grace, he began to cry, being so thankful for the food. He shared a little about his life story. He and his family were taken to Siberia when he was age twelve; after two months on a train, they were all dumped out unceremoniously in snow over their waists. Out of a thousand people, only one hundred survived. He was there six years before the Russians came and got him to fight in the war. The only supplies they got in Siberia were those goods the Americans got through to them by bribing the government. I asked him why he thought believers suffer; he told me it was so God could see how they handled suffering, and in America we are blessed in order to see how we handle blessing. I asked him which scenario was worse, not to have the money for a house payment or to have your son tell you he has become a homosexual, a drug addict, or any of several other maladies normal among America's youth. He just stared and said that to have the emotional problems would be worse. I said that we all suffer, but perfect peace comes from focusing on Jesus. When suffering comes, at first I may only think about how it affects me, but if it lasts long enough, I will begin to think about God. Jesus lived in a body and was perfected through suffering. What is perfection if not a perfect focus on God? Suffering kept Him near the Father.

I usually stop each year to tour the Occupation Museum; it is a very moving experience. There is an exact replica of a small wooden hut, the one many stayed in after deportation to Siberia. It is probably 15X20' with two large shelves on which the people, up to sixty in number, would sleep next to each other, packed in like sardines. There is a note explaining that the people were so packed in that during the night, one person would give the command to roll onto an opposite side, and everyone had to roll at once. In the hut is a fifty-gallon drum with a board laid across the top to sit on, a Russian toilet. All of the prisoners smelled of this "red Russian perfume" wherever they went. Once the drum was full, the Russians took it outside, dumped it, and gathered the drinking water in it. Someone said that in fourteen years in Siberia, he had never seen a piece of toilet paper. A friend is a concentration-camp survivor; she was accused of being an American spy and sent to Siberia. At that time she had never even met an American, but that did not prevent Stalin's regime from persecuting her. She shows me a painting by an old master she knew personally. "When he was a young man, not old enough to wear pants, he was tending his father's flocks. He crawled onto a rock, looked around at the beauty, and said, 'God, I want to see the world.' Well, God did answer his prayer. He saw Europe, the East, and Scandinavia; in fact, God even let him see Siberia for 25 years!" He was asked to design a poster that would boost milk production. He thought he would be clever and draw a cow with two udders. The Communists were not amused and gave him a sentence of 25 years for that drawing. He came out an old man with only one regret: He had not taught his children about Jesus.

I was served a large grated white radish, of which one woman explained, "In Siberia, we would trade our clothes for a radish. We were all starving. One man would be chosen to eat a particular weed. If it did not make him sick or kill him, we would all eat it. I lived for many years on grass. It makes a very nice meal." She also told us the concept of "islands" that developed in Siberia. Ice floes would come down the 20-kilometer-wide river and always provided a little surprise in an otherwise dreadful, drudge-filled day. The incarcerated thus came to call surprises "islands." Now that the woman is elderly, she gifts us with "islands" such as special desserts or vegetables. She has a wonderful glow about her and is such a blessing to be around. She told me that the secret to cooking is doing everything from love. She told me more about her stay in Siberia. She pulled out a little notebook that was her journal while there. The letters were brown because they did not have ink, so they wrote their notes with milk, afterward placing the paper over a candle's flame, and the heat would turn the letters brown. I also saw a picture, hand drawn with great detail, of the house in which they stayed. It was really an unbelievable "shelter" for being well within the Arctic Circle. It had no floor, windows, or doors, and the inhabitants were not even given a blanket. In the morning after awakening, her hair would be frozen stuck to the wall. The Soviets came out with a new policy that everyone had to go get his or her own bread. The daily portion was only three centimeters—three fingers—wide. One man had frostbitten feet and could not walk; he would drag himself on the ground to get his bread. The prisoners were constantly starving, living like dogs, yet many managed to stay alive there for more than twenty-five years, though no one really could account for how that happened apart from the will of God. One night they decided to steal potatoes from the Russian supply shed. No one knew the Russians had set grizzly-bear traps in the potato room. Fortunately, a woman who walked with a stick was the first to enter. Her stick went into the center of the trap and was snapped in two. It would have taken her leg off. I saw a photo of a former factory owner; the woman looked half-dead and was wearing a coat made of scraps. When someone died, he was laid in the snow; as spring came and the ground thawed, the others could dig a hole for burial. This lady and her brother were still rather young when their mother died in Siberia; some two years later they were taken to an orphanage. They were not given shoes. To provide some protection, they took the small rope sewn into potato sacks and pieces of paper. The paper was placed on the bottom of the foot and the string wrapped around to hold the paper on. This woman gives a new appreciation to the term Siberia. After seven years, a communist countrywoman bribed her way to Siberia, bribed her way to the orphanage, took all twenty-seven children, bribed agents to secure the tickets, and returned them to their home country. As soon as they returned there was another wave of persecution and deportation. They were all rounded up to be returned once again. The authorities wanted to know why they were back. The briber was sentenced to Siberia. It was a miracle for our friend, for those in power decided not to send the children back to Siberia if they did not have parents. She made her way to her uncle's house; she had been a very young girl the last time she visited and was not sure she would find it. As she came down the road, her uncle recognized this orphan. He ran to her and said, "You are the one we have waited so long for." He picked her up and carried her in his arms. It felt so strange and so safe. He carried her and placed her in the lap of her grandmother, where she just sat, feeling secure.

One young woman spoke in excellent English and was interested in any topic related to Christ. She said that the best years of her grandmother's life were stolen by the Soviet system, with her years in prison and personal losses that go beyond one's ability to quantify. Yet her grandmother glows and never has a harsh word for the former occupiers. She recently asked her grandmother why that was and was told, "I could not live with that kind of bitterness in my heart. I had to forgive to be free. I forgave the whole Soviet system, and when I did, I forgave every single person." There is a Way and a not the Way. Christ is the Way, and every other way is not the Way.

Asia

A fellow told of one man who was both an owner of several gas stations and an elder of a church. Being extremely controlling, he tormented and finally drove off the pastor, placing spies at each filling station to see in which direction the pastor left town. Two years later the pastor was passing through the town and stopped for gas. The attendant recognized him and called the elder, who sent word to the pastor to come meet him at his house. Naturally, the pastor did not want to go, but the man nearly begged him. He arrived for dinner, and all the food was set in front of him; the elder had only a bowl of oats. The pastor asked, "Why are you eating oats and giving all the delicious food to me?" The elder responded, "The day I drove you out of town my appetite left me. For two years I have only been able to eat oats. If I eat anything else I will throw up. Will you pray for me? I have sinned against you." The pastor prayed for the man, and his appetite returned. The fellow ended by saying that believers should always invest in prayers for their pastors and their wives. He also made the point that pastors suffer when only businessmen and intellectuals are made elders of the church; then the pastor managing spiritual affairs is overseen by persons qualified to be in charge of financial affairs. He contends that the two must be separated as in Acts, but because of flesh and worldliness in the church, many prefer to have powerful men in charge rather than spiritual. Another pastor told about how one time in his church a very controlling elder pulled him aside and said, "Your bread and butter is in my hands." The pastor said to all of us, "I must be honest, I wanted to tell him to go to hell!" Everyone got a laugh out of that. He went on to say that he did not say anything; he waited until a board meeting and then turned to the two who were causing the most trouble and gave them a word. "If you do not stop your contention, by this time next year you will be dead!" One year later both were dead. It is very refreshing to see how seriously these believers take the ministry and position in the church. I liked this fellow. At least the message he received from the Lord was not so vague, like much of what is said today, such as, "'There is something wrong,' says the Lord"; instead of, "I have this against you," followed by a specific charge. The Lord is not vague or confusing about what He has for us: "You have been given fullness in Christ!"

I am off to visit the church of a fellow with whom I have an instant friendship. He is sixty and has built a compound, a small classroom with four rooms above that allow him to have Bible classes. The pastor is such a joyful fellow; he is explaining that when he started the church, the place had only a few buildings, and now there are nice homes as far as our eyes can see from money that has come from the men who joined the foreign forces; they are paid $1,500 per month with all food and housing provided. Hence, all monies are sent home to build the houses. It is a strain on the family with the father gone for years. It will soon be the 25th anniversary of this church building, which the congregation never got to dedicate, because the police came on the proposed day of dedication and stayed. They would like to do it this year. One problem that has been overcome is that initially the churches here had their services on Sunday. Saturday is the Hindu holiday, so this caused quite a stir. Since then the believers have switched to Saturday, and though some will hold another service on Sunday, the major conflict was resolved. One pastor who has been beaten repeatedly told me that the police once came and stopped his service. He just invited them in, fed his enemies, and they left. They were also telling me of meeting the Seventh Day Adventists, who thought it was great that they shared the revelation that the holy day was Saturday, until they discovered that it was just done out of compulsion. The pastor said, "They are Christians, but is not every day God's day?"

The minister tells me about his most recent trip to Europe. It seems an aid agency there had for years been sending money for the poor of his country and had never sent anyone over to look into what all had been accomplished. The minister, because of his good reputation among believers, was contacted to evaluate the work. He knew the man to whom the money had been sent and disclosed that there was not, nor had there ever been, any work among the poor achieved by him. All that time the man was simply spending the money and sending in false reports. A request was then made that the minister travel to Europe and give a report. This he agreed to, but he made it clear that he would not work for the organization, since his call is to the lepers and their church; no one will budge him from that. My calling is for the revelation of abiding, and his is for the revelation of abiding to the lepers. We stand in the same foundation. While in Europe, the minister went from church to church looking for someone who knew Jesus. In his innocence, he just could not understand huge church buildings that had only a very few worshipers in attendance. No pastor or bishop wanted to talk to him. He found it all quite baffling, or as he simply puts it, "Sad." Finally, he met a pastor that knew and loved Jesus; the man was happy to fellowship, and, upon hearing of all that is occurring with the lepers, invited him to speak to the small group of youth among whom the man works. The minister went and began to speak about both the lepers and his starting and directing schools for the children. When he mentioned his work with children, one of the boys raised his hand and asked if the minister were a child molester. At that the pastor closed the meeting. "See what I have to deal with?" he later told my friend. "These kids are so hard and unchurched. What would you do?" The minister gave some really good counsel. "Take the boy that is the

115

roughest, spend your time with him, and see what happens. Just work with one boy to whom God leads you. When that boy breaks through, he will reach the others." This minister knows, having grown up on the streets himself. All in all, he has no passion to return to any part of Europe. I was so happy to hear that, because topnotch men like him are so often lured away, never to return to serve the people in their home country. The organization in Europe even offered to pay for his graduate studies, but the minister is happy in the leper colony. Wonderful.

As we wait for the men to return with the van, the girls have many questions for me. They were definitely listening to the sermon last night. Since we have some time, I decided that I would take their histories, do a profile, look at issues of discipleship, and help them to understand each other more readily. The older daughter is a Thinker and a Feeler and is amazed that I can give her a list of how she acts and feels. Her sister is a Doer and has yet to meet an obstacle. Their concepts of God are very interesting to them. Soon their mother comes alongside us to listen; when she begins to talk, she points to a picture of a young girl of eight on the wall. I had assumed that it was one of these two daughters, but it was a younger sister. They tell me that the children's uncle had come over and wanted to show them all a trick using gasoline. The mother protested and told him to take the gasoline outside; then she said that she had to go to the market. As soon as she left, the uncle brought the gasoline back into the house to perform the trick. The stunt went wrong, the petrol ignited, and the uncle, in a panic, threw the gasoline away from him; it landed on the small girl, who was then burned to death. The mother returned home to find her daughter dead. She was going to call the police, but the uncle asked for forgiveness and said that if they were Christians, they would have to forgive him. I was not expecting all of that to be disclosed while we were waiting for the van! I could see the pain in the mother's eyes. I talked to her about grieving, false guilt for not having done more to prevent the death, the permissive will of God, and the impossibility of having the feelings of forgiveness so soon after such a tragic event. The mother could no longer hold back the tears. I was happy to be there with her and to be able to talk to her; it was really God ordained, and if this trip were over now, I would go home happy with all that the Lord had accomplished.

Africa

An engineer was telling about going to court and how corrupt the proceedings are. Before paying a traffic ticket, he was instructed always to tell the judge that he was guilty and that he was trying to learn the judge's language. He did as instructed, for these are Muslim judges who despise the Christians. The judge then said to him, "Six months in prison and $500"; he paused, "No, no prison, but $250"; another pause, and finally, "$20." At that the judge went off to the back room to drink beer that was put in pots so the other Muslims did not see him drinking. Another time a houseboy stole all of his stereo equipment; he went to court and the judge did nothing, for the boy was Muslim. Later the engineer was walking by the judge's house, and the judge called to him, "Come." He went and the judge said, "What did you want in court? Just tell me!" Before he could answer, the judge said, "How much money is in your pocket? Show me!" He displayed $500. The judge took it and said, "I will see you in court." In the end the judge gave the boy two years in prison, but the engineer only wanted his stereo equipment! There simply is no justice, no law, and no advocate for a person in this place.

We had a discussion on how to fix government. "There must be a war to throw out the bad and bring in the good." My response to that was that the nature of government cannot change; it does not matter who is riding the horse; the horse is still a horse. Man in the flesh will be corrupt. I do understand how they feel, though, since they suffer under the weight of injustice, bribery, theft, and deceit.

One pastor friend has been very vexed by what he has seen. While book after book could be filled with man's inhumanity to man, and that is not the purpose of this book, I believe this pastor's story gives us comfort in reminding us that the Lord never leaves us nor forsakes us and is among us and in us as we suffer. Indeed, He never wastes one drop of our suffering, but steadfastly turns it to beauty, even in others who watch us undergo pain. In one church, the warring insurgents came to a pastor and said, "You are of our blood, but your wife and children are not. We have not come to kill you, but them." They stood the pastor aside and killed his wife and children in front of him. The sad thing is that the rebels were members of the man's own congregation. After the murders, the man went to the church every morning, fell on his knees, and held a Bible up in the air toward the church; this was all that the man did for three months. He would not speak. At the end of the three months, he passed on from this earthly existence.

On a walk to town of several kilometers, I found my way through a park that contained cactus the size of large trees. I heard some shouting and could make out a few words, "Jesus . . . Father . . . forgive." I went deeper into the woods and found men 100 feet apart crying out to God in loud voices. People were everywhere. It was really a blessing to observe.

On the way to the hotel we passed a military funeral. The soldiers and police had blocked the street. There was a band playing and a crowd watching as they carried the coffin. The pastor said, "You can see that those men are fresh from war. They would be very rugged." Yes, looking in the faces reveals those that are fresh from war. It is written in their being. Sometimes I wonder if it is not better to be killed than to kill. Killing can do something to man: it scars, but it can also turn demonic and make some men bloodthirsty.

It is a bit depressing to listen to the radio station, which for the last two years has been trying to unite orphans/street kids with parents that went missing during the civil war. The child's name is given, year of birth, and month, if known. Then the child gives the description of his or her parents, where they lived (what part of town or the name of a village), the father's name, and sadly they often only knew their mother as "mama"; for example, Victor Tubu and Mama Tubu. I cannot bear the thought of child after child hoping beyond hope that mother or father will hear the ad and answer it. Come quickly, Lord Jesus!

I have a full, thirteen-hour day of counseling with the senior students at a Bible school, and that gave me a much better understanding of the people. There are a few clear observations, such as that everyone has stuffed his emotions; it hurts to feel, and so most do not. That is understandable in a place where most women will lose two to three children born to them; it is no wonder that they are a bit detached. However, they treat the children much better than do the fathers. I did not find a single fellow with a decent father figure, and all but one of the fellows' fathers was a drunkard. One student's father, while they were fleeing the civil war, just abandoned the family, left them, and went on ahead. This boy and his mother nearly drowned crossing the stream. He was then given to an uncle who beat him and would not help in his schooling. The Padre at the school would beat all the boys without mercy. There was nearly an identical story from another graduating student. His father made him walk ten miles in elephant grass as they fled the war; he was only eight and running to stay with his father, but he kept losing him. His father was a demanding perfectionist who was once buying a suitcase and made the son spend three full days opening and closing it to make sure he would do it the exact right way. If he made the least little mistake, he was beaten. These types of stories just went on and on. One thing I found consistently throughout the group was that these students also had temptations to go to the witchdoctors and believed that aunts, uncles, and so on had put spells on them. It became quite obvious that their concept of God had come from observing their earthly fathers, so it was no wonder to me that they had more hope in witchdoctors than in God. I took each one of them through the God concept test and listed how they felt about God. I would list things like demanding perfectionist, follow Him and you will be abused, He forces His will on you, He is waiting to judge you, and more. Each man would say I was describing Satan, and then I would write "father" as the title of the list, and the revelation would come. It was no wonder that these fellows had very little concept of grace. Each believed that if someone did something wrong, he would go to hell. There was no rest in these young men's souls, where the first things, the basic foundation, were not right. I explained that God had a big job in dealing with each one of them, but He was up to the task. He would have to allow them to fail and then still love them; only then would come the revelation of who He really is. They were great sessions. Many had suffered from witchdoctors' spells. It was clear to the school's directors that something would have to be done to correct students' false feelings about God, or else in times of pressure they would move toward the witchdoctors and not toward God.

I so enjoy this church. One the of the elders came to me and said, "You are a difficult man!" I said, "Yes, I have heard that from Betty." He then explained that he could not get the statement out of his head, "If you do not forgive an enemy, the enemy will live in your head and pay no rent." Then he explained that men had broken into his house and beaten his wife, daughter, and granddaughter. He came, stopped the attack, called the police, and the men ran. He later left to go find a replacement for the broken door. He did not know that the criminals had just hidden in the bushes; they came back in when he left to rape, steal, and more. He was so angry that he wanted to kill all thieves. He realized that, through his hatred, they were living in his head and paying no rent.

These meetings are three hours long. I have a great time of sharing, though the fans do not work, so it is so hot in the church while I am speaking that the sweat rolls off of me. I speak on what are typical themes, yet something they have never heard. They are seeing that we are talking about real life. These people have suffered way beyond what we would consider to be severe pain, injury, loss, or unpleasantness. They are all just plain sick of war and can see absolutely no benefit to it. I talk about blessing those that curse us, because they lost so many family members in the conflicts. Now when they see the people who killed their relatives in the markets, they are tempted to strike. They do not, because they would not want the war starting up all over again. Blessing those that curse us brings others' evil acts down to only affecting a few days of our lives, which is far preferable to letting the evil infect our whole lives through our bitterness and lack of forgiveness. They understood and could see the wisdom in it.

India

I have a vexing meeting with an acquaintance who has come a very long way to talk about his work situation. He has been working for 25 years in ministry for an American. He is confused at the man's attempt to build a kingdom. He was due to be made a director, but several of the younger workers from the U.S. said that they would not work under an Indian. He has worked hard and really sought the Lord. The American rarely sees him; however, when he takes him to the U.S., the American proudly points out that this preacher is his creation. The Indian man is so loyal that he will not leave, though he has been in a state of confusion for years. We have a good time of sharing. He remains committed to following the Lord and serving the man as he would the Lord.

The pastor calls in to see how I am feeling after my severe bout with salmonella poisoning. He tells us that he would like to share with us his testimony. So often we get to hear the stories of people and what God has done in their lives. His parents were Christian. He grew up among the tea growers, the poorest of the people in this area. At a young age he was sent to live with a Hindu teacher. Everything went fine until age nine, when for no discernible reason the teacher beat him mercilessly with his sandal. The boy never knew why. Life returned to normal and went well until age eleven, when there was another beating. He feared for his life, took the Bible his parents had given him, and ran away. He was caught having jumped a train and given fifteen days in jail. God protected him there. Afterward, he was told to go to work carrying luggage outside of a hotel. He discovered that the older men would not let him carry any of the bags to make tips. [I muse on how many hundreds of times I have had kids grabbing at my bags to carry them. I wonder if any of them could potentially be pastors.] In the end he went to begging, where he met a man who let him work for him. However, as he listened to the boss talking one day, he remembered something he had heard in jail about a man in town that sold people into slavery. He realized that this was the same man, so he packed up and ran. Finally, a man told him he could work at his hotel. That went well; he earned fifteen rupees a week plus five rupees for smokes; since he did not smoke, he had the full twenty rupees (about $2 back then). He had dreams of going home one day and entering town as a rich man. He became very sick; he had contracted TB. He kept trying to work but got sicker and sicker until he was nothing but skin and bones. The owner of the hotel told other employees to lay him beside the road to die, in order that none of them would have to tend to the body. He coughed up blood all that night, but he had a vision of heaven, and a peace came over him. He knew he would go to heaven, and death no longer frightened him. In the morning, covered in blood, he was picked up and taken to a TB hospital that only had room for twenty, and the boy's bed was number 20; one man had just been released. The nurse discovered that he was a Christian and said to him, "I will talk to you last each night." At bedtime she talked to every patient and prayed for him or her, and then she would take the boy outside and share Jesus with him, giving him Scriptures to read. John 10 stuck in his mind. Once he got well, he decided to return home and give his life to the ministry. He went home and said to his parents, "You must treat me as a son that has died; I belong to Jesus, and my life is given to Him." They blessed him and agreed. From there, through a series of miracles, he received an education. He has never forgotten his call to the villages. The next greatest change in his life was the day he read the book, *Back to the Cross*, by Watchman Nee.

Latin America or Caribbean

I met an interesting woman, an old blind woman who motioned me over to her. She felt my face and said that she wanted to tell me her story. Her daughter had been married to an abusive man for ten years. At the end of that time the daughter developed cancer, and as she laid sick and dying, the husband never visited, and the mother (the woman talking to me) was filled with hatred for him. Whenever she saw him she would cross the street and walk on the other side; she refused to meet him or face him. However, there was a growing conflict in her. She hated the man, but Jesus in her loved the man. The conflict within became greater and greater until finally one day she shared it with an elderly missionary woman, who gave her some very simple and practical advice, "Act the way you want to feel." The now blind sister took it to heart. The next time she met up with her son-in-law, she went to him, put her arms around him, and said, "I love you, and there is nothing that you could ever do that would make me stop loving you." He was shocked and walked away. She was not shocked, for as he walked away, she still hated him. However, the next time that she met him she said the same thing, "I love you, and there is nothing that you could ever do that would make me stop loving you!" Again he was shocked that she said it, and she still hated him. It went on for three years, with every encounter. "I love you, and there is nothing that you could ever do that would make me stop loving you." He stayed shocked; she hated him. What happened after three years surprised her. She awoke in the middle of the night weeping because of her great love for him! She really did love him, and there really was nothing he could ever do to make her stop loving him. She said it with a smile. God had put a great love in her heart for her abusive son-in-law. While she related this story to me, she had been holding a fellow's hand, which she then held up and said, "This is the man I love, my son-in-law, and there is nothing he could ever do to make me stop loving him." He was there with his new wife, and both of them take care of the old blind lady. Why? Because she loves them so!

A pastor takes us to his home, where we find a couple of fellows that have traveled fifty miles to see him, because last night they had a vision of him. One man came to pray for the pastor, and the other man came because in his vision, he was to give his life to Jesus when he met the pastor, and that is exactly what happened. Later, the pastor said that years ago, when he was protesting and marching for Jesus, pressing the government not to renew its contract with the voodoo spirit, the police came to the house to arrest him. He looked at the policeman and said, "I pity you for the job you are doing. It will not go well for you to touch the servants of the Lord. It will cost you your life." The man looked blankly at him and took him off to jail. A few days later the policeman quietly fell over dead! God will permit what He could prevent. The Christian does not merely bless the world; God's presence in the believer can curse, also, when confronted with obstacles.

Some believers are like finely cut diamonds. They really are pure men of God. Every morning this pastor comes to the table and proclaims, "I love God, and I love you!" This morning is no different from the other mornings. I ask him to tell me a story. I am sure that from his thick accent I do not get the details right, but the gist of the story is accurate. He had a vision that he was going to be arrested. He told the people in the congregation, and they were praying for him. What brought all this about was a run-in with a powerful religious organization. The pastor was preaching every day in the city center. The youth were being drawn away from the other organization, and its head protested to the police, saying that the pastor had hindered him from doing services for the President's father. Of course, this was not true. The pastor kept preaching, and the other organization started a disco for the youth, many of whom went, but the whole thing backfired when the parents started questioning why their children were out so late and away from home. In the end, the head of the other organization took a "rest" and never returned. His allegations had already been put into play, however, and a few days after the vision, the pastor was taken to the police station, where the head officer accused him of being a troublemaker and drew back his hand to strike him. Just before he struck, the officer asked for whom the pastor was working. Since he had a weekly radio program, he said that he was working for the radio station. At that the policeman paled, for he knew that the owner of the station worked for the President. The pastor was released, to the praise and rejoicing of many people.

I am invited over to meet my coworkers' neighbors, a wonderful couple that reminds me of my youth and my best friend's parents, Mr. and Mrs. Lagerberg, a wonderful Swedish couple that never seemed to recognize as a stranger anyone who came to their door. The lady immediately begins speaking in good English, and so does her husband, for he was stationed at an Air Force base in Arizona for several years. On his wall hangs an interesting painting depicting a true occurrence during WWII. A Brazilian plane sunk a German ship, and as the plane circled back to assess the damage, the crew spied men alive in the water without life preservers. The Brazilians flew over again and dumped out all of their own life preservers for their enemies to use (there is a sermon in there somewhere). The gratitude of the enemies was such that on the fiftieth anniversary of the event, the surviving Germans came to Brazil and thanked the survivors of the plane. After a really a nice ceremony, they flew together and dumped out balloons. I just do not think Brazilians like having enemies; they have too much passion and love. In so many ways they are unique.

I have a session with a woman infatuated with her pastor. This can happen when, as in many countries, the pastor is the first man ever to listen to a woman. It is easy for the pastor to kill this emotion by simply pointing the counselee to Christ, but in this case, the woman went to him to talk about her marriage, and they ended up talking about his struggles; now they have developed a mutual infatuation. This vexes me. I am not saying I am a stronger person, but there is a danger in using one's position in such a way. People come to pastors for help in the name of Jesus, and it is dodgy business to use someone's emotional pain for one's own gain. Well, amen, it happens, and that is where ALMI comes in. I listened to her and then said, "Oh, you left something out. You are sure this relationship is of God because of the amazing peace you have and the fact that both of you pray and witness together." She just stared, "How did you know that?" Well, it was not prophecy; I have seen it more times than I care to think. A marriage is in trouble for years, so with the mind a spouse runs away from divorce, but with the emotions he hastens toward it. This creates an incredible amount of conflict. Therefore, when the decision is made to separate, mind and emotions now agree, the conflict is over, and a false peace sets in. Next, to validate the whole mess and show he is on the right track, the spouse actually begins to pray, read the Bible, and witness. In this particular case, further examination reveals additional cause for the behavior. She is a setup for an older man, which the pastor is. To make a long story short, she had never had a positive experience with a man. I spent a good bit of time explaining to her that the pastor was not ministering to her at the level at which she thought he was; he was actually only ministering to her flesh and not her spirit at all. It is possible, through counseling, to make the flesh feel good. However, that does nothing for the spirit. She got the message. I did not tell her that she had to leave the pastor and stay with her husband in the condition that has previously always existed for them. A new marriage with her spouse would have to be started with different attitudes, goals, and a center in Christ. I did ask her to withdraw from the situation with the pastor in order to listen to Jesus and allow Him to meet her needs. She looked shocked and said, "I was fearing that you would just tell me I was a terrible person!" She agreed that she needed to go to Jesus and listen to Him. She could also see the cross and how it applied. She had been taking the blame during the entire course of the marriage and needed to take up the cross to deny that part of her and let her husband wear his own failures.

I am off to another counseling session with a person who knows English quite well, so I can go it alone without an interpreter. This man has had a personal failure in his life, and the question is simple and straightforward: "Is God punishing me?" Several situations had occurred that could lead someone, under the influence of the enemy, to think that he was still being punished after repentance. Often the voice of Satan is predictable; he has whispered to someone that he is forgiven but must suffer the consequences. Christians are actually taught that this is the case: "Oh, God may forgive you, but you will suffer the rest of your life." The passage often used is, "If we sow to the flesh, we will reap to the flesh." That is true, but the logical conclusion is not emphasized, which is that if a person stops sowing to the flesh, he will stop reaping. Every farmer will witness to the truth, for it would be nice if he could sow once and then reap the rest of his life, for sowing is hard work. However, a year's worth of sowing is followed by just a few weeks of reaping, and then the farmer must sow again. The principle is that once we stop sowing, we will stop reaping. In the end, I tell this person that I am bored talking about his failure, and I believe that God is bored, too. I ask that we press on to the topic of Jesus. We do, and there is an obvious lift that comes from the Spirit within.

There is an odd, demonic practice throughout this area of killing babies. The enemy can extract from a person what fear allows. I was told of a practice where the men of the tribe can come and demand the heart of a baby to eat. I heard of one woman who had become pregnant but did not want to have any children. She stayed in the jungle so no one would know that she was expecting. She gave birth to the child, covered it with leaves, and returned to the village. A man walking heard cries and at first thought it was a spirit, so he began to run; but he stopped, listened, and could tell it was a baby. He found the baby, which by then was covered with ants, and brought him to the missionaries. Three days later the infant died in the hospital. The women in this village have each had, on average, seven children that have died, been buried alive, or abandoned to death, before they had one child they kept to raise. One missionary told of a woman that gave birth to twins and became distraught at the news, asking that the babies immediately be buried alive. The father, upon hearing the news, shouted, "Is my wife a dog to give birth to a litter?" The missionary begged them not to bury the babies, though this is not something that can be done under the government's current Indian policy; interference in the culture is not to be tolerated. Of course, culture and religion run hand in hand; change one and the other will always change. The missionary begged, "I am married, but I have no children. Please give the children to me!" The young parents agreed to give one and keep one. Next the missionary pleaded, "I do not know what to do for the child. Can I pay you to live with me and teach me?" The woman agreed, but on one condition. "I will teach you what to do for the child, but I will not do anything for the child!" For three months the missionary labored with the child. Then came the day when the sister of the mother came and explained that she only had a son and wanted a daughter, and asked if it might be possible for her to have her sister's baby girl. The missionary agreed, and now all are living in the same village. Among the unsaved, many of these ungodly practices continue. However, among the saved, things are changing quickly. It is so nice to have a God that does not demand the death of a baby! Many tribes are completely despondent, lacking hope and just seeing death as a much simpler way.

CHAPTER 4
Honoring Father and Mother

Pacific Islands

The whale's tooth is of great significance in some cultures. All business—from requesting help from the Prime Minister to asking a father for his daughter's hand in marriage—is conducted with the giving of a whale's tooth as a seal of the commitment. Land can still be given if requested with a whale's tooth. It is also a sign of honor to have a great tooth; some are as long as the forearm. One older saint told me how once as a younger man, he happened onto two very large whale's teeth in an Oriental store in a remote area of his island. He purchased them, which took all of his money, and took them to his aging father. He led his father into the bedroom of the house and opened the trunk in which a man keeps his most treasured possessions. He removed his father's possessions and then showed him the two whale's teeth, which he then placed on the bottom of the trunk and put the other objects back on top. He turned to his father and said, "When you die, your mother's family will come for your trunk, and when they remove your possessions, they will find the great teeth. They will know you were a great man." At that his father was content and stood with a great smile. As in the rest of life, I imagine that it is what lies at the bottom of the trunk that is most important.

One young man had been a Bible school student in a foreign country when I met him; he invited me to his home country, and eventually I made it to that remote place. He has a great heart, and I wanted to work with him. He told me that as soon as he got back here and was hired by the church, his mother called to ask what he was getting paid. She told him to send fifty percent of it to his grandmother, who lives on another island.

My friend tells me of some recent occurrences in the village. These community-minded people can so strongly count on the dependability of their word; it means everything. A lady came to her father and said she had caught her husband with another woman. The father confronted the son-in-law and sought his word by asking, "Do you want my daughter or not? Let your yes be yes, and no be no." The younger man repented and said he would never again do such a thing. The father spoke directly: "Our word is what we have. Your words to me that you want only my daughter are now written on my head and on my heart. Nothing can change that. If I hear anything different, I will come for you and take my daughter." From that day the daughter's husband has not been the same and has been a devoted husband.

Eastern Europe

A visiting lecturer from the U.S. told us that his father was originally from a country taken over by the Soviet Union, but while he was still quite young, his parents, in order to escape the communists, moved with him to China.

However, both parents died, leaving the five-year-old boy an orphan in China. He was shuffled from home to home by those who had "adopted" him. More accurately, he was moved from abuse to abuse. At age seventeen he found his way to Paraguay, and later went on to the United States. The lecturer once asked his father if he ever got angry at God during those long, hard years. His father replied, "How could I? He was the only One who understood me, listened to me, and loved me." The lecturer told us, "I am a Christian because of my father's witness."

A very young woman in this country suffering from want had been working for a ministry when she was seduced by a missionary man nearly forty years her senior; being from the U.S., he had lavished her with gifts and promises. She was sorry for the situation and wanted to be rescued, but she needed a dad to make a decision for her that she could not make for herself. Her own biological father is very ill and not a Christian. I prayed for two days before meeting with her to explain that we are one in the family of Christ; therefore, I am her father, and fatherly love compels one to stand between a person and her destructive behavior. Should a father allow his daughter to continue in such a situation? She wept and said no. I told her I was making the decision that she would quit her job, the relationship would end the moment we prayed, and that I would talk to the wolf in sheep's clothing. She beamed and said, "I will do it!"

The pastor's parents arrive from another city. They are not yet Christians, but they are beautiful people. They remind me of another couple I know that so overprotects their son that he is nearly suffocated. Their arrival seems to signal the beginning of a scene from a reality television show on remodeling. They act as though they have twenty-four hours to restore the entire apartment. His mother has a bucket and a friend in tow. One nearly instantly begins to scrub the floors while the other cooks breakfast. The father has his tools and is fixing all the doors, windows, chairs, and anything else that gets used. I come out of the bathroom and am expected to move aside for a swift cleaning job in there. We are called for a wonderful breakfast of chicken-fried pork with walnuts and all the trimmings! The pastor sits back passively, having lived through this scene a hundred times; he does a good job of taking up the cross and denying himself. His parents are really, really loving and pleasant, just overprotective. His mother would chew his meat for him if he would just let her. I would love to stay and just watch, to do a little case study, but I still have the sermon to work on, so I excuse myself.

Asia

I spent several hours with a Chinese pastor; I feel there is a lot to learn. The Chinese have been a mystery to me for many years. In nearly every country there is a small enclave of Chinese that stays true to its culture. No one really knows what they do; they seem to have a few businesses, restaurants, and nearly always their own schools. He explained that from birth they are taught the rewards of family; ancestors are worshipped, grandparents revered, parents obeyed and pleased. For the one who can do all that and become a success, the rewards of the community are great. From literature to family dinnertime, the young are instructed to be like so-and-so. Community is everything.

The downside is the near impossibility of not feeling like a failure, because great pressure is applied on each child to succeed in school, since he or she is an extension of the parents. At that I interrupted to say, "You must spend your whole lives either attempting to change the negative identity (of being a failure) or maintaining the positive identity (you are so-and-so's son)." He exclaimed, "Yes!" There is very little variation at the root level of man, which is why every man needs Christ.

One of the brothers told about his Muslim friend who converted to Christ, so his father beat him until the neighbors called the police. The new convert never lifted a hand, nor would he lodge a complaint against his father once the police came. The next day he was disowned and completely stripped of everything. "He is very bold for Christ," I was told.

I arrived at a little village of 10,000 people with 8,000 Muslims who do not like the 2,000 Christians, including Catholics. When things get too loud at church, the Muslims come and throw rocks at the building. A pastor and his wife brought me to this place, and on the way, he told me about how he came to Christ. His story reminded me that the way in which we most honor mother and father is to live a life glorifying to God, even though all too often the parents will despise us or reject us for that very thing. He was the fourteenth of sixteen children. His mother had her last child when she was 51 and died at age 65. He did not like coming from a large family (at which my only comment was that it was good his mother and father did not stop at thirteen!). He told me that he grew up with a speech problem and was not coherent. One day he heard a voice say, "Repent!" He wondered what repentance was. He went to his room and had a vision of a great light and a piece of white cloth on which were written all of his sins. Again he heard, "Repent!" As he began to confess the sins printed before him, his speech became normal. Earlier a sister had told him about Jesus, from whom he knew this vision to be, and he believed in Him that moment. He went running to the family, and all were amazed when they heard his speech. He then told them that he was going to become a Christian. They said, "No, you are not!" He said he would. In the end they threw him out and refused to pay for his schooling. The Lord provided the money he needed, and he went on to school. Later he was used of the Lord to see five of his brothers and sisters converted. Eventually the family accepted him back.

My son was called on to speak in my stead and give the concluding thanks. He shared that many have thought him brave to leave home and go to remote places. However, he has not left home, he has found a new home. It is nice to hear that people are family and nice to say it, but it is much nicer to see family, love, and home demonstrated. The same is true of Christ's life in us. It is nice to say, nice to hear, but even better to experience not the acting like Jesus, but exactly Jesus living within!

Latin America and Caribbean

I started one service by talking about the "others" in Hebrews, those who believed God, did not receive, and continued to serve, love, and believe in Him. At the end a couple in their early fifties came to me in tears. "God spoke to our hearts. We lost our only son, twenty-three years old, for no apparent reason, and yet we continued to believe. Tonight God showed us we are the others. We are so excited and so encouraged." Amen! There is one thing with which every parent must come to grips, or else the task of parenting can be overwhelming. We must all come to the revelation that our child is not our child; the child belongs to the Lord. Psalm 24:1, "The earth is the Lord's, and everything in it, the world, and all who live in it." Having learned the absolute point that the earth and all that is within it belong to the Lord, the next statement will be equally absolute. The child who is fatherless is also the Lord's. Our foundation is not the parent, but God; the issue is not the parent but the child who belongs to the Lord. I meet people who are raising fatherless children; this is an increasing trend in the world. These children are left feeling uncertain where or if they belong. When the mother describes the origins of the child, the explanation will often confirm what the world and the child's emotions have been indicating. Whether the child was planned and welcomed or not, this absolute fact remains; the child belongs to the Heavenly Father. If you look in the mirror and see this child staring back at you, or if you look across the room and see this child sitting across from you, you must both cherish this same thought: Every child belongs to God. As the child or the parent, have you recognized it?

In the morning I meet the interpreter, who speaks English so clearly that I immediately ask him to tell me his story. In the 1950's a single woman from the U.S. came here with no money or language skills, with only a vision to help abandoned street kids. She was in Brazil one week when a pastor told her of an abandoned three-year-old, whom she immediately took in. Since she did not know the local language, she only spoke to him in English, and English became his first language as he grew up in Latin America! She then put him in an English-speaking school, where he studied until age twelve, at which time the anti-American sentiments were so great in this society that she feared for his safety and put him in a public school, warning him not to speak English outside of the home. Once again I see that I am the weakest of all, for I would never be able to speak to this group of believers without all the tremendous works God has done beforehand. The man actually had a Midwestern accent like mine! We clicked, and I was happy to be dependent on him to communicate. I shared with him my firm conviction that the fatherless were chosen and set apart for God, and that if being fatherless on the earth was good enough for the Son of God, it was definitely good enough for the rest of us, for God intends to be our Father.

A pastor explains how he met his wife. She is from a Catholic family that was rife with nuns and priests. She attended one of his evangelistic meetings and gave her life to Jesus. In this place the practice is courtship, and a couple cannot get married without the parents' approval. The pastor fell in love with her and had to go to the parents' house to tell them that he loved her. He was very nervous, for not being a Catholic meant that he did not have a chance for the girl. However, the night before he came the mother had a vision in which she saw the young man's face and heard a voice that said, "Do not turn this man away!" When the mother-in-law-to-be saw him, she said, "I saw you in my dream; how can I say no to you?" So the pastor and the young woman were free to marry, and he continually shared with his father-in-law, reading him the Bible. One day the father-in-law asked, "What does the Bible say about baptism?" When the pastor showed him, the man said, "That is not what the priest told me! I must go to him and ask him to explain why what he is telling me is different from what the Bible says." When he did, the priest could not explain why his teaching was different from that of the Bible. At that the father-in-law became a Christian. Smiling, the pastor says, "My wife is my daughter in the Lord and my wife." He explained that the conversion in both families was so great that it resulted in many brothers and brothers-in-law becoming ministers and in many sisters and sisters-in-law marrying pastors. He said that when he meets family members, they immediately say to him, "Thank you for bringing Jesus!"

A counseling session was interesting and so illustrated that there is a legitimate and an illegitimate side to every issue. The woman is frozen in panic over the possibility of losing her only son. While it is legitimate to be protective, it is illegitimate, unproductive, and unrealistic to live in fear. As we talk I discover that her whole identity is wrapped up in being a mother; it is where she proves her worth, and therefore, she is not just protective of her child but also is shielding her identity. Being a mother is actually an idol. The tragedy is that through bondage to fear, she is not enjoying being a mother; there is no lightness in her work. She sees this and is almost immediately set free from it. She leaves a better mother, and actually, the best kind of mom, for she is one trusting in Jesus.

During dinner the pastor told me that he met his wife in the slum area. She was a student at the seminary in which he was a student teacher, but he had yet to have her in class. They worked together, and one day he sat her down and said, "I am going to ask you a question, to which the answer, 'Yes,' will mean yes, but, 'No,' will mean maybe. Will you marry me?" He asked her mother, who refused to allow her daughter to marry him. He asked why, and her reply was, "Well, you have not finished college, you do not have a home, you do not have a job, you have no source of income, and you work in a ghetto." He responded, "Oh." However, they continued in the same seminary, and they both loved the slum area. It took three years for everything to come together for them, but in the end, they got married and started a family in the ghetto. His family is great fun with two sons, ages four and ten. His wife had great difficulty bearing the first child; he was born prematurely and had a disease. The attending physician was a spiritualist, but by the end of the ordeal was a believer! The child has had several operations and is fine today. However, the young boy wanted a brother and in front of his mother prayed, "Jesus, I want a brother. Thank You for giving me one." The mother laughed, because she was on birth control pills. Three months later, she was pregnant! The home they live in is typical in this area of the city: a block home on a small lot on which every square inch is poured concrete. Surrounding the home is a wall with a padlocked gate, for security is high. The home is quite modest with small rooms, no ventilation, and no ceiling fans. A few months ago, his FIAT was stolen and the next day found burned. He determined to walk and take buses, when he got a call from an American asking if he needed anything. He explained what had happened, and the U.S. pastor said that he would bring it before his congregation. That night he got the call saying, "Buy a new car!"

India

I had a counseling session with a woman who remains in a marriage that has failed. Her husband was abused as a child, does not function well, and is constantly depressed and very abusive. He threw her out but has agreed that she could come back if she paid half of the expenses and never said anything, not one word. It was really a good time, since we covered many things. In the end I asked the most important question, "How do you see God in all of this? Your father arranged the marriage, and your one chance at marital happiness has escaped you." "Oh, I was very bitter, very angry with my father, for he should have seen the problems that the boy had. But one day I realized that God was using all of this to keep me near to Him. If I had wealth and emotional security, would I still love Him and seek Him? I see God in it. I even went to my father and confessed my bad attitude toward him." I was so happy to hear that.

It is hard to describe an elderly man I know; in this culture he is considered to be father/teacher/wise one/ he who has gained all the respect of those younger than he. This man is small with long white hair nearly to the shoulders, thick glasses, and the traditional lungee (skirt). He is a good friend, and we have remained close through the years. He is probably the best-read person that I know. He loves books, loves imparting knowledge, and is very soft; he stays up on all of the latest thoughts circulating through the Church at large. On a personal walk and talk, we moved slowly through the jungle trees past a cow enjoying the slop that it had received and making a sucking sound as it inhaled the day's leftovers. Passing by a mahogany tree, the elder confided, "I was offered 4,500 rupees by a neighbor for this tree. I waited and discovered from another man that it is worth 18,000. I do not have much to leave my children; therefore, I will leave them this tree." There is an unknown about this man; I never know when he will stop to point out something of nature or to make a statement. I am accustomed to the teachers I have making one-line statements, but this man only drops a word. "Do you know my niece has a beautiful voice?" Then he just stares at me. After a long pause he says, "Nightingale." Another pause, staring, then he speaks, "Lark." He looks at me long enough for the mental image of the two birds to merge with the image of the girl. He would not waste words telling me all about her; just two words are enough. His eyebrows go up slightly when he realizes I have gotten the picture, and then he turns and walks away. He shares many stories that I will have to think about, and we end up back at the house discussing whether it is men or women that are to leave their parents; which is more concerned for the parent, a boy or girl? In Genesis there is mention that "for this reason a man shall leave his father and his mother." My elder mentions a verse I had not thought of before in Psalm 45:10: "Listen, O daughter, consider and give ear; forget your people and your father's house." Conversation is a finely-tuned art form in this part of the jungle! His daughter had recently gotten married;

the whole wedding took from seven in the morning until seven at night. Tradition requires the bride to drive to the house of the groom; in this case, the whole wedding party on the bride's side drove for three hours. She wore a beautiful white sari. After the initial service (somewhat similar to that customary in the West), the groom brings a special, after-wedding dress that he has picked for her; it is brightly colored and very nice. He dresses the bride, and then one thread is taken from the brightly colored dress and inserted through a small golden locket. The groom stands behind the bride and "ties the knot," adorning her with the locket, the final part of the ceremony that seals the marriage. This groom is working in the gulf, and she has only seen him a few times since the wedding. This is normal in this culture.

A fellow arrived at the church, a young man from a wealthy Sikh family. He had secretly given his life to Jesus and began to collect Bibles. His parents found them and told him that he must throw out the Bibles or they would throw him and the Bibles out. He picked up the Bibles and left. He has found himself in this place, many miles from home. He asked to be baptized and has removed everything that identifies him as a Sikh: the beard, hair, and turban. The church pastor wants him to continue to wear the turban and beard in order for him to be more effective in witnessing to the Sikhs. "He will become a Christian sadhu," asserts the pastor.

A young man, an unbeliever, upon hearing the story concerning the blood of Christ, related his own story. "Three months ago I was traveling in the mountain when suddenly I fell down the mountainside. I was so injured

145

that I almost bled to death. My father carried me to a doctor, who, after a careful examination, declared that he could do nothing for me. 'If his bones were broken,' said the doctor, 'I could do something for him. If he had an illness, I could give him medicine. But he has lost his blood. The life of the body is in the blood. If we lose our blood, we lose our life; I cannot give the patient any blood, so I cannot help him.' When my father asked if there were nothing at all to be done for me, he said at last, 'Yes, if there were someone willing to give his blood—that is, some of it—for him, I could save him.' My father, who loved me wonderfully, said at once that he was ready to do this. A vein was opened and my father's blood flowed into my body, but because my father was an old man, the operation was too much for his strength; he was so exhausted that he died, but I was saved. So," said the young man as he finished his tale, "my father died for me. Because he loved me beyond measure, he gave his life for me."

I visit a young couple; the husband practices internal medicine and sees 100 patients a day; the wife is an obstetrician and sees up to 120 patients per day. This kind of exposure makes for well-trained physicians. After ten years of that, day in and day out, they are quick to analyze a problem. I was really impressed with the breadth of the fellow's knowledge. At night we talk about their arranged marriage. The concept sounds odd in the West, but it has its place and value. They were saying that parents, who have lived life longer, are much more perceptive about the merits of a prospective mate. A meeting is arranged, and if the parents agree, the groom interviews the bride, and vice versa; if approved by all, there is an engagement, and the

146

wedding follows shortly. The bride and groom get to know one another after the marriage and seem to enjoy the lack of pressure that comes from dating and having to find a mate on their own. The family structure is very tight, so there is a lot of support to make a marriage work. It seems there are about the same percentage of dissatisfied marital partners as in the West, but much fewer instances of divorce. One nice thing is that a couple does not bring all the baggage of dating—and maybe even living with another—into the marriage. In fact, there is very little baggage. The couples move on to work through all the same issues that we do in the West, primarily self-centeredness and flesh. The couples genuinely grow to love each other. Infatuation, which I see in Indian marriages, comes after years of living together, and therefore is something much more lasting than in the West. I am not opposed to it at all, but again, a person must be here a while to see the wisdom in it.

Africa

I arrive for morning services at a packed church with standing room only. A very special younger brother in the Lord starts by telling the people of being in a village where the chief watched as visitors danced before him. He said, "Bring a chicken for my guests." However, the people continued to dance and sing the chief's praises. Soon he said, "Bring a goat for my guests." The visitors refused to stop celebrating the chief. At that the chief called for his wife to "Bring the cow!" With these words of encouragement the church erupted in song and dance before the Lord. Taking up a collection is a great celebration. A basket is placed in the center of the floor and the people very

147

joyfully dance up to it and put in their offerings. After the collection the pastor announces that he has a special visitor, his mother. He tells of her care for him and then says that he is going to charge his mother 500 local dollars to introduce herself. He asks, "Do you want my mother to introduce herself, so you can meet her?" Everyone says, "Yes!" Next he tells the people that they will have to pay him the $500 ($.12 U.S.), so he can give the money to her, to pay him, to introduce herself. It all worked; as the pastors sang and danced among the people, one by one, they gave him what amounted to the $500. He gave her the money and then introduced her. Later the pastor pulled me aside and explained. "That woman is not my mother. In 1994 I was in the U.S. to escape the war. My mother was in the village. The rebels came in and butchered and ate my mother raw. This happened to many people. It was not until one year later that I discovered what happened to her. The woman I introduced this morning adopted me. She told me that she wanted to drive every terrible thought about my mother out of my mind. She wanted to meet every need a mother would meet. She never wanted me to feel lonely or unloved. She has done everything for me and has become my mother!"

Many of the Bible College students counseled here are Doers, but then, a person would have had to be a Doer to survive in this place of war and starvation. They have masked their emotions, too, since it does no good to have any. Of course, they are all working hard for what they feel is a perfectionistic, high-strung God; that concept mirrors their fathers, but I can only imagine the pressure on those fathers in this environment. The fathers explode under the stress of unemployment coupled with the need to provide; the sons watch and react the same way in a vicious cycle. I am surprised and delighted to see the very last counselee, for he has a great concept of God. His mother died, and the father took care of him and his siblings quite well. Punishment was always meted out in a just way. He was taught to go to authorities when he was in trouble; authorities are safe. He was a very amiable and capable person, but not the best student. The professor made this observation: "He is not the best student, but the best prepared for ministry." I did not point out any problems with him, because good counseling involves knowing when not to counsel. I just encouraged him in the ministry.

CHAPTER 5

Holding To The Traditions Taught

Africa

I met with a pastor who had been recruited to and trained in the seminary, after which he was committed to teaching Jesus and the Bible. When he returned to his local church to preach Christ, because of the mixture of magic and religion there, the congregation shrank to one-fifth of what it had been. The elderly were really upset because he would no longer follow or listen to their visions. Undaunted, he started two more congregations based solely on the Bible. I also met a pastor of a small community of believers; there is not a single unbeliever in the community. This, to me, was incredible, but I was quickly told of a larger city of 12,000 wherein every person belongs to the same church.

Late one Saturday night my host said that we would visit a church and, "You will speak for twenty minutes." In the morning we arrived at the church and were ushered to the platform. There was a balcony all around the sanctuary. There were four different choirs I wish everyone could hear; the beauty of the music prompted worship, and many were wiping away tears. All of us on the platform started dancing in single file; we left the platform, went to the open area in the center of the room to make a circle, and then returned to the platform. With that each section of the church rose, one by one, and danced in single file, weaving back and forth in the center of the open area before returning to their seats. Finally, the leaders formed a circle and one by one went to the center with a special dance. It was great! Then it was my turn to preach with an interpreter who is excellent and has a policy of protecting the speaker. If I say something that should not be said, for example, the word "fool," he will not use that word but will pick one that communicates what I need to say in a less offensive way. I talked about being a "not" in the sense of denying self and obeying Christ, and I gave the illustration of being angry with Betty and having to go to her to apologize. There were lots of laughs. I finished in the twenty minutes, and when the pastor arose, he said, "Normally if I ask a man to speak for twenty minutes, he goes for one hour and tells me it is the Holy Spirit. Mike only went twenty minutes. Also, have you ever heard of such a thing as a man telling his wife he is sorry? This is not heard of here, and never would it happen with a church leader. We have been proud, wanting glory; this must change." Then he explained that they had prayed for God to deepen their faith, and God had answered their prayers by sending the message that day. I believed him, because I never planned to be at that church. It was the Lord's plan all the way. After the service, when we met with the church's leaders, I clarified the message, "It is impossible to increase your faith in Him without decreasing the faith you have in yourselves. You must fail. Power is in weakness. Weakness is a magnet to God's power."

I have known for many years that Christianity's cultural roots are not Western but Eastern. It does not center on what we know and can recite. In many ways as I travel through Africa the Bible makes more sense to me. Often I feel that I am in the midst of some Old Testament story. In this place are people who still fear God, who are punished, and who have been spoken to through a vision. In fact, my brilliant interpreter told me that the last time he was here he had a dream. Before he had left his own African country, his mother was quite ill. In a dream a man told him that his mother would die. The next day in church a woman gave him a prophecy, "Your mother has died." Later that day when he called home, indeed his mother had died. He inquired about the hour; it was the exact hour that the woman had spoken to him.

I am shown a church's drilled water well, complete with water stands, and told, "We pump the water with generators to the tanks above. It is good water. Outside the wall is a tap; the poor can come and get good drinking water for two hours each day. On Saturdays, there are four hours in which to get water."

At the end of one evening's service, I was escorted away to give an interview to a local newspaper. "In your opinion, what are this country's Christians lacking?" I responded, "Nothing, absolutely nothing. My message is not to tell you what you are lacking, but to bring the revelation of everything that you already have. No Christian is lacking in anything. We are complete in Christ." Another question: "Recently five men from Europe came to Africa and said that they must pay Africans for the injustices and abuse that their fathers committed against the people. Do you agree?" My response: "I most certainly do not, for several reasons. What is the end of such a teaching? Land was taken from a tribe, but the tribe had taken it from another, and that other from another, so how do they plan to follow through on remunerating the original occupants? Secondly, do these men really believe that some Africans are in the condition they are in because of something the Europeans did? If I believe that my state is solely due to the actions of another, then I become that person's continuous victim and slave. God is for us, so who can be against us? We either see God or we see men in our condition. We can see God in everything, for He causes all things to work together for our good. For men to insinuate that they have directed events in Africa is the height of presumption, making themselves out to be God, as if they caused the misery and now can fix it. They would have you looking to them, and worship means *to give attention to*. Third, how many people in European cities have never heard the Gospel? Why are they here discussing with you how they can fix you, when there is plenty of work for them to do back home? In these end times we do not have time for such piffle!"

Often—and not just on this continent, but nearly any time I am going to speak to remote village people—I get unsolicited advice to "Keep it simple, for these are simple people." I must admit that I always wonder what that means. Is the Gospel not simple and tailor-made for simple people? If I am preaching something that is not simple, I do not see how I could be teaching the Gospel. "But I am afraid that, as the serpent deceived Eve by his craftiness, your minds will be led astray from the simplicity and purity of devotion to Christ" (2 Corinthians 11:3). Jesus really is for the weak. When I am told that my approach is too difficult for "simple" people, I think that statement is a revelation of the speakers' pride, bigotry, and unbelief. All of God's people are simple, and a person cannot call himself a teacher if the people do not comprehend what he is saying. My father pounded that into my head growing up. He was an engineer who had to explain to janitors how to operate and repair equipment. If they did not understand what he said, the blame was his for not making it simple. I believe that. I have noticed on my travels that all of the "simple" people are doing quite well at getting the "complex message" of how Christ wants to be our life, while the educated and seminary elite just want to argue to a non-constructive end.

At the end of my speaking session in a village, the choir came forward to treat us to beautiful dancing, hand gestures, and a song about Jesus' returning, angels taking us away, and the evil men and murderers embarrassed that they did not walk with Jesus. They continue singing and dancing for the next three hours. There is a movement in the worship services in the West to add some dancing, and it is seen as radical and new. In this culture it has been happening for centuries without the goal of whipping up emotions or forcing the presence of God. It is quite a natural expression. No one looks at anyone else; they just cannot sing without moving their feet.

When a flight was canceled due to the plane's mechanical problems, so many people at the check-in counter were angry. Not that I have never been in that state before myself,

155

but honestly, the plane cannot fly. It has not even arrived. In the end a fight breaks out, with one fellow climbing over the counter, the airport manager screaming, and people gathering from all around. I know it is a true blessing not to understand the language! While yelling and gesturing wildly with his hands, the airport manager started looking in my direction and made me the focus of the screaming. I had said nothing. I motioned for him to come to me. He was ready for a fight and assumed I was even angrier than the others. I immediately extended my hand; he looked shocked and grabbed my hand. I pulled him over to the counter and put his ear against my lips. I whispered, "It is not your fault. You are doing a wonderful job. The mob does not understand that you cannot make the plane fly. I would not want your job." He stepped back and just quietly observed me. Then he smiled, others smiled, and all of the yelling stopped. It was amazing. Truth is not preached but demonstrated. "A kind word turns away wrath."

Before you read what follows, I want to say that I know several social-gospel based ministries that see their aid as a means to an end, really do love the people, and are constantly preaching and giving of themselves. One is in Central America, another in the Philippines, one in Israel, and now that I think of it, I could go on and on and never list all of the fantastic people I have met around the world, from the Salvation Armies to Pacific Garden Mission in Chicago. If pressed, I would side more with a social gospel than against it; having seen starvation firsthand, it would be difficult not to be so inclined. We are admonished to remember the poor, yet I also have a sound conviction concerning God's use of suffering in man's life. It is, to me,

His greatest evangelistic tool. Because of pride, men do not accept Christ, and suffering breaks pride. I am also against nearly every form of intervention. The angels ministered to Jesus AFTER His time in the wilderness. Many need the same type of ministry after the wilderness, not while they are in it. God is doing something in the experience. Generally speaking, I believe that the Church today has so little confidence and experience in what fellowship with Jesus and His expression through us can mean that we have opted to work in the realm of the social. When the Son of man comes, will He find faith on the earth? I still believe that the guilt-motivation style of preaching is the easiest and most suited for unbelieving believers. Any of us can close our eyes and picture scenes of starving peoples, abandoned children, and the homeless. I am not dismissing the legitimacy of that need or the people; I am addressing those who are showing the pictures. What do those pictures have to do with the Gospel? The Church is flooded with such presentations. I would like to have the pictures shown and someone say, "Do you know, do you believe, that if these people gave their lives to Jesus, the Father in heaven would change everything in that country? Despair could give way to hope, greed give way to sacrifice, and deception yield to truth; for in reality, these are the things that are at the root of starvation in the world today." We do not hear that because it is not believed. During this trip I have been in the epicenter of world aid. The Africans themselves do not respect it and see it for what it is. World aid is a business. I was told today of two different men who made appointments to describe their works to a Christian aid group; one appointment was in the morning, the other was in the afternoon. Somehow, they had actually collected the same photos of hungry people and a building that was going up. They did not even know each other; they just wanted in on the aid machine. "Well, if just one person is helped, it is worth it!" I think someone needs to reveal who that one person is. The U.N. directors are getting paid pretty well; they live in nice homes, have servants, and drive big cars. "Well, if just one is getting helped!" What is the help being given, and why? I really am appreciating the Africans to whom God has led me; they are excited about giving the pastors Bibles and Bible teaching and seeing them mature in faith. They believe the rest will take care of itself. One Christian brother told me of being in the U.S. and sitting at the back of a church when a missionary to his country was speaking. The brother knew the missionary, knew where he lived, and knew how he lived (a house with servants). However, the missionary told stories of how rough it was, of the snakes, of the constant danger, and then he looked up and saw my friend. At the end of the service, the missionary came up to him and said, "I need to tell those kinds of things, or the people will not give." My friend replied, "No, you do not. If God wants people to give to your work, He will lead them to give. Your responsibility is to walk in truth." I could tell you many more horror stories, but then those might soon eclipse the reality and work of the genuine missionaries. I know how they feel, for I have to carry the mistakes of every self-serving white person that has ever spoken before I did in a church. Hudson Taylor was a missionary with a call; he went without money or any support other than those who would pray. God proved to him that with the call comes the provision. I am once again preaching my own funeral, because no doubt in my early days of missionary work, I wanted so badly to go and minister that I only told of the dramatic occurrences. As I keep saying, "I have done it all! I have made all the mistakes, and it is only God's grace that has delivered me from the 'cleverly devised.'"

I arrived at a Bible college connected to a branch within the Anglican Church called God's Army. A fellow in the last century could not understand how people could sit in pews while people were going to hell. He started an evangelical movement but, unlike others, refused to leave the Anglican Church. It became a sort of order within the church that still exists today. These men, though in what would be considered a very liberal church in the West, are firmly committed to evangelism in a great way. I met the director, a British fellow who is a genuine missionary. I cannot think of a better compliment. We shared, and there was not a hint of competition from him; we were completing each other in Christ. We had tea and a nice time of sharing about the most important thing in counseling, which is gifting, since a gift will carry a person way beyond education; if we pray before we counsel, how effective it will be. We also talked about the need to be connected to the Lord in order to move where He is moving in the life of the disciple. Most importantly, did we really believe Jesus could meet every need?

I have a long flight ahead of me; it will take two days to get home. I am tired, and my voice is nearly gone. Earlier in the day the director of the seminary came to me. "You know me, I have never asked for anything. I commute over five hours a day, and sometimes ten. I really need a computer. If you hear of an old laptop, could you get it for me?" I explained that we would see what God would do. As I was packing, the Lord spoke to me: "Give him your computer!" I was honest and said, "I do not want to! I like this one and will find him another one." Earlier I had been teaching on greed. I made the statement, "Greed is keeping something for which a brother or sister in the Lord has a greater need." I remember the pastor's words after teaching on being a servant: "It will not be easy. I know God will come for my words and put me in the position of being a servant." God had come for my words; I was just being greedy! After all of the things the family of God has done for me, I could be greedy. In the morning, I handed him the computer. He gasped in shock. How did God give the ALMI support team to me, send me, have me bring a computer, and give it to a fellow who was praying for one with no practical way of ever getting one? See how the Lord works through all of us?

The courtyard is filled with cattle; a large denomination's founder who lived here long ago loved cattle. Every morning they were released to go to her, and she would sit under a tree and feed them bread. She also kept chickens as a hobby, for she liked selling the eggs very cheaply to the poor. On this property are a museum and a large statue of her. During church conferences the statue is strictly off limits to the visiting pilgrims, for the simple reason that many new converts will bow to the statue and pray for a blessing. The pastor here—he truly is the chief servant and loved by all—keeps things Christ-centered and is opposed to the practice; he always announces to all that a statue will not help them.

I was told of a man who was an idol maker. One day he thought to himself, *I will cut the head off of one of the idols and see if anything happens to me.* Nothing happened. Next he cut off the hand and nothing bad happened. In the end he cut the idol in two and nothing happened. He then realized that something made with hands could not be a god. This revelation led him on a journey that found him at the feet of Jesus. I was told by one missionary that people can be born again through a clear conscience without having to hear the name of Jesus. I do not believe it. Truth is where fact and faith meet. He could not present a single person who said that God gave him a new life before he later discovered that the new life had the name of Jesus. However, though an unbeliever in a remote area cannot be born again, he could have a conversion in his thinking, as did the idol maker. Revelation can lead someone to search and find Jesus.

My friend was telling me about a fellow that got him interested in counseling. The fellow would see hundreds of patients a day, providing most of the psychiatric care in the area. He would stand all day and walk down a line of people, asking a few questions and giving out prescriptions. He had three daughters; two had rebelled and one had stayed at home, a model child. One day this daughter overdosed on malaria tablets (common in Africa) and died; the autopsy revealed that she was carrying a two-month-old fetus. After the funeral was over and he was back treating the people, the psychiatrist had to sit and let the people walk past him. In a few weeks he could not walk, and they came to his office. In a few more weeks he could not move, so they came to his home. Soon no one could come. When my friend visited the man, he found him sitting in a chair staring straight ahead, chain smoking, with a case of beer on one side and a trash can on the other. In just a few months he was dead. What a sad ending for a man who had lived to help so many. That image is burnt into my friend's mind as a remembrance that our counseling must be Christ-centered or the world will overwhelm us.

Another interesting missionary tells me a story of a woman who asked Jesus to see what heaven and hell were like. Jesus first took the woman to hell, where she saw a large table set with beautiful food. However, the people had no elbows and therefore could not get any of the food into their mouths. There the people looked quite miserable. Next she was taken to heaven and saw the exact thing, except everyone was happy. She stood there wondering why until the people started to feed each other. That is a wonderful illustration of how we can experience heaven on earth.

A Bible teacher was attempting to change his image, getting frustrated when he could not, and subsequently acting like his abusive father acted. He is on complete performance-based acceptance and has invited in the lie that God is not love. This allows the father of lies to make constant visits and accuse him. He must learn the love of God. We have a great visit, and he is so open. The time together is beautiful, and Jesus moves in his heart.

It will be a busy week. The founder is here to help celebrate the ten-year anniversary of this Bible school. Students are graduating, there is a pastors' conference, and more. I am here to lead the evening sessions and the pastors' training in the mornings. As I begin to study, I hear the Africans singing. It is unbelievable how many sounds can be made by the human voice. There is not an instrument in the crowd, but the harmony of voices is soothing and beautiful. The sun is setting and presents a beautiful orange/blue background to the silhouetted mountains and bush trees. The lecture hall is of red brick with a metal roof. The evening is cool, which to an African feels like freezing. Many have on thick coats, while others came from the plains, assumed that it would be hot, and brought no such wraps. The two front rows are filled with the local pastors. Something amazing was done here last year; students started leading the local pastors through a Biblical training course; at its completion, one pastor testified that he had been in complete darkness, teaching things that were heresy, but just not knowing any better. It is an incorrect judgment to assume that someone who is teaching something false is false himself. These men just never had any training and did the best that they could. For this evening I chose the topic of legalism and hit it hard. The reception was wonderful! I asked, "For every one thing you tell people to do, could you tell them ten things Jesus is doing for them?" At the end, the major professor said, "Brother, legalism is the exact problem. Every question ends with the answer of needing to be obedient. I am sick of even hearing the word *obedience!*" At the break I was talking to another pastor who is working toward his Ph.D. in counseling; he shared his approach, one that is popular in Africa and is some kind of narrative approach wherein a person tells his story and finds what he has done in the past that helped him; then he is encouraged to apply it to his present situation. This man is more mature than I am, so I hesitated to say what I wanted to say. However, it slipped out: "What if that which worked in the past is just good flesh or is something like intimidation? Would you encourage that? Also, can the approach be done without Christ? If so, how can it be Christian?" The proof of his maturity was made clear in his response, "Thank you for those thoughts!" Later he said to me, "Has anyone ever accused you of just saying too much about Jesus?" We had a good laugh. He explained that one pastor kept talking about Jesus at a conference until another pastor stood up to disrupt and said, "Do not be deceived! He is saying nothing about the Father or the Holy Spirit! He is only talking about Jesus! He is false!" He also said that he was so locked into thinking about psychology that it was easy to forget Christ, and he could see that there was a problem when Christian counselors were secularly trained people who happened to be Christian. I like it when there is fellowship and not debate.

The second service I preach one morning is to a Black congregation of twelve, and we have some fun. The service is in English, because it is becoming the unofficial language here. The singing, often with no accompanying instruments, is beautiful. It comes time in the service to recognize the guests. A fellow from a warring country introduces his friend he met on the street, and they knew immediately that they were each members of the opposing tribes back home. This young man of 22 that had been on the streets is destitute, the only survivor of his family that was slaughtered before his eyes, and his eyes still tell the story. He had made his way to this relatively peaceful country, and the fellow who was a believer saw him and brought him into his own home. The refugee did not have a job, so they were sharing the food. The Christian brother wanted to introduce the itinerant man to the audience and stress that he did still have a family, the family of God, that he was not alone, that they were one with him, and it was quite beautiful. I shook the refugee's hand and placed some of my supporters' money in it. He was shocked, but I just held him and said, "Family!"

Asia

I met with evangelists based in Singapore who told of their trip to a land parcel in the northeastern Himalayas where no foreigners are allowed (they were born on the same continent and would not be considered foreign); the place is kept sealed because it is strategically located. It has been on my heart to go there for many years; Sam Jones was the first person to tell me about the place. During the time the country was sealed and all missionaries were thrown out, the few believers in this mostly Buddhist/Muslim country began to cry out, "Father, what are we to do?" God began to pour out His Spirit among the Baptists, and in the end over 80% of the people there converted. The evangelists told me that they had spoken in a church of 3,500.

The same evangelists told me of one of their earlier trips to the interior. After they held a meeting, the village men informed them, "The English came and our fathers cut off their heads. The Japanese came and their heads were also cut off. One day an Englishman appeared, pleading for the head of one of the men and saying that the man's wife could not rest until the head was returned to England.

He offered us a special spear in exchange for the head. We took the spear but told him to leave without the head." The evangelists just stared at the group, so one of the men said, "They do not believe us." They took them by the hand and led them to a special building in which was found all of the heads of the village men's fathers' enemies! The evangelists were also allowed to examine the spear that was made and engraved in England. That night as they lay sleeping, first came a huge knock at the front door that woke them up and shook the small hut. Then came another knock at the back door that made the building shake and the roof start to split apart. The witchdoctor had cast a spell on the building to try to force them to leave, because he knew what would happen to his business if the people of the village converted. They jumped out of bed and saw a light just a few feet in front of the building; it was a gaslight, beside which was the village pastor, who was keen to see their Christian work succeed. He had heard the sound, knew what was happening, and ran to kneel in front of the building, praying aloud that Jesus would intercede. The Lord moved, and the sound stopped. They went on with the ministry, and the Church in that village grew. The earlier part of this narrative is reminiscent of when the Apostle Paul said that he had wanted to go to a place, but Satan hindered him.

The evangelist gentleman is seventy and really an entertaining speaker. He told of meeting a chief that kept trying to rub the black off the evangelist's face, and about working in a village where the adults hide in the tall grass to undress, come out naked to bathe in front of the entire village, then return to the tall grass so no one sees them dress. In this village he made an important discovery: only when the chief sat beside him did the people listen, because it meant that he was speaking on the chief's behalf, and the chief wanted everyone to hear it. From then on there were conversions. The evangelist was encouraging the staff to go out into the frontier and continue ministry. There are many women missionaries, one of whom for ten years has crossed the river weekly, ridden first on an elephant and then on an ass, and climbed the rest of the way on foot up to the village. She said the most dangerous possibility is rape by natives.

In a church on a prominent island nation, one woman was really noticeable. She was setting up chairs and helping. At the end of the service she was serving the meal and then doing the dishes, all with a big smile. The pastor told her story. At university she would look to the hills and pray for the tribal people. One day she discovered a young man in the fellowship that did exactly the same thing. They married and moved to the base of a huge mountain on which tribal people lived. They built a large church and put lots of lights on it so the people could see it. After five years, still no tribal people would come. She was eight months pregnant with their second child when, during a meeting, as she played the piano and her husband gave an altar call, a tribal man stepped in. His hair was cut as though a bowl had been placed on the head, he wore only blue, and both of his hands were shoved into their opposite big shirtsleeves. When the pastor came to pray for him, the man pulled a knife out of his sleeves and stabbed him in the church. The wife went into labor. Both were taken to the hospital. While she was still in labor, the Lord spoke to her, saying, "I am going to take your husband." She could not attend his funeral, but it was there that all of the area pastors vowed to provide for her. They came to the hospital to tell her. She gave the baby to the elder pastor and said, "Raise him in the Lord." The elder pastor agreed, but asked, "What are we to do for you?" The woman said, "Where my husband fell, I will continue." This was the woman with the smile. These events had happened many years previously. She had helped found many churches and was a well-known evangelist.

One evening when I was being taken from one meeting in the city to the next one in the country, the driver stopped at one of his satellite churches in a remote, poor area. He told me that a year ago he had heard of a Catholic man who had died in an accident. His body laid for two days while the Catholic Church refused to perform the funeral, because the man had not kept up his church membership. The fellow I am with called the family and asked if he could be of help. They requested that he perform the funeral service, which he did, and at the end issued an altar call. About forty people came forward. Three days later a reception was held, and more came forward, nearly a hundred altogether. The people wanted him to return and continue ministering to them. None of them had been attending church, because bus fare was $20 roundtrip per person to get to the church in the closest town. My driver had started the church and continued to make sure someone was there to minister on a regular basis. The believers have built a little building that is quite nice.

The head fellow of a Bible Society is delightful. I explain the ministry and that I am just here to present what we do, distribute some books, and ask people to pray if I should return for the training. His immediate response was, "The message is needed in this country!" He follows it up with telling me that the pastors who verbally beat up and abuse the people vex him. He knows we are to lead even the weakest of people with love and respect. He is smiling all while we share our lives together in Jesus.

We are introduced to a ministry that took our friend out of the leper colony at age six, housed and educated her in nursing, and now has hired her as director. The ministry originated in New Zealand. Twenty women at a time are brought for five months to be housed, fed, and educated here. Classes are from eight in the morning until five in the evening, instructing in such topics as medical treatment, Bible, sewing, knitting, and more. At the end of the time each student is given a foot-pedal sewing machine and sent back to her village to duplicate what has been done for her. The idea is to make the ladies self-sufficient. It is really a great ministry for forty young women each year.

A new church building is being constructed and is nearly completed. The people are going to enjoy the new building; it is very nice, has lots of light, and displays crosses in the windows as a witness to all those who pass by. Also, the baptistry is built on the outside of the church as a reminder to every Hindu that walks by that believers are cut off from their roots and have a new life in Christ. In some ways it seems that baptism has more significance to Hindus than it does to most Christians, for to Hindus, Christian baptism is a complete cutting off from the Hindu world and family.

I started with the lectures on marriage that kicked off a four-day seminar. I first had to lay the foundation of seeing God in everything. It is a labor, but taken slowly and repeated often, the people are having the revelation that Jesus is in all things. The predominant culture of Hinduism strongly influences every aspect of life. Loving a wife is not done. Serving or helping a wife is not done, and I know that what I have to say will erect a barrier of incredulity. Therefore, I also began by talking about the place of culture in our lives. We have a culture of our heart, of our humanity, of our village, of our district, and of our country. If the culture of the heart changes, then the ripple effect is that all other cultures that surround us will also change. This makes sense to them. Then I told them of the poor man in Africa I saw fishing while his naked wife and children looked on from their mud hut. I was curious about that simple lifestyle and requested that the interpreter ask the man what his two main worries in life were. He responded that he did not understand his wife and worried about what would happen to his children. Those worries were the same as mine! I told the seminar attendees, "In your culture you do not teach to love the wife; in my culture we do, and yet there are few doing it. I am not the one who says that we are to love our wives, but God says it," and we read portions of Ephesians. I also explained the place of the commands of God, that they are there to make us happy. Not loving his wife will punish a man. That settles the matter and I can now move on. At the very end, two pastors are allowed to give their testimony. The first pastor said that he had never heard such things or seen a presentation in picture. He then outlined the whole seminar. He had gotten every bit of it; the Holy Spirit had made it clear. It was wonderful. Another elder spoke and was choking in tears most of the time. He said that he finally understood his wife. He was a Doer and she a Thinker; he had falsely judged her and could see what a blessing it was to be married to her. One high point of the day was when one man stood up to say, "I have wanted to hurt my wife, and now I see I would only be hurting myself." Beautiful! Christ is the Way and every other way is not the Way. Forget culture when it is not based in Christ. Finally, we heard from the pastor credited with establishing the modern presence of the Church here, the pastor who had been so badly beaten by the Hindu authorities. He is full of surprises! Most pastors in developing countries will not share about their failures. In fact, I have been told that I am forbidden to speak of my failures, but I refuse to be silenced on that. I have a good marriage, but what help does it give to tell of only the wonderful things when others are struggling? The pastor tells of going to a seminar in the capital city, where an American was speaking on loving your wife. A local pastor had stood up and said, "My wife is very naughty; what am I to do to her?" The pastor that had been beaten was thinking to himself how his wife was the same. The American said, "It is quite elementary; you must simply walk up to her and give her a kiss." The beaten pastor is very humble and willing to follow the advice of Christians. He immediately went home and found his wife in the kitchen. She was kneeling down, blowing through a pipe on a smoldering fire attempting to get a flame. In this country a man does not kiss his wife unless they are behind a locked door. He shut the door and went to grab

171

her and give her a kiss. She did not know what he was about to do, so she took the pipe and hit him on the head. [At that the crowd went wild with laughter. It was hard to go on with the people laughing so much.] He went away and came to her four days later, shut the door, gave her a kiss, and explained what it was he had been trying to do for her. He said that the marriage began to change. Prior to any of this she had at one point even broken his kneecap. I laughed and said, "Brother, the police have beaten you, the Hindus have beaten you, and now I see that your wife has beaten you! Who has not beaten you?" I am happy about this week, in that 250 couples were able to spend their first nights ever alone in a guesthouse, there was no cooking they had to do, no kids, just one another. The whole meeting was a blessing for me to experience. We have all bonded, and the worship team stays to sit in a circle and sing.

A large ribbon has been placed across the front of the platform, and we are invited to participate in the building dedication. In a very nice ceremony, the minister gives the message, and I have the privilege of cutting the ribbon. Next I am called upon for the ordination of my host into the ministry. He told me that over the past eight years, many have wanted to ordain him into their respective denomination, but he was never at peace with it since his church is here with the leprosy colony. He then had it on his heart to wait until I returned to ordain him. I spoke to the people about how ordination is not the setting apart of someone for a job, but the recognition that God had set that person apart. I read the passage concerning the call of a leader and asked, "How can any man do all of that on his own? Therefore, not only must the man be recognized as set apart, but the congregation that ministers WITH him must also be recognized as being set apart. The whole congregation must support the man." I explained why we anoint with oil; it is the power and fuel of the seed, and without oil, man has no light. Oil represents the power, the fuel, and the light of God. It represents His Holy Spirit. I then asked the men to come forward and pray for my friend as I anointed him with oil. The Holy Spirit was present with us. My friend had asked that I also ordain the elders, but I explained that he was the one recognized by God to lead in this work, and so after I ordained him, he was to ordain the elders. He could see the reasoning in that and called the elders forward at that time to anoint and ordain them.

At the break one of the visiting pastors came to talk to me. He was very excited as he proclaimed, "I just knew it was true! I always believed what you have been saying. It is true that if God gets all the glory, then God must do all the work. Jesus wants to live through me, and I am so sick of the legalism that tells me that I can live like Him. I just want to know more and to take my church in a different direction."

The students have invited their parents to come to a meeting and listen to me speak at the school. Several poor Muslims attend the school, and many have parents that are illiterate and are very appreciative of the opportunity that the school affords their children. I began by talking about problems that man has without having a God. I moved on to talking about the Way we should live. I ended by saying the Way was a man named Jesus. I then explained

173

more about this man and His ability to live in us so His victory could become ours. I am not an evangelist in the conventional sense, but at the end of the meeting I asked for a show of hands if there were any who wanted this man, Jesus, to live in them. I stopped counting at forty. I know I am standing on the back of the host pastor to see such a thing, but I also know that he is standing on the back of Jesus. It was beautiful.

One partnering pastor is pure gold. The prophecy is true, "In the lesser day, God used greater men, but in the greatest day, God will be using the lesser man." With each passing year, the call on this pastor's life is more evident. He does very little that will benefit him. Many people from various groups have tried to hire him, but the price is too high for him to pay. The offers generally include time-consuming administrative tasks that would cause him to neglect his outreach to the remote areas in his country. He is of a Brahman family; his last name reveals his high-caste status. Therefore, seeking Hindus and converted Hindus have no problem coming to his church, because the pastor is of the high caste. In this regard, his name is of benefit to him, but the reverse is true of those pastors of a lower caste. They have a terrible time getting people to come. Christianity is illegal here, but the insurgent threat has made that more of a minor issue. However, baptizing someone against his will is a mandatory three-year prison sentence. Therefore, this pastor makes every person sign a certificate that he is being baptized of his own free will. He keeps the papers in case someone returns with the police, wanting a bribe and saying that he was forced into baptism. The pastor was questioning some other pastors as to why they preach two hours a week and spend 48 hours on the internet, surfing the web to find a church or ministry with which they can "partner." I get several of those types of letters a week from various developing countries. However, I have to remember that if I need extra income, I can go to work somewhere part time, an opportunity that is not available in most of the places in which I minister. Also, the men need to grow in faith and discover that with the call will come the provision. This will take having them become exhausted with the disappointing lack of response to their "appeals." In the end, they will have to trust the Lord for the supporters that they get. He also tells me of an Indian couple that traveled the worldwide conference circuit, and at each place they cried about losing their purse. A large donation was always taken up for them, even though in reality the purse was never lost, but they returned to India and built a mansion with the ill-gotten donations.

Eurasia

I was speaking in a sixteenth-century church building that had no heat, and around 200 people were there—all bundled up—to listen. I had a great interpreter who loves his people, loves the message, and loves that they are able to hear it. In fact, he said to me, "As an interpreter, for the message to flow, I have to get out of the way. I am not the message; I communicate the message of another. When I am out of the way, there is no pressure on me. I know when I am in the way and out of the way." I said, "Well, amen. That is the attitude every believer should have toward God and His work through us." Even before we began the sessions at the church, I had received a letter

175

from a woman who had earlier been listening to bits of one of the books I wrote being read in her language on the radio. Her letter said: "I am a music teacher. Four years ago Jesus came into my life. I was so happy, but soon God became a complication of laws that I cannot keep. Events came that I could not understand. I asked God what it all meant. My problems were very serious, and I was afraid there was no one I could talk to. Little by little my old sins and old life returned. I felt miserable and guilty. I tried to read my Bible but was afraid that my spirit had died. I thought, *Where is there help for me?* Then I listened to my radio and heard a reading from your book. It came at the perfect time. I decided that I must get this book. I heard on the radio that you would be in my city. I thought, *Maybe this man can answer my questions. 'God, if it is Your will, I will see this man.'* Then I heard at the last minute that you are coming. God did what He said, 'When they call to me, I will answer them; when they are in trouble, I will be with them. I will help and honor them.' I can say your book is God's answer to me! This is a key for my problems. I thank God. God saved me from myself with your hand. Maybe in the future He can do something for you by my hand."

In one city we had meetings that included two groups from two different Bible schools. I was wondering how the students would hold up to a full day of lectures on a hard bench, but they were wide-eyed the whole time. It is really exciting to see people coming into revelations of Christ in them, of His power to work in "average" problems, and of the application of His life to marriage. Many issues such as relationships, the struggles they bring, God's method of refining us through them, sex, depression, and personal defeat are not discussed in their churches; those would most often be viewed as being inappropriate. However, I have a policy of bringing up these topics, because many silently wonder how Jesus is relevant to them. Since I am a visiting foreigner, a psychologist, and an American, even those who oppose it say very little; they do not have control of the messenger so do not have to agree with what I say. The advantage is great in that we can bring ministry to those who are hurting. Our interpreter is pulling triple duty, since three of us take turns speaking all day and all evening, and then later we have some meetings with the staff. A university professor in English at one of the business schools, she has only been a believer since May; her student interpreter, who was allowed to translate a couple of the sessions, is not a believer at all, but at each break both of them make a point of saying they never before heard these kinds of things. They are all smiles and continually thank us for coming, and sure enough, the morning before I left, the student interpreter asked to speak to me and said, "I accept God, I accept God, I accept God!" She had definitely come only to learn about interpreting, but the lectures made her think about her life, about God, and about how everything in life had been made so simple. She could see her need for Jesus. When we left, she cried. Her transformation was really a beautiful little blessing for us all.

According to popular thought in the States, if ever there were a people that needed to understand the concepts of denial, co-dependency, and the power of positive thinking, would it not be people from the formerly oppressed cultures in the Soviet Union? However, those topics, when mentioned there, are responded to with blank stares. I like

177

to deal in spiritual absolutes. In any situation I will ponder how an emphasis in the U.S. and other countries applies here. When I visit Christians in developing countries to speak, it is my habit to tell them up front what I will be saying. "I will present the abiding life of Christ. You pray and judge if it is needed here. If not, I will apologize and leave. If it is, we will do our best to make the books available in your language and return to train believers to train others."

A driver taking us from one city to another told me about when he and his siblings were small; the schoolteachers had warned all parents that if they taught their children about Jesus, the authorities would take the children away from the home. However, his parents continued instructing their children about the Lord, but they also served at the school when others would not and ensured that their children were model students, so the teachers did nothing. The communist youth club would follow them periodically on their way to church and beat them up. He explained that many who had been persecuted in those days are proud now of having stood fast, and it is tempting to view the new believers as not deserving. But, he pointed out, some laborers start in the morning, some at noon, and some at nearly dark, but God gives the reward to us all. One of those new believers was present at the last meeting we did in the city from which he was driving us. I had noticed that a woman was sitting on the front row and weeping. At the break, her friend came to me and made a request. "Could you have an altar call at the end of the teaching? My friend would like to come forward and accept Jesus." We did, she did, and the whole church rejoiced. She said she had heard of Jesus but never knew of all that He could be. It is true that there is nothing that His nearness will not cure. Another woman there had been a drug addict. She wanted to know how to help others, but I spent time helping her by talking with her about her alcoholic mother, how she had never known her father, God's wanting to be her Father, and what it would mean for her to have a new life, Christ's life. I watched as the Lord provided revelation and she grasped that she could be something new. It was really fun, and the interpreter was also getting trained in helping others.

Speaking of all that we can be in Christ, I would like to mention two men with whom I work here. One is a man of vision and integrity, and he is one of the few people I have known who moves flawlessly between the business and the spiritual worlds. He is a Doer and yet has a humility that can only come from abiding in Christ. If he had 24 hours a day to work, he would need a 25th hour. His demeanor is one of sternness, yet once he is talking, real warmth emanates from him. The other man is a longtime friend I met at a conference years ago. I wanted to come to this part of the world, and he has done everything possible to make each trip enjoyable, though he experiences long hours with no pay to interpret my seminars and oversee translation projects through to completion.

One mother is worried about her three teenaged sons who are all smoking. What to do? Actually, there is very little one can do except fight! She must decide what is worth fighting over and then realize that they may still do it. Where does this leave the parent? With a simple prayer of, "Father, allow enough into our children's lives so

179

they will see that they need You. Allow nothing that would cause them to be destroyed." She must move into faith. She does, and the Lord gives her peace. Her story unfolds: a husband who was a pastor and left her, a daughter with a broken back, and a carrot-juice-making business that supported the family. No one here is accustomed to talking about problems to a pastor, for here the universally accepted assumption is that people do not have problems after receiving Christ, and to admit to them is to admit to a defective Christian life. She was disfellowshipped from her church for having the women write their sins on a piece of paper, confess them, and then burn them. Somehow this was seen as being akin to witchcraft.

A woman brought her daughter, age ten, for counseling, because the girl has trouble with exploding and tearing up her room. We spent a good bit of time talking about feelings and explaining what it meant to abide in Christ. I used several examples and finally hit on one the little girl understood. She was very intelligent and really listened. Days earlier the Lord had spoken to me that there was a little girl for whom I was to pray in this city. I had forgotten about it, but as we were talking, the Lord said, "This is the girl!" I looked at the little girl and asked, "What voice do you hear, and what does it say?" "I hear a voice that tells me I am evil!" "Why would you be evil?" "I am not, but it is the voice telling me." I explained the difference between the voice of the butcher and that of the Shepherd; she had been listening to words from the butcher. God has called her for something, and she must listen to His voice. I asked if we could pray for her. She agreed, we did, and I knew this was the one whom God was setting apart for her generation for reasons to be revealed. I explained to her what it meant to be set apart for God and that the full meaning would be revealed in the future. Her mother was a bit taken aback, since she saw the girl as a problem child, but God chooses the weak and ignorant to shame the wise and the strong! I was really happy after talking to that girl.

There was talk about the times during the Soviet collapse; the people were talking 24 hours a day about their newfound freedom. They were going to bed smiling and waking up smiling. The place must have been electric. One sad bit of news involved the passing of the initial burst of excitement, when many educators, intellectuals, and leaders began to talk about the next step. It was suggested that they might read ancient literature that had withstood the test of time. Many writers were mentioned, and finally one man said, "What about the Bible?" It was agreed that it would hold some solutions. Many pastors were asked what to do, since the people were actually listening to them and were willing to follow. Unfortunately, many of the pastors who came to the forefront were those who had collaborated with the Soviets and were actually wolves in sheep's clothing. They got the opportunity to share their ideas with the people, and few even mentioned Jesus; they just gave their own thoughts. At that time the church buildings would not have been able to hold all of the people who would have flocked there to find God. Before that time pastors were held in great respect, but soon they had little. They had only come presenting philosophy and the wisdom of man. The people wanted God, and it was a lost opportunity.

I began a training session with counselors by sharing the doctrine of problems. We must have it right, we must see that God works in problems, we must see that problems drive us to Him, and we must not work to solve a problem until it has driven us to Christ. I take a woman's history in front of the entire group. She had earlier come up and thanked us for the book, *Problems, God's Presence, and Prayer*. She had been at the bottom when someone had given her the book, and she had underlined every page during her repeated readings. Her father was an alcoholic (typical during the Soviet era); her mother had not wanted another child, but got her! When this woman grew up, she married an alcoholic and had an affair with a different alcoholic for ten years. In the end she, too, became an alcoholic. She could not stand herself and went to a church to confess her sin. She had seen a small statue with a priest holding out his arms. "This is what I need: someone that would welcome me." At the church the priest said, "You are 45 and have never come to a church until now! What makes you think you can come now?" At that he threw her out. As she was walking out, she looked up at a statue of Mary. The Statue spoke to her, "Do not give up; go to another church!" She said, "I know that sounds crazy, but it happened." She went to another church, where Christ was shared with her, she stopped drinking, her husband became a Christian, and so did the fellow with whom she had pursued the affair! It was really a good testimony, and she used concise and quick expression. At one point of describing her miserable life without Christ, she said, "I felt as though the frontline had marched through my heart!"

The director and her associate of an aid ministry come to talk to us. They begin by recapping the story of an alcoholic fellow who would come saying that he was having conversations with people and gangs that were forcing him to do things he did not want to do. They determined that it was demonic (this country has an ancient history involving witchcraft). They prayed for him, and all the voices and images went away, but in time he was drinking again and the same things were happening. Then the other shoe dropped when they revealed, "He was found dead in the sea. We could have done more. Did we miss something?" The women began to weep. I understand, for I have had the same type of thing happen to me. First, if we are not hurt and upset, that only proves that we never really had anything invested in the person. Second, we cannot insure that our own children will always make right decisions, so how can we insure that a stranger will? Third, if we take the blame when things go wrong, then we will take the credit when things go right. Since God gets all the glory, God must do all the work. If He does not perform or prevent something, we cannot take the blame. Fourth, we must get off the throne. We are not God. Fifth, we must do two things at the same time: mourn and rest in His peace. The ladies received what I said. Next came many questions about the propriety of feeding the poor when the poor take the money they have been given and buy alcohol. "Are we really helping them?" I explained that we feed as a tool to preach. If they give advice and it is not followed, and the person shows up again for food, they must let the peace of God rule in their hearts as to whether or not to give more aid; but, generally speaking, this type of person is in pride and working in his own system. In a city with over forty percent unemployment, this ministry is the only one doing anything to help the needy. There is no social welfare system of which to speak; this ministry takes on the full load.

One fellow wanted to know what to do about false teachers. "Do we let the people be deceived?" There are three issues here. First, we are to confront those things that are false and warn others. Second, a false teacher can be followed in two ways: We can follow and agree or we can follow the teacher in order to rebuke; either way we end up following him and not Jesus. Third, often false teachers are not creating wrong hearts but revealing wrong hearts. If a teacher gets a following of people when he teaches that Jesus wants us rich, what kind of people are they? What are their hearts for the Lord if they perceive that the goal of Christ's suffering is our wealth? Fourth, everyone works for us. Let people follow what life will not support, and when they come to the end of themselves and the end of their trust in others, we will be there to offer Jesus.

The debate continues here over the teachers from America who emphasize prosperity as God's promise. Why does that message appeal to people? I think it is because they really want something other than Jesus. Also, there is the teaching that people are living in Plan B; they have made a mistake in the past, married the wrong person, did something stupid, and they are always going to be second best. I am so glad that my God loves not only the second best, but also the dead last. I remember that the first will be last, and the last first. Working here at the Christian ministry's facilities where we have our accommodations is a dear older sister who cleans our room every morning, keeps up in the office, and does our laundry. She is a real servant. Today my coworker and I bought her some really nice hand cream; when we gave it to her, she said, "Why? I do everything for Jesus and have my reward." She really means it! What an attitude and a pure motive. It was just for Jesus.

We finish all the questioning after completing a seminar in the middle of winter in a frigid area and only have a few minutes to pack and get in the car. I am amazed at how people here drive flat out on ice, and it does not seem to bother them. So often I thought that we would smash into the rear-end of a car ahead, and yet we would stop just short. Well, amen. We take off in a hurry to meet friends for lunch and come upon one of the deacons of the church; he had run out of gas. We do not have the time to stop and help, but I say to my friends, "That could be us one day!" We find a container, stop at a petrol station, make a funnel, and return with the fuel. The fellow is quite happy. It seems that my pastor friend's wife went past him in her car, and shortly thereafter a large truck went out of control and went spinning around down the highway. She had to take to the ditch to miss it and was buried in the deep snow. The deacon we just helped "just happened" to come by after the accident and was able to dig her out of the drift.

Man has a spiritual thirst that if not filled with Christ will lead to a variety of otherworldly activities. As we walk along the main street, there are at least ten cars lined up one side, and I am told that often there are twenty or more. In them are people waiting in line to see an old woman witch, a "white" witch (somehow that makes what she does—

which is exactly what a "black" witch does—sound better) who has healed many people. That does not surprise me; since Satan can bring a sickness, why would he not be able to take it away? Though it is all done at a price, of course. We also walk by three houses that have been burnt. One family has lived in all three homes. It is believed that there is a curse on the family, and the result is the burning of their homes. From the time we left the front of the witch's house, something was placed in my heart. As we continue our walk and head back to our rooms, we stopped again in front of the house, and I said to my interpreter and the young pastor, "I believe that if we pray, we can stop the spirits from functioning, and no healing will take place in this house again." They agreed, and we prayed. I have seen that prayer answered before, but only when God had spoken such a thing to me. We were all happy when the pastor reported the next year that the townsfolk, who were no longer being healed at the witch's house, ran her out of town! God moved, and then the woman had to move!

We finish the meetings in time for supper and are asked just to sit with the group and answer questions. One woman is plagued by guilt. Her intention had been to talk to a certain unbeliever about Christ, but the person died before she could. She had been taught that this person was now in hell because she did not act quickly enough. Talk about guilt manipulation! We address the issue that if God gets all the glory, then He must be doing the work. I ask a simple question: "If the Bible has the power we are told it has, why do we preach to one hundred and only see two people believe?" I got the right answer, "It is because the Holy Spirit was working with the two and the Bible was a witness to that work." The next observation is clear, "Then there is no 'Master Plan of Evangelism' that will guarantee results!" We walk with God, rest in Him, and witness to those He brings our way. I asked how many people died while we were sitting and studying. If salvation is our responsibility, then we let some die while we were studying the Bible, having our quiet times, or attending church. Another lady has this question: "My husband made a vow to the Lord to serve Him every day if God would heal him. He did for a while, and now he is not doing it every day. Will his sickness return?" Well, the husband should repent, but not of the failure to keep his vow, but for ever making one. What do we think we have to offer God that we can make such bargains with Him? We must walk with God. Anyway, it is more of what circulates as a form of Christian Buddhism. If we do bad, is God obliged to punish us? If that is true, then when we do what is good, God must be obligated to bless us. Can we manipulate God? Is He working for us? One of the pastors cut in and said, "I see that such thinking and praying is sick!" Anyway, God does not punish us just to get even; God has a goal in His discipline, which is the revelation of Christ in us. One pastor tells of two great revivals in his country. One was begun 800 years ago with a monk who came into a relationship with Jesus. It is not known how many peoples in the mountains (at that time they were cannibal savages) came to believe in Jesus. There was also a revival among the Protestants in a brief period of history after 1917, when there was freedom of religion. Hundreds of thousands came to know Jesus. We also have a good discussion about pride. I like these pastors. I have seen many evangelists that follow the fire around the world; that is, they go where the Holy Spirit is moving and have huge meetings. I have witnessed some of these fires myself. However, when the fire becomes embers and the "fire chasers" depart, the hard work of discipleship is left to pastors like these. One was so encouraged recently, having been to the U.K. for a gathering of pastors. The largest church represented had thirty members, and the smallest had five. They all drove old cars. He was so heartened that these pastors of small churches believed themselves to be called and blessed of God. It was a completely different scenario from the mega-church model constantly promoted that just makes them feel they are out of the will of God, punished, and doing something wrong. He pointed out that it is impossible for a staff of twenty to minister to individuals in a church of thousands; hence, small groups come into play, where real ministry takes place. He asked, "If it is true that small groups are where ministry takes place, then what is the point in huge multi-million-dollar buildings? The small groups are the church. Why spend all that money to come together for one hour? It appears to be kingdom building and pride. Under the mega churches' own definition, we could be called small group leaders or pastors. We are small groups and we are the Church. We just do not have a huge place in which to bring all the small groups together." Well, amen. I do not know about all that, but it is vexing when, through comparison, some are made to feel insignificant by a standard that is worldly and fleshly, not Christian. We had several discussions on sin until I interrupted with, "We can end up talking more about sin than Jesus. If Jesus is the focus, if we are abiding, if His life is flowing, then how could we be sinning?"

After my sermon for Memorial Day, the pastor takes me into his office. "Michael, should we not always just forgive?" My response, "Most certainly! Bring the person to me that is asking for forgiveness, and I will give it to him as quickly as the Father has always given it to me. Brother, how do you forgive if no one asks? God puts forgiveness on the table, but it is man's choice to pick it up. If He is forgiving with no one asking, then why even mention Jesus?" The response: "I see, and thank you. This is a point at which we have been stuck. You are right; we must love, bless those that curse us, and we must have a heart of forgiveness. Yet, no one has asked for forgiveness for the many thousands of deaths, and the people do not know what to do. I will encourage them to love and bless and have a heart of forgiveness. We have put the burden of confession on the foreign invaders." Well, amen!

My interpreter has become someone that I minister WITH. He is just as capable at presenting Christ as I am, so I often wonder why I am here. He has been used before as interpreter for presidents, but recently he quit, unable any longer to bear listening to the political drivel. I think that speaks well of him; few would give up the position and the pay. He is principled and rooted, is not moved, and has a like goal, so we move as one. I spend much of every year speaking through an interpreter, and I actually prefer it, because the flesh of the speaker—in this case, Mike—cannot add anything. Either the words witness to the message of Christ or they do not. A speaker who must talk through an interpreter may jump, scream, or tell amusing stories, but every form of manipulation dies; Jesus, and Jesus alone, must touch hearts. An interpreter with a like heart is unique because of the oneness that develops, and I like that. It makes being dependent enjoyable. Not to make too much of it, but in some small way a good interpreter is similar to the Holy Spirit in guarding the lips! If I say something stupid, the interpreter will give me a knowing look, and I know I am to say it differently.

Pacific Nations

One of the elders told me about his daughter getting married. One night after church, she asked to see her father. When he arrived, she said, "I want to be married tonight." He did agree and took her to the equivalent of our courthouse to sign the papers. As he signed, he told his daughter, "God has given me the authority and right to sign this paper. I do it from my own free will. I give you to the man." Three years later she returned after leaving her husband. This time she brought a different paper—a divorce paper—for her father to sign. He told her, "God has not given me the authority nor the right to sign this paper, and I will not." Without her father's authority she had no option but to go to the pastor and work out the marriage. God did a miracle in her and her husband and turned the whole thing around. The father told me he could see how God had used every bit of the situation for good.

In this tropical paradise is something unique and pleasant: a living fence. Fence posts were made from trees and placed in the fertile ground, which receives so much rain that the posts actually began to root and sprout leaves!

The fence protects people from danger. Those who guard and protect in the Church should also be living fences, not dead posts. I once heard a friend in another country say, "The church today is similar to a dead hen lying on top of living chicks."

The village chief is dying. He is my friend and has been a faithful support to me. He has always helped and prays for me constantly. I am vexed, for I do love the chief and will sorely miss him. He is so soft and honest. He cannot get up, but I go to visit him lying on his mat, not long for this world. His attendants yell at him to say, "It is Michael, it is Michael, it is Michael." With that the old chief opens his eyes and recognizes me. His hand, the size of a shovel, slowly opens, and I place my pale white hand in his. He whispers, "Michael, thank you, Michael." He asks a few questions about what I am doing and then drifts off to sleep. As we leave I speak to the village elder who is presently the pastor and caretaker for the chief. "Will you talk to the rest of the elders for me? I have a request. Will the village allow my wife and me to buy the tombstone for the chief's grave? You know that I loved him." The man smiled, "I will make the request." I had heard that it often took the families many years to get the money for a stone. For me, it would be an honor to purchase one.

Saturday morning we sat down to discuss several aspects of the ministry there. My friend's faithfulness has been exemplary; he has been here seventeen years and was doing Bible training until, for a variety of reasons, the work was closed. Now those obstacles are nearly all put to rest, and he is getting on with things, such as hosting four Bible camps in the last few months, each one packed with nearly fifty students, and he is getting more requests. We hope to start the Bible training again and get more teachers involved. We worked on an outline and brochure that will describe the work. We will need to build more structures: a home for the director and a center for discipleship training. However, we are out of land, and because of foreign investment along the coast, a small plot big enough for a house is around $50,000 U.S. Here is something wonderful about the culture: my friend's son-in-law has ancestral land just a thirty-minute walk over a hill; it is the most beautiful piece of fertile plain, protected from storms on all sides by mountains, and traversed by the river that sustains the city. The son-in-law suggests that we look at that land, and when we did, it was odd to stand in the middle of the field with the men and have them tell me, "Pick what you want." We are all at peace and wholeheartedly agree that it would be perfect. I would estimate that the place would be worth several millions of dollars. Once the son-in-law sees that we like the land, he sets up a meeting with his father and brothers the following day before church begins; the request for the land will all be settled with words, a drink of kava, and an agreement, no contracts. I like that. The next day we arrive early, passing over a river on a couple of fallen coconut trees. The recent hurricane has certainly done its damage to the village: five houses completely gone, the steel from the washed-away bridge twisted around a few trees, and the mountain walls stripped of their trees. It is a shock to me. The son-in-law leads us to the house of his father, which is actually his own house, but his father is living in it since his was one of the houses lost in the storm. We all sit on the floor; everything is said in the native tongue.

First, the old man welcomes us. At the end of his speech we cup our hands, as is the custom, and clap once. Then he asks why we have come. My friend greets him, which takes some time, and in the end, we clap again. Then my friend places in front of the elder one kilogram of the finest kava (ground root from the kava tree used as ceremonial drink) and begins to explain the history that the two families have together, that they are one family because of their children and grandchildren. My friend is in need of land to build a house in which to live; his son-in-law's father has the land. Not only could the land benefit the school, it would benefit the village, and when the family is farming there, they will have a place to stay from this generation to the next and the next. The proposal is entirely agreed to by the patriarch, who claps once, reaches forward to take the kava, and all clap, signifying that the deal is done and sealed. The land now belongs to my friend, secured with a bag of kava. Everyone is happy.

I got a call from a missionary I met the day before and gave a book to; he had read it through the night and wanted to talk. Again, this message is never taught but is a witness to what the Lord has already placed in a person. He arrived and said to me, "Nothing in your book is new; I always knew this but have never read it in print!" He had a typical past: a father that he could not please, a wife he could not please, a church that he could not please, and a self that could not be pleased. It was through valley after valley—including a broken home, a destroyed marriage, and a failed business—that he came to see that God was exactly what He said He was, "Love." This man knew the mercy, grace, and forgiveness of God. Beautiful!

One woman is really a blessing to me. As I began taking her history, I asked if she had any hurts in her life. She immediately mentioned the one thing that continues to haunt her, which is that she was raped at age seventeen. Before I let her say anything else, I said, "I know that how you feel is stupid and guilty; you blame yourself, thinking that if only you had not walked that way, if only you had avoided the boy, and if only you had obeyed your parents, the unfortunate attack would never have occurred." She looked shocked and said, "Yes." I explained that I had spent enough time with Satan to know what he whispered to others, such as that she was to blame for another's sin. In reality, she was allowing an event from the past to dictate how she lived today, and not only that, but the body is being renewed physically, cell by cell, every few months, and therefore there is no part of her existing physique that has ever been touched by another man. Another current outgrowth of her past was that while she enjoyed the journey toward sex, her husband only liked the destination, and therefore, she was having trouble not dragging up the baggage of the past and feeling that he was forcing himself on her. We talked about breaking through an emotional obstacle when we know what is right but we feel something totally different. At some point we must break through and say no to emotions that are stuck. It can be done, but only through choice. I gave the example of walking several kilometers to another village and finding that the bridge was out. "Would you turn around and consider the journey a waste, or put a log over it and cross?" She said she would put the log over and cross; it would be frightening, but it would be better than a wasted journey. In the same way, I pointed out, our emotions get stuck at washed-out bridges. We can withdraw, or we can move past the obstacle. I can feel defective and not want to speak, turn around, and remain in my condition. Or I can invite Christ to be my sufficiency, move against my feeling (putting the log over the stream), and go forward. She would have to say no to these feelings of being defective and go forward. Amen, she got it, and I could see the weight lift from her.

In the village, no one owns anything. A person can walk past someone's breadfruit tree and pluck a few for dinner that night; nothing will be said to deter the fruit picker. Actually, it is unacceptable to be in possession of things in the sense in which we view ownership. A villager who finds himself with extra money first asks if there is anyone with a need. This has created some problems for villagers who move to the city, where those of foreign descent abound and actually have the notion of wealth accumulation. Also, it is difficult in modern society for the native villager to plan for retirement or the unexpected. One of my friends is really wise in the way he helps his village. He refuses to go there and give what he calls a handout, but rather invites the youth to come live with him in the city and attend school and university. While they are there he teaches them financial responsibility, systems for seeing a project through to the end, and other aspects of business. He wants the coming generation to be trained in running a government, which also does not run on village rules. He wants the indigenous folk to prosper and not be left behind. It is a good approach.

There is a student here from an island nation. For the first time in her life she has seen frost, and she is never without a coat. She has taken a leave of absence from her job of working for a Muslim couple in an Arab country; she is very excited about ministering to them. The wife has told her that she is closer than a sister. Muslims believe in dreams, because that is how "the prophet" got "his call." She is always praying that they will have a dream about Jesus. It is so encouraging to see someone so focused on what many might consider a trivial matter—just ministering to one unbelieving family—yet she sees it as a huge and important calling. She is very bright and wants to know more and more about discipleship and how Jesus meets every need.

Folks in this large nation just do not see the need for church and say that when they make the effort to attend, they get nothing out of it. This is not true of the church I am visiting, where the pastor was told about ALMI by a mutual friend and listened to the material, which witnessed to what the Lord had been doing in and showing him. He reckons that understanding abiding is breaking through the matrix (playing on the concept in the movie by that name). He was initially presented a Christianity of performance and lived in that system as all that he knew, until one day he began to see its falsehood as not the real system. Real Christianity was exactly Jesus dwelling inand living through a believer. Slowly, through revelation, he began to see that Christianity was weakness, not strength; suffering, not always comfort; expansion, not change; and faith, not creating. He is a reluctant leader who has defined leadership as consisting of four main things. 1) God must call a man to lead. 2) The day a leader is listening to everyone else, he is not a leader. 3) Leadership is taking people where they do not want to go. 4) Leadership is like a bus that has the destination marked on it. Once the leader sets out and people have gotten on the bus by their free will, if they later decide they do not like the destination or it is the wrong one for them, they need to get off; they should not strive to change the direction of the bus. He explains how some practice white witchcraft by attempting to change the pastor's will through prayer. I find it all quite interesting.

"Uncle" tells me of the "sugarcane-cutting Christian," a young man who always has his Bible with him while working. Sugarcane cutting is some of the hardest work done in this island paradise. It seems the boy had been leading an evening Bible study, and a Hindu girl was coming just to see the boy, because she had a crush on him. She kept telling her parents that she was going around town and to the movies with friends. However, one day they followed her and discovered that she was actually going to the Bible study just to see the boy. Upon finding this out, they threw her out of their home. The next day as the boy passed by, he noticed her plight. He took her home and told his mother to give her his room; he would move in with an uncle. In three months the girl converted, at which time the boy fell in love with her and they were married. What impressed me the most about this story was the boy's going about his daily task of cutting sugarcane. He was living life; life was not living him.

India

As I addressed a group of graduating students, I told of being in a conference and being asked who was the best counselor in the world. I immediately responded, "I am, of course." The people just stared at me. Finally, one intrepid young woman said, "How can you say that?" I replied, "Because when I am counseling someone, I am the only one there. Therefore, God must believe that I am the best. There may be better counselors, but they are not there. Only I am there. I am the best of the best if I go in weakness, asking God for His wisdom." I went on to explain that we, the speakers and professors, were not going to leave and go throughout the country preaching, but they were. God was not sending us but them. They are God's best in each of their individual cities. I encouraged them not to be nervous, but to go in confidence with His wisdom.

I am reminded as I hear so many testimonies about conversions among Hindus and Muslims that there is nothing in the New Testament about forcing a believer to stay in the faith, and we are not commanded to make people stay. This freedom in Christ is unique to Christianity. Converts to Christianity out of Hinduism or Islam are cut off, taken out of the will, considered dead, and may even have murderous attempts made against them. I think the Muslims, Hindus, Mormons, Buddhists, and every other religion should take the challenge and announce to every member, "You are free to leave with no retribution." I believe that over half would leave.

I traveled with one of our sons to a city near a restricted area to which I had been invited; I had hoped to go there for years, and I had come this far, but the bus on into the area did not leave until nightfall, and that gave us some time to burn. We decided to visit the temple that is on top of a mountain outside of town. The mode of transportation is auto-rickshaw, very popular here as a variation of the man-pulled rickshaws we are accustomed to seeing on TV. This one is in poor repair and leaves us wondering if we will ever get there. We pass a huge lake on which there are several dilapidated boats serving as living quarters for locals. These do not look seaworthy, but people are loading on to one for a long trip to the other side. We start the climb out of the valley up into the mountain. After several minutes we climb above the heavy smog and have a very nice view. Along the way, we pass students on an outing, boys and girls all wearing uniforms, and the schoolteachers constantly scolding. It appears that in this area, scolding is the normal way of talking to people. At the top we approach the temple, take off our shoes, and climb the marbled steps; attempting to sidestep all the pigeon dung is useless. The first temple is carved out of one piece of rock. Everything is dirty. We move on to the main temple, encountering several Hindu priests wanting to show us around (for a fee, of course). The place is very ancient. Flowers and colored dye are strewn about. Up and down several other steps we go. It is cool up here, and that makes the trip worthwhile. We head to the auto-rickshaw for the trip back down. We barely made it up; many times the vehicle came to a complete stop. My son notes that the trip back will be easy if the brakes have been fixed. The engine is cut off for the trip down; our driver rides the brakes the whole way, but we arrive in the city in one piece. I went back in the hotel and asked, "Are there any churches here?" The dry reply was, "There is only one; churches are not popular here." I was able to ascertain the part of the city where the church was located, and when we arrived, we were surprised at the church compound with many buildings. It was all quite nice by Indian standards; however, in the West one might think that the place should be closed. We ring a doorbell, and one of the students tells us to come on up. I told him I was looking for the pastor; he pointed the way. After encountering a few more students, we realize that these are not Christian students, but those who come from the surrounding towns to attend the local university; they are merely housed here. Finally, we find the pastor's house. His wife answers the door and tells us to come back at exactly 5:00 p.m. or we will miss him. We give her two books and say we will return. We walk to the lake and back, arriving at exactly 5:00 p.m. The fellow comes to the door with a gentle smile and welcoming countenance. He has another fellow with him. We all sit, knowing our time together is short, and I begin to share about the ministry of ALMI. "Many know they are going to heaven, but they are living a daily hell. I am a missionary to believers, pointing them back to Jesus." I raise one hand and say, "On this hand is Jesus, on my other hand my problems." I move the hand that represents Jesus closer to my face, blocking the view of my other hand. "When Jesus is my focus, though the problems remain, they do not overwhelm me. There is nothing the nearness of Jesus will not cure!" The men are interested, and now it is their turn to share. The first fellow tells us that he was in government service for twelve years and then worked for a mission organization for another 28. At age 58 he was forced into retirement (which can come even earlier than that for many in this country). He came to this area because so few believers live here; it seems that the only Christians are from one of the lowest classes, the uneducated tea pickers. He wanted to help train the believers. Each person must take a turn at being a pastor for one year. He explains that it is difficult getting people to be pastors, because they are not respected in the least. The working people see someone who is a pastor as someone that is lazy and does not want to work. The Hindus also mock the pastors. Young believers in the churches in the big cities are willing to give money for Christian work, but they do not want to do the work themselves. It seems that the missionaries here many, many years ago were interested in "soul winning," not building a church. The pastorate is a difficult and lonely work. I ask about their doing some translation work, but it is not possible. They just introduced their first small book that took two years to translate and publish. There are only four believers in the whole area that can do translation work, and they must do it in the midst of their other activities; it is very difficult. The pastor began to tell us about introducing the book and the prayer time that preceded it. The village pastors were all swinging madly at the air beating Satan back with their Bibles. "They do not know that battle has been won." He has a heart for the village people and has told the church that if he does not get three days in each month to minister to the tea pickers, they will have to find someone else. "It is a call," he explains. "What do you do when you have a call? Nothing else matters!" Amen! As I have experienced, the call of God will carry someone when nothing else does. I am so enjoying being in this out-of-the-way place, talking to people that I never knew until an hour ago, experiencing that oneness of

Spirit, and enjoying the Body of Christ. We talk some more about the ministry of ALMI and the fact that the materials have been useful in over eighty countries. Then I surprise them by saying, "I will send all the materials to you. Review them, and if I do not hear from you, you will not hear from me. You are too busy for something that will not work here; I am too busy to go where the message is not needed. If I do not hear from you, I will know that you did not see what we do as workable in this place. If you call, I say, 'Amen.' If you do not call, I say, 'Amen.'" At that, they laughed. I explained the importance of saying "amen." Little did I know that God was soon coming for my words. I told them of walking in the garden with the old man that told me to pick a plum. "How will I know if the plum is ripe?" "Plums are like Christians. If you squeeze them and they yield, they are ripe. Is there any pressure in your life?" he had asked. I laughed, "I am a man under pressure with family, ministry, finances, time, health, and travel." "Pressure comes from resisting the situation that God has permitted to push you toward Him. You must yield and let it push you close to Him. What does the word amen mean? It means 'so is it' or 'let it be.' When you wake up in the morning and realize that you do not have any money, just say, 'Amen, amen, well, *amen.*' Do not fight it; let it move you to God." I could see that this concept was ministering to them. "Trouble is not in the trouble," I continued, "but in the heart's attitude toward the trouble. Nothing ever goes wrong; we just go wrong with it." We discussed these principles in some detail. It was now time to go. I explained that we were going to "the restricted area" on the 8:30 p.m. bus. They looked at each other and asked if I had the pass that is needed for entry. "No, it is to be given to me when I get there." "Brother, you cannot get the pass there. You must have it before you attempt to go. A New Zealand couple tried to go there without their pass. They waited here for three months believing that it was going to come from Delhi. It never came, and in the end they had to leave. Brothers, do not go. You will go eight hours and then stop. You will be questioned repeatedly, and they will not understand why you are there. Do not go." Immediately my own words came for me. A few minutes earlier, I was preaching my own funeral, and with such zeal. "Amen, nothing ever goes wrong; trouble is not in the trouble." Well, truth is not only preached, it is demonstrated. I have for years gotten up in the morning and said, "Jesus, like a shepherd lead me." My grandfather had sheep; I know what that means. He leads as we choose; that is what faith is. To have a list of what you are to do before you do it is unbelief. Look at the detail that God has put into the creation of the eye, the brain, and the thumb. If there is that much detail in His highest creation, is there not that much detail in the way He structures our life? Do I believe that? I do, more than ever! When Paul was hindered from going to a certain place, it did not mean that he was to stop, but to continue with the message in a different direction. He was led in natural events that opened or closed the door. I will not be going to the restricted area. I need to go ahead, for He has something else for me. The peace of God is always ministering to us. All of this went through my mind as I listened to the brothers. I said, "Amen, I will not go. The purpose in my coming here may have been to meet you!" Then we asked if there were a cheaper hotel in the area. They knew of one, and the pastor said that he would walk us there. It was suitable, twenty dollars per night, and the staff was very happy to have us. We walked to the bus station. What happened next truly amazed me. The pastor, in his late fifties, began to tell us his testimony. He had been a believer living in defeat. He only had a few books. However, someone gave him a copy of Watchman Nee's *Spiritual Man*. He read it and one night decided to believe that he was crucified with Christ, to believe what God said about him. He chose to believe he was with Jesus, and wherever Jesus was, he was there. The following day at church was the celebration of the New Year; he proclaimed to the congregation that every moment was a New Year for him. He was in Jesus, past, present, and future. Until then, he could not preach, but he discovered that the Christ in him could preach! He found a new power, the power of Christ in him. It was so similar to my own experience, only I had been reading Andrew Murray. My son was smiling and whispered to me, "We are on the same page." Could it be that I really was just here to meet this brother, this lonely pastor in this place? Well, we began to share and share as we walked. We got to the bus station, obtained the refund for our tickets, picked up our bags, and shifted to the new hotel. In India it is hard to adjust to the noise, crowds, and pollution. Oh, yes, there is one other thing: beetle nut! The nut is ground and put in a leaf, mixed with other spices, and chewed. Those who are addicted have red-stained teeth. The sidewalks are covered with the red juice that is spit out continually. Arriving at the room I asked the pastor if we could have another meeting. He had said to me, "If only there was a way to share Christ's life within simply, with pictures." I showed him some of our materials and diagrams, and it was really nice to see the look on his face as he saw that his experiences were portrayed in pictures.

I had the privilege of speaking in a very liturgical church wherein everything is done, sang, administered, and preached in order. I talk about seeing God in all things, and the message is well received, though of course at first the people are not accustomed to my loose style of preaching. Soon, even in such a setting, people begin to laugh. They try to hold it in but it just comes out. I actually like these kinds of services, where everything is very quiet and calming. One practice is especially sweet; the bishop stands at the altar holding his hands as though praying, and two men approach with their hands held upward, palms together, in the same prayerful position. The bishop opens his hands, encompasses the hands of the first man, and says, "The peace of the Lord Jesus be with you!" After this is done to both men, they walk down the center aisle and do it to the first person in each row. That one, in turn, does the same to the person next to him, and so on until everyone down the line has received the peace that comes from, as it were, the throne. I suppose it is something like the practice in the U.S. of turning to the pew neighbors and shaking their hands to welcome them. However, this is softer and seems more significant, in that the peace of Jesus is recognized as being passed along.

"No greater love than a man laying down his life for another." My friend has blessed so many in his counseling office and worked long hours and even years for people. Here they call him "Uncle." We met a young woman with whom he had worked for many years. She was happy to see that he was feeling well and said, "Uncle, I am so happy that you are feeling good after your open-heart surgery. When you were sick I prayed and asked the Lord to take fifteen years off my life and give them to you. That was 1999, so you have twelve more years to go." She said it with such joy and contentment that it was really quite nice.

I was reading about an Indian prophet who visited another country. He was there only one day when he made a rather harsh observation. Some of the Christians confronted him, saying, "You do not know us! You do not know what we are like! You cannot make such a comment so quickly!" He responded, "To study botany takes many years, that is true. However, it only takes a moment to discern the smell of a flower." This same prophet refused requests to pray for people. He would stand by them as THEY prayed! He wanted them to realize that Jesus would hear them, and then he felt that when he left that place the people would have confidence to ask on their own.

Latin America or the Caribbean

We arrive to be met by a very pleasant brother, in pleasant surroundings, and pleasant weather. He drove us to his small city and we hardly saw any other cars. What a contrast from the gargantuan metropolises! We arrived at the estate, and the couple had done everything to make us feel at home. Every amenity and detail was done to let us know that they did welcome us. They truly practice the uniquely Godly principle of loving and then getting to know us, in contrast to the world's method of knowing and then deciding to love or not. In the morning we were given a tour of the factory. The founder of the plant came from Asia over seventy years ago when the economy was very bad, and over here free transportation was being offered to those who would come and work in the coffee plantations. The man came, worked hard, started the factory, and is now the largest employer in the city. He is an upright man and uses the Bible as his standard of living, yet at age ninety he is still not a believer! This proves again that the Christian life and principles are those on which the universe is built and through which it operates the best. I have often thought and taught that even if a person did not want to accept Jesus, he would have a better life attempting to follow His teachings. The man's sons, who now run the company, are all Christian men of integrity with a social consciousness. They really care about their employees, and the employees care about them.

We are on a medical mission boat stopped at a typical village with houses on stilts, a shop with rice for sale, one tractor, and the clanking of a distant generator. The doctors were very busy today; our appreciation for them grows daily as we see them taking their precious holiday time to do the same thing that they do every day of the year, only even more intensely. Two of the women on our boat are excellent with children and start the meeting out with songs, hand shaking, marching, and more. The "hall" is a dirt floor building with no walls and a metal roof. Rough wooden benches in a row offer seating. A couple of us speak; then one of the young interpreters gives her testimony. She said that she had been going to church from the time she was in her mother's womb, but that Jesus did not mean anything to her until she began to question the meaning of life. That, of course, is a great question, since Jesus is life. We end with an altar call given by the boat captain, and three women come forward; he prays for them. The boat's dentist is one of the most interesting Brazilians on the trip. He is of Japanese ancestry and very joyful. What makes him interesting is the source of his joy, which is serving people, and this service makes him other-conscious and very happy. He does a beautiful job repairing teeth and then is either off to his guitar playing and singing or fishing. He is a delight, as are the locals staffing the boat. They are such servants and do everything for us. It is very humbling.

Often when traveling around the world I see plants that have been moved from one climate and transplanted to another. They never last! Certain things are not to be taken home, transplanted. In the same way, I do not think it is always appropriate to see what is happening in one place and try to transplant it to another. God gives a plant for a particular climate; He moves for a particular church in a way that does not have to be taken everywhere. I think of that as I look around the room at pastors in unbelievable heat wearing coats and ties.

Sometimes believers from developing countries have traveled to the U.S., studied, and then refused to return home. One pastor was telling me his story. God sent him to the U.S. to be trained in a Bible college. Immediately upon arriving, he decided to stay. The Lord spoke to him, "Why have you deceived Me?" For he knew that the Lord had only sent him to the U.S. so he could return to his countrymen. He went on studying for another two years, after which, still determined to stay, the Lord spoke again

to him, "Why have you deceived Me?" At that he yielded
to the Lord and returned home. The end result is a very
happy man! He is completely yielded to the will of Jesus,
and the peripheral results of this are eighteen churches,
schools, and countless converts. The joy that surrounds
him is so visible in this place of demons.

For one session I got started by talking about marriage
and its purpose in the plan of God to perfect us, move us
out of self, and make us take up the cross. I am quite sure
that in this place, this is the first teaching on marriage that
addressed things from that position. Actually, it may be
the first teaching on the dynamics of making a marriage
work. I took questions and one man openly said that I was
describing his marriage, and that his wife was constantly
mad at him and did not understand his motives. It proves
again that people are the same all over the world. By
the look on the people's faces I could see that there was
something that caused more internal conflict than poverty:
a bad relationship. It was a great morning. Again, it is very
hot. I spend most of my time on top of a chair drawing
pictures on the chalkboard that illustrate the concepts I
am sharing.

The interpreter is just great. A "big-name evangelist"
came here and my interpreter's services were called upon.
However, as the evangelist started his "miracle show," the
interpreter determined that there was not even a message fit
to translate. So he just started letting the evangelist have his
say and then preaching his own Christ-centered message.
He did not want to waste the opportunity to present Christ
to such a large crowd. The next day the evangelist was told
that what he had said was not being repeated in the other

language, so he rebuked the interpreter and warned him that he must stick exactly to what was being said. In return, the "evangelist" was warned, "If you do not preach Christ, then I will." The interpreter was fired on the spot.

I meet the director of the mission house, who stops me in the street and tells me his story. He and his wife were working in the big city making eighteen times the minimum wage. Busy did not begin to describe them. He was a deacon at church and heard a missions appeal. He walked forward, though because she had her head bowed, his wife never saw him walk forward. She, too, had heard the call to missions, so she kept praying, "Father, when I open my eyes, I want to see my husband standing at the front; if he is, I will know this call is from You." He was standing at the front, praying, "Father, if this is not just emotionalism, when I open my eyes, my wife will be standing next to me." She opened her eyes first, saw him, and stepped forward. He opened his eyes, and there she stood, right beside him. He told of the journey of coming to the remote area, going without, and God's providing. Once he and a friend trekked three days through the jungle to reach a tribe, stopping only to make soup and sleep. He was making a fire for warmth and began to tell stories of the old days, when a fire meant sausages cooked over an open flame. He turned to his companion and said, "I would not find sausages in such a remote place." His friend said, "God is able to do anything." In a few minutes they noticed lights and discovered that they had camped on the fringe of a giant ranch. They saw what appeared to be a truck coming toward them. The rancher approached, and they assumed they would be thrown off the property.

Instead, the rancher said, "I knew that missionaries came through these parts, and I have come to encourage you. The tribes need your ministry, so do not lose heart or faith. Move forward, and keep moving forward." He prayed for them, went to his truck, and returned with a box, which he left on the ground without saying a word. After he had left, they opened the box and saw that it was full of sausages. The traveler found himself, as in the old days, roasting sausages. God is indeed able to do anything!

The Bible school had purchased a medical boat and a dentist is heading the medical work. I asked the dentist to tell me how the work was going. He is the head of the medical commission here and got a letter from a tribe that needed help; he asked the commissioners to go with him to see the tribe's condition. He said that the whole encampment, sixty-six people, were sick with malaria, some having contracted the disease five times in as many months. The people were so weak and malnourished that they could not speak. What vexed him the most was that the tribe was Christian. It was scenes such as this that had caused him to transfer from a large city to this area of greater need. The man is a missionary first and a dentist second. He is looking for other doctors that will come and spend a couple of weeks with him treating people. He explained that this part of the river had very high acids, and therefore, few fish. The land will not grow anything; the people have nothing. Therefore, the tribesmen will kill anything that moves. Some had eaten a cougar, and when asked, "Did you like it?" they simply responded, "It was all that we had!"

CHAPTER 6
Things Hidden To Some Eyes

Pacific Islands

One Sunday morning I went to a small church to preach, and the head elder kept apologizing for the small number of people present. I got up and asked, "If the Prime Minister invited you to come to his home alone, would you be honored?" The response, to a man, was yes. "If you were invited with fifty other people, or 100, or 1,000 others, would it be such an honor?" No, that would not be such an honor, they agreed. There is more glory in a small meeting with a dignitary. We come not to fellowship around each other, but around Jesus, the King of Kings and Lord of Lords. We can rejoice that where two or three are gathered together, He is in our midst. We got on with the meeting, and though they were few in number, God really moved in the people.

I was speaking at a camp where in between sessions I had the opportunity to walk up and down the beach, listening to Jesus. I needed that time alone, for I am seeing more and more that I can prepare either my message or my heart. Preparing the heart is much more beneficial and rewarding. I watched for some time as the ocean current worked to push a floating coconut to shore. Eventually the

213

task was accomplished and the nut placed in a position of rest, where its inner life was now available to be revealed to anyone who took the time to look within it. Some coconuts, so I have been told, can be carried on waves for years before finding a place of repose. The ocean, with all it has going on in its vast depths, takes time to work with the seemingly insignificant coconut, tossing and throwing it to its settling place. How amazing that an infinitely big God puts effort into me, this nut; He continues to work to put me in a resting place, where the life that was adrift can begin to expose itself!

I was attempting to pack for the next place of ministry when a pilot appeared. His grandparents had immigrated to this island to work three-quarters of a century ago and never left. His wife had twisted his arm to come see me. After about an hour we established that he was a "loser" using the job, kids, and wife to change himself into a winner. At the end of the session he decided to give up his attempts to change and exchange his life for Christ's. The relief on his face reflected the rest flooding his being. It all clicked for him; he could now work for the glory of God. I call it a setup, the fullness of time, or reaching the end of self. He left the room and was asked, "How did it go?" "Powerful," was his response. Amen! It is God's glory. It certainly was not my speaking of the truth that entered into his heart and moved him, but the words and work of the living Jesus. I had just wanted to pack and go to bed!

Along the beach the Hindus had scattered flowers and were praying for rain in this unusual year of having had no rain for two months. Much of the cane harvest was ruined. We arrived and prayed for rain ourselves. That night it began to rain. We commented that God had heard our prayers. I said, "But the Hindus believe that gods heard them, also." The Lord brought to my mind all the beggars around the world He had lain on my heart to give something to. In the same way, He is ever mindful of His creation's needs and will from compassion meet those needs. The Hindus might not have known it, but God in His graciousness had given them rain.

A friend gave his opinion on the high cost of goods in this tropical island by saying, "Living is very cheap here. What would we do if God decided to give us a tab for what He provides? How much would it cost to turn the earth, give sunlight, fill the ocean with fish, or invent the coconut? God does it all without charge." Amen!

It is interesting how flexible people are and how plans change day to day in many parts of the world. In one way I like it when people can be told about a meeting that same day and they will come. On the other hand, it is inefficient, but maybe that is simply my erroneous assessment. One of the church leaders said, "It was a very big meeting we had tonight. Jesus thought that most meetings would only include two or three; that is why He said, 'Where two or three are gathered together, I will be there'! Any time there are more than two or three people, it is a very big meeting!"

One morning I visited a pastor that had burnout. I really enjoyed my time and believe God sent me to this man. He had been on disability for four years. I explained to him how there were several advantages to having a breakdown. He was too spiritual to get drunk when stressed out; therefore, he made the conscious decision to break down. The attempt to present the best of the flesh actually becomes the worst of it. He smiled, "Many business executives actually wish for a small heart attack. Not a big one, just a small one; one that will give them an excuse to stop and shed some of the pressure." That was a good insight. The better option is to get a life, get Christ's life, not just as Savior from hell, but Savior from daily living. Admit weakness, stop covering it up, and allow Him to come and be life. Man's glory is an ugly thing. God's perfect plan was to create an imperfect mankind and then show His strength in weakness. God safeguards His glory in His perfection and the weakness and imperfection of man.

I arrived at the hotel that is my normal abode when here. However, there has been a change. The previous "owner" did not actually own the place, and when the real owner found out all that the fellow was up to, such as stealing, he was put out on the street. The owner's son, then sent to run the hotel, related the following to me. As he took over the running of the hotel, he hired his cousin, who turned out to be quite mad. He was a mechanic and would stay up all night taking apart each piece of the vehicles. In the morning the son would arrive to find the whole lobby filled with parts. He tried to talk to the cousin, but to no avail. The cousin would run away and begin eating cow dung by the handful or drinking seawater. The whole family is of East Indian descent and Hindu. Finally, one of the hotel maids, a Christian, said to the owner, "You must take your cousin to church, for he has a demon. The pastor there will deliver him." The Hindu, having nothing to lose, packed up the young man and took him to church, where during the service, the pastor called him out and cast a demon from him; he has been free since that day. That is a minor detail compared to what happened next. The uncle, the hotel owner, returned home and called all of his family together. When all had gathered, he announced, "Hinduism is baloney!" You can imagine the shock of the family. He continued, "We should have cast aside that stupid religion with its sacrifice of chickens many years ago. I want a bulldozer here tomorrow to destroy the two Hindu temples that we have, the one at our house and the one at the hotel. We are all becoming Christians." The son was quite shocked but explained, "What could I do? It was my father saying it, and it was the truth. Hinduism really was baloney!"

All around the villagers were working on their new houses. I walked by a small house that obviously had not been inhabited for many years; I asked where the occupant was. "He is the son of the chief and has not been back to the village for 27 years." None of this seems of interest except when noting one thing. Though others are in need of supplies for their own buildings, nothing has been removed from this rundown house, not a pane of glass, a board, or a door. I like the village life. Another thing often not recognized is that people in the village are very smart. They do not spend their days and nights in front of the television and are not constantly looking for entertainment, so they have highly developed relational/conversational skills. A thought can be thrown out, such as, "Why did God create man?" There will be heaps of dialogue at a very high level. They think things through and will continue to think on things as time passes.

Walking across the street I see an old friend with whom I have always gotten along well; he is a Hindu without guile and is always my driver when I am here. We meet with a hug and agree that he will stay with me for the day to help me run several errands. It is very easy to share Christ with this soft friend, and we never have an argument. I listen to him, and he listens to me. He tells me of having rheumatoid arthritis and going to a Hindu witchdoctor, who had requested that he show up with two packs of cigarettes, two small bottles of vodka, and some bread. The witchdoctor advised my friend to go home and bathe in hot water for seven days. After just one day he felt better, and then he discovered that such baths are normal treatment for the symptoms of rheumatoid arthritis. He did not want to go back to the witchdoctor, because he had seen that he was deceived into paying for common knowledge. His wife, however, fearing what the witchdoctor might do to him if rebuffed, forced him to go. He went at night and was instructed to stand in the dark until the witchdoctor had seen many people. He noticed the table piled high with ill-gotten gain. The mosquitoes were biting and he wanted to leave, but his wife kept pressing him not to anger the so-called healer. When he could take it no more, he started screaming, "This is rubbish! Your magic is rubbish! Everything you teach is baloney!" The witchdoctor warned him that he would never sleep again if he stopped coming, but my Hindu friend took everything the "healer" had given him and threw it in the fire. That night he slept better than he ever had.

Next comes some marriage counseling. In this culture, respect for the husband is demanded, and, if not given, physical abuse often ensues. We spend a good bit of time looking at the Unique Self, which allows me, in a non-threatening way, to talk about deeper issues. The ideals held dear by a perfectionist Doer-Thinker extend to the entire family, and those imposed rules must be adhered to quickly, or else intimidation or force come into play. Family members under such a system will only cooperate for so many years, and then they will have this thought: *I am the cause of your misery, and my best has not been good enough. I do not have more to give, so for your wellbeing and my own, I am going to leave.* This sends the Doer into a deeper spiral of trying all the harder to control through condemnation, always pointing to the law not kept as the justification. It is quite a mess, but in this case it ends beautifully with the man changing direction. He made a good observation: "A strong branch cannot bend, and it will only break. A weak, tender branch will bend. I must be weak and tender." Amen.

The Bible School director takes me the long, majestic route to town over stone roads, through sheep pastures, over gorges, past white water, and without a single person in sight! He says he brings the students to this area every year and sends them off by themselves to pray for the day. When they return, they find a tablecloth on the ground with communion cups and bread. They sit, pray, share, sing, and take communion all night. For him, it is the best part of the year. I told him about a friend who gets youth pastors out to a remote ranch, where from the bluffs they can see for miles. He gives each one an envelope to open when he has hiked away and there is no one else around. Inside the envelope is a piece of paper on which is written, "You are now looking at all the people YOU can help or minister to." What a message. Ministry is 100% dependent upon Christ living through us. At our luncheon engagement I met a youth pastor with a common question, "How do you know if you are dating the right person?" First, we must let the peace of God rule in our hearts. We must have peace. Second, assume a green light to proceed unless and until a red one appears. It is the Good Shepherd's job to lead and our assignment to keep moving so He can lead.

Eastern Europe

An elderly lady who spent time in a Russian concentration camp told me her thoughts on the purpose of illness. "God cannot send a whole person to the hospital, so He sends the sick to minister to the sick." She told of a woman who had cancer, went to the hospital, ministered for months to patients and staff around her, and then the cancer left. "You cannot send a free man to prison; only a prisoner can go to prison, so God sends the prisoner to minister."

There is a fairly strong emphasis on hell here. For me, the overemphasis begs for a response. When the groom woos the bride, he does not end the proposal with, "If you do not marry me, I will send you to hell!" He may, however, end with, "If you do not marry me, any other life you choose will be hell. I have beckoned you to choose me, for I will love you always and take care of you."

I love the little things God does on our mission trips to believers. For some reason, one evening at a conference I started one topic and ended up talking for some time about the blessing of being an orphan. I asked, "If you beat three million people in a race, how would you feel?

You could rest in the knowledge that you are the best. The day you were conceived, three million sperm put on their tennis shoes to compete with one another, and you beat them all. No one is a mistake; no orphan is an accident. Orphans are set apart from birth to have God as their Father. An orphan who is not a Christian is missing his destiny." I then told of a brother I know who pastors a huge church in Europe. He grew up an orphan. I had everyone take a break, but I was thinking, "I am way behind on the presentation of the material, so I should not have gotten sidetracked." Then I was told that a woman who runs an orphanage had brought several of the children there that night, and they were filled with joy at the message. Well, like I had already said, "God loves the orphan." After the seminar we were invited to the orphanage for coffee and treats; the children really took care of us and showed us a beautiful evening in the family of God.

Sometimes people get so caught up looking for the spectacular miracles that they neglect to recognize God's supernatural working in the quiet confines of the heart. A husband and wife came to me telling me they had each married the wrong person. My first thought was that some things in the former Soviet Union are not so different as in the West! I went through their histories and pointed out how they related and misjudged each other, how the marriage had been bankrupt through lack of deposits of love and respect. I proposed a question, "How can you say you have married the wrong person when neither of you are doing anything right in the marriage? When is the last time you looked your wife in the eyes and said, 'I love you'? When have you looked at your husband and said, 'I respect you'?" As I was leaving, the husband started telling me all the stupid things his wife does. I stopped and drew a line in the dirt. "Brother, can you step over the line? On one side is the past, and on this side is the present. Live in the past if you want, but you have bankrupted the marriage with your constant withdrawals and lack of deposits. You are head of the house, and I hold you accountable; redemption begins with you." He paused and stepped over the line. Well, amen!

In a very ravaged country, it was interesting that the pastor took up an offering and explained, "Many of our people have yet to get the principle of 'giving as it has been given to you, giving freely, giving when you do not have it, and watching God supply.' Too many hold on to the little they have when they need to give. My wife and I gave when we did not have anything, and God just kept giving back. Therefore, we have taught our people to do the same thing."

I had a session with a pastor who had attended my meetings the past year. He explained that he had asked the Lord why there was so much division in the places he ministered. The Lord had spoken to him that the rifts were caused by him. As he grew up, his family was in constant dissension, and he was always the go-between for his parents. Therefore, since he only knew how to function in strife, he created it so that he could operate in his own comfort zone. It was a tremendous revelation. We spent the rest of the time talking about ministry and how to turn rejection (in the ministry there is plenty of that) over to Christ. I am reminded of an Aesop's fable wherein an old man and a boy are walking a donkey. A fellow walking toward them said, "Silly man! Why would you own a donkey and lead it? Let the boy ride on it." They agreed, and the boy began to ride. The next man they encountered said, "Silly man! You are old. You should be on the donkey letting the boy lead you." They agreed. Another man they met chided, "Silly man; you should both ride on the donkey." Again they concurred and acted on the new suggestion. Yet another man scolded, "Wicked man! You are abusing the donkey." The man and boy rolled the donkey over, tied its feet together, stuck a pole between its legs, and began to carry the donkey. However, after that a man objected, "Silly man; you should lead the donkey, not carry it." The pair had come full circle. No matter what is done, there will always be someone to complain. We can never please everyone, nor are we created to minister to every person. Our attention must be toward pleasing our Heavenly Father.

At the end of one service a legalist came to me. How did I know she was one? Her head was covered, she would not shake hands with a man, and she wore the stern look that accompanies the loss of joy. "I think I have found in you someone that actually believes the way I do. I do not like Christians that do not have outer behavior that testifies to being a Christian. I have to be around people that follow all the rules. Can I write you? Are you interested in reading different material?" Well, I have been in this type of conversation often enough to know where it was going. The materials I was going to have sent to me would have something to do with Christians' being hypocrites, what she perceived I had left out of my teaching, and what we need to do to be holy. It would all be fringe Christianity.

Also, I would not want to be admired by a legalist, only to be put down later when I did not measure up to her pet standards. "Yes," I said, "I like any material that talks about Jesus. But I refuse all other materials. You say I am someone who lives like a Christian; if you were with me very long, you would find that I am just like all the other people that ultimately disappoint you. In my flesh dwells no good thing! If I am abiding, you will see Christ. When I am not, you definitely would see my flesh." That pretty much ended the conversation. I will not perform for another believer to attempt to prove who I am or where I am in Him. Performance comes from Him. If I impose it on myself to project a certain image for others, of what benefit is it?

These churches are involved in a lot of self-righteousness and works. My host was pleased today to see a particular man in church, a man I, too, had noticed, for he was weeping when I was talking about the need to love an enemy. I was told that he was a great worker in the church and led the choir until something happened. His fourteen-year-old daughter became pregnant by an unbelieving boy in the village. Her father was called before the leadership and told that had he done a better job as a parent, such a thing would not have happened. They proceeded to disfellowship him from the church. I spoke to the leaders today. "Why do you cover your weakness? Power is perfected in weakness, so why do you cover yours? For glory! If you give the impression that you have no weakness, two things happen. First, if it is true, then you are only ministering out of your own strength, not as a spiritual man. Second, you prevent others from seeing that it is not God's plan to make us stronger, but weaker, so He can be our strength. Adam and Eve hid from God by covering up their real condition. Seriousness is the clothing put on by the religious before they enter church. It does not hide where they are or their true condition from God. I am glad that it does not." I believe they were all relieved to hear that, for it takes a lot of effort to cover up weakness.

It is interesting to watch legalists operate; they suck people in yet never really let them arrive. People are manipulated to join, manipulated into working to remain, and yet are never quite acceptable. When one complains, he is told he is in rebellion, bringing dishonor to the Lord. He is finally put out, for the task of a legalist is to continue to make laws until finding one that others cannot keep. The rejected person is left depleted, spiritually abused, confused, lost, and wondering if he even has a faith. Such is the case here for many suffering under very legalistic pastors. Exclusiveness is encouraged in those churches; the altar near which the pastor sits is symbolically placed many feet from the congregation. In one way, I see a positive when we honor the past and honor the person God has placed in a headship position. I cannot see it, though, when he is treated like Christ's direct and only representative. I am reminded of Sundar Singh, who refused to pray for people; he made them stand and pray themselves. Why? There is one mediator between God and man: Jesus Christ. The legalistic pastors persecute nearly every person I have met here that has come into some kind of personal relationship with Jesus. One couple wept telling about how they met Jesus but are not allowed to partake of communion as long as they do not agree that the only person who can administer communion is the pastor, and that the pastor is God's voice. They questioned where that was in the Bible, and that just put them in a worse situation with the pastor.

We have arrived to visit a young pastor married to a lady he met while in seminary. They live in an old farmhouse that has been very nicely remodeled by this lovely couple that has really gone out of their way to be hospitable toward us. We have a nice time of fellowship and eat a Russian dish that is quite nice. It looks like boiled pasta with meat in it, but really different. Upstairs we find our room heated by what looks to be a ceramic stack that is nearly three feet thick. It takes very little wood to heat the stack, and once heated, it gives off a consistent heat throughout the night. We take the next opportunity to go to the church to visit a woman that is staying there. She moves about on all fours. Her mother was in a tractor accident during the pregnancy and immediately thought something had gone wrong. Her daughter, the woman crawling toward us, was born an invalid. She has thick calluses on her hands, and her feet turn in. She is absolutely beside herself with pleasure to see the gentleman with us, the director of the Christian radio station, because listening to the broadcasts is her lifeline. She hangs on him with shouts of rejoicing, so grateful for his work and this visit. Each week she sends the station a beautiful letter that is so moving, the director reads it on air. For all practical purposes, her physical attributes look to be a mess; it takes great effort for her to slur out a few words, and her whole body jerks as she talks. Her mother just died, so relatives are pressing to have her put in a home, even though she is quite cognizant. The pastor has an obvious great respect for the woman. I am just vexed looking at her, and in my heart I whisper to the Lord, "What would You have me do for her?" The reply comes quickly, "Why would I want or need you to do anything for her? Can you not see she is directly under My eye? She is proof that the sparrow neither sows nor reaps, but I take care of it, confirmation that she is of much more value to Me than the flowers of the field. In her devotions she leaves her bondage and is free with Me." Well, amen. From the countenance of the woman, one can easily see that something very deep is taking place within her. Often if there are two people with severe infirmities, one will be a joy and a blessing to be with, and the other will be draining. The difference cannot be the infirmity; it must be the heart.

I heard about a couple in Russia working as sculptors during the Soviet times. One day they were looking at their thumbs and thought how their thumbs enabled them to make beautiful things; someone had to create their thumbs. Hence, they started a cult called "The Maker of the Thumb." The Russians had taught them there was no such thing as God, but they did believe that someone had to make the thumb. When they went to an evangelistic meeting and heard the message of Jesus, they believed that He must be the Maker of the Thumb and gave their lives to Christ.

For some time I have known one nun here that has been such a blessing to the people over the years. She delights me with some pleasant news: "Michael, often God will wake me up in the middle of the night to pray for both you and your interpreter." I was thanking her and she

227

said, "No need to thank me! He is the one that has told me to do it!" Amen. Someone has given her a book on breaking generational curses and the ten steps one can take to have emotional healing. I have not read the book, but she presses me to read the list of steps and give a response. I am thinking, *This list is interesting. Every one of these steps to freedom could be taken by an unbeliever. If so, how can it be Christ-centered? Jesus is not mentioned in even one of the ten steps. Any list that calls for the flesh to do something to improve itself is ultimately doomed to failure. There may be initial success, but none in the long term. These steps done in the power of the flesh would have to eradicate flesh, which the flesh just will not do. Therefore, there can be no system, save suicide, that could do that. If this list is the definitive one to follow and chant to bring ultimate freedom, why would the Bible not give the list? Did the Apostles keep the secret hidden from us?* Then I think, *Well, what is the fruit of saying all of this to her? I can tell she likes the book, has had some measure of success, and will defend it. I can end up on a track I do not even want to go down.* In the end, I settled it by saying, "Honestly, Sister, I do not know about the book!" None of us are in charge of another person's growth. That is the Lord's job, and He will witness through us to them along the way. I have settled on not arguing anything except the core belief that Jesus, without additions, is what we need. However, it helped me set the theme of the conference: "I have a guest! My heart is Christ's home. At the highest revelation of Christ in me, there will be no opposition."

The "schizophrenic" boy attending a few of the lectures has agreed to come and see me. Something that just baffles me is medication prescribed by a physician after only a ten- to fifteen-minute consultation, even though it could lead either to a lifetime dependency on the drug or a manifestation of proven side effects. This boy has absolutely no signs of schizophrenia and has been on the medication for months with no perceptible improvement. The mother asked the doctors when he might get off the medication or when she should expect some change. No one knows. All they know is that she will have to continue to come up with the $240 a month to pay for it in a place where a well-paid man gets $200. Amen, I am all for medication when needed. I take his history (he was in the psych ward for a month and no staff member interviewed him) and find out that he is a normal obsessive Thinker. We go over the list of characteristics. He is loyal, hates change, believes what people say about him, and, like all high thinkers, believes that something is wrong with him. I then discover that he has moved eight times in as many years. Thinkers hate to move. At each new school he was picked on. This makes him feel even more abnormal. Next he begins to put himself under a magnifying glass every day to try to pinpoint the things that are abnormal in him. It does not take long for him to discover more things that are "wrong," because his standard of normalcy is the behavior of a Feeler. The spiral tightens as he withdraws and creates in himself the very thing that he hates. He "feels" abnormal, tries to act like a feeler, and then judges himself as being really odd. Further attempts to try harder to be "normal" find him panicking, shutting down, and going off to sit in his room. I explain this and much more to him. He is getting it all, and the change in his countenance is unreserved; he is smiling the entire time. We then look at the way

229

out, Jesus. Finally, we come up with a plan. It was a great time, and the Lord intervened once again. I will write up a profile and have it sent over to his doctors. He needs to come off the medication, but slowly. I am familiar with the medications and do not understand how those particular drugs could have been viewed as having the potential to fix the problem. I believe that Jesus will pull the boy out of his troubles, and why not?

In the morning there are two separate church services at which I am to speak. In the first service I preach, but in the second I am only to greet the people and never mention the name of Jesus, because the church is monitored by government agents, and the pastor's life will be made difficult if a foreigner is caught preaching. I give a five-minute introduction to abiding with a few illustrations and finish on time. Later my host said, "I told the pastor he was taking a risk putting you on the stage, because you cannot speak without talking about Jesus. Well, he will have to wear the consequences." That was a real shame; I honestly got up just to say, "Hello," and then I started talking about the need for peace that only Jesus can bring. We plan the next eight days wherein I will be counseling people by day and speaking at night. In many countries Christianity tends to concern itself merely with good behavior and getting into heaven; it is not viewed as having anything to do with bad marriages, depression, abuse, unemployment, sickness, rebellious children, or annoying in-laws. In the lectures, I open Pandora's box in order to be real with the people; I share my struggles as a husband, a father, a son, and a believer; and soon they are coming for help, excited about the message. One woman in her sixties said, "My family is a complete mess, everything around me is in a mess, but now there is no mess inside me, and I feel that Jesus will work in everything around me." Beautiful!

A young lady, a believer, has a question. It seems that when she was little and dying from liver failure, the doctors could do nothing, so they told her mother to take her to a witchdoctor in case he might be able to heal her. This her mother did, and the girl was healed. Even to this day the mother says that she does not need Jesus, because the witchdoctors were who healed her daughter, and the daughter should consider that. I explained to her that only Jesus heals. I have witnessed many, many witchdoctors in Africa, Asia, and Central and South America. The fact is this: Jesus holds us together and permits healing. Satan does not heal anyone, period. So why would Jesus allow witchdoctors to heal? I believe it is for the revelation of hearts. In the end, who gets the glory? If a witchdoctor or an agnostic physician takes the credit, Jesus will say, "You did a miracle in My name, and why would you take the glory? I have never known you; depart from Me." My point, I told the young lady, was simple. Jesus heals and looks to see who gets the glory. "Are you willing to give Jesus the glory, or do you give the witchdoctor or your mother the glory?" She said, "No, I give Jesus the glory!" Next she asked another pertinent question: "Is it true what many tell me, that since a witchdoctor healed me, the enemy has a stronghold in me?" This is common thinking for many. I explained that Satan is the father of lies and can visit his lies and oppress. If she were to believe that the witchdoctor healed her, Satan could visit that lie and oppress her through it. However, if she gave the glory to Jesus, she would be in truth, and the enemy could not visit her. Amen, we got heaps sorted out, and once again, I would not be counseling without the wisdom that He gives freely to all who ask. The bottom line is that her mother is full of pride and uses the experience with the witchdoctor as an excuse to avoid Truth. Amen. I just told the young lady to wait. It is amazing how much of the Church is geared around "what we can do" to get someone to believe in Jesus. It is that "what can we do" that will turn Christianity from something living to something dead. The secret of it all is that the leading Buddhist scholar living in the center of the temple and turning his heart in the slightest toward Jesus will find out that He knows his address and will be there in person, by way of the Holy Spirit or by His indwelling presence in another believer. He will find the seeker, period!

Asia

Cultural sensitivity is the mantra of humanism and many missionaries, yet I am not convinced that acting like and speaking the language of another people group will endear a person to that society. The "culturally sensitive" mindset seems to covertly present itself as lowering oneself to another language and way of life. We never hear people saying they are moving up into a culture, as though the customs and language were superior. I have also noticed humanists constantly referring to other cultures as "them" or "they," while referring to themselves as "we" or "us." In so doing, they maintain the separation in assumptions such as, "We know what they need!" If flesh is flesh, that is quite a statement. To be honest, the most ineffective people I meet when working internationally are those who never get away from talking about culture and language. They may spend years learning the tongue and traditions and never get around to preaching Jesus. Perhaps in this way they never offend anyone, but neither do they get around to ministering. Do not get me wrong, for there is a place for respecting societies' differences! If it is rude to eat with the left hand, I try to eat with my right; however, people are much more forgiving than the culturally delicate and linguists would have us believe. I have been witness to the fact that someone can know very little of language or culture and yet be full of love to which people respond, and then ministry happens. I once met a most effective missionary, and he never learned the language. He depended on others, kept true to the message of Christ, and he witnessed thousands coming to recognize Jesus. Also, the culturally oversensitive forget that a person completely assimilated into a different culture loses his distinctiveness, and then so often he loses his audience. People said of Jesus, in essence, "Oh, we know Him, we know His family and His village. What could He have to say or give to us?" The gist of it was that He is no one special. Jesus said, "A prophet is not without honor except in his hometown . . ." (Mark 6:4). We do not have the same hearing in our hometown that we have in another place. When I meet an African king, he shows me his staff, his throne, and his ivory; and I can promise you that I am learning and listening. My neighbor showing me his possessions does not have that kind of impact on me. A white man showing up in a small village on the border is an interesting sight. The richest man in the village heard I was there and asked if I would meet with him; that day I shared Christ with him. I did not notice his asking any of the locals in to tell him about Christ. Again, we must put Jesus first, ahead of cultural awareness.

A brother with whom I stayed for a week had really been beaten up in the ministry. For three years he was a pastor in a small European country, where he saw nothing happen. This is not unusual; I know a group that spent four years in a neighboring country and witnessed only one conversion. This fellow was very dour, told me what he does not like, did not ask one question about the ministry, and was happy to drive and say nothing at all. I gave him some of my books and audio sets, and after a very brief perfunctory scan, he threw them back in the box. I was shown to my room, and then he entered his and shut the door. Let us simply say that I was not surprised not to find a welcome mat! At first I thought, *Well, Mike, just hush. You cannot put water into a full cup!* But then the Lord reminded me that mine is an ambulance ministry, and people do not schedule an ambulance like they do a haircut. The Lord can send the ambulance before a person even knows he needs it. Well, the ambulance had arrived, and just as an ambulance with no one in it is useless, so am I if God is not present in this ambulance. Of course, He is, and I would wait to see what happened. This fellow believes he failed in ministry in Europe, but what if God desired to reveal His love not through allowing thousands to be saved because of this fellow's ministry in Europe, but instead through sending him all the way there to perfect a work within himself? What if God were concerned not merely with the needs of the lost, but even more so with the needs of the saved? The brother continued rejecting me through the week, walking away while I was speaking, opening the door when I arrived and knocked, but immediately walking away. I believe if I could have explained quantum physics to him, his response would be, "Yes, yes," as though he already knew all about it. I got the clear message that I am boring. Any word I spoke about Jesus was construed to be a teaching, and he had no need for teaching. At one point he told me of three visions that he had of me. First, there was a very old antique doll in my house that was exercising an evil force over the home (we do not have any antique dolls). Second, there is something black in the back of my eyes, an evil influence of some sort that I picked up traveling in some distant place. Third, he saw a being in heaven with a white flowing and radiant robe. *Finally a positive*, I thought. But then he ended by saying, "That could not be you!" The Lord whispered, "Mike, you cannot trust your own thoughts; do not listen to his." I went on to share with the brother the life of Christ within, continuing to believe that God had me in this place for a reason. One morning, as I awoke to more "prophetic words," my roommate told me that I was focused on teaching and not on Jesus; I needed to lay aside my notes and focus on Jesus; I love my notes more than Jesus; if Jesus were my focus, all else would follow; when I speak and see the people blessed, I will have pride and believe I am reaching them through my notes. I listened, and God spoke to me, "This is a judgment, a revelation of himself, not a prophetic word." I asked him if he had notes. "Just a few," he said, "so that I know when to stop." Just as in every form of legalism, if a person fails at one point, he fails at all. I asked, "Why are you not trusting God for when to stop and what to say?" His answer was a long reinterpretation. I said, "As a father, when I want to talk to my children, I talk to them plainly in a way they can understand. When one child is representing me to another, it is nearly always to cause trouble." The up side to all of this was that since his judgments reveal him, I had somewhere to go with our talks. I knew that he was in self-hatred that leads to other-hatred. I knew he believed that he would be rejected by others and therefore looked for reasons to reject others first. I knew he wanted to feel exclusive and special for being rejected, and therefore he could not be taught. Taken as a whole, his comments revealed his vested interest in finding fault in others. He needed to come to see that God loves him, and so my message to him would include just that. In every situation, God has something for me. For one thing, it was a good exercise in self-denial to respond to his need without reacting to the rejection (something Jesus has always done for me). Also, God had brought someone along who does the things I do on such a grand scale that I could not avoid being confronted with my own behavior. This man amplified to an extreme what is in my flesh. Could it be that I do not give my full attention to people, that I do not listen, that I cannot be taught? Well, I saw it as the self-centeredness it was and gave it to the Father, praying what I always pray: "Father, could I have that precious ten seconds I need before I act or speak? That way, I can first turn to You before turning back to listen, see the importance of every person, and bless those around me. Amen." Finally came the morning when I awoke for my spiritual check-up, and he greeted me by saying, "I am feeling better about your spirit today!" The thaw was beginning, and within days he began spilling over like a waterfall, sharing and sharing, communicating with me for the first time. He had gone through a wilderness experience, his parents had cut him off, and he had lost everything, from money to health. He tried to figure out how a parent could hate a child, but Jesus took him and loved him in his isolation and brokenness; he could never forget Jesus for that and loved Jesus so much. He had decided—as many people do—that people equaled pain, so for fear of the pain, he avoided people. Though many people came to stay at the mission house, they think he is aloof, unfriendly, and uncaring (*Really! No kidding!* thought I). He said it was touching to witness the moving of Jesus among the people at the meetings; "It was not really you speaking," he said. I saw more clearly that my roommate's heart was beautiful, but wounded. He said he had not cooked for a single person who had stayed at the mission house (he is a gourmet chef), but after I had been there a few days, the Lord told him to cook for me (wonderful fish in ginger, curry, garlic, and eggplant). He had made it clear that he was not cooking for me, but for Jesus, and the food was blessed because of that. Well, amen! Whatever we do, do to the glory of God. It was very interesting that he made me beautiful corn muffins; normally if I eat corn, within one hour I have a migraine headache, but I ate his muffins for four days and never had a headache. Again I see that there are two sides to a person, behavior and heart. I started our relationship only focused on his behavior and only now am seeing his heart, so I got the misery I deserved.

Race relations in this country of mingled cultures are very simple: "We tolerate one another." That well sums it up, except for those who live in the spiritual culture, where

237

many will continue to lay down their lives for others. There is a real prayer effort taking place on behalf of one group of illegal immigrants. We passed by a market that serves that particular group; the government wants to tear it down. The pastor I am with is making plans for an outreach into that immigrant community and is working toward a mission church for the refugees.

A man told me he understood what I was teaching about abiding, and now he would leave the church rather than work with so many blinded people. I said, "Brother, that is amazing. Just yesterday you were blind! Why do you see more clearly today? Are you especially clever, or did God grant you grace?" He knew the answer was grace. I went on, "If you judge those who do not know what you know, then God will simply close your eyes to further revelation of Jesus. Do you want that?" He was getting the picture about the thin ice on which judgment puts us (I have fallen through that ice myself). Second, this fellow was in a panic to get a problem fixed in ten minutes that had plagued him for years. I stopped him, "Brother, I know all that is wrong with you and that you want it fixed now, but stop! We can thank God for what is right tonight, in this very moment. 'Father, You love me. There is no obstacle, for You have used everything in my life up to this point. You sent help before I knew I would need it! Everything is right; everything is under Your control. Thank You!'" He looked like a blowfish when the air goes out and said, "I see it!" I asked, "Do you feel the peace?" He answered, "Yes, Brother." I ended, "Now you know a secret: Focusing on Jesus brings peace; your problems can wait until tomorrow."

A Hindu temple is laid out exactly like the Old Testament Temple. An evangelist took an American—the unsaved father of a missionary—to watch a Hindu festival. The evangelist explained what each part of the temple meant to the Hindu and to Israel. The man watched the people reveling most deeply in idolatry and later called his wife and said, "Pray for me; I want Jesus!" His wife had prayed for his salvation for years, till God used a Hindu temple to preach Christ.

Here, just as in many places around the world, the altar call is seen as a sign of a special touch of God when believers come forward for prayer. I was questioned on why there is no altar call when I am in charge; since the Lord is moving in the meetings, the leadership wants to see people coming forward. I said, "For years you have had altar calls with the people coming forward, but what has changed after doing that? The people that come forward ask that we pray for them to receive what Jesus has already given them, such as victory or peace, which a believer has naturally when he turns to Him." Well, my point was well taken, for they knew things had not changed. Altar calls can be a blessing, but the emphasis should always be on how we have already been given fullness in Christ, who is the Head over every power and authority (Colossians 2:10).

A man said he once saw Jesus sitting upon a great white horse in heaven and inviting him to come and see His glory, but that he did not believe he was truly being invited until Jesus called him friend; that word went racing through his whole being. "Yes," Jesus said, "you are my friend. I talk to you as a friend and invite you as friend." The man wept. John 15:5, "I no longer call you servants, because a servant does not know his master's business. Instead, I have called you friends, for everything that I learned from my Father I have made known to you."

It is interesting that the definition of religion, at its very root, is a system of laws. Therefore, government is religion. To say that we want a strict separation of religion and state is impossible. Take religion (a system of laws) out of state government and there is no longer a state government. Therefore, there must be religion (a system of laws) in government. The crucial question concerns from where the laws are to come. The Christian world, which is Truth as opposed to religion, operates effectively; the non-Christian world does not. Truth is not only preached; it is demonstrated. God gave laws in His Kingdom; Israel wanted its own king and kingdom modeled after other nations. This new kingdom was a new religion. Does the system of government offered to the people by an organization such as the United Nations offer a higher standard than the religious government (Hindu, Muslim, or Buddhist) it attempts to replace? Religion is religion. All religion leaves out Jehovah and His Son. Government in the U.S. was originally modeled after Biblical principles; the fruit of it is seen everywhere. The Christian principles written into the government are what allow dissenters to oppose Christianity! Humanists are only preaching to the choir; the only people that listen to their message are those who already believe it. Those who get up in arms about the whaling industry are only those who would not participate in whaling, but the people who do are completely unaffected. Dissenters count on Christian compassion to come to their aid. In some countries, the people feel justified not only in abusing their neighbors but also in killing them. In Mecca, no non-Muslim is even allowed off of the plane. No social activists go there or push for an embargo against that place. In some places, barbers that give a Western style of haircut are put in jail. No activists there. I am not even touching on the continual persecution of believers in every part of the world. One who converts from Judaism to Christianity in Israel cannot hold land or vote. No activists there. Conversion in the Muslim world means prison; in the Hindu world, it can mean death. Still there are no activists to be found. Pollution in this and many other parts of the world is unbelievable; no activists. Traveling for twenty years, I believe that I have a fairly good grasp of abuse. I am sickened when weak Americans long for an image and set out to find some form of victimization on which to hang their hats; these people do not have a clue about genuine victimization, but they perceive that there are advantages in espousing that it occurred. They say it is because of others that they cannot get a job, use their freedom to sin, or take drugs or alcohol. They are actually saying they are slaves to ALL other people, for it is others' whims that dictate their lives. People who believe that have great difficulty with the deviants to their social doctrine of victimization, for there are those from the ghetto, from minorities, with abuse in childhood, and with physical handicaps that have gotten educations, stayed free from drugs, held public office, given to society, and become very wealthy. How to explain them? They must be discounted, so they are minimized as simply being puppets of those in charge. Choice and human responsibility are so avoided in the American culture. What even makes me sicker is the fact that I have played the victimization game myself. In my relationships, I have a tendency to think that if I were treated differently, if others went along with me, and if I got a little more support, my life would be better. Where does the Bible say that? Driving through an Indian reservation in the U.S., I noticed that a farmer had put up a sign for all who entered to read: "If God is for me, then who can be against me?" Do you believe the things of God, or must you have them proven? He will show you, in the midst of everything's and everyone's being against you, that He is for you. If He is for you, then who else matters? Does anything else matter? I do not see social activists changing things where they need to be changed, and I do not see anyone as a true victim if he has God. Why do I bring this up? I have to spend the day driving through the filth that a Hindu kingdom has produced. The caste system, the Brahmans, the dire poverty, and the lack of hygiene are all testimonies to the tenets of this religion; and in the midst of this mess, Christianity is outlawed! We go to the "holy river"; one has to wonder at the Westerners that come here for "spiritual renewal." The temple area is filthy. There are many lepers begging. Past them are the dens of trinket salesmen and -women selling everything from the ritual holy paints, to knives, to eyes of Buddha, to carvings, to food for the monkey gods. As we pass into the temple proper, we come to the river, its banks lined with ancient stones and round protrusions on which we see two bodies being burned; the ashes will be dumped into this "holy river." The stench of the river is unbearable; a cow reportedly drank from it and immediately died. Yet many people are wading in the foul water, and the holy men are pretending to drink it. Downstream a carpet factory dumps its chemicals into the waterway. It is a dead and poisonous river, just like the religion whose adherents it serves. We walk along the bank and discover in the rocks the abode of several Hindu priests. Monkeys climb everywhere. I go up through a wall into the temple grounds containing many monuments to the 350,000,000 gods. We ascend the long stairway to the top of the mountain where a few more small shrines of worship are located. In the doorway of one shrine sits what looks like a large monkey with a red face, but as we draw nearer, I see that it is a "holy" man; his forehead is painted red, and nothing else can be seen because of his hair. I stop and ask if I can question him. "How long have you been growing your hair?" "I have lived in this rock for 56 years, and I have never cut my hair." He then unties his beard from behind his back, smiles gently, and reveals a beard that flows to the ground. Looking for spiritual insight into his way of life, the kind of insight that must drive Westerners to come to this place to find, I ask the obvious, "Why do you have your hair so long; what is the significance?" He readily replies, "It is my hobby!" Well, amen. If all he has done is sit for 56 years, a hobby like growing hair may seem quite exciting. I ask him what he believes is the most important thing to know about God. "You must be one with God." I reply, "Yes, I know. But how is that achieved?" His quick reply is, "Take plenty of baths." My pastor friend guiding me on this tour was fearful that in this temple I was going to start preaching, for there is a man from Norway spending three years in prison for that very thing. I gave the red-faced man two dollars and told him I would return next year to talk to him again. He then offered to give me a blessing. I explained that I was actually more qualified to give blessings, but we parted amicably. I was told that this "holy" man was arrested last year during a disturbance in the temple area that drew many people, even the press. What they found was this fellow sitting and talking to a naked European woman, naked himself while sharing his "deep insights"! Well, back to the river, where there is another body burning. The duty falls upon the eldest son to set the head on fire. The belief goes that the mouth is the exit place of the spirit, and smoke and flames help it to come out. To keep the body burning, and as part of the religious ceremony, ten-pound chunks of butter are broken into pieces and laid around the body as it burns. We work our way through the crowds of hawkers to the taxi. In the car the pastor/friend explains that there are two types of crimes in this region, religious and civil, and both can send one to prison. A religious crime would include the killing of a cow, for it is said that the perpetrator killed his mother (or father in the case of a bull), and he would spend seven years in prison. A Christian preaching in an open area is sentenced to three years in prison; one who baptizes a person into Christ gets seven years. Then I was astounded when told that at midnight, the Hindus go ahead and kill cows, goats, lambs, and anything else that they want. Religion is for the express purpose of controlling people; those who make the laws never intend to keep them. As soon as they are given, people begin to sneak around to break them. In all religious writing, freedom is not mentioned. The Bible speaks of freedom and about being free from the law, but Christianity is not a religion; it is a relationship with the Person of Jesus Christ.

We meet a gentleman at a leper colony who is very short, 72 years old, and only has half of his feet, but in spite of that, he walks four hours to get to church and four hours to go back home. The pastor has offered to give him bus money, but his response is always the same, "But as I am walking, I hand out tracts about Jesus. How would I hand out my tracts?" The old man is one big smile as he begins his journey home. We have told him that we will visit his home today, a fact that elates him. After dinner we make our way to his home down a small trail, through the mud, over a few makeshift little bridges, past a churlish dog that I was very happy to discover was attached to the end of a chain, and to the house of this old man. His wife is all smiles as she greets us at the door of their three-room house. She has no nose and only stubby hands. The living room is just a couple of benches and a bed for their adopted daughter twelve years of age. The elderly gentleman is not there, since he has gone to the village to purchase soda pop and bananas for his guests. His wife has told us that this is the happiest day of his life. He had never expected to entertain such visitors in his home. She takes us to the kitchen, where there is what appears to be a desk made out of mud, and on top are two goats, tied up and lying down on straw. Under the desk are sticks that form a gate, behind which some fifty chickens are kept. All of this is next to the wood-burning stove, the site of all cooking. We return to the living room in time for the leprous man to return. His face aglow, he hands over flowers strung together to put around our heads. Each relative is given the task of

245

putting a garland on a different person. There is the pastor, my son, my brother, and myself. Next come the sodas, the bananas, and fresh boiled eggs. The food is just for us, and no one else eats. I asked the elderly gentleman to tell me the most important thing he has learned about Christ. He told me the story of Zaccheus and the fact that Jesus called to him. Then he explained that when he discovered that he had leprosy, he went to the road and for three days kept lying down in front of trucks to kill himself; none of the trucks could hit him. Then he went into the forest to starve himself to death, but he was discovered and taken to a leprosy hospital. There, upon eating rice, he began to sway like a drunken man. From his hospital room he could look down on a church and knew that Jesus was calling him like Zaccheus. He got well enough to attend the church and gave his life to Jesus. We had a great time visiting in his home. We prayed for the family, and I presented him with a Leatherman multi-purpose hand tool that totally amazed him, and I gave his wife the money to fix the fence for the goats. As we walked away, I said to the pastor, "I would not trade my freedom to meet these kinds of people for the biggest ministry in the world." He wholeheartedly agreed that he was a blest man to be in a small ministry that could watch the Church grow, one person at a time; he has labored in many areas for years before there was fruit. The film about the life of Jesus is shown to huge audiences around the world; here this pastor is only allowed to show it to one family at a time, and he feels so blessed to be able to do so. He also mentions that there are no efforts made by the Hindus to help the many sufferers of leprosy, since their "holy" book states clearly that leprosy is a curse from

246

God. That was the biggest reason why the old man was so happy that we had actually entered his home. The next year, during my seminar at the leper colony, he stood up to speak and gave a brief testimony about what God had done in his life; then he sang a song that he had written. He was going so well until he began to share about this man (pointing to me) that came to his house, this man (still pointing to me) whom he was not worthy to receive, nor was his house good enough. In my spirit, I could not let such talk go on. I stopped him and asked the minister to interpret for me. I explained that saying such things would not be allowed. I am the weakest man there. Others paid my airfare to get there, others paid my expenses and wages, others sent me, and others had to interpret for me. Without others, I could do nothing. If we want to talk of worth, I had no worth in this country. Then I explained once again that Jesus is for the weak; that settled that.

I was asked if God brought wars. Yes, He does, but for reasons much different than when man brings a war. God's wars are for judgment, and man's wars are for kingdom building. God is a pacifist when it comes to having a war to change a political system, for killing certain men will not change the flesh of other men. The flesh is flesh. If a war could change those kinds of things, Jesus would never have stopped Peter, who was attempting, in my opinion, to start the only just war in history.

Generally speaking, I am imposed on people my first trip to a developing country. Of the people issuing the many requests I receive to come and minister, most do not really understand what I do or the message that I have. I was invited solely with the hope that I would help provide

247

finances for their ministry, but in order that I will not be disappointed, meetings are arranged for me. I understand this system full well. Often when I arrive at a church, the leadership will barely acknowledge me, for I am being imposed on them by the pastor who had invited me for the purpose of receiving funds, so in their minds they will not reap any of the financial benefit of my visit; they know it is first come, first served. Then I begin the message, "Jesus, Jesus, Jesus! Jesus is all we need! Jesus permits what He could prevent. You are in the perfect place for Him to accomplish His will, the revelation of Christ in you." I keep preaching, and steadily I see Christ's Spirit begin to witness to the people; their countenances change. Their attitude toward me changes. At the end of the meeting I am being invited back and getting many hugs and handshakes. I see once again that the Lord knows what I need. My flesh needs that initial rejection and my spirit needs to see the witness to Christ in others. This meeting is no different but is going according to Plan. The people are hearing something different and they are responding to what is not the same old stuff, the same tired old legalism that exists all over the world, regardless of class or education. This is Jesus, what they had hoped Christianity could be. Well, amen! I so enjoy the service. Afterward, individual meals have been wrapped in paper for the people to take home. Some of the street children were hanging around outside the meetings in hopes of getting some of this free food, also. They are rewarded; my host feeds them all. Later, my host wants to know my plans. They are simple. 1. Present the message. 2. See if the leaders want me to return. 3. Translate the materials. 4. Complete the seminars and training. The questions from my host continued, and then I could see the issue. A "famous" American had made contact with him when she wanted to come to this country. He organized several meetings for her, and then the woman asked, "Do you know the pastors of the biggest churches?" He did and introduced her to them. She immediately dumped him for pastors of more notable repute. After that, she asked those pastors, "Who is the greatest pastor in the whole country?" They said they could introduce her. She met him and dumped them. I put my hand on the shoulder of my host and explained, "The Lord told me something many years ago. I was to go, and if I were received, I was not to depart from the person that first received me. You received me. If the Prime Minister were to ask me to work with him, I would not depart from you. If you like this message, we will continue to work together."

The pastor took me out and told me his testimony. He had been an atheist who believed that Lenin was God and we all evolved from apes. Even after the fall of the U.S.S.R. he believed in Lenin. He had been a Soviet athlete and had traveled throughout the Soviet Union. Then he went to a church service and could see the reality of Jesus. Great! He converted and worked in the church for one year, going well until he fell back into behavior even worse than he had exhibited as an unbeliever. The reason was that he was strengthening the flesh through the doing of good. After five years, a Korean missionary shared the grace of Jesus with him, and his life was changed. For the next five years he went flat out in ministry and business until his wife said, "I cannot tell a difference between your being a drunk or being a Christian. Either way, you are absent from home."

This broke him; he quit his work and began to devote all of his time to his family first and then his church. Amen.

Someone gave a shepherd a tract that talked about the only living God. As he watched over his flock he would read the tract, and with the passing of time, he came to admire and desire this living God. There was one problem: The tract only witnessed to the living God but never gave His name. Even so, he came to worship this living God. One day he went to the Hindu temple, asked the priest if he might know the name of the living God, and explained that this living God was the God that he now worshipped. The priest became angry and, with many threats, threw him out. The shepherd continued worshipping and seeking the name of the living God. Then one day the Hindu priest became ill and called for the shepherd, explaining that he was dying and needed the living God to help him. The priest requested, "If you still have that piece of paper that talks about the living God, place it on my heart, and your living God should heal me." Without hesitation the paper was placed on the priest's heart, and immediately he was healed. The priest, in his joy, told the shepherd of a man in another village that worshipped this same God; but he warned the shepherd to be careful, for that man had suffered much for his living God. The shepherd made his way to the man's house. The wife answered the door, and the shepherd asked if there were someone there that knew of the living God. The wife assumed that he was a Hindu spy that would accuse them of a forced conversion in order to have them killed. She said that she knew of no such man, but in truth, just such a man was hiding in his bedroom. The shepherd told his story of the tract, the healing of the Hindu priest, and more. The concealed man could hear and soon emerged from his bedroom, believing the shepherd to be a genuine seeker. The man proclaimed, "This God who has met you in the field, this God that you worship, this God that healed the Hindu priest, is named Jesus Christ. He is the Son of God, God who became man and died for the sins of the whole world." It was with great joy that the shepherd received the name of Jesus, and today, that shepherd is a pastor.

I get busy counseling the Hindu manager, who has requested some time with me. I take his history, and then he begins to weep. "I have done everything for God. I am kind to all strangers, to my people, and I do good to all that enter this place. My wife was pregnant, and every week I took her to the doctor. I watched over her. Then one week before the due date, I took her for the examination, and it was discovered that the baby had died that very day. I do not understand why God has so cursed me. I do not know what else I could have done." He is a God-fearer, though he may not know the way or His name yet. First, I explained to him that he was a slave to all men. This surprised him, and he had difficulty understanding my statement. I made it again. Still he was puzzled. Then I explained, "You are happy, successful, kind, loving, competent, and more." He agreed. Then I explained that all of the positives in his life had made him a slave, for as soon as someone says, "We have hired you because you are the best," then he must live to that and be his best every time he sees the person. When someone tells him that he is the kindest man to live, he must always be kind. I explained that he did not know the rest that my God offered. If Christ were his life, he would no longer have to defend his positive image. This was revelation that intrigued him. I explained again the bondage that comes from being controlled by a positive image, wherein we must live to the image before men rather than living to God. He got it. Next, I addressed the death. I was led to speak of David and the loss of his son. I mentioned David's statement, "I will go to him but he will not come to me." His child was in heaven. The reality of love and loss results in the only option to grief's being never to love. Naturally, this was an option in which he was not interested. I told of how God would be the God of all comfort (only our God is described as such) and would come and take him through the process. In the end, we have decided that we need more conversations. Amen. Days later I get a phone call saying he would like to meet with me. He arrives in my room and throws down the piece of paper that I had given him. "I understand my personality, I understand what you call flesh, I understand how I live to men. I do not understand how to fix it." The door is wide open, and I explain the Way of the Lord Jesus. I tell him that religions are all the same in that they end at the feet of man, and if he could fix his situation, it would be fixed. I tell him that in reality, he is a Christian, but as a Hindu he has yet to confess Jesus as the only Way. He agrees that all that he does that succeeds is consistent with Christ's teaching. He sees clearly that Jesus is whom he needs. I then ask, "Do you recognize Jesus? Do you see that He is the Way? Do you see that there is no other Way?" He answers quickly, "Yes." I said, "Then you have become a Christian, and it is that simple!" He then confided that he had been reading the Bible and it witnessed to what must be the truth. We had a great time, and I appreciated such honesty, such humility, and such faith. Amen. I can only witness to the work of the Holy Spirit. "The Spirit of the Lord is in this place." Yes, for where the atmosphere of God is, men see that God is the only thing that makes sense. Beautiful.

India

One man has illustrated to me perfectly that the weakest believer who goes to Jesus is better off than some with great understanding and little time spent with the Lord. He was Michael Francis, a leper who lived his last years on the street, homeless and begging. Before he developed leprosy, he was a believer and a law student; once he became infected, his wife took the children and abandoned him. He was an acquaintance of my mentor, who one day asked him, "Michael, what is abiding?" As he sat on the concrete platform, ears, fingers, and toes eaten away, Michael moved his palm across the area on which he laid and said, "See this cement that I sleep on? It is as soft as velvet to me, for it is the very lap of Jesus. Every night He holds me here. That is abiding."

A man I affectionately call "the Indian Angel" shares with me an approach to life that he is using. Each time he breathes, He thinks of Jesus. He breathes in and thanks God for the breath of life, he thanks Jesus that He dwells in him, and he thanks Jesus for peace. Each breath he wants to breathe in thankfulness to Christ. He wants to be reminded every moment of Jesus. He says it is amazing what living in thankfulness with a mindset on Jesus can do for us. I am reminded that the sacred is everything that we have neglected as being sacred. All of life has become sacred for this man. Jesus is all that matters. He shares with me the danger of focusing on self with each breath. "When there is a dead man in the river, the body is often pulled to the side of the river to be examined. As the body is examined, the whole area becomes polluted. If the body, the source of pollution, were allowed to just wash down the river, the damaging substances would be taken with it, and each place the body passed would be clean." The self-life, the flesh, is not to be continually examined. Let the blood of Jesus wash it away.

I met a believer, an "uneducated" man whose mind is obviously enlightened by the Holy Spirit! He told me of the acacia, a tree that grows in the forest and has hard, deep thorns all around its trunk. Even when the tree is hewn and made into pillars, the little thorns remain. To come into contact with this tree is to be injured; yet this is the tree God selected for use in the pillars of the tabernacle. The man explained, "We are that tree. To touch us is to be injured, and yet God chooses us! He took us from the forest and placed us in the very temple. We still have our little thorns, so God covered us with gold, His love and glory. We can no longer be seen; only He is seen." Next he told me that there were three spirits of counseling, the Holy Spirit, the demonic spirit, and the human spirit. Only Holy-Spirit counseling can deliver people. He listed four types of people:

1. One who knows not that he knows not! This is the man of pride and ignorance, the atheist, who has no clue that he really knows nothing.

2. One who knows that he knows not. This is the humble man, more ready to learn.

3. A person who knows not that he knows. This is the defeated Christian, continuing to look after finding Christ. What he could best do is stop to examine what is already in him, for he does know the Truth.

4. The man who knows that he knows, the victorious believer. He knows that Christ is everything and can meet every need. He will not waver.

Then this "unlearned" man told me the following, a depiction I use in discipleship even to this day:

He wrote on a chalkboard some classifications of his qualifications for being a Christian. Under talent he put zero. Under ability he put zero. Under intelligence, zero. Under people skills he put zero. In every category he put zero. He looked on the board, and all he had written was a line of zeros. Then a man said to him, "Let me show you something. All you have are zeros, six to be exact. Now we will add one before all the zeros, the only ONE that matters. We will add Jesus at the head of all of your zeros." The man then put a one at the front of the zeros and said, "See? When I added the ONE to the front, where Jesus belongs, your zeros have now become one million. Add Jesus to your zeros and your weaknesses become your strength."

Several of us spoke at convocation, and one fellow relayed a story of two pots. One knew he must be empty before he could be filled; he knew he would have to be lowered into the depths of darkness in the earth to be filled with the sweetest water. Emerging back into the sunlight at the surface, he would proclaim, "I went down empty and

I returned full!" The other bucket, however, would just be beginning the descent, and he always cried out, "I am sick of all the greedy people that keep taking my water when I am full! I hate always sinking into the dark, dank pit." People share the same experience of life but often display very differing attitudes.

I know of a man who is a great-great-grandparent. As a youngster, his family had slaves, and when he would come home from school, he would find his favorite slave, an elderly man, and make him give him rides on his back, up and down the road. Once the boy had grown up, guilt came and visited him. He was vexed by his selfishness, his way. He thought, "I never considered whether the old man was tired or not. He had worked all day, and I made him continue to labor." He was guilty of selfishness. He could not go back to that time as a child to make things right, but he could change direction that day. He did, and he chooses always to help anyone who had been a slave. Guilt had produced a positive. After the change in direction that is evidence of true repentance, guilt had played its part and was no longer needed. If guilt did return, it would be false guilt sent by the enemy for condemnation. Guilt that leads to the change in direction is true guilt. Guilt that leads to condemnation is false guilt.

I arrived just in time to speak at a meeting and was met and greeted by the Catholic bishop, a really pleasant and soft man who warned me that the counseling students in the audience were Hindu, Muslim, and Catholic, so it would be appreciated if I said nothing about Jesus' being the Way! This was a challenge, seeing that the topic was guilt and forgiveness, and my talk was to be three hours long. I had never done that; could it be done? The Lord graciously interceded, and I did not mention the name "Jesus"; I just talked about the Way that is written into every man. Guilt does not come from what I do to others, but what I do to myself. When I invite something into myself that goes against the Way that is written into me, I become guilty. I cannot go back to undo the event. The purpose of true guilt is to make me change direction today. I know what works and does not work, for there is something in me witnessing to the Way. Guilt that comes after I have changed direction is false guilt. Incredibly, the place was electric with how well the message was received. The people were so excited just getting caught up in the Way. They flocked to the front to purchase the Indian editions of my books, *Sidetracked in the Wilderness* and *Problems, God's Presence and Prayer*. They all went away with a book, which would tell them in detail Whom the Way was. I was so thrilled with the way the Lord led, not turning them off with the overt preaching of Jesus, but letting them hear of His Way nonetheless.

A fellow who was really broken came to me; I have met him in the past, and he has been reading and rereading *Sidetracked in the Wilderness*. Since our last meeting his wife, who has many problems, has turned his world upside down. She has for years overtly rejected him and emotionally, verbally, and psychologically abused him. It seems that she was telling him how worthless and immoral he was in front of the children. He reached over and slapped her once. He takes full responsibility that his behavior was wrong and did not blame her for it. There was no hint of, "She made me do it." Of course, this was the event that she needed to justify her behavior and have him arrested.

In India there is a new law that was greatly needed; it protects women from being beaten, and it can give a man nine years in prison. Once the complaint is made and the warrant issued, the offender must rush to the police station and post bail. If not, when the police find him to serve the notice, they beat him. I took his history, and as he was listing his greatest hurts in life, the primary one was that he was born with a light complexion (there was a past Iranian influence in the genetic makeup of the people). The other children called him "Snipe," which is a derogatory term for a white person. The deriding never stopped all the way through school, and to this day he hates being too light or white. He is a Doer, and Doers must always find a fix to the problem. How could he change his color? He decided that he would never look in a mirror, since he hated what he saw. To this day he can shave, comb his hair, and brush his teeth without looking in the mirror. Well, in Truth, the facts of earthly life and the faith of heaven meet in a man named Jesus. I see the consequence of the fall of man in the Garden of Eden as being "Christ in you." I see suffering as God's greatest evangelistic tool. I believe that nothing ultimately works against us. I know that the earth is the womb in which the child of God is birthed. I also see that a situation does not create problems but reveals them. He said his wife had made him so angry, vindictive, and bitter. I stopped him, explained the purpose of life on earth (which is the loss of glory, pride, righteousness, strength, and kingdoms), and then said, "How can you tell me that your wife made you angry, vindictive, and bitter? She did not make you that way. She is God's shovel digging down and finding it in you. You have been angry, vindictive, and bitter since the children started calling you names years ago." There was a long pause and tears before he said, "Yes." I said, "You want one answer for several issues," and I pointed out thirteen things with which he was dealing, and the last was the most important. "You do not really believe that God is love. If you did, you would know it is love that is allowing this in your life. You believe that God shows partiality. You do not believe this situation is the best for you. Under your ID picture there should be the name 'Unlovable.'" We continued until I saw the lift in the countenance of this suffering person that only comes as the Holy Spirit brings the revelation of the work of God. It was hope that I was seeing on his face. We discussed the fact that he can mourn, take action, and have peace all at the same time.

The Indian people are wonderful, and if a person gives himself a chance to really know them, they are very gentle and hospitable people. In this particular area, there are very few tourists (I have seen none), and the people are very helpful. Ask a question on the street corner, and immediately the corner fills with helpful passersby. The Indians are so industrious. The British took them all over the world as basically cheap slave laborers. Once set free, they set up businesses wherever they were and started building and educating. Indians do not have a victim mentality, and I so appreciate that they have not succumbed to that addiction. As we drive along, we pass women carrying rocks in baskets on their heads and pouring them on the ground to make the base of a new highway. What we would do with a truck in just a few minutes will take them all day. What we would do in a day will take them many, many days. Westerners believe this hard physical labor to be abusive, but many of our grandfathers and great-grandfathers worked just that way to build the railroads of their day. Also, finding jobs for a billion people is not an easy task. I remember when a friend in India was given a washing machine from a brother working in another country. His wife never let him turn it on one time, because it would have taken away the job of the woman who for years had worked for them, and what would she then do to feed her family? At the airport I got a nice surprise. The police questioned us, took down the information from our passports, and then as they were walking away, one turned back and said, "Jesus." He quickly turned away and kept walking. When we were finished going through security, the officer said to me, "I, too, am very happy. I also am a Christian!" We had not said a word to him!

The pastor is an interesting fellow. He had been an atheist and so miserable that he and his friend made a pact to commit suicide. They took many pills but woke up a few days later, feeling quite ill. Their next plan was to jump off of a cliff. They tried that and ended up so frightened while standing at the edge of the cliff that they were paralyzed. Next, they rented a very nice room in the mountains that looked like the perfect place to hang themselves. As they sat on the bus that was taking them to the mountains, our pastor friend noticed that the man in front of him was reading a Bible, so he asked what he was reading, and the man began to give our friend passages to read. The Bible-reading man "happened" to be a believer and the head of a psychiatric hospital; he could see that our friend was distressed and invited him to come stay for a while; it was during his time there that our friend recognized that Jesus was God. His friend continued on and did accomplish the task of killing himself. These events took place eight years ago, and the pastor is a vibrant and excited Christian. I noticed what appeared to be many Hindus at the church. When I questioned the pastor about it, he said, "I do not clean the outside of the cup." He will not tell a convert to stop practicing Hinduism, change his style of dress, or remove the face paint that reveals which god the family worships. "If you change the outside, you will not know where the people are at in their spiritual lives, because they will change just to please the pastor. You must keep working on the inner man, and when they put off—without command—the outer garb, I know the truth of their conversion." He refuses to make light of the Hindu religion, seeing in its adherents a people needing their desire for God rechanneled. The meeting begins for a roomful of eclectic listeners, including the women sitting on the floor (many obviously Hindu) and men lining the walls.

Europe

I know a lady whose husband has had many, many affairs. The husband has a beautiful heart, and though he fails, he is always repentant. I believe that one day he will be free. Over the years she has been tempted to leave him. Family members and even pastors have told her to do so. However, the peace of God has never allowed it, so she has remained, faithful to Jesus. One day I said, "Sister, when you get to heaven, you will be much closer to the Savior than will I, who have only told you to forgive and look to

Him for your needs. But you have done it. You will be in His glory when He says, 'Good and faithful servant, enter into the joy of your Master.' When you are standing there and He welcomes you, what if He asks you, 'What do you want me to do to your husband?' What will you say?" She thought and said, "If not for his behavior, I would not have had to live so fully in God's presence. Therefore, I would say, 'Bless him!'" I was so excited, for she had gotten hold of the purpose of her suffering.

The believers really have to labor in a place where the "Christian Religion" has such a strong upper hand. Born-again Christians are not embraced where the religious spirit has driven the least little desire out of the people to look for something spiritual. Therefore, Jesus is not easily considered. I cannot say the people are hardhearted; it is merely that their definition of Jesus includes suffering, crawling, misery, bondage, lack of joy, confinement, and total deadness. With that definition, why look any further into the prospect? Several believers have worked here for twelve years, and the end result, in part, is a little meeting at which I will speak in the morning. They have invited their friends and coworkers and have made much preparation to make it a beautiful experience for them. We are to be in a small room in a new "meditation" lodge. We will have four hours of teaching and then a vegetarian meal. Nine people arrive, two of whom are unbelievers. I have been told by the Lord the direction to take in the teaching. I will spend the first three hours talking about how we live, how we feel, what we think, and the struggles of man. I will not mention Jesus until the end. After three hours, it was obvious that Jesus had, as He always does, the right people there. If He gets all the glory, then He must do all of the work, and He does. As I talk about Jesus, everything must be redefined, for the words that we commonly use have one meaning to us but another to them, having been steeped their entire lives in the prevalent religiosity that distorts the meaning of nearly every term. I just stick to Jesus, His uniqueness, His love, His difference, His life, and all that He is. Then we talk about His being our life, not praying, "Jesus, help me," but praying, "Jesus, come and be my words, my life, my love, my joy, my everything." I was not saying anything that I have not said a hundred times before, and yet when I looked up there were only a few dry eyes. The one girl who was an unbeliever immediately came up to me crying and said, "Something has awakened in me! I knew I needed something; I knew I was being called!" The fellow who surprised everyone by coming was also right into the message. As the group moved to dinner, the topic was Jesus. One brother with a beautiful heart has labored for years and only seen a few couples come to Jesus. He was excited and said, "This approach of life, of getting in the person's skin, of showing in that context the need for Jesus, will be received. We will pray about putting a conference together for the couples I know around this country." As I was being driven home, my friend turned to me to say, "In twelve years, that is the most openness that I have ever experienced with a group of people and the deepest conversations that we have ever had." It excited me, and yet it vexed me, for I could see how he and his wife had suffered here in loneliness, going it by themselves, how much they forfeited to be with these people and to labor in such a religious environment. As I have mentioned before, the ugliest religion in the world is Christianity; there is nothing like it to so quickly kill the spirit of man, for every other religion is made to be a religion, but Christianity is centered in a great God Who lives through us. Try to make it a religion of lists, and the standard will become so high that the people will be wiped out; they then will focus on some insignificant speck that they CAN accomplish, as though it were of ultimate importance, in order to avoid the fact of their failure to "be like Jesus." It is obvious that at some time and place during the history of the Church, it became expedient to the carnal to have a "Christian religion" that would stir the pride of the masses and make them forget that they should not be fighting for the earthly kingdom of man, which is actually tantamount to forsaking Jesus. The whole thing sickens us in light of the fact that Jesus is alive (mind you, we would not have that light without the revelation of the Spirit, and this will always soften our criticism). I have a silent disgust for all things religious, since Jesus struggled so with the religious men of His day, and His emphasis was that there was no obstacle between man and God. Religion is religion, and Jesus is not a religion; He offers a relationship. I was able to spend extra time with three of the people from the meeting above in order to go over the material and show how it works in a practical way. The obstacle in the life of one young woman had to do with definitions. She is a feeler and so enjoys life. However, in her belief system, instilled in her by the religion in which she was raised, were she to allow Jesus in, He would trap her, take away her joy, give her lists she could not keep, and give her a life of suffering. I gave her an example: Imagine that you were told I was a terrible person, and all day I noticed that you stayed away from me. Then imagine we were all going to leave here and go in separate cars. I would make sure that you had to ride with me and that there was no other person in the car; I would essentially trap you in the car so I could spend time with you, and you could discover I was not the bad person you thought. "God," I said, "has been cutting you off from your friends, your relationships, your parents, and your boyfriend, so it would only be you and Him in the room. He has not done it to hurt you, but to bless you." She began to cry; that had been her experience. Then I explained, "It does no good for me to tell you that Jesus will make you free and alive. Your emotions would not let you believe it. I have a secret, though: Jesus is not dead. Right now, bow your head and ask Him, 'Jesus, do You want to trap me?' He will answer you." She bowed and was quiet until she looked up at me, smiling. "He said, 'No!'" "Then ask Him another question, does Jesus want you to be free?" Again came the pause and the smile, "Yes!" In the end there were no more obstacles to Jesus. As we were talking, she went quiet and said, "I once saw you in a dream, drawing this very diagram to me. Do you believe me?" Of course I believed her, for that is exactly how my ministry works. It is not one of creating but of coming behind and witnessing to what He has already done.

Well, in one way the country I am in is, as my Nepalese interpreter would say, "Sad." In general, the percentage of believers is quite low. People have deep needs, but the subculture has taught them not to trust those who talk about Jesus. Neither do the people practice their traditional religion, yet they are afraid of denouncing it, being somewhat superstitious. The end result is a group of people refusing to talk about spiritual matters, those topics being just too confusing, condemning, and fearful. I challenge anyone to find a more pleasant group of people, and they remain ready to befriend a person, but once he mentions his desire for them to come to a Christian meeting, it is akin to inviting them to join a group of Satanists. People just will not have it. If a country of this type were Nineveh, no one would have listened long enough to repent! Into this impossible situation, God will do the possible. He has sent a missionary that headed an African mission seminary for twelve years, during which time the church grew to over 4,000 and many young men were trained for ministry. He went from all that was happening there to a church of fifteen here, but I know him and believe him when he says God called him to come. We were talking about why he would be in such a difficult place. The typical answers came up, such as that in the future he might discover that his ministry allowed one person to be touched, that perhaps God had sent him to reveal hearts and give people in the end times a chance to hear truth, and that God does not care about numbers. In the end I said, "Brother, I used to think of those kinds of things because I go to small, remote groups. Now I think differently. I know I am where God wants me. Period. That is enough. Wherever you are today is where God wants you."

Latin America and Caribbean

At times it is difficult to deal with issues that should be beside the point in the Church, such as when two tiers of people are believed to exist. One is the upper rank of ministry staff with its positioning, politics, kingdom building, and image mongering. All of this is done at the expense of those perceived as existing in the lower tier. It is obvious from watching some in "ministry" that the "lower level" people are to them just—to borrow an accounting term—widgets at which to be preached in the manner of being warned to keep coming, trying harder, and, of course, giving. This type of ministry staff experiences no vital connection with the people as children of God. Behind the scenes, the widgets are talked about as the "people" who do not know thus and so, do not understand this and that, and are lacking in commitment. What is beautiful is when the Lord Jesus shows grace to one in the pulpit and allows him to recognize his connection to the Vine as a branch right along with all the other branches, a spiritual awareness of true oneness and ministry.

I call my host from the hotel, and he informs me that I will be speaking in the favela, the slum! That is exactly where I wanted to go! The husband and wife are both pastors of this church, and we are warmly (mildly put!) greeted. We get acquainted in the pastor's office, and everyone is so excited about my being there. Emerging from the basement, the stark difference between the "proper" city churches and this one is made evident. The people are jumping, dancing, and shouting. Pointing to the worship team, my host says, "Most are ex-drug addicts, thieves, and murderers." I must emphasize the "EX," for the countenance of the Lord is burned into the smiles of all those I see. All day the messages in my mind kept changing, but now, as I walked toward the platform, one message had stuck with me. I opened my mouth and said,

"We must talk about revelation and the cross." At that, the place erupted, and I continued. Throughout the service I would notice someone crying, shouting out, or just staring fixedly. I was talking, yet not I; it was Christ in me, living through me as though it were me, but it was not. Now, here is what I did not know. The pastor and his wife had been praying some three years ago and asking for direction. The Lord had spoken to both of them, saying that He was sending someone from the U.S. to speak to them. They would know the one He was sending, for the man would use two specific words: one word would be "revelation" and the other would be the "cross." Some time ago the pastor had been in my host's new bookstore in the downtown area and had noticed the book *Sidetracked in the Wilderness*. He had asked if this author ever came to this city, and my host had answered in the affirmative. Then the man asked, "Would he come to our church?" My friend told the man that his church was exactly where I would want to go. After the service the pastor spoke to the people, saying, "See? I have been announcing this speaker's coming for three years, but I just did not know who the speaker would be!" It was an incredible evening. So many people came up to hug me, and finally my host and the pastor had to take me away to the basement where the people had brought food just for us to eat. My host told the pastor that it was not right for us to be the only ones eating with so much food. The pastor agreed and invited all the people to eat with us. It was a feast. Of course, the smallest meal served with love is a feast; however, this had love and a variety of foods. So many people had questions for me that my poor host—who is also my interpreter—could not get a bite to eat. That is the life of a good interpreter; he never has a chance to eat. One woman revealed that she was married to a pastor who was an abusive alcoholic. He was a successful evangelist, and she wanted to know if she should stay with him or if she should expose him. My question was, "Expose him to whom? Nothing is hidden from God!" My second question was simply, "What is the peace of God telling you to do, stay or go?" She just smiled, "Stay!" I refuse to presume to tell someone what God is telling him or her to do. We all belong to Him, and He is faithful and true to tell us what to do. At length my host had to put me in the car so no one else could get to us; the crowd was that great. What an evening in the favela, and I am invited back tomorrow night!

It is Sunday morning and a pastor has organized over fifty pastors to leave their pulpits to others and come to a breakfast meeting. The church has quickly organized the food for the breakfast; it is easy to see the hearts of these servants of Christ. They have taken great care to decorate, prepare, and make this a very special event. The first question from the pastors is: "What do we do about stress in our ministries?" One pastor has fifty small churches to oversee, and another has 100. I said, "Brothers, we must first recognize that if we were all to die from some calamity at this very moment, all of our ministries would go on. Why? They are not our ministries, but the Lord's; He could raise up someone for ministry from the rocks. We are not that important. If God gets all the glory, then God must be doing all the work. We must learn what it means to let Him do the work and understand how to let Him do the work." We also talked about the fact that ministry will perfect us before it does those to whom we minister. We are in ministry because it is our place of growth; others work at their jobs because God sees it as their place of growth. Christ is all in all.

It was fun to meet with an elderly woman who is getting married for the first time. Some in a position of "spiritual authority" refuse to give their approval; they are in charge of her life, you see. However, she has pressed on with the engagement. I just warned her, "After you are married and you have a few problems in the relationship, do not let the enemy whisper to you that you should never have gotten married. You are convinced in your own heart, and that is enough." She had already thought about that. Also, she is writing a letter to some of those leaders and wanted my advice. Any letter that is written can always be used against the sender, so I advised that the letter should be short and center around what we believe about Jesus. Often we cannot have fellowship around what we think, but we can around the Christ in whom we believe. Any letter attempting to explain ourselves and our positions must always be redemptive. She is very soft toward the Lord and agreed to it all.

One fellow kept wondering if he should have married his wife and if he were truly in love with her, then or now. He had been to many counselors, and they had all attempted to work through the issue with him. Here is where the Christian has an advantage over the most educated person in the world; he has gifts of the Spirit, and a gift will cut through places where education muddles along. I asked, "How many obsessions have you had since your childhood?" "Many," said he. I again asked, "Then have you considered that the issue is not whether you love or do not love your wife, but it is just one more obsession to keep your excessive mental energy from being directed toward a self you hate?" His face lit up, and he said, "I know that is it. I hate myself. I hate everything about myself. I cannot fix it, so I have always put my mind on something else." Truth cuts, but it also feels good, like removing a splinter. We talked about having a self that he could love, walking in Christ with Him as his life.

A gifted evangelist has done a lot here, like running a camp, a circus ministry, a bus ministry, and traveling 36,000 miles in the interior. He is never without a smile. He was telling me of being in the interior when the oldest man of a tribe—and thus, the chief—appeared in the city with six wives. A missionary heard the boy speak and knew his dialect, so she began to interpret for him and discovered what their situation was. That chief was sixteen years old, and all six wives were sick, so he was seeking medical attention. The government is practicing the passive genocide of native tribes by refusing to allow outside contact, and even if a missionary has previously had access to a tribe, he is only allowed in a few weeks each year and is not to provide medical treatment. Of course, these stringent rules do not apply to the atheistic anthropologists that are allowed to stay for prolonged periods. Anyway, that night the chief came with his wives to the evangelist's meeting. He was listening intently to the message but could not understand, so the missionary was asked to interpret. At the end of the message, the chief came to say, "I see why my people are dying. We are not worshipping God. We must throw the witch out of our village." Upon inquiring, the believers discovered that a female anthropologist, a foreigner, had set up camp amid the tribe to study their ancient remedies in an attempt to discover the cure for cancer. She refused to allow any outside influence other than her own. The people were sick, and she refused to allow in anyone to come help. It is a misconception that remote peoples live idyllic lives.

The interpreter is a blessing. He is in his seventies and pastors a church in a city. It would be difficult to find a softer soul. He quietly takes in everything. No more than shoulder high, his countenance alone commands the respect of many. He has been listening to the messages and smiles at the end of every session. Today he shared with me the fact of progressive revelation. He said that he gets a question in his mind and spirit that only God can answer. He will begin to pray, and little by little the answer will come, even if it takes three or four years. He wanted to know if a Christian could commit suicide. God spoke, assuring him that one could. He then wanted to know what people think of while they are dying. God spoke several years later, revealing that each person thinks of something different; the children of God are thinking of Jesus, and others are trying not to think about Jesus. His last question was, "What does a baby think?" The answer is yet to come. It is interesting that maybe a thousand Christians, liberally speaking, have had visions, walked on water, raised the dead, or been caught up to heaven. This is out of 1.2 billion believers and leads me to believe that those experiences are not to be considered typical. Anyone who wants to know what the normal Christian life looks like should stop reading and go look in a mirror. Our lives, gone through daily with God speaking and revealing slowly, demonstrate the normal Christian life.

We have several other meetings, and it is a joy to see the Lord work. After one meeting with a pastor, he was driving me to the hotel, and I said, "Brother, I did not want to say this in front of the people, but you did not say one thing that was right tonight." He did not act shocked as he asked for an explanation, and from his heart's attitude, I knew he would receive it. I continued, "All of your teaching ends at the feet of man, and man cannot 'find' God, 'please' God, or 'work' for God; for it is God who is at work in us both to will and to do of His own good pleasure. It is all about God, it is all about Jesus, it is all about the Holy Spirit, but it is not all about our efforts. He keeps us, He pursues us, and He puts us in situations where He can work all things together for our good. We are not 'Prayer Warriors' in the way you are presenting it. We do not just keep annoying God until He gives us what we think we need. We do not know what we need and should not want our will but His will for us, for He is smarter than we are. Prayer will bring the peace that comes from the revelation of being in His will." The brother stared and said, "I see now that the Church has gone left when it should have gone right!" It was a great time of fellowship.

Africa

A Bible School principal whom I really admire made an interesting observation: "Some churches in America are not very creative." I asked what he meant. "If one church does something, others copy, and soon it spreads over the whole world. That is not creative!" He also explained that the Fetish Priests have a lot of the exact behaviors he has witnessed in U.S. churches. In Africa, when a Christian behaves in a manner that imitates the Fetish Priests, the Christian must use the Bible to explain why his expression is different from that of the priests and is of the Lord. If he cannot, then it is not allowed. I felt it was an inarguable point. It seems that Americans have grown weary of attempting to find Christ in understanding and are seeking to find Him in emotions, while the Africans are weary of attempting to find Him in emotion and are looking more in understanding. Both emotion and mind are of the soul, and God is in our spirit.

I was told a story: Each day a poor man walked by a rich man's property and said, "I wish I had that." One day the owner heard the man and called out to him: "I am leaving and will put you in charge, but when I return, everything must be as I left it." The poor man happily agreed and came and took possession. The first night, as he was beginning to go to sleep, he thought, *What if someone steals something?* He got up and stayed awake all night, protecting the place. The next day he called five friends and told them his fear of not being able to return the place just as it was. They all gave different counsel, and every bit of the advice gave him something else to fear. He did not sleep for four more nights. At last he made an agreement with his wife that he would guard all night and she would watch out all day. For months the man did not relax in the dark at his post of surveillance over the fortune. Finally the rich man returned, and the poor man begged him to take the place back, saying, "I have not rested since I was given this place. In my own little house I slept well every night."

I was on an overnight flight, which is hard on everyone. It is nice that when an announcement was made on the plane's speakers, it ended with, "Have a blessed day in Jesus." When we landed, we heard, "Thank you for flying with us, and we trust Jesus will bless your journey!" Amen!

God gave me a story before the start of the service. As soon as I told the people God had given me a story for them, they leaned forward, alertly listening to every word. "There was a beautiful flower by the river in the valley, and only one such flower in the entire world. A young boy would come every morning to gaze at its beauty and to water and care for it. He loved the flower. One day the boy came, but he found many mean boys fighting over the flower. They grabbed and pulled at every petal until it was destroyed and the boys had nothing remaining over which to fight. The boy went home weeping; his father asked why. He took his father by the hand to take him to the place of the flower. His father surprised the boy by not being upset. Instead the father showed the boy all the seeds that had been hidden in the flower and were now scattered on the ground. With joy the seeds were planted and tended by the boy and the father. Where there had been one flower, now there would be many." I asked, "What is the flower, who is the boy, and who is the father?" There were many suggestions before I explained, "The flower is the Church in this war-torn country. Evil men destroyed it for nothing. However, Jesus was watching over it. He brought the Father, and your Church will grow again and multiply." At that the place erupted. There were many shouts of joy.

I decided to wade off into deep water one morning in the training seminar. Up to this point, I have been telling stories that lead to Jesus and making some basic principles known. I do not have an overhead, nor is there electricity. However, this morning, with a makeshift chalkboard, I went into the "Concept of God" lecture. I read the test and had them take it. Everyone there (all are in some type of ministry) was excited to see why they had so many bad feelings about God and why there were so many unbelieving believers in their fellowships. They could really relate to how a bad father on earth can give bad feelings about a Father in heaven. I decided to go a little deeper. We began by looking at the two bags we bring into marriage: flesh and unique self. I knew that the concept of a personality and uniqueness had not been taught here. They all stared as I explained thinker, feeler, and doer; then the heads began to nod knowingly, and soon there was lots of laughter. They were getting it because they had lived it. Marriages are in trouble here; many just give up and resign themselves to thinking that things cannot get better. At the end an elderly man came up to me and said, "I was interested that you said thinkers do not need lots of hugs, and that if they were tired, they will go stiff when the mate tries to hug them. In our country if a man begins to hug his wife and she becomes the least bit stiff, it is assumed that she has another man. The woman will then be abandoned, abused, and sometimes killed. I have noticed that those women are exactly as you describe the thinker. This is why they weep and say that they never had another man. We must know more of this." I agree that it is an important bit of information to possess, especially when someone can lose his or her life over the lack of information.

I asked a group if there were some who could not read. Many hands went up. They were surprised when I said, "You do not have to read to be a Christian and to grow." I certainly had their attention. I explained that when someone has trouble reading, it does not limit God from speaking to him. I gave several examples and then talked about learning about God from the things that God had made. Again, I gave more examples. The people were beaming they were so encouraged, not because they were feeling good about a deficiency, but because it was true (John 7:15, 16). I did not even want to encourage them to read, because the schools and materials are not available. God touched the people as I continued on the theme of our weakness and God's strength. I talked about self-righteousness, pride, and strength, the things that make our daily lives truly miserable. I was hoping they could see their favored position with Him because of their state. They did. In fact, several of the pastors said, "The old women with no education are in the market telling people what you said. They understand you!" Well, thank You, Lord. You are the One who never proclaimed Yourself, in no way crushed a worthless (to all appearances) reed, nor put out a smoldering flame.

In a village I am asked to say a few words. "Two boys in a village began to fight, and one boy killed the other; upon seeing what happened, the villagers began to chase the boy to put him to death. The boy ran to the house of the chief and fell at the doorway, crying out to the chief for his protection. The chief came and, seeing the crowd, asked for an explanation of what was happening. The crowd yelled, 'The boy killed another boy in a fight, and we have come to take him and kill him.' The chief said, 'I cannot allow you to take him, for he has fallen at my doorstep.' At that the chief lifted up the boy and put him in his house. Then the crowd yelled, 'The boy that he killed was your son! Give him to us!' At that the chief became despondent and went silent; after a long time he spoke again, 'Then I will adopt him.' At that the crowd dispersed. Do you believe in the love of God? Do you believe that He would do the same for you? He has, and no matter what has happened in your life, the love of God is up to something."

On another long drive across town to find computer parts for a Bible school, a professor tells me, "I have two rules that I live by. If I see someone buy something that I want, I have trained my mind to turn away from it. I will not buy what I want, but only what I need. Second, if I see another being blessed, I turn my mind from asking why such things have not come my way. These two things make me happy, and many wish that they could have my attitude." A professor that has not had a day off in thirteen years, does not have a car, and lives on just over $100 per month says with a smile that he is content. I can see by the look on his face that he really is happy with his state in life. Wonderful.

There are many questions after our sessions concerning God's acceptance. One man was saying that if a believer died while committing sin, he would go to hell. At this another woman said, "If only God's love were unconditional." We see how those who do not understand the basics themselves have used fear to manipulate the people into good behavior. The pastor asks the man, "Do you have children?" "Yes, a daughter." "Does she ever disobey you?" "Yes, she does."

"Do you then reject her?" "Never." "Yet you would believe that God, Who is Love, would reject you!" The man just smiled and the woman rejoiced.

The men share more about the Church's starting up after the civil war that lasted from the mid-seventies to the mid-eighties. Proving the point that God does in suffering what He cannot do in comfort, it is related to me that the Church had disappeared in this country and only got started again by the displaced people in refugee camps in neighboring countries. We see on television the worst possible situations for people, and yet out of the suffering, the Church can be birthed. The situation in which a believer finds himself is perfect for him if he wants the revelation of Christ in him. God is not fighting this fallen world but using it in a mighty way. However, does it not floor you how little credit He gets? Man starts the wars and diseases and then asks, "What kind of God would allow this?" God uses the terrible situations to bless men by bringing them to Him, but those without eyes of faith see the tragedies as worthless.

My last counseling session of the day was with a Doer, and I was really happy that two pastors were sitting in with us. This type of fellow would only represent 3% of the people that I see. As a Doer–Thinker, the dysfunctional family in which he grew up did not bother him at all, for that temperament type does not look to others to formulate a self-image. At that one pastor made the comment that the whole system I had been presenting all day was based on identity messages given from others' overt and covert behavior; he was thinking that now the whole system would fall apart. However, a Doer–Thinker builds his own image in the power of great talent, abilities, and intellect. He has a strong enough sense of self to build a positive image alone without looking to others. The clue that this was the case was revealed when I made a simple request, "Tell me three failures in your life." He could not think of three. It took some time to convince him that good is the enemy of the best. Flesh is like a coin with two sides, one side bad flesh and image, the other side good flesh and image. I showed him a picture of a white horse standing close to the gate and wanting out of a corral. A black horse was standing back, seemingly unconcerned that he was penned up. However, it was a ploy, for when the gate was opened, the black horse raced forward and left before the white horse had a chance to. When we work to maintain a good image (his was being a success, a good father, intelligent, and capable), not only are we in as much bondage to image as the person that is trying to change a negative image (worthless, unacceptable, and unwanted), but by opening the corral to let out the good flesh, we also let out the bad. This explained why, when his family and others under him did not measure up, he would insult and become critical, something he hated to do, since this did not maintain his favorable image. He just sat back and smiled, "You have undressed me! I see it clearly!" Then I explained that we all think a bad man should die, but we do not believe that a good man should die. He needed to die so he could be free from image and stop boring all of us with his image building. His persona did not matter; Jesus is who matters! Letting exactly Jesus flow through him was much better than projecting his image. I made it clear that I did not want to beat him up; I wanted him to be free from spending his waking moments thinking about image. It was a move of God, and I was witnessing to what Jesus had already put in him. Beautiful.

One missionary worked hard here for ten years, at the end of which he simply said to his elders, "I have done all I can do for you. I have nothing else." They were quite shocked. We talked about a trap we get into as ministers, parents, and spouses, the trap of thinking that we can make choices for others. I do not know a single person who has pressed on in Christ because of me or anyone else. If someone presses on in Christ, it is because he chooses to. Ultimately, it comes down to choice, and choice is not something we can do for another person. He was explaining the complexities of African family life. Many of the people do not love one another because they do not know each other. In many places the woman is not allowed to look at the husband when she talks; she must turn her back. In other places, if the woman wants to tell her husband something, she must send her brother to talk to him. Often one's own children do not get the inheritance; it falls to the children of a brother. The uncle has more say in some homes than the fathers. It is a mishmash of tangled relationships. The concept of being "in love" rarely exists in the village. He told me that after the ten years of ministering here, he still could not get the men to tell their wives that they loved them. He has given up on that for now and is just working on getting the men to tell their wives that Jesus loves them.

The service is really nice. I do like worship songs and bands, but I also like a pipe organ and old hymns that have meaning. The church is full each night, no small feat since most have worked all day and must rush home in order to race off to the church. The time passes quickly and at the end of the service I must be off for a cell group meeting of university students. We talk for two hours before I believe that they must be tired and stand to leave. At that we continue our discussions while standing for 45 more minutes. They are really hungry for the things of God and have been trying to put their lives together from discipleship models that have every aspect of life landing at their feet, and not the feet of Jesus. Because of the change in government, their opportunities are very limited, and so there is an incredible pressure to get things right from the beginning. At eighteen they must know what they are going to do for the rest of their lives; there seems to be no room for waste. They are pressured not to miss the will of God for their lives. Is it not interesting to be told that God has a wonderful plan for our lives, but we must discover and fulfill it? If He has the plan, is it not His job to fulfill and reveal, while we enjoy our lives as the sheep the Shepherd leads? Then there is this pressure of evangelism: "What if your neighbor dies and goes to hell, and you did not talk to him about Jesus?" The whole concept that I am responsible for another's salvation is a bit odd but often taught. It certainly does not sound like abundant life to me. You can see that we had a lot to talk about. Their English is nearly perfect, so that is great.

I was told of a man getting a haircut while sharing Christ with the atheistic barber, who categorically said, "There is no God." The man left and, as he was walking across the street, saw a man that had never had his hair cut. He turned back to go tell the barber what he had seen and said, "I do not believe in barbers! I just saw a man who has never had his hair cut, so barbers do not exist." The barber said that was a stupid thing to say; the man had never had a haircut because he had never visited a barber. "Barbers exist, but for that one man they do not, only because he refuses to visit." The man then said, "And because you refuse to visit Jesus, you say that He does not exist!"

The hosts had invited forty pastors from the interior, but one pastor told another, and another, and another, with the end result that 125 pastors so far and growing are showing up for the conference. ALMI has committed to feeding the pastors; therefore, our budget just tripled! Then I discovered that though the pastors can read, only 25 have Bibles; the rest are preaching from tracts and bits of information they have picked up here and there. Upon further investigation I find there is a Bible society here that has Study Bibles in the local language; it is just that no one has any money to purchase one. Amen! I am certain the supporters would not mind if we purchased each pastor a Bible. We have decided to wait until the last day to distribute the Bibles to the pastors and women involved in ministry. At any rate, we cannot hand out the Bibles until a church stamp is first imprinted on each one to show that though it was given away, it is ultimately the property of the church. This is done to keep the people from getting a Bible and immediately selling it for profit. Amen, I understand tough times and doing what one has to do to get by! The morning came for giving out the Bibles. Other than the interpreter, the bishop, and me (the guest speaker), the only person who knew about the Bibles was the driver hired to pick them up. Unfortunately, he spread the word, and the place was packed with people wanting a free Bible. The pastors had heard that we were going to give them to those who did not own Bibles, so they left theirs at home and came forward to get another Bible; one pastor who had four Bibles at home left his to come get another one. As disappointing as this is, we must keep a heartened attitude despite the methods some have of taking the joy out of anything we try to do. We wonder why African leaders only think about themselves, but we are seeing the principle permeating the society! The supply of Bibles ran out, and many of the women that I had wanted them to go to were left without one. It came time to teach, and I mentioned how not all things that are true are the truth. I had a ready example by saying, "You might have said that you did not have a Bible today, and that was true; but the truth was that you left it at home so you could take one from a person that did not have any Bible at all." I stared at the men, and several put their heads down, but no one ever came forward to return a Bible.

Chapter 7

When Caesar Seems To Have The Upper Hand

Actually, the kingdoms of men and their politics are not that interesting. To me it becomes like a wheel within a wheel, and I will tell you a secret: My life is not determined by any election or political force. I am pressing forward to the high call in Christ. He is not fighting systems but using them. They will not hinder me; He will only use them to direct me. I look forward to the future because He is my future. Actually, for the next year I have challenged myself not to mention politics one single time. I think I will have a far greater lift in my spirit. For now, the doors are open; I can go anywhere, and I intend to go where the Shepherd leads me. When believers from any country whatsoever focus on Jesus, the differences are minimized. The problem is obvious: there is just not enough abiding in Jesus.

Eastern Europe

I met a leading pediatric surgeon, a Gideon, in a satellite country of the former Soviet Union. While he was working in a hospital during the Communist occupation, prayer, worship, and even the mention of Jesus were illegal. He had heard that a woman he knew to be a Christian was dying; as she lay there taking her last breaths, he whispered, "Would you like me to pray for you?" She said yes. In front of everyone he dropped to his knees and began to pray aloud, and thus she passed into the presence of the Lord accompanied by prayer from a brother. In less than 24 hours he was informed that he had lost his job. This is only one of thousands of such stories.

I remember as a university student having the unpleasantly foul job of cleaning out a grease trap in a kitchen. All I could look forward to was a shower to remove the stench. It seems that all of the satellite countries of the former Soviet Union are in the process of taking one gigantic bath, washing and cleansing their culture from the foul smell of communism. As a whole, they are singing in the shower! They remind me of the stork, which migrates hundreds of miles to nests that are hundreds of years old. If a nest is destroyed, storks will rebuild it. The people are beautiful and have determined to rebuild that which was destroyed. With each passing day there is renovation, new paint, and men and women dressed impeccably in the latest fashions; more and more European models of automobiles can be seen. Church buildings are going up everywhere, largely financed by Christians in the West.

I had a wonderful meeting with a translator; she was born in Siberia, because her parents were forced to work as geologists for the Communists, who informed her family's village that if they raised the money for her father's return, he and his family would be allowed out. However, once he was let out, the Communists proclaimed him an escapee, recaptured him, and returned him to Siberia. She and her husband had recently moved into her grandfather's house, since as often as possible, property was returned to original owners by the government once the Soviet Union fell. Like all the others, the house had been gutted during the long siege of Communists and all her grandfather's furniture sold, but at least the home is theirs.

The Communists were like locusts; they did not just move in, but came and set up camp in old mansions, stripped everything from the walls, never added a coat of paint, used the halls for toilets, and otherwise depleted their surroundings. I visited a collective farm that had been an estate—complete with castle—until the Communists took over. In eighty years there was not a drop of paint applied, nail pounded, nor roof shingle replaced. The castle had been gutted and trashed years ago by the workers. The whole place was completely dilapidated. Just outside the "estate" I watched as two fellows pulled a harrow by hand, using ropes. What has been done to these people is not just stupid, but demonic.

I found that the average person is not interested in recounting tales of Siberian woes, relatives snatched away in the middle of the night, nor fears of glancing the wrong way. Rightfully so! They want to move on in the Lord, and yet there is not much encouragement to be found when it comes to the economy. I stayed with one concentration camp survivor whose emphasis was not on the past but on how to live on $100 per month when the current government has purchased her downtown apartment complex and raised the rent to $800 per month. It will drive her out. She did recount her flight as a child during WWII. One night as her family walked on the road, her

287

father felt they were lost and must sleep in a field until daylight. That night the road was bombed, and had they kept walking, they would have lost their lives. What she remembered most were the body parts, smell, and carnage of the families not so fortunate. She told me that she laughed to avoid crying. Nothing much bothered her.

Persecution under Communist rule was different than I had been led to believe. Upon taking power, Stalin had put to death 50,000 to 70,000 pastors. During his many paranoid purges, several million free thinkers were also killed. To be sent off to Siberia, one needed merely to be accused of thinking something against the state. Literally millions went to Siberia for basically nothing. I was told of a meeting in a full auditorium; a party leader gave a cheer for Stalin (he was not there). Everyone started clapping, but all were afraid to be the first one to stop. The clapping went on for nearly one hour. Finally, a party member on stage quit and sat down. The crowd immediately followed his lead, but he was taken away the next day and never heard from again. At the end of the cold war, 200 Christians were released from prison with several thousand other dissidents. It was realized (much too late) that to continue to purge the people would in the end deplete a much-needed resource. Thereafter, the persecution took on different forms. Church meetings were held, but those attending were fined half of a month's salary when caught; Christians were mocked in school, refused admission to universities, given lower school grades, and demoralized in other ways to make a miserable existence even more frustrating.

A city heated by Soviet "central heating" meant there were boilers in one location for the whole city and hot water piped from that location to every home. Communists engineered this to facilitate their control; heat could be cut off to homes at the least sign of rebellion. Even today, heat turned on all over a city is set for a certain autumn date, when freezing temperatures may have already set in for a month, or the weather may still actually be pleasant, resulting in homes and buildings that are way too hot. In one such hot hall, people arrived, wondering what to expect from my talks. I began with a short introduction on suffering and spoke for three hours. The Lord so encouraged the people through that message. It had not been my plan to go in that direction, and I was as surprised as anyone. Christians here have long held the belief that suffering is the judgment of God on them; they had not thought of suffering as a tool to bring them deeper and deeper revelations of Christ.

It was interesting to see how God provided for the only Christian radio station in one of the Soviet Union's former satellite countries. A ten-year project had been completed and a broadcasting tower had been built that was taller than the Empire state building. However, two years later Communism fell, and before the Russian soldiers left the country, they returned to attempt to destroy the equipment in the tower. They fired several shots into the door that would allow them access to the stairs and tower, but for some "strange" reason the lock never gave way. The soldiers gave up and departed.

There are so many broken dreams. One young believer told of her military officer father's being promised a new apartment and enough money to purchase a car if he would work for three months at Chernobyl after the nuclear accident. He agreed, but not only did he never get the apartment or car, he lost all of his life savings when the currency changed. He now suffers the effects of the radiation poisoning that include a nervous disorder that makes walking difficult, diminishing eyesight, and hair loss.

In a country such as this, wherein soldiers and rulers from another country abused for years the citizens and treated them with contempt, there is the opportunity for those citizens to turn around, after the collapse of the intruders' power structure, and treat the soldiers with the same type of bitter scorn that they had meted out. However, to the degree that is practiced, the citizens will become the very thing they hated. Blessing those who curse us is truly the only Way. When we are offended, there is separation, next confession, which should be followed by forgiveness and restoration. There cannot be restoration until there is confession. God offers forgiveness but does not give blanket restoration without confession. However, there is another option where there is no confession: "Bless those who curse." This simple command brings peace in the heart of the offended that can spread to the whole land; it can bring closure and can keep the offended from becoming like the offender. In fact, I had an interesting talk with a prominent believer here concerning the attitude we are to hold toward an enemy. It was concluded that God does not cause all things, but that He does cause all things to work together for good. This brother, being a Doer in a country with so much out of the control of the people, has found a way to live. His formula is: preach Christ. "There are really only two types of people, those who know Christ and those who need to." When I was with this brother after a meeting, a fellow came up to him and said, "I do not believe what the American said. I have been bitter about my wife for the last twenty years. She divorced me and still has a position in the church. The American said to forgive to be happy, but it is not that easy." He then went on to explain, "My job is to fight this injustice; if I fight the good fight, my heart is at peace for a moment, and God handles the other problems." Well, it made sense to him, but not to my brother in Christ, who explained that the fellow really must let it go. "To look at the splinter in another's eye is really to take that splinter out and drive it into your own eye." He showed the man the church songbook. "On the outside is written 'Jesus.'" He then opened to the index and said, "The index is just like your list of injustices. You only see them when the cover is bent back and you no longer see 'Jesus.' Close the book, hide the injustices in Jesus, and get your eyes on Him." The man began to weep, for he had been scratched where he itched. The pastor is a top brother, a blessing to work with, and a man of vision.

One night we went to a pastor's home for a feast of herring covered in potatoes, beets, jelly, thin slices of liver covered in sour cream, mashed potatoes (included with every meal in this city), and paper-thin pork, battered and fried. It was the first protein I had eaten this particular trip, for food was scarce. Every home has an outdoor toilet. I was vexed by what the pastor told me. Before the fall of the Soviet Union, people worked and got paid minimal wages, but there was no inflation. At this time things were actually much worse. Many were going to work month

Untold Stories & Unknown Saints

after month in hopes that someday they would be paid, but when it happened, it was only for the current month, no back pay. Farm workers had not been paid for three years. However, they were allowed to take milk, eggs, meat, and other food. All summer the farmers had weeded the beet fields, but in one month there would be a frost and none of the beets would be harvested, for there is no fuel to run the tractors. The wheat crop was harvested by hand as the combines sat idly beside the road. All foreign aid had been diverted to the former communists, who are now the present government officials, the new Mafia. The family subculture is nearly destroyed for many people. Alcohol has done a good bit of damage. Many of the little shops that sell bread and meat also sell vodka by the ten-ounce glass. The men buy it, drink it in a few gulps, and then walk off. All manufacturing has ceased, and it appears as though the country might decrease in population and become a hunter-gatherer society. The end result for the Church is twofold. First, many of the pastors that were involved in the revival that swept the country after the collapse of the Soviet Union made contacts with churches in other countries and abandoned their congregations for a better life elsewhere; leadership is lacking throughout the entire country. I looked at the pastor and said, "There is a higher call than the call to another country. Though there be need all around, in every area, we must remember that the Lord's Prayer does not say, 'Dear Wealthier Country, give us this day our daily bread.'" It was his assessment that many had merely been hirelings, not really concerned for the flock. Second, the men of the Church are forced to go to other nearby countries to work and leave their families for six months at a time. The pastor cannot even find deacons, let alone men who will answer the call to minister in the hundreds of villages that have requested a pastor. Since materially things were better under the Soviets, now that they are gone and there is freedom to believe in God, some reject Him with the opinion that He is judging them through the Soviet departure. There has been a sharp increase in satanic worship, for the Satanists have presented a very clear message: "You will go to hell, but at least today Satan will give you something to eat." The pastor believes that God is judging the country because many have professed Christ but abandoned Him in their quest for comfort. I ended the conversation saying, in effect, "God's will be done." There is no salvation in governments, in men, or in moving to a wealthier area. We must continue to point people to Jesus. This pastor was proof of the abundant life with Jesus as his focus, for he had not missed a meal nor slept one night on the street. Having said all that, I am reminded that Peter said, "I do not possess silver and gold, but what I do have I give to you" (Acts 3:6). It is easy to spiral into a false guilt over what we have that others do not, but that is not the issue. Peter had seen human need and its accompanying belief that there is nothing that money will not fix, but Peter knew better. Many times a pastor will allow me to speak in his church when he does not really care about the message of Christ as life. This is made evident when I talk to him about Jesus and he continues to turn the conversation to how bad things are, what his family or church needs, the shame of not finishing the construction of the building, and other tangible necessities. When a conversation will not turn to

Christ, I know the motive is to secure silver and gold, but I do not care. I want to facilitate ministry to the weak, even if it is only for the one suffering person who cannot understand how Christ can keep him in perfect peace. If other motives have dictated that I am given an opportunity to speak, that is fine, for I have my own motive: to present the God of all comfort to any who will listen.

I met with a wealthy industrialist who has taken every advantage of the new situation without the control of the Soviet Union. He loves Jesus and started a business. It is nearly impossible to move in this country without encountering the Mafia, and soon they appeared; when he resisted their advances, grenades were thrown at his house. He agreed to a meeting with them, where he looked at the Mafia boss attempting to extort payments and said, "The money I would have given you I will be giving to the Lord!" Well, this took the boss back a bit, and he responded, "I, too, think about God!" "Well, then you will understand that I will be giving my portion to the Lord!" The boss did not quite believe in God to that level. This was the first Mafia boss to approach him. The second was from a rival gang, and the industrialist told him the same thing. In only a few weeks the two Mafia bosses killed one another in a feud, and the industrialist has not had any further trouble. He continues to give to God what the bosses had demanded.

We visit a victim of the Soviet Holocaust. His story, unfortunately, is typical of what is heard concerning the Stalinist approach to people. It is difficult to understand how we can hear so much about what the Nazis did to the Jewish people and so little of what the Soviets did for a much longer period and on a grander scale. This slight, elderly man walks bent over and has a twinkle in his eye. Before he begins his story (with a heavy accent), he first goes to the wall to take off a black-and-white photo of a family taken in the mid- to late 1930's. He begins with a soft smile, "My house was bombed. I went to visit it and found nothing. I was told that the Russian family down the block had gone through the rubble. I went to their home, and they were kind enough to give me this photograph. It is the only memento I have of my family. No other possession." He then begins to describe with great delight each person pictured. His father was a very good man. His Uncle Moses was in the soap business. A brother studied chemistry in Germany until Hitler began the persecution of the Jews. The year 1941 ushered in the Soviet occupation and also the first persecution of the Jews in his country, the first "deportation." Of course, not only the Jews suffered; many other countrymen were also deported during this "Reign of Terror." He notes his country had been the best place in Europe to dwell as a Jew. The government encouraged Jewish schools and the speaking of Yiddish, and business opportunities abounded; there simply was not any discrimination. Too, the country was becoming an industrial power, and its neighbors sought many of its goods. He continues with his story. "At four a.m. the KGB [then known as the NKVD] appeared at the door telling all of us to get our documents and come to their headquarters. We were processed; the men were put on trains and taken to a remote area of Siberia for Soviet mining. They left with only the clothes on their backs and were not to be seen again." He pauses long enough to have the pain and loss of the event sweep over him. "The women and children were taken to a different part of Siberia, where we worked eighteen hours a day and were given only this much bread daily," motioning that the size of the bread was only about as large as a third of his hand. After four years of imprisonment, he was returned to his country, but after just a few months, the KGB returned. He is much more of an expert on the KGB than he would like to be. At KGB headquarters he was told that once again he would be deported to Siberia. This time the reason was that his father was an industrialist, which was not true. His father was a hard-working and well-educated man, but not an industrialist. They would not believe they had confused him with another, and the final condemning factor was that his first name, a Jewish name, was not on the approved list of names. When a child was born and registered, his or her name had to be approved as part of the Russification plan. He had taken the name of his grandfather. He made an appeal to a Jewish woman who was part of the deportation machine (yes, there were Jews that betrayed Jews, just as in the time of Jesus). She told him to go; she would check into matters, and if he were not the son of the industrialist, he would be returned. To his surprise, after four more years in Siberia, he was called to the headquarters and given documents that allowed him to return to his country of origin. The rest of his family perished in Siberia. His response to a question was interesting, considering that he is Jewish. "What do you see as the greatest problem in America?" "The greatest problem is that you have gotten away from the Bible. Americans are Christians, and they need to follow the Bible!" I asked what the purpose of suffering is, but he would not answer me. Next, "Why does God allow suffering?" Again, I did not get a response. I believe that the effect of Stalinist oppression on people is that there are areas of thought into which they simply dare not venture and have been trained not to think. It is terrible. However, he made a great comment. Every day, in every school, in every place, they were taught that the Soviets, through compassion, had come to deliver them from the deception of thinking that there is a God. Yet, after nearly sixty years of indoctrination, as soon as the Soviets left, the people in wholesale numbers turned to God.

I am traveling with a very joyful brother who is very knowledgeable about many things and a real asset to many ministries. He told of being in the capital city as a kid and seeing the starving Russian troops of WWII come through; when the children threw a piece of bread on the ground in front them, the soldiers would all scamper for it like dogs. The capital city fell in 1944. His family was to escape on a boat, but before boarding, the boat was bombed. They could leave over a bridge, but the bridge got bombed. The bridge was repaired, and they got out on the last train to Germany, though the bridge was being bombed even as the train crossed over the water. At every place they thought they would die. They were taken to a German concentration camp; conditions in the camp were miserable. He received each day a "German Brick," a piece of bread. Pumpkins were smashed, boiled in water, and served as swill. "To this day if I taste pumpkin, the nightmare returns." He remembers looking through the fence as a boy of ten and watching a large German make some of the scantily clad women prisoners run in circles in the freezing weather; any women too weak to run would fall down and be beaten to death. Eventually the German officials discovered that his father had been forcibly drafted by the Germans to dig trenches on the front lines. This meant that he, his two brothers, and his mother were friends and were allowed to leave the camp. His mother and father had made an agreement that if he lived through the front-lines experience and returned home but did not find her, she was to have buried, in a particular place in the garden, a jar that contained any information about where she might be. The father found the information and traveled to Germany to find the family. But in the meantime, the boys and their mother left the concentration camp and were moved into a fifteen-by-fifteen-foot shack, still with no food or water. As the Russians neared they decided to flee on a two-month journey into Western Germany; the brothers, being very sick with tuberculosis, were strapped to a board with a wheel mounted on the front; they had to be pushed. This man could tell one miracle after another about how God kept them. They walked each day, eating grass, drinking the water in the trenches, and digging through the dirt for a frozen potato. He would often see people cutting the flesh off of animals that had died along the way. It was a long road filled all day and all night with refugees. If the Russian airplanes would see people on the road, they would drop their bombs, making everyone scurry toward the ditch. One night they asked a farmer if they could sleep in his home, but he angrily turned them away. The farmer's abuse ended up being a blessing, for that night his farm was bombed, killing everyone there. Once a farmer gave all the children milk. They finally arrived in a city close to Berlin and watched as the city was completely destroyed. The Russians that entered with the allies at the end of the war would call to the refugees, "Come to Mother Russia with us! She will take care of you." He said that all of those who went were never heard from again. He ended on a very positive note. "The nightmares stopped when, at age fifteen, I asked Jesus into my heart. I was flying high, carrying my Bible, talking to everyone about Jesus." Again, truth is not only preached but also demonstrated. There is nothing that the nearness of Jesus will not cure.

The head of the Salvation Army here was given a farm by Christians in a Scandinavian country; this place is reminiscent of manna, something from the dew, because the Lord provided it to sustain His children. As we headed back to the Salvation Army building, the director told me her story. Her father and mother were the first Salvation Army officers in this country. In 1941 the KGB came and shot her father to death. The two daughters were transported to the capital city and separated for months from their mother, who had been left on a farm with the other smaller children. Her mother kept praying, and God gave her a verse, "Though a thousand fall on your right and left, you will not be harmed." Soon she joyfully discovered that the two girls were still living. They went through the Soviet times suffering just like everyone else. In 1989, things began to loosen; a Swedish man wanted to interview her mother, who did not notice the microphone and just kept talking about the Salvation Army in the early days. The man went to Sweden and published the article. Soon people were calling on her to reopen the Salvation

Army. By this time she was 95 years old, and this is where the present director, her daughter, came in. She donned a uniform and went to the officials to register the ministry for the second time in her country's history. They allowed her to register, and since the old Salvation Army building had been destroyed, the government gave them the present building, formerly a children's hospital. In the last eleven years this place has experienced one miracle after another. We bought some electric heaters, since they are staying and working in this large building with no heat. You would think that as cold as it gets, there would not be any mosquitoes. Not so! They can bite right through a person, and they bite all night.

We are to meet our friends at a Chinese restaurant. This city of the former Soviet Union was not built for restaurants or the peddling of capitalistic goods, so now the lower apartments of the high-rise buildings (they are everywhere) have been converted into retail space. It all looks deceiving and makes for difficulty telling where things are located. We do find the restaurant, and the food is scrumptious. We are close to China, and someone has definitely learned how to cook. We have a private room and the conversation is wonderful and Christ-centered. Our host does not have a lot of money, but this meal will be well over $100 U.S. in a country where a doctor makes $25 per month. I am told that he is pleased to do it. The topic of government comes up; I do not comment on their opinions of what the U.S. does or does not do but respond with a different observation: "Can you imagine that our governments would have had us fighting each other? I cannot bear the thought of killing those brothers and sisters with whom I am now in fellowship." That observation kills the discussions concerning governments, for we clearly see the insanity of the world and its system. Our governments would have us all moving into pride to defend their ways, just as they allow us a measure of the deception that we have something to say. In reality, it is money that has something to say. Well, amen! We do not predominantly belong to these kingdoms. One of the fellows asks many questions, and then reveals, "When I get home, I have a problem. The tax/mafia men will expect a payment. I do not have the money. What am I to do? All the talk of letting Jesus live through me sounds good here at the table. However, tomorrow is another story!" I answer, "Brother, you have a history with the Lord. Have you not found yourself in this place before, and has not God provided? Our goal is not comfort, but the revelation of Jesus. Go home, trust Jesus, and watch what happens. I will see you next year, and you will tell me that everything went just fine." He had to agree that Jesus had helped him out of so many jams before.

As we walk along, a young pastor describes an intriguing part of his country's history. It seems that after Russian soldiers entered the area in WWII, the national partisans continued to fight on. Over a thousand of them moved to the swamps, which only a few could even navigate. The group lived and fought from the security of this place. They had a priest; they were married, but they left the swamp only to attack the Russians. Finally Russians assembled between three- and four-thousand troops to attack the partisans of the swamp. It was a disaster for the Russians, for these loyalists had German "bone cutters," machine guns that put out several hundred bullets per minute. They even said that they felt sorry for the Russian soldiers, who had the KGB marching behind them driving them by force into battle with machine guns. If they hesitated, they were shot in the back, and as they proceeded toward the swamp, the nationalists shot them. It was a horrific loss for the KGB. In time the countrymen knew that they had to get out of the swamp, so a few days later they mounted a false offensive to move the Russians to the point of attack, thus opening a way of escape for the rest of the partisans. Many who thus escaped divided up into smaller bands to fight against the Russians. Once the Russians were winning the war and offered these loyalists "amnesty," it included torture, interrogation, and a prison sentence. The leader of the group of partisans refused to turn himself in and, in fact, went on for another six years fighting the Russians by himself. Eleven years earlier Russians had gone to his house, run the children out, and hung his wife by the neck over a well. They made sure her corpse hung for several days. This one leader continued to fight until captured in 1955. He was hung in the city square and his body left for many days as a reminder. When they finally took his body to the swamp and buried it, a young woman watched where they buried him and kept the place in her memory by continuing to mark it for nearly fifty years. She finally told some of the partisan survivors, after they were released from their imprisonment, where the body now lay. They took the body in order to stage a great burial and make a political statement. There were many people at the funeral, even three of the man's four children that had escaped to the neighbors' place when their mother was hung. Now, this is where the young pastor relating this history enters in. He was struggling along with no one willing to listen to the Gospel, no results, and no help, when out of the blue he was invited to speak at the funeral in his area. Famous people from all over the country attended, and this turned out to be his open door to preach the Gospel to many. The death of the partisan fifty years previously actually gave birth to the church in that area; many were willing to listen to the pastor who had spoken forth the Gospel to so many on such an important occasion.

A young lady describes in detail the points at which God spoke to her and set her free over the weekend. She said, "None of us knew what to expect from the conference! We had never gone to such a thing. But God had prepared my heart and I am free." Amen! She was always free in Christ but has now come into the revelation of it. She had been controlled by others and at the conference began to experience what it meant to recognize that Jesus is in control. She was beginning to judge her emotions so that they would not rule over her. She told us of her mission work each summer in a remote area, where the Muslims are making a push in little communities by building large new mosques, and they continue to persecute Christians. This lady's group worked for a week to show a movie about two men—one a believer and the other not—who climbed a mountain. In the end, the Muslim mayor said that the movie could not be shown. The believers yielded but prayed. In a few days someone from the government wrote the mayor a letter explaining that he had no legal grounds for preventing the showing of the movie. She said that it is hard to move around in that country, and citizens of her own country are granted a one-month tourist visa but must register each week with the militia so their movements can be tracked at all times; the militia is stopping all evangelistic meetings. However, half of the cities to which they go refuse to allow them to register. This young lady shares many stories about the suffering Russian believers and made a great observation: "The people need to be loved." At the camps for the youth, she will go to each child at night, give a hug, and say that she loves him or her. "I have never had a child want to go home early."

I would like to share the story of when my interpreter in a former Soviet bloc country first went back there years after his family had escaped the country during WWII when he was a baby. The Lord led him back there for ministry once he was an adult in the early 1970's, at which time it was nearly impossible to get in. It took six months to get a visa, and then they told him that he could not come from Sweden, since he happened to be standing in Sweden. He had kept abreast of the KGB and knew the name of the colonel in charge at that time, so when the Soviet embassy in Sweden told him he could not gain entry into his native country, he looked at the fellow and said, "If I do not have my visa today, I will call Colonel So-and-So, and by this time tomorrow your head will be on a platter." The man disappeared, returned, and said, "In one hour you will have your visa." He went to a Soviet bloc country neighboring the country of his destination and was immediately met by KGB officials, who put him in the first-class train to his country. As soon as everyone went to sleep, he went to the back of the train with the peasants. When the train arrived, he ditched the KGB and appeared at the hotel. The woman at the desk realized that he had ditched the KGB, and despite knowing it would mean trouble, gave him a room. Soon a KGB escort appeared to spend the week with him. The KGB agent was confused; no one could understand how the fellow knew the colonel, how he came to the country, how he could speak the language perfectly, nor whom or what he was. Was he a spy? Who was he? The KGB official took him out and, in a feeble attempt to get him drunk, got drunk himself. My interpreter got on the trolley car with him, but when the car stopped, he got off and went into the center of the city to try to meet with true countrymen. Immediately met by a gang, he thought, *Well, I am done for.* However, this happened to be hooligans that were fighting Russian bands of criminals. The gang leader, with a shaven head, had just been released from prison. It seems that he and his bunch were crossing a bridge when met by the Russian militia. The gang threw them off the bridge, but the gang leader noticed that one of the officers was drowning, so he jumped in and saved the Russian man's life. This resulted in two years of prison. The gang befriended my coworker, and he was able to meet with his ancestors. Since then there have been so many more trips and stories.

In the morning we are to speak in a village that had been a Soviet collective farm. I will not bore you with the stupidity of that idea. In Kansas, one farmer could work 640 acres; on a Soviet collective farm, the same area of land took 400 laborers. We arrive at the center of the communal farm, a "city" of at one time 800 now shrunk to 400. The fellow who drove us here is actually prospering on about 100 acres, but probably not for long, because the EU is moving in swiftly and will snuff out the small farmer. The driver is a genuine believer and has advertised the seminar for months. The topic is addictions, an apt issue for a place where so many people are alcoholics. Since misery loves company, I just wish you could see how terrible everything here looks. These places really cannot easily be improved, and I often wonder at the person who introduced concrete and white bricks to the Soviet system. Of course, those working on building the structures were passive/aggressive in their work ethics, and I cannot blame them. They suffered under a stupid system, but if they were to complain, it would be very cold at their next stop: Siberia. I have one friend who did his job as "unto the Lord" and for five years straight got the award for "Worker of the Year." Then it was discovered that he was a preacher, and they took him in front of the very people he stood before to get the awards to have them stripped away. Wow! What a morale booster.

Asia

One Asian country is very corrupt, with most of the income coming from military shakedowns and drugs from an area profuse in heroin. I was shown what had been a cemetery from which relatives or friends of all of the people buried there had to dig up the dead and move them, because the government had struck a deal with some foreign businessmen to buy the land for a hotel. The teak tree is one of the richest commodities in this country, so the military proclaimed that all teak trees belong to them. One church administrator told me of the military's coming right into the front yard and cutting a sixty-foot tall, eighty-year-old teak tree. The internet is illegal here; all faxes, phone calls, and computer activities are screened. A pastor told us of the days when church meetings were not allowed and he made a place in his yard for 450 Christians to gather. Once he had a band playing Christian music and held baptisms; many of the neighbors came to watch. The next day the police arrived to question what had been going on. He had planned the service to occur on his birthday, because the government allows birthday parties. He told the police that he was having a birthday party, so he was warned to tell them about the next party.

I have just finished a three-hour conversation with a retired electrical engineer who heads a ministry in the Catholic churches called "Releasing the Spirit." He parted with this advice: "In all literature promoting your meetings, you must advertise at the very top, 'NOT FOR MUSLIMS.'" He then related all the discrimination that exists for someone who converts from Islam to Christianity and can no longer use the name Mohammed Ben (Son of Mohammed). A name change requires a trip to the government office; however, the government does not allow a name change. Trying to change sends a signal to all other Muslims that this person converted; he will no longer be allowed entrance into the better schools or granted promotions within the government. A lie is a parasite on the back of truth. A lie cannot support the world; only truth can support it. The Muslims are able to discriminate against the believing world because our Lord commands us to love our enemies. If the Christian realm ceased to exist and all in the West were allowed by conscience to treat the Muslim world the way they behave toward us,

307

the Muslim system would soon collapse. It is not Muslims who are buying all of the oil that allows desert nations to survive and thrive. Interesting that everyone needs us, and everyone needs us to be Christian.

I stayed with a wonderfully interesting family, whose grandparents had first come to this place from India after a family feud; all of their belongings were in a sack. They were so poor that the mother would cook rice each day and feed it to her children, while she would merely drink the water in which it was cooked. One of their daughters displeased this couple by fleeing an arranged marriage to marry a Chinese man, who also was very poor and was an alcoholic; this couple had five sons, and these are the topnotch men with whom I stayed on a plantation. The eldest son received a college scholarship to be educated in the U.S. He always sent the living-expense allowance from the scholarship back home to his family. Once he returned home he became an accountant in charge of the merger of two of the largest companies. With the money thus made, he educated his four brothers. The second son showed up at the plantation—owned by the older brother's company—and worked his way from field hand to CEO in ten years. The third brother was educated in diesel mechanics in the U.S. and runs all of the equipment; the youngest brother manages what is now a large family estate. The second brother became a Christian; his brothers and mother followed, though conversion to Christianity is illegal in this Muslim-ruled country. Because the estate is in the frontier and employs so many workers—many of whom are illegal aliens from six other Asian countries—the hostile government does not know that the main goal of this vast corporate structure is to reach men for Christ; most of the managers are also teachers and evangelists, and the Gospel is presented in meetings to which the workers are invited. It is obvious that this plantation is owned and managed by committed believers; normally the plantation workers fend for themselves and build shacks. Here a very nice village has been constructed with efficiency houses— painted and decked out with flowers—plus a grocery store, a canteen, and a play area.

One fellow was a government official and a believer, something quite odd for the country that houses the world's largest Pagoda and outlaws preaching. His father is from a chiefly family, so they had a large home. The British forces during WWII took over their home as headquarters for 300 troops. After a Japanese assault, the British troops retreated. His mother and father were placed against bamboo poles; the Japanese commander took out his pistol to murder them both. His mother, holding him in her arms (he was only nine months old), asked if she could speak before being shot. The commander granted permission. She explained that she had taken excellent care of the British because they were guests, but guests of a different color. The Japanese were a similar color to her and her husband and would get even better treatment. She found favor and was spared. Next, the British came in aircraft to bomb the Japanese from the very place they had previously found shelter. However, this man's older brother was a member of the bomber crew. When he realized the target was his own home, he drew his pistol and very apologetically said, "I have fought for you, and now you would kill my family? You must turn the plane around or I will kill you all!" They called off the air attack and instead sent in artillery. The house was mildly damaged, and the Japanese fled. He believes that it is a miracle that he is alive, and that since he was dedicated for the service of the Lord, he must serve. After thirty years as a public official, he almost died in a plane. The engines cut off and the Buddhist pilots called for everyone to pray before they died. Everyone was praying, and he shouted, "Jesus, deliver us!" Immediately the engines started. He quit his job and started his service to the Lord. Since his brother had started translating the Bible in their language, he has committed to completing the task, and, as descendant of a chief, he has the useful ability to call the people together.

We stopped in at the headquarters of an internationally known ministry. It is interesting to note that this ministry can function without being able to do outreach. The believers have discovered that during certain Hindu festivals, nearly everyone is having a meeting of one kind or another, so they are able to have their meeting in a large, open-air place for a few hours without drawing special attention to themselves, a quick hit and run. The same plan works well in the villages. Go speak for a couple of hours, pack up, and completely leave town! The director observes that the Church in this country was built as people talked one-on-one to neighbors when the Lord allowed. But now it seems that organizations only want to work with the big, spectacular meetings.

Often in countries ruled by those of non-Christian persuasion, believers simply cannot go about sharing freely; they must pray and count on their unspoken witness. I met four men who rented a building, remodeled it, hired some teachers, and opened a school where there was none. They then gave scholarships to the children who could not pay. When the people discovered that Christians were in charge, they became very angry, believing it was a trick to convert their children. However, the school never mentioned Jesus; they just started teaching and serving. Remember how St. Francis of Assisi said something like, "Preach the Gospel in every way, in every place, and if you absolutely have to, say something"? This is the approach of the men who founded this school. After eight years they shared the Christmas story with only the teachers, and a few accepted Christ. One of the men lives in the neighborhood, and the Hindus call him a god simply because of his lifestyle. After time has passed, the people now say that these Christians are good men doing a good thing. Little by little they are making inroads. I have a good time of sharing and prayer with these men; when I explain that I am a missionary that evangelizes Christians, they look surprised until I explain how Christians lose focus, become consumed with the things that surround Jesus, and forget Jesus. The head nodding showed that they understood.

One pastor was called to the home of a wealthy converted Hindu, upon his death, to perform a burial according to the man's wishes. Before the pastor could arrive, the Hindu relatives grabbed the body, took it to the river, made a stack of wood, and cremated it. Upon learning of this, the pastor returned home, but when he arrived home, the rebel soldiers, who had gotten involved, called and asked that he come back to the house for the burial. He knew the reason they wanted him to come back was to kill him, so he stayed away. One of the captains called him to

311

obtain by the threat of killing his family several thousand rupees. He sold his motorcycle, borrowed some money, and Christian brothers gave some more. He met with some of the guerrilla leaders and told them that he would pay them only the sum he had, but if it were not enough, or if the soldiers were going to come back for more later, they must kill him now. One of the men said that he had been a Christian but was now following the guiding principles of the rebel faction. The soldiers were friendlier once they got the money, tried to persuade him that they were helping the people, and sent him on his way. It is the last that he has heard from them. What is vexing is that some of the pastors are sympathizers to this insurrectionary cause and turn in other believers.

The Christians are oppressed in this country—as in any Muslim country—in so many covert ways, from job discrimination to building permit denials. One amendment to the constitution institutes the death sentence for anyone speaking against the Muslim faith, and another dictates a death sentence for conversion to the Christian faith. It therefore baffles me that these believers are all so proud of their country, a nation that does everything possible to make their lives miserable. They truly are giving honor to an antichrist government. I admire their faith and resilience.

A church here is not legal, so the people start schools and then let them double as churches. As we arrive at the walled building, I cannot help but notice the armed guards that surround the place. To avoid any mishaps, the guards have been hired to keep the meetings safe. I visit one of the elder's houses where we are served tea, and I have an opportunity to meet with the pastor. Most pastors here work another job besides the one at the church. This fellow worked for and retired from the government, which has given him some contacts that have proven to be very valuable. I am asked, "What will you be saying about Islam?" I responded, "I do not preach Islam!" "Yes, but what will you say that is negative about Islam?" "Again," I said, "I do not preach Islam. To say something for Islam or to say something against Islam is still making Islam the focus. I will only be talking about Jesus." That settled the issue.

The pastor tells of an adopted daughter. It seems that many years ago, before the rebel war, he went to a village and found a girl whose parents had died, and he adopted her. When he was leaving the village with her, she was captured. From that day, it has been impossible to find her. Since the war has ended, he has gone back to the village to find her. He was successful, but her story was not. She is now a young woman and related what had happened to her. It seems that the insurgents took her as a slave. When she reached a certain age, she was presented with a choice. She could either pick one of the guerrillas to be her husband or be passed throughout the camp from man to man. She chose one man and began to live with him. In the passing of time, they had a son. Her son was eating a peanut and choked to death, while her husband was killed in the war. The pastor has purchased an 8,500 square-foot plot of land that she can use to sow crops. This will yield enough income for her to exist for six months. He was very, very happy to find that she was still alive and, more importantly, still moving ahead in the Lord.

I was told an interesting story of when soldiers were going into the villages and forcing the Christians to join their anti-Christ regime. Nearly all of the believers refused. Then a leading man in a village, a believer, was ordered to join and told that he would be appointed commander over many men. The fellow talked to the pastor and said he was wondering what to do. The pastor said, "Tell all of the Christians that are commanded to join the forces to join. God will work through you to save the churches and many believers." The pastor made it very clear, "I did not speak these things on my own, but it was the Holy Spirit through me." The man accepted the assignment and was praised by the leadership for his effectiveness as an officer. Any time the soldiers were going to burn a church and kill the Christians, the man would go, and the soldiers would yield to him and leave the believers alone because of his reputation. Believers could have debated the merits of being pacifists for years. The pastor heard and spoke what he heard from the Lord. I am only reporting to you what I hear and see, something that is never reported by the media. They are the secret stories of unknown saints.

Pacific Islands

I witnessed what was obviously the work of western lobbyists trying to change the constitution of a traditional country's government to embrace sinful behavior. At a rally I was the first to the platform. I spoke on the Way, the Way written into our being, Jesus. I spoke on the need for systems to support the people. Many alternative systems nestle themselves around the Christian system and claim to be better; however, when the Christian system is removed, the others crumble. I explained that Christianity is never on trial, because life proves it. The sinful behavior is not on trial, because sin and punishment are one and the same. However, the government is on trial. We do not have the authority, so we do not have the responsibility, but it does. Finally, I ended with a plea to the churches. "What gets your attention will get you. Do not let this issue become the focus of the Church. We are called to be redemptive, not to be anti-sin preachers." There were three more speeches (and lots of music) after mine. The last speaker was a letdown. My personal experience is that every time someone stands up and proclaims to be God's apostle and God's mouthpiece, it spells trouble. I knew everyone from the Hindu to the sinners would bear the brunt of his condemnation. I just wished he would stop. Well, amen! After the rally, the church folks decided to march around the city park, requesting that as a foreigner I stay away, since they did not want the government to view me as protesting against it. They decided to do a "Jericho" march, lining up eight across and walking around the city park seven times very solemnly and without making a sound. When they came to a stop in front of the platform, a trumpet sounded with a deafening blast; and all the people, with arms stretched upward, in unison shouted, "God hear our prayer!" Then the band erupted as the crowd sang, "I went to the enemy and took back my soul from him." It was all truly moving to watch.

I went by a house today that is magnificent. It is interesting how the government came into possession of the house. The owner had worked in this country, made a lot of money, and paid just as much in taxes. He got back at the government for the incredibly high taxes by giving them the house with the stipulation that it be maintained but never sold. It costs $400,000 annually to maintain! Now the government gets a taste of its own medicine by always having to pay him for the upkeep.

Africa

Entering one country, we were packing forty pounds of donated medication in old suitcases; as usual, we are never sure how the Lord will get the supplies through customs. What happened in this country was truly amazing. My father and I were standing in line to get our passports checked behind an African woman who was carrying two bags and a baby; we offered to carry her bags until she was ready to leave the secured area. We could see ahead that the customs officials were checking everything. She revealed that she was only in this country for a funeral, that her relatives worked in airport security, and that if we would like, she would take us with her; we could bypass customs altogether. Hopefully we did not look too gleeful as we accepted her offer and walked out of the airport with a perfect stranger sent by God. Our suitcases held thirty-six thousand dollars worth of medication that could well have fallen into black-market hands. As it was, it was safely delivered to a church preparing for a medical-missions outreach to villages.

After a seminar in a church, several people came up to say the same thing: they were so discouraged with the oppressive government, inflation, and the uncertainty of the future that they had not realized how much they needed encouragement. They recognized that there was hope when Jesus was the focus. Later I was sitting in a home listening to a couple talk of crime, unemployment, the fear of death, and reprisals from a government apparently pitted against the citizenry. I thought to myself, *I want to mention Jesus and see if the serious mood changes.* I said, "An African, Andrew Murray, stressed the verse, 'I will keep him in perfect peace whose eyes are stayed on Me.' There is no peace when eyes are on government, the thief, the murderer, or the future. Peace arrives when our eyes are on Him. God deals with man's trouble spot, the heart: 'Let not your heart be troubled.'" I watched as everyone smiled, the mood changed, and lightness was in the air. God dealt with the most precious thing to Abraham, that being Isaac, knowing that if Isaac were dealt with, all lesser things could be laid aside. God deals with our Isaacs; mine is any prolonged looking to anything other than Christ. Even in the worst situation, turning to Him, dwelling on Him, and looking at His goodness brings light.

On a long drive on what was by African standards a surprisingly good road, we are in a caravan of cars traveling to the home of the present leader of a church. All of the pastors wear a white collar and white robe today, because as we travel there will be numerous roadblocks set up by the police to extort money. They will spend very little time with the pastors once they notice the white robes, because they know pastors will not pay bribes; this means our trip will not be delayed as much. This works well except at one sentry post, where the police accuse us of having a car with forged papers. Again, it is simply an attempt to wrest money, but this diversion takes some time. At last we were on our way, and my pastor friend said, "We must be

317

careful; they will shoot a person and say that he was trying to do something illegal. When the person is dead, he cannot defend himself." Another pastor chimed in and told of a friend who was in a neighboring country when civil war broke out. "He was fleeing with four other pastors, and all were wearing robes. The soldiers asked who they were, and all said they were pastors. The head soldier asked, 'Then where are your Bibles?' The pastor's friend showed his New Testament, but was asked, 'If you are a pastor, then why do you not carry the whole Bible?' The man responded, 'I was escaping and could not run with something heavy.' The head soldier sat the man aside and asked the same questions of the other four, who unfortunately did not have Bibles and were shot; the first man was told he could pass." As we passed through the next city, I was told, "This place is very hostile to Christians; its king openly practices witchcraft. When he dies, many people will go missing, for he must be buried with many heads." I look over our driver's headrest to get a quick glance at the fuel gauge, hoping there are no unexpected stops in this city.

It was discovered that our taxi driver was a Christian. He told me several interesting stories of when a notoriously cruel tyrant was president and Christians were persecuted, which our driver thought was generally a good thing for the Church. He told me of a soldier's coming into one of the churches, his gun ready to fire, and announcing, "Anyone who does not want to die for the faith in Jesus has only a few minutes to get out of the building!" About half of the people got up and ran. As they were running, the group that stayed behind was yelling out, "Tell our families how we died!" The soldier then said to the group that remained, "I know you are devoted to Christ, and true Christians never cause trouble at their secret meetings. Go on worshipping. As for those who ran, my soldiers have already shot them; they are the ones I do not trust." I asked if the Christians ever fought back. "No, we gathered together in secret meetings and prayed, and prayed, and prayed until God removed the man." The world is a better place because the Christians do not return evil for evil.

We rush off to the private office of the vice-president of the country. I am skeptical of politicians here. Remember that the continent with the most billionaires with Swiss bank accounts is said to be Africa, yet the general population is ground into dirt-poor conditions. As always, if I judge, I will judge wrongly. The vice-president is an ordained pastor, a gentle and humble man who says, "We want Christian teaching. Our schools must return to Christ. Where Christ is, there is less crime and more love. I will help you in any way you need: invitations, customs, whatever." He was a deviation from the crooked politician, for truly he loved the Lord and wanted that for his people, seeing it as not only his hope, but the only hope. I wanted to put him in a suitcase and take him home with me! We would do well with this fellow in politics in the U.S.

A couple helping us get around were missionaries for five years before the man took a job with the embassy as chief of disbursement for humanitarian funds, or in other words, ascertaining that the money actually goes to the cause for which it is given. It would not be far off to say that less than five percent of the donated money for helping Africans actually gets distributed to the target recipients. The people of Africa are industrious, yet their governments are generally greedy and push the people down at every turn. There are exceptions, of course, but few. I find it frustrating when government traps people who have next to nothing. In this particular nation, all they might dream of affording is a bicycle, so what does the government do but slap a 110% duty on every bicycle and then require bicycle riders' licenses. Men are stationed at the side of the road to ask each cyclist to show his license. If one cannot be provided, the roadside "officer" is allowed to take the bike, and the owner must pay a fine. This activity is permitted because it forces the people to buy a license. However, the government still wanted more, so the bike owners also had to buy a registration for each bike and carry that with them all of the time. It went still further by mandating that even the person who is just riding the bike and does not own it needs to buy a registration. There appears to be no end to it. This government was actually given forty tractors by an aid agency; they were brought in by ship. The border guards said the tractors could not be unloaded unless a 100% duty were assessed. The shipmen told the guards just to confiscate the tractors, which would have accomplished the same purpose of gifting the government. The government would not agree. Aid agency representatives asked if the guards could take half of the tractors, sell them, and with the proceeds pay the taxes on the other half, which could then be brought into the country as a gift. This request was also denied; the government really wanted the money for the assessed duty. At last the ship had to move on; it was being taxed for each day it was in port. The agency gave up, and the ship went into the open waters and dumped the forty tractors, where they sit today at the bottom of the ocean, charitable donations that are now an ironic silent testimony to greed. One pastor was given a motorcycle to assist him in his work. It was caught up in paperwork for six years, and when he finally got the scooter, it was completely useless. If only the governments would ease up on the people a little bit, everyone could be more productive.

I ask a missionary to tell his story. He grew up in South Africa; his forefathers came from Europe over 400 years ago. The white settlers were moving north at the same time that Africans were moving south. They met in the north of South Africa, a land that was not filled with indigenous peoples. People from both races can say they arrived in the area at pretty much the same time. South Africa would have been too cold for the Africans to settle early on. This fellow was in the youth party in favor of apartheid and elected to the national council. Once a man came from Europe to tell the South Africans that apartheid was dead. This fellow actually organized a protest at the airport to tell the man to go home. However, he next got involved in missions and so enjoyed it and its call to evangelize Africa. As he began to fellowship with the Africans, he became increasingly unhappy with apartheid and began to speak against it. This caused no little persecution from his former cohorts. He stood fast, and when it looked as though apartheid would end—but at the cost of a civil war—he was struck by a passage in the Beatitudes, "Blessed are the peacemakers." It was then that he threw himself into reconciliation efforts to the point of stressing his body into severe sickness. He was nearly killed too many times to count, but in the end, a peaceable end to apartheid was worked out. He made the observation that there were people who for years made their living being anti-apartheid, and now that the system is gone, they do not know what to do, so they are constantly looking for something to be "anti" about. He enjoys the fact that South Africa is now a democracy, the thing for which he worked so hard. Many of the South Africans would like to get away from the stigma of apartheid, just as Germans would like to be free of their Nazi stigma. He told me of one black friend who went into a store, and the clerk said, "What do you want, Kaffer?" *Kaffer* is a derogatory name for a black. The black man was highly educated and just smiled, later saying, "I feel sorry for the man." I do, too, for one day Jesus will make the statement that He was naked and not clothed, hungry and not fed, and the man will say, "When did I see you in need?" Then Jesus will remind him of the Kaffer rebuffed in his shop. A pastor that I really like (well, it is easy to like everyone around here with all the smiles) was sharing about the struggles that he had during the time that he spoke out against apartheid. A "secret" organization existed among the churches to support the apartheid stand. Those pastors who did not go along would be slandered and accused of mundane offenses, and the congregation would begin to turn on them. He was just shocked when a leader of his own church came, revealed his affiliation with the group, and threatened him by saying, "I will lie about you!" Amen, I can see the difficulty of shifting gears for someone raised in the atmosphere of apartheid, for we all like to believe that what we have been taught was true. But in the Church it is so wrong to harbor men who threaten with lies. After writing a few more anti-apartheid articles, the pastor was called to a radio station to debate on air a rightwing pro-apartheid leader. He was frightened, but prayed, and when the appointed day came, the radio broadcasters could not get the equipment working. He had to return the next week, but this time they had also invited an anti-apartheid leader to help my pastor friend. It seems that the two men were really blessed and won the broadcasted argument.

Set up in the market is a witchdoctor with all the paraphernalia of the trade laid out: hairs, bowls, roots, animal parts, and, of course, plenty of whiskey to keep him drunk. We are told there are certain areas in town from which children are told to stay away; witchdoctors live there, and children do actually go missing and turn up again dead, missing body parts that were sold to other tribes and used in rituals. This is not the only place that I have heard of such things. A special brother had to leave a country for this very reason. He was counseling a psychotic boy whose family had been in the trade of human organs for a couple of generations. The brother worked with him and shared Jesus with him, and upon believing, the boy was cured. All of this was documented and put in my friend's doctoral dissertation. However, the government learned that he had documented such a thing as organ trade and froze his bank account, took his home, and gave him one day to get out of the country.

The older pastor traveling with us told of starving during wartime and leaving the protection of his home neighborhood because there was news of good fishing at the mouth of the river. He snuck out and had to swim the river to get to the other side. As he was about to reach the bank, the rebels came and started shouting for him to hurry. He came up out of the water and was immediately told to surrender his money. He had none! They threw him into a 55-gallon drum, put a lid on it, and started a fire on the lid. They assumed that the heat and pain would draw some money from him. Finally, they brought him out, bound his hands behind his back, and tied together his feet. He then let them know, "I am the last man you would want to bind." The leader of the rebels just looked at him, and his men began to become concerned; one of them said, "I know that man. He is a pastor. It is not wise to bind a man of God and incur God's wrath." Next, a higher-ranking general came and heard that a pastor had been bound; this general stood before the detainee and called for the rebel leader that had commanded him to be bound. Once the rebel leader reported in, the general took out his gun and immediately shot the leader in the head. Then he announced, "Release the pastor!" Turning to God's servant, he requested, "Pray for us." The pastor went home without any fish but with his life intact.

During a civil war one pastor went into the city for food and was captured. It took nearly five years for him to find his way back home. At one point in his captivity, the rebels were trying to teach their men how to read and write. The pastor came forward and started reading. The rebel leader was amazed and put him in charge of teaching and filling out forms. He then lived with the Arabs, took to wearing their clothes, wore a beard, and carried the beads. In this state he was allowed to begin to move freely. At long last he was able to escape and return to his home, but there he found that his wife, assuming he was dead, had remarried and was with child. The man explained that it was his fault for going to the city and not her fault that she had remarried, but he tried to persuade her to come with him. She refused, gave birth to her new husband's child, and got pregnant again. Finally, she gave the escapee his three children and moved away with her new spouse and children. I think this wound is much deeper than any other this brother received in the fourteen years of war.

Latin America

I was told a story about 24 judges put in prison at the same time for corruption. The chaplain was called by the unbelieving warden to come in and help. Naturally, the judges were isolated in one wing of the facility, since all of them had sentenced men who were currently serving time in that prison. Many of the judges came to Christ and had their wives go talk to the chaplain's wife. Even the wives came to believe. Is prison bad? If we recognize a system of belief that says God's goal in life is to break down pride so we can have eyes that see and ears that hear, is prison bad? What would a man give for his soul's salvation? Would these powerful men have ever taken time to listen to the Gospel outside of prison?

One woman I met told of the Lord's deliverance for her family when she was just a few months old; her father and mother had her on a boat as they, with over two hundred other missionaries, headed for Africa. It was before the U.S. was in WWII, and the ship that they were on was flying a British flag, since the ship carried supplies for Britain. A German boat saw the flag and sunk the boat. Up until that morning, the baby had required her bottle at exactly 5:30 a.m. Her father would go to the galley and warm the milk.

However, on this morning she awoke early, and the father had to fix the bottle earlier than he would have liked. He was back in the room by 5:30 when a shell penetrated the side of the ship and passed through the exact place in the galley where he would have been standing. There was time to evacuate the ship before it sank, and the German officer was quite surprised to discover 200-plus missionaries in his "loot."

The missionary will spend the afternoon getting permission for us to visit the people across the river. The government has the final say on who will be guests of a remote tribe. When the request has been granted, we head off in a dugout that is skimming through water just a few inches below its top rim. The river is very beautiful, and even in this low season we are seeing the rapids and the whirlpools; to fall out would spell certain doom. Another missionary coworker has met us. This mission outreach was begun by a woman in 1984; for seven years there were no conversions. The couple who invited us here came to work from 1991 to 1998, and during this time the tribe began to convert; this work in Christ continues to this day, with the result that half of the tribe has converted and there is a mission house in the village. Many of the tribes practice a strange dietary habit; when someone dies, the body is hung until sun-baked, then ground and sprinkled in food. Many parents here have killed their children. For one thing, if twins or triplets are born, they must die, for a multiple birth is seen as a curse on the village. Also, at the occasion of any birth, the witchdoctor has the power to say whether or not the baby has a soul. If not, parents must bury the child alive. One couple refused and fled to the missionary, who gave the couple sanctuary, and now the missionary is being prosecuted for helping the couple and not allowing the child to be killed. The government policies are directed by godless anthropologists and are absurd in effectively dealing with the tribes. The tribe we are visiting was enslaved to a neighboring tribe for several generations and now ekes out a living. When set free they had no land until, after a long period of merely existing, they were granted a plot 300 yards by 600 yards. A nearby plot is used to raise crops. However, to access that land they must pass through another parcel that is protected by the owner; he has offered to sell it for 150,000 in local currency, something impossible for the tribe. Alcohol is the greatest destructive force in all of the tribes (something that was not introduced by roaming foreigners; the tribes have long known how to make it). The physical system of Indians cannot metabolize alcohol like Europeans. They drink and are very prone to becoming alcoholics. Even very young children are alcoholics. From this tribe in one year fourteen men drowned while drunk and attempting to cross the river; they fell out of the dugout. Alcohol, slavery, the killing of babies, illness, and out-and-out despair had at one time shrunk this tribe to 63 people. We are told about the first convert. The missionaries noted the drunks lying around the town and one day picked up a tribesman that was passed out in his vomit. He had previously suffered a fractured leg and been in the "Indian" house in the large city downstream, waiting months for medical care that never came. He returned with a leg that only allowed him to walk with a crutch. They cleaned him up and brought him back to the tribe. He stayed with them until he was sober. Then they began to teach him pragmatically, explaining that he could do what he wanted in his own village, but the city was like a different village with rules unlike those to which he was accustomed. The rules of the city were that a person cannot be drunk and have honor, he cannot defecate on the streets or in front of the market, he would need to wear clothes in the city, and more. He found this interesting and very useful, and he determined that he did not want to be a drunk and end up dead like so many others in his tribe. The coming months proved quite difficult for this Indian. The urge to drink and the alcoholic beverages offered him became an overwhelming temptation. He therefore decided that whenever and wherever the temptation came, he would go hunt and do something useful for the village. Soon he had a different perspective in life. It was then that the Gospel was shared, and he wholeheartedly accepted Christ. Today he is the pastor, and the tribe has grown to 109.

There is a native of particular interest from a people group of 2,000; he is quite respected among his people. He became, as do many Indians, an alcoholic at the very young age of ten. He converted and could see that to help his people, he must be educated in the white man's world in order to understand them. This is because a typical meeting between whites and Indians lasted three days. The white men would present their position, and the Indians tried to understand it. On the second day, the same thing would occur. By the third day, the Indians were beginning to understand and could respond, but the whites were now frustrated and refused to come. Therefore, he is the first in his tribe to get a university degree. He is pressing the

Indians to become active and fighting the idea that the government can decide who may visit their villages, or in any way tell them what they can and cannot do. I do not see the present situation sustainable by the government. Even in this very remote corner of the world, the Indians are experiencing some globalization and will not put up with the heavy hand much longer.

India

The caste system, "abolished" by law in the 1948 constitution, is slow to disappear in the predominantly Hindu north. The whole notion of a person's being an untouchable is wicked; can you imagine the identity message that would give a person? Normally, being born into a family with a particular occupation is what would define a person as untouchable. Shoe cobblers, firewood haulers, those who mold the cow patties for burning, and more make up the lowest caste. These people are not allowed to enter the temples of the higher caste, shop in town, drink from the same well, and so on. In the south is found very little appearance of the caste system. What changed it in the south are two things: first, the predominance of believers, and second, the policy of one man, one vote. The higher caste, in wishing to be elected to office, had to relate to this large bloc of voters.

Is it possible for you, the reader, to indulge me in making an assessment? Jesus is coming, and everything is getting into play for the appearance of the Anti-Christ. In the last twenty-plus years of traveling the world I have watched as the sentiment of Anti-Christ was writing a bible. It is now being read and followed without hesitation, except by those who question it and are viewed with suspicion by the adherents, who cast doubt on their sanity. It is a very odd religion espoused by this bible and practiced by the policy mongers of the Western world. Those in the developing nations tend to follow it, assuming that its commandments must work, since the West has more and nicer cars, toys, and comfort than do they. The basis of the new book is something like this: Humanism alone is powerful, and no one shall come before it. Humanism is the evolution of Christian thinking and will take us beyond the cryptic Christ. Humans have rights, the main right being the right to sin, and any who speak against that shall be held accountable. It is all worded in a way that makes so much sense, such as that the greatest evil presence in the world has to be the U.S. that is using up all of the resources; also, conservative believers, those who call themselves "born again," are actually messing up every country. The only kind of person that needs judgment is the one that has spoken out against sin. There is no individual responsibility; thus there can only logically be others' responsibility; someone else is always responsible for misery. Therefore, in war-torn countries the focus is never to be on the men pulling the triggers, but rather on the ones that sold the men the guns. For the higher good, there will be AIDS education; never mind that there has never been a correlation made between education and a decrease in the rate of AIDS. This "AIDS education" is presented in such a way that any who had not thought of casual sex before are now giving it a first look. It is stupid to have those kinds of campaigns on remote islands, where village and family are still central in a person's outlook.

Of necessity we must have think tanks (assigned by the Anti-Christ) that can sort out all the world's ills and, of course, cast aspersion on the haves for the existence of the have-nots. We must portray lesbians in a wholesome manner to allow children with that leaning to have the freedom from social pressure to pursue such a bent. All the thinking is a half-a-click off; even the sentences that start out so well become twisted and end as anti-Christ. In all this it is the Christian, not the Hindu or Muslim, who is vilified. There is also a very odd distortion to justice, in that a person can never take law into his own hands, because that right and definition of the law is in the hands of the powers encroaching upon us; no assessment can be made that is outside their boundaries. If one were to state the truth about a continent—that it is a cesspool because of corrupt leaders and organizations that only beseech aid in order to scam funds—one would immediately be called a bigot. In the end, these people are noisy in the world, like a subculture that is very difficult to understand. As a child when I would be in the car driven by my uncle, he would decide to take us for a wild ride; he would come to a corner and say to my aunt, "Hold onto your pants, Juanita!" At that time there were no seatbelts and nothing else onto which to hold! I think we are not far away from taking an amazing ride, and it will be time to say, "Hold on to Jesus, Juanita!"

CHAPTER 8

Greater Works Shall They Do

If ever anyone had the capacity to be tempted to display spectacular signs to validate His divinity, it was Jesus. He rejected the notion of people's seeking such signs and chose to live by the great refusals in Isaiah 42. A miracle will never carry a person as far as will faith. I was told of a man who experienced miracles and then left the church, wrote a book about them, and brings Christian tourists from the U.S. to see where the miracles took place. I believe I have seen the Lord accomplish things through the course of ministry that are even more amazing than what are normally considered to be miracles: marriages restored, depression lifted, lost children returning, and enemies loved. These take place in the hidden part of a person. However, Jesus is alive and does do miracles as needed in places of His choosing. Those I have heard about as I traveled the globe are recounted in this chapter. I remember reading whole books devoted to spectacular events God allegedly performed in conjunction with revival in certain countries. When I was actually in those countries years later and would ask believers about those events, I would only receive blank looks in response. Were those events fabricated or greatly embellished for the

333

purpose of writing a book, or were the tremendous works of the Lord given only for a certain time and a certain group of believers? I cannot say with any degree of surety. I assure you that I trusted the people who gave the accounts that follow, or I would never have given the tales a second thought. Not all of the stories involve the miraculous, but they do show people who answer the call of God and by His grace and doing perform some very uncommon feats. Consistent with the rest of this book, I do maintain anonymity for the people involved, for their protection, and none of the miracles had widespread impact, at least at the time the miracle occurred. The ripple effects from those may still be impacting lives many years from now. GOD IS GREAT!

Asia

In one poor country we were shown a believer's well. For years adjacent property owners had attempted to drill wells, but none had ever been successful in finding water. When our believer friend called the well driller and told him to begin, the workman resisted, saying there was no water in the area; however, he was paid and told to drill. The Buddhist worker said, "I will drill, but first let me seek the spirits for favor." The Christian brother warned him that he would not be seeking spirits, for our friend's God was the living God. The believer pointed to a spot on the ground and said, "Drill." In short time there was such a large and copious well that the driller had to stop going deeper, even though he wanted the additional income further digging would engender.

A Christ-centered brother, a recognized friend, described his early ministry to me. At age fifteen, one of nine children in a traditional Chinese family, God touched him. He canceled plans for university and went to Bible school. He sensed God telling him to start a church in a remote area, where there is much in the way of demon worship. God told him to begin as Paul did, with the demon-possessed. Though he did not speak the language, he was soon told of a demon-possessed girl that was tied to a chair each day to keep her from ripping off her clothes and running naked through the streets. Many in the outback believe that they are to host and take care of the demons that come, a job normally assigned to the father. Before the father dies, one of the sons is to agree to take his demon and care for him. In this girl's family, the eldest son refused and then died in a tragic accident. The second son refused and fell victim to a head injury. The first daughter refused and went crazy. The demon settled on the second daughter. The minister went to the home, heard the demon yell out, and he cast it out. This girl was the first member in a congregation that grew to over thirty within a language group that had not ever before heard the gospel. This brother says, "I will rejoice when in heaven people of every language praise God and I see those people. No one knows the impact of his own life while living, but only after death. It is God Who ultimately gives us grace even to meet with Himself." Today that young girl is married with children. When the demon departed, so did poverty for the family; the demon demands care, yet by complying the family stays in poverty. My friend says, "Sometimes a believer thinks it is easier to feed a beast than try to ride it!" The flesh promises satisfaction but always leaves us in want, in poverty. The man also told me of cases where spells were cast to get someone to fall in love. He had cases where Christians came to him because they could not get a particular person out of their mind; they prayed together and the obsession would leave. Only later was it discovered that someone had cast a spell. The demonic activities in these remote regions are such that believers become accustomed to them, simply stand against them, and get on.

They have a saying in this place: "When you get old, you get the face that you deserve." I had lunch with an interesting lady with a radiant face who, forty years ago as a schoolteacher in a remote area, started a church under a large tree for the children that she taught. Only one little girl came. However, within a few years it had become a large congregation of new converts, and today it has sent out hundreds of missionaries and started many churches. It all began under a tree.

One man I met had an interesting ministry; God called him to minister to people in rural areas. He was nearly killed in a small country where he had gone to speak in a revival. As he cleared customs, he was told he could not go, because the Hindus would kill him. Sure enough, during the meeting a mob of Hindus stormed the gate; the pastor handed out clubs and asked the men to try to keep the crowd from the guest speakers. The congregation was in great fear, and they prayed and prayed. Eventually there was silence, so the church people turned off all the lights, opened the gate, and there stood the Hindus. The Christians got in cars and drove through the crowd; it appeared that the Hindus did not even see them.

I was told of a church in the interior that my friend has visited and verified with the people involved the following story. A businessman decided to first build a building and then start a church in it. When the building was completed, he advertised that the first service would be on Sunday. On Saturday night a huge crowd gathered to burn the church building. The man was at his home. On Sunday the crowd that had gathered to burn the building arrived to attend the church. They all wanted to know why there was a fence all around the church, great lights, and beings in glowing white robes. Who were they? And why was the fence gone on Sunday? This had occurred three years previously, and that church had grown to the extent that it planted three others in the interior.

I enjoy ministering among a certain denomination; like the others, they have their own spiritual subculture, certain catch phrases, movements, and preaching styles that are expected. While sometimes I cannot understand why the preaching goes where it does or what need it might meet—God knows—I like the fact that they do expect God to do something and do not limit what He can do. I also like the long prayer services. One fellow came to me and said he could not get over a neck pain, but if I would pray for him it would get healed. Well, amen! I prayed for him, and he was healed. One fellow told of a prophet that looked at him and his wife and said, "You are oppressed with a spirit of rejection." They had not previously met the prophet, but from childhood the husband had been rejected because of his parents' mixed marriage (Indian/ Chinese); at the Indian school he had been beaten up for being Chinese, and at the Chinese school he was beaten for being Indian. His wife had always been rejected by her mother, told she was never wanted, and made aware of the two different attempts to abort her. I asked, "What did the prophet do?" "Oh, he prayed for us, and the feelings of not being wanted gave way to the realization that God did want us." For freedom Christ has set us free! Another told of being in the deep jungle when a couple said, "If your God is real, pray that the monkeys that eat our garden each night would stop." He did pray, and only this garden was not attacked the next night. Over 2,000 tribal people were summoned to view the miracle, after which there were over 1,000 conversions from a prayer about monkeys.

One pastor, a very humble and sincere person, told me more about his ministry. Though Pentecostal, he does not believe that everyone experiences the Lord in the same way. He kept using the term creative. "God is so creative in bringing people to Himself." He told me of a Buddhist temple wherein Jesus appeared to the worshippers and all were converted. He said, "See? God is very creative." He told of being in a village and watching a man eat burning objects and scream. He moved toward the man and a demon said, "Stay away! This is my house, and I like it here!" He cast out the demon as the man attacked him. After the demon left, he told the man to repent, and the man told him that he liked the demon! However, many onlookers did repent and accept Christ. He also said that God has given him dreams revealing things about people in the congregation, not vague or spectacular things, but very practical, specific things. Once he dreamed that a young woman was sleeping with her boyfriend and had an abortion. He confronted her, and she wept and repented; she is now a key person on the pastoral staff. On another occasion he dreamt that one of the members, while in a distant city, joined a cult. He confronted the man and related the dream, even describing the house wherein the cult meetings took place. The man was certain that the pastor had been to the house. Once assured he had not, the fellow confessed that it was true, repented, renounced the cult, and now is a church worker also. The pastor told me he needed more education. However, I explained that operating out of gifting is much better than education. Having the Lord help him in the way He does far outperforms a degree!

We met a radiant woman who was introduced as one of the Evangelists. A converted Hindu, she was thrown out of the house upon conversion, and her husband took another woman to be his wife. The believer was penniless and homeless and constantly pressured by her own family to return to Hinduism. However, she stood fast and refused any compromise. She could not read, and though someone had given her a Bible, there was nothing that she could do with it. What she did was a real act of faith. Every morning and every evening for three years she would open the Bible, stare at it, and pray that Jesus would permit her to read it. At the end of the three years, words began to become clear to her, then more words, and more, until she was actually reading the entire body of Scripture. Everyone in the church knew that she could not read, and soon she was reading at the services. It was a great witness and encouragement to everyone.

I followed to his church an old man of whom it was said, "There in the form of a man is the history of the Church in this whole area. He was the first pastor in this area.

Christianity came here in the early 1700's but was then banned and died until this man began the work here in 1951." As we walk along the streets the old man tells me their names. He actually named these winding side streets himself. Now everyone knows the streets by the names he has given them. He points to one and says, "This is Butterfly Street; I like it." Arriving at the church I discover that he is an artist, and the walls are lined with murals of two types: Bible scenes (there is the progression of the building of the ark and the flood before me) and the mountains and valleys of his homeland. He has nine children, one of whom has died, as has his wife. He has two children by his new wife. We sit drinking pop in antique bottles as he relates his story. I will try to the best of my ability to relate it accurately. It came through two languages and an accent, but if I have erred, it is in minimizing the incredible life and story of the man. He was a young man in the British military. During his service he gained a great reputation as an artist. Many officers would come to him and ask to have a portrait painted. He was making a good living doing this as a second job. He was looking for answers to life by examining several religions. A Hindu priest gave him some Christian tracts with portions of Scripture in it; the Hindu had found them somewhere, liked them, and handed them out. As he was reading the tracts he had a vision; a voice from the top of a building more than five stories high spoke to him and told him to return to his country, return to his people, and preach Jesus. He saw Jesus and begged not to leave the place of his revelation. Jesus spoke to him, "No, you must go back and preach, but know that I am coming for you later." This experience began to form his theology. He now

340

knew that the instant that someone died, he went to be with Jesus. He also knew that Jesus would return. He went back to the Hindu priest and asked, "Do you even understand what you are giving people?" The priest did not, so he shared with him, and the Hindu converted. Afterward, he obeyed the vision and returned home, where naturally his extra income quickly disappeared. His wife was very upset with him, and for a period he was depressed. Then he began preaching from place to place. The police came and arrested him, the first of more than 25 arrests in his life. They took him to the police station for preaching Christ, tied his feet together, then his hands, and finally the hands to the feet. Next he was hoisted in the air, and the guards beat him for the next eleven hours. They would beat him until they became exhausted and then would rest and return. When the blood began to flow from his nose, he assumed that he was dying; he went unconscious. In this state he again saw Jesus and begged to be able to stay with Him; again he was told to return to the work. The police believed him to be dead and stopped the thrashing; they untied him and called for his friends to come and get the body. Their official report stated that the man had been very sick when he came to them, and they had tried to help him, but he died. The friends took him to a home, where he was nursed back to health. The man's body is covered with scars. When he was well, a complaint was filed with the police. In time the matter came to court, and the judge asked him what he had been doing. He said, "I was preaching Christian," but it sounded like he said, "I was preaching Krishna," the Hindu god. The judge asked the police what was wrong with preaching Krishna. The police would not correct the judge but only said, "He was using the Bible." The Hindu judge was indignant, "There are four great books in the world, and the Bible is one; I read it, and so should you. It may help you from being ignorant." When the hearing closed the judge said that the man had done nothing wrong and wanted to know why the report said he had been sick, they tried to help, and he died. The police were afraid. The final decision of the judge was that the police protect the man, take him to the airport, and allow him to leave. His persecutors had become his protectors. They were warned that no harm must come to him. The judge did ask one final question, "What is your obsession with Christianity?" His answer was quick, "In Jesus I have had revelation, and in no other place have I found revelation. The Hindu religion cannot offer it." Later he was preaching in a village where the Hindus became so enraged that the crowd beat him until they believed that he was dead. This time he was unconscious for three days, and again he had the same visions. Some from the church came and got him. There were a few women that were so upset that he had been beaten that they immediately went back to that city to preach and see if they would be beaten (a Hindu man will not touch a woman on the street. If women are protesting and sitting, only female police can remove them). The women went, preached, were not beaten, and decided to stay there and start a church. He had a vision for a church building and purchased the land next to his house to begin construction. The police kept telling him to stop because it was not legal for Christians to meet. He continued. On the day of completion, the local government officials came to him and said, "We are taking your building for the purpose of government office space." During the night, he got the answer. He went out and painted on the front of the building: "Personal residence of (and put his name)." This created a stir in the morning when they came to possess his church, for legally they could seize that, but not if it were a private residence. He maintained that it was on his land, adjoining his house, and used by his family. Yes, he might have a few people over, but they were guests. This technicality brought him again before a judge. After hearing all the arguments, the judge said that he was going to send him to jail for one year. When given an opportunity to speak, he did so forthrightly: "If the devil is in your heart and you want to send me to jail, then so be it. But if there is any of God in you, you will release me." The judge dismissed him, but later called him back and set him free with one condition: he had to return with a bribe. The neighbors gladly gave the money. On another occasion he was caught baptizing, which is a mandatory six-year sentence. He went to jail. This did not bother him. What did bring pain that still lingers with him and is written on his face was that the police had stood outside the church and told all the members that whoever returned would get the same six-year sentence. This scattered the church. When this news reached him, he was very vexed and is to this day. He basically had to start the work over again once he was set free. Inside the church is a painting of a tree. The root represents his first church, and every time a church has been planted or spun off, an additional branch is painted. The tree is growing. He was hurt by the years in jail, the times of neglecting his family, and the many times that he returned to find the family without food. He still suffers from that guilt and the amount of time given to preaching and not to his children, most of whom are pastors today. Beautiful. I am sitting at the feet of Christian history. Now the Christians are able to move freely in this place, even though Christianity officially remains illegal. Because of this man, they are actually respected. New churches are constantly being planted, and there are many outreach stations that have not yet attained the full-fledged status of "church." We leave and walk back; I am feeling so small, thinking, "What do I have to say to such a man?" Jesus gently whispers, "I am coming for you, too, one day." I am encouraged and move on.

Pastor Q recently returned from the interior and gives a report. A few years back he trekked several days to some of the remote villages. This is no easy hike, since it requires scaling one mountain to reach the summit, only to descend it and scale the next. It may not be that far as the crow flies, but it takes days. No pack animal can make the journey due to dozens of "bridges," some of which are merely a wire on which a person walks while holding onto a wire above his head; others are a bucket the trekker climbs into for someone to pulley him over. Also, the animals cannot scale the faces of the cliffs. The typical village is governed by a Buddhist monk and a priest, both of whom are very protective of their territory, not because they are devoted to it, but because their livelihood depends on the people's remaining of Buddhist persuasion and giving them money and food. (Again, all religions are the same and not at all what the anti-Christ groups portray them to be.) Pastor Q arrived in the first community and began to preach. Many believed. In fact, so many trusted Christ that the Buddhist leaders came to take him by force and stone him to death. He fled for his life and ran for two days, not stopping for anything. Arriving at another village he preached again, and many there also believed, but the Buddhists from the first village came and stirred up the Buddhists against him. Once again he had to flee. A few months later a small group of young men from the first village found him. They described how they had been beaten by the Buddhists and asked to deny Christ. They refused, because their conversion had been real. The persecution became so great that they, too, had fled. They stayed many days with Pastor Q, and he taught and encouraged them. Then one day the Lord spoke to the pastor to send the young men back to their homes. He wondered at that, since they were persecuted and the Buddhists tried to kill them. That night he told the young men; they glanced at one another and said, "Yes, the Lord Jesus has spoken that to each of our hearts. We will return!" They returned to additional very heavy persecution that was great enough to call for them to once more take flight. They came back to Pastor Q, stayed, and were taught, until another time when the Lord Jesus said, "You are to return." This time when they got back their families believed, their neighbors believed, and those in surrounding areas believed. The conversion was so great that the new converts (not the young men) went to the Buddhists, began to stone the temple, and drove the men out of their village. It is now a Christian village. As for the second village from which Pastor Q had to flee, it seems that a young woman converted after his preaching and began to share Jesus. The Buddhists chased her out of the village and into a forest, where they stoned her to death. When news of the event reached the residents of her village, they marveled that she could love this Jesus so much. As they discussed the matter and the message that they heard, the village began to convert, and today it, too, is a Christian village. I cannot imagine that all of the paper in the world could describe the works of Christ. He is alive.

There was a man who prayed for the healing of a very sick person. He said that the Jesus who holds us together is always present at the point of illness. While he was praying, the Lord asked him a question: "Would you take this illness?" The man responded that he would, and Jesus moved the illness to him as the person for whom he prayed immediately got better. He said that he understood, at least in part, what it meant to complete the suffering of Christ.

India

I had lunch with a pastor who had worked in India. He told of showing the "Jesus Film" in a remote Indian village to a crowd of more than 300. However, during the movie it began to rain. He felt led by God to stop the movie and speak thus to the crowd: "You have seen that Jesus on the screen? I will now pray to that very same Jesus, who is alive today, and ask Him to stop the rain." He prayed, and immediately the rain stopped. He restarted the movie, and at the end more than 200 Hindus converted to Christ!

Another Indian walked up to tell me his story; he had been a Hindu priest and teacher. He developed sores all over his body. After spending over $2,000 pursuing a cure, an elderly man said, "Come to my house; I have the medicine that will cure you." He did go, and the old man looked at him and said, "Your disease is sin; your medicine is Jesus Christ." The old man shared the Gospel, and the Hindu repented and asked Christ to be his life. In less than three days all the sores had disappeared! His father became very angry, but the son said, "See the snake lifted up, the highest of our gods? That snake was cast down in the garden. It is Satan's pride and our deception that has lifted it up. Father, you worship Satan." It must have been the fullness of time, for instead of banishing or trying to kill his son, the father immediately gave his life to Jesus, as did the rest of the family.

Middle East

I was told another verified account of something that happened in one of the public primary schools of a wealthy country. During class, Jesus appeared to the children and spoke to them, saying, "Read My book and learn about Me"! The children wanted the book, which caused quite a stir in that prominent Muslim country. The police interviewed every child about the occurrence, and each one related the same story. They were not given the New Testaments, but I doubt that the children will forget what they were told to do.

Eurasia

We got a tour of the Christian Radio Offices on the fifth floor in an old attic, a very attractive place with people everywhere. I was shown the construction of an upcoming sound studio, where everything is first-rate and provided through one miracle or another. Some Canadians have given 1,500 radios that can only be tuned to the Christian radio station; these are to be gifts for prisoners, so that not only will they get Christian teaching, but the radio station reads letters from inmates' families on the air, the only communication with the outside world that they get. The founder of this radio station is a man of vision, humility, and talent; truly one of whom it has been said, "There is no limit to what God can do through someone who does not want to get the glory."

One man here has studied several of the eastern religions and was sharing some of the teaching paramount to those religions that pointed clearly to Christ. He shared with me that his country was the center of occult activity in the post-Roman period; it is written that many came from as far away as Western Europe to consult the oracles that were said to live in every house. This would explain why at nearly every conference a couple of witches show up and genuinely seem to enjoy the conference! There is a very popular sect of witches that hang around the graveyards. They get the water that was used to wash dead bodies, the sand from graves, and more to use in occult activities. The man related how, when he began thinking about Jesus, he started seeing auras around people, saw people healed, and saw the future. He was troubled by the experiences but was assured that all of it was God and that he was one of the elect to whom God spoke. One night in prayer he became so uncomfortable with the experiences that he cried to Jesus. Next he fell to the floor, encompassed by evil (an evil he said was terrifying; death held no fear compared to the evil he felt). He yielded to Jesus and began to shake, throw up, and finally pass out. After several hours he came to,

FREE! The evil had left him, the visions left, he was born again, clean, and since that day has not had any trouble.

The man shared his testimony. I have not tired of listening to people's life stories; I have only lived one life, but as someone shares his or her life, I get to participate in it. He was a boxing champion. During his military service, the KGB repeatedly attempted to get him to join them. He was not interested, for at that time he was reading books of spiritual importance that were discovered in the attics of relatives. He would read the works of Nietzsche: "I hate knowledge that comes without power to change my life." He would talk privately with friends at night about spiritual issues, and then when daybreak came, he would be forced to fall in line with the Soviet propaganda. Eventually he began to plan an escape through Finland and trained for months to ensure he had the physical stamina required for the journey. As he and a friend approached the border, a wrong turn was made, and they found themselves within sight of a guard tower. They dove into the grass and assumed that they had not been spotted. In a few minutes, dogs, guns, and soldiers surrounded them. He had taken nothing with him that might reveal that they were attempting an escape, of that he was confident as he removed the contents of his bag and each item was inventoried. However, as he was emptying his pockets, he remembered that his back pocket held an address book with a note inside from an American he had met; on it was written her name, address, and a brief, jesting note: "I am looking forward to seeing you in America when you come." This note was a death sentence. When the soldiers were not looking, he slipped the book in the front of his pants. After he was put in jail, he asked to use the restroom. The guard kept lookout through a peephole as he sat on the toilet, so the man mocked him for watching until the guard turned his head, and at that instant the whole book was dropped into the toilet and flushed. Thus he narrowly escaped detection. Interrogation ensued that lasted for five days. He admitted only that he was merely lost, not that he was attempting to escape. The officials investigated his teachers, friends, professors, and anyone who knew him. He was amazed that they could know so much about him, but no hard facts surfaced against him. By climbing up the cell walls and cocking his head just right, he could hear the confessions of his traveling companion. In this way, he was able to keep his story straight and avert a minimum of 25 years in prison. In the cell he had a vision of a golden cross. His companion mocked, "Yes, that is the sign of death that we see in the graveyards." But he began to think that it meant something different: a call to God. Back home he was viewed as both a hero and a leper; many admired the failed escape attempt and yet had the good sense to keep their distance. He was constantly harassed, followed, and threatened by the KGB. One day he looked at the sky and noticed its beauty. "I should be dead, but I am alive." He looked across and saw the doors opened into the Catholic Church. He and his friend walked in. Because young people did not enter churches, an old woman asked, "What do you want?" She went for a priest, a man of about thirty. When he saw the young men fit, tanned, and large, he assumed they were KGB agents coming for him. The priest took them outside and began to share and quote Scripture. Our young friend's heart burned within. In time he gave his life to Jesus and was baptized in the Catholic Church. Soon the news spread; many wanted to see this athletic boxer who had become a Christian. The Russian media came and took his photo, then put it in the newspaper proclaiming him as a Rambo-style priest with a group of followers that wanted to overthrow the Soviet Union. Though none of it was true, it still had its effect, and still to some he was a giant, but others could not afford the grave consequences of being associated with him. The BBC, American newsmen, and others interviewed him, which helped make the Soviets afraid to have him go missing by gunning him down. They had spread propaganda in the West that there was religious freedom, so to kill him would be a public-relations nightmare. Some came and wanted to join the resistance movement; he would assure them there was no movement, and then he would preach Christ. The KGB would send people to say they wanted to join. He would surprise them by quoting I Corinthians 13 and talking about loving our enemies. He had freedom to move about preaching, and many came to Christ. One time he had filled his bag for a journey; among the items were Bibles and anti-Soviet tracts, the possession of which would garner an immediate death sentence. Guards searched the bags and found nothing, for apparently God supernaturally blinded them. As he was walking away, a second group of guards got a call and were told to search the bags one more time. They did, taking the Bibles and tracts out, laying them on the table, and still not seeing them. He has so many stories of little miracles that strengthened him in the early years of faith. One night he had a dream of men coming and searching his house for books. When he awoke, he took the books and hid them. In a few hours the men arrived.

One brother had an interesting story about being diagnosed with a brain tumor that had filled half of his skull. The complex surgery to remove the growth was accomplished, and the doctor said to him, "The brain is like a muscle. Exercise it and it will get strong again." Therefore, he endeavored to tackle the most complex theological doctoral program in Europe. At first he would break out in a sweat just trying to think. In the end, he accomplished the course, and in a very rare move, he requested that the government take him off of the disability rolls. It was then that he discovered that a group of Jews, when they had heard of his initial tumor condition, went to the Wailing Wall in Jerusalem and prayed until they had God's assurance that he would be healed. This so moved him that he responded to a call to a ministry to and for Israel.

There are two airports in this city, one a few kilometers from the site of the conference. I arrive at the one that is over an hour from where I need to be. I must get a bus to the other airport and then find a shuttle. However, when I get off the plane, there stand my hosts! They are busy organizing the upcoming conference but came way out of their way to drive me to the conference center. This couple looms bigger than life, glorious amplifications of everything unique about their country. Both tower above me at six feet plus and wear the clothes that would be seen on a fashion runway. He was a former manager of a top hotel and then became the international representative of a famous tile company. He can cut a contract in seven languages. He and his wife came to Christ out of a solely religious background and never looked back. They had thought very little of Jesus until they heard a converted priest tell of Him. On the same day they converted. At that time they were still raising their daughter, but they refused to force their new faith on her, choosing instead to live it and let her observe it. Their daughter came to know all about the Christian faith because of witnessing the doings of her parents. In time she believed and married a believer. I enjoy the daughter very much in the sense that it is no good being a water hose hooked up to living water if no one drinks. The daughter had been struggling fifteen years with her inability to have a baby, and upon hearing that Jesus is not just Savior but our Life, she embraced the Truth. I rejoiced when she was asked, "If you could ask God for anything, what would you ask for?" I expected her to say, "A baby." Instead she said, "More of a revelation of Jesus." In time I learned that she was with child, and when I saw her at the conference, she said, "Michael, over the past two years, I released my life to Jesus. I stopped the constant, desperate longing for a baby and longed for Him. I know this will sound odd, but when I learned I was pregnant, I did not go crazy. I opened my hand and said, 'Father, it is always my desire to know You. I hold the baby with an open hand.'" Well, my heart was singing. Jesus, Jesus, Jesus, it is all about Jesus, and she had that message in her. Amen. She was not a "baby at any price" woman; she was a "Jesus at any cost" woman. This family brings a level of proficiency to the Church that is really needed; the conferences they organize run like Swiss watches. The husband also organizes evangelistic Christian meetings in Africa that will have between 100,000 to 150,000 people attending. The first year he took over, he saved the evangelist thousands of pounds. He and his wife must be the best dressers that I have ever met. He appears in orange pants, a brown corduroy coat, and a pink pinstriped shirt that all works and looks fabulous. They have lived in the upper crust of life and yet find LIFE in helping believers and are dedicated to the truth of spiritual equality. I love them. As interpreters, they are both excellent. She was translating books for free and one day was told how much a translator got paid. She did the math and could see how much money she could be making. However, she decided to complete the project that she was working on for no charge. That night, from an unexpected source, she was given the exact amount of money that she might have made had she demanded what she had earned. She could see that God would provide and she could go on translating for free. Since that day she has done dozens of translations (four for me). Her husband is exacting in everything that he does, and having him for an interpreter is a blessing. I only have to add a minute or two to the lectures because of the speed with which he interprets, and he understands the meaning of what I want to say.

We head off for the Baptist Church library, a nice little building wherein I am surprised to meet two Texas missionaries laboring in a place where results will be slow coming. Again, we must never forget that the Lord uses the mission field more for the missionary than the people. They are a very interesting couple that home-schooled their children until the age when they could go to the States for their education. They also once planted an inner city church in the worst part of a metropolitan area, where after years of taking the youth to games and various activities, the area's largest drug dealer, who watched them the whole time, acknowledged Jesus as life.

Pacific Islands

Tonight a believer for whom I have a special love had a very serious talk with me, weeping as he spoke. I did not know he had almost lost his grandson to convulsions and fever. He said, "Dear Brother, I must confess to you that I lost my faith. I left the room weeping, then stood in front of the house crying out loud, 'Dear God, please do not take my grandson! If I or my children have sinned, do not count it against my grandson!' As the boy lost his pulse and his eyes rolled back in his head, I lost faith in God. The ambulance showed up six hours after being called, and the nurse walked slowly into the house, picked up my grandson, and held him close to her chest. There was no life in the boy. As she left, she turned to me and said, 'Where is your faith? Have faith in God!' At that moment my faith returned; I only needed that encouraging word. In my spirit I immediately knew God would give me back my grandson." Miraculously, the nurse revived the boy. Do you know that we can often allow others to live on our faith when theirs becomes feeble? A simple encouraging word from a saint can stir even the weakest among us to reality. Amen! Had the Lord been preparing and dealing with my friend in a different way and the grandson had died, He would still have restored the man to faith in the fact that God causes ALL things to work together for the good of those who love Him and are called according to His purposes.

While walking across the street, someone shouted a greeting to me. It is a good friend, a famous sailor, a jewel of a person that worked for years taking Bibles for the first time to the various island countries of the South Pacific. He has incredible stories of his maritime adventures. He was one of the first fellows to sail the Atlantic alone. He has told me before that after so many days at sea, one can forget to wear clothes. One day a passenger ship passed by him and hailed him to make sure he was all right. He came out on his deck and began to talk to the passengers on the other ship. After about ten minutes he realized that he was not wearing a stitch of clothing! On his first Bible-delivery voyage to one of the island countries, the schedule was so tight that he had to leave one island out. Eventually he discovered that they had waited for twenty-some years for his arrival. They had felt left out but did not give up hope. Once he finally did arrive, he got the red-carpet treatment and was introduced to a girl named after his boat, because she was born while the people were awaiting his arrival. He has lost two ships and says his current one is "a fantastic old lady." Presently he is sailing around the Pacific showing the "Jesus Film" with a volunteer "crew" from a large Christian organization. He is a great believer with a big heart and is willing to take some risk with an unseasoned onboard staff. My kind of fellow! He has agreed to take several cases of our books with him to distribute in the islands before we arrive there with him in a year. It is a real blessing.

There is revival here, and when one old man stopped me for a chat, I asked how he had become a Christian. He explained that he had hated Christians, and all relatives who became Christians were not welcome at his house.

He became quite sick; though he had taken in both food and drink for five days, no bowel movement or urination had occurred. His niece, a Christian, came to visit him. He asked, "What do you want?" She said that she had come to talk to him about sickness. He asked if she were sick. She said, "No, I have come to pray for you; you are the one sick. May I?" He agreed, she prayed, his stomach began to feel funny, and he went running to the stool and was physically and spiritually cleansed! When he came out from the toilet, he immediately gathered up all the idols, pictures, and incense burners, put them in a bag, and threw them as far as he could. He said to all of his relatives, "Vishnu, Ganesh, Kali, and all the rest are like dung! They have done nothing for me, but this Jesus has healed me! You will not tell me whom to worship, for I worship the God that heals!" As a Doer, no one is going to tell him how to live. He told me of two more miracles. After a storm, the beach is often covered with black trash, broken bottles, trees, and much dead organic matter. It costs $2,000 to $4,000 to have a bulldozer remove it. He was praying and reading his devotions when he read that if a person had faith, he could tell a mountain to move. This formerly devout Hindu went to his wife and daughter and told them to pray at church that God would remove the black junk from his beach. The mother forgot, but the girl remembered, and the pastor began to preach from that very text. The man, too, was home praying for an hour under a tree as he looked at the mess. The next morning, his wife left to go for a walk but returned shortly, crying, "Come, come; I must show you something!" The whole family went out, and the beach was completely cleaned off. In two years he has never had to clean the beach. The garbage always goes on the other side of the jetty. Another time he had to make a $1,700 payment to the bank but only had $1,000. He called the bank, but they were not willing to show any grace. He had to appear at the bank with the full amount. He went to leave wearing a red shirt. His wife stopped him and said, "Why are you wearing red? Go change your shirt." He was surprised, because she normally did not care how he dressed. He had trouble picking a shirt, but after finally settling on one, he put it on and stuck his pen in his pocket. When he did that, he noticed something was already in his pocket. It was exactly $700! Another time he was given $100 and wanted to give a ten-dollar note in church. He forgot and only had five dollars on him as he was going to church. His son said not to worry; he would loan him another five and that would make ten. That would not do, for he wanted to give exactly a ten-dollar note, not two fives, and so he asked the son to take him to the bank. The bank was closed. Then he asked the son to stop where they could exchange the two fives for a ten. The son forgot, and the man found himself in church sitting away from his son with only the five-dollar bill that he had looked at so many times in his pocket. The collection plate came; he reached in his pocket and pulled out the five-dollar note, but something strange had happened; it had become a ten-dollar note! He was so excited he borrowed twenty dollars from a friend, put that in the offering plate, and kept the ten-dollar note that had previously been a five-dollar note. He still carries the ten-dollar note in his pocket. God has used the spectacular in this Doer's life to minister to him. He is two years young in the Lord and reminds me of Peter.

He may have many rough edges, but hidden beneath beats the heart of a true saint.

I was told this as true by this man's brother-in-law. It seems that he needed to get hold of a fellow and lost his number. He thought that he remembered it and dialed the number. It was the wrong number, and the woman on the other end never even said hello but just yelled, "Why did you call me now?" Then the phone went silent. After a few minutes she came back on the line, asking, "Why did you call me now?" This went on for nearly thirty minutes. He was ready to hang up the phone and call 911, but the Lord told him not to hang up the phone and to pray for her. The next time she came on the phone he just started praying aloud for her. In the end they got off the phone. In the coming months he would occasionally try to call the number again, but since it was a number that he had guessed, he could not remember it. Six months later he was preaching, and after the service two women came to him. One woman asked if he remembered the event. She said that she was that woman. She had gone to her sister's house on the coast to commit suicide. She had just cut her wrists when the phone rang. She was trying to hold on to the phone with the blood going everywhere and kept dropping the phone, but she was able to stop the bleeding in time for him to pray with her. After the prayer she had believed in the love of God and given her life to Jesus; she now had a great peace and wanted to thank him. Amen!

I was introduced to an old man who was working in the garden. He said that when he was young, he looked up to the sky and it split open, allowing him to see directly into heaven. He told his parents what had happened, and they told him that he had eaten some bad food. However, since that day he has been able to pray for people and they would be healed. If he were living in the West, this would be grounds for a spectacular weekly TV show. However, this is no showmanship for him, but his life in Christ. He cannot talk long, because he has been hired to do some gardening. He goes back to praying while he works. Beautiful.

Latin America or Caribbean

An elderly man has worked for 35 years as a prison chaplain and is so well respected that he has an office behind the prison walls. A few years ago he was dying from cancer, the Lord healed him, and he immediately returned to the work of the prison. As we approach the prison for ministry, we are told to prepare for anything from a strip search to being turned away at the gate. We arrive, are searched, and then wait; eventually we are led through a series of lockdown doors, then down a long tunnel next to the prison's butcher shop, the stench of which was a bit overwhelming. The old saint said to me, "They cleaned it up for you!" There are difficulties with doing time in a South American prison. Many of these men have been here for ten years awaiting sentencing in a prison built for 1,000 but holding 5,000 inmates. I said, "How would you like to be walking down this hall beginning a twenty-year sentence?" The old saint is very concerned for the prison leadership. When he began, the prison had only a handful of Christians; today there is a congregation of over 1,400, with 200 men trained to be leaders. I am scheduled to speak to those leaders. We wait and wait before finally being taken through the prison yard to the chapel. The old man says, "Many hate these walls, but I love them. I have given my life for this place." He is very interesting, and as I learn more about him, I am becoming more and more attached to the spirit of the man. He was the head accountant of this government's tax department. Thirty-five years ago he heard on TV that the prisons were going to be socialized. He could not sleep; God was telling him to go to the prison. He did not understand the call but went to the prison the next morning, not knowing why he was there. He showed his credentials to the guards, who immediately recognized his position. No one likes seeing the taxman in this country. He was quickly taken from post to post until he found himself standing in the presence of the warden, who behaved very cordially, not knowing why the accountant was there. The man told the warden, "I heard that you were socializing the prisons." "Si, si." "I believe that the prisoners would be better served by being taught about Christ." The warden was still very cordial, because he still assumed the visitor might be there on official business. So the warden said, "When would you like to start?" The man said, "Oh, oh, uh, next week." The warden said, "No, no, you can start right now!" The taxman, who had never preached a sermon or taught a Bible study, found himself, within minutes, standing before the prison population! He preached in weakness, and many got saved! After the meeting a man approached, and he recognized him as a man who had come forward in church the same day the taxman had and who was also an accountant. He had been put in prison for "cooking" books. He was shocked to see the taxman and explained that he was "cooking" the books for the administration in this prison. That was the beginning of the chaplain's ministry. "You cannot believe what God can do with nothing!" That is true; God does the very most with nothing. The chaplain looked at me and said, "I would cry if tomorrow they told me I could no longer come to the prisons. I live, breathe, and think about these men."

After I spoke to the group of inmates, several came to kiss me on both cheeks, as is customary in this culture. When I had been speaking, a bird had come in through the open window, sat down, and, oddly enough, looked as though it were listening. As soon as the meeting was over, the bird flew out again, unhindered by the prison walls. I paused to watch the bird leave as the men were still shaking my hand. I thought, *What does this bird teach me?* The Lord spoke, "I come freely through these walls; they are no obstacle to Me." YES! I had spoken for less than an hour, and it took us an hour and a half to clear back out of the prison through various locked areas. The next day when we returned, entry went a little more smoothly, but it still took so long to clear through all the posts that we were two hours late for the meeting. I discover that the cause for our improved passage is an off-duty guard who had come to Christ while guarding the prisoners as this elderly caretaker of souls preached to them! He loves the old man and does all that is possible to expedite our check-in. A young man enters; the prison chaplain turns to us to say, "Only 24 years old and two murder convictions, but did you see how his face glowed? He recently gave his life to Jesus." We make our way from one locked room to another. Passing a makeshift cage under the stairs, a young man's eyes of hopelessness catch our attention. Finally, in the meeting room, a brother convicted of a double homicide leads us in singing, "We will celebrate Jesus, celebrate!" Today I am speaking to the leaders of this 1,400 strong congregation on the topic of "The Theology of Problems." So few have a theology of problems, for they relegate problems to the realm of God's punishment, their own stupidity, or the unknown mysteries of life. However, if we move to a completely different system—God's system—we can see how problems are His greatest tool to reveal our glory, pride, and weakness. A problem that makes us weep bitter tears can, in the hand of God, make us weep tears of joy. I also shared what it is like for me to be gone from home so much and have the enemy begin to whisper to me, "What if something happens to Betty or one of the children? What if someone needs help? What if there is an accident?" I asked if any knew what that felt like. There were a lot of heads nodding. This led into a discussion on faith, rest, and expanding our belief system, not just saying that we have a God, but living like we do. It was a beautiful meeting and a bond is growing between us. Later, the old saint said to me, "I want more of this teaching; it is something that the men can use. We do not need worthless things. When these men accept Christ, they have to come forward in the prison yard and bow down. The other inmates will often pour scalding water on them from above. They must be serious, for they will have many tests." It is interesting that God is not fighting the unbelievers but using them to perfect the believers.

The saintly gentleman chaplain, age 72, told me two very interesting stories. One New Year's Eve, he turned on the TV news and heard the report of a riot in a cellblock;

one of the prisoners was holding a knife to the warden's neck, and two other guards were held captive. He told his son he wanted to take a little trip and borrowed his car. He went to the prison and pleaded with the board of directors: "Let me go in! In ten minutes I will subdue those men." After much arguing they allowed him into the first room, locked it down, and unlocked the next door. He knew the man with the knife, never said a word, walked straight up to him, yanked the knife out of his hand, put it in his own pocket, and said, "All of you will return to your rooms. None of you will be moved to other prisons." [It is the habit after a riot that all prisoners are dispersed.] "No one will be punished, and you will repair everything you destroyed within thirty days." The inmates had destroyed all of the medical and dentistry equipment and argued that they could not repair it because they could not get the parts. He promised to get all of the parts. They just looked at him and walked back to their rooms. That was the easy part. Now he had to persuade the board to comply with his promises. It took much negotiating, and in the end he again had to promise to provide the materials to repair all damages before they would agree. He arrived home several hours later to a wife and son who had seen him on TV and were furious that he had not told them where he was going, since he could have been killed. After the son's rebuke, the chaplain said, "I have a problem; I have promised to provide all that is needed to repair the medical equipment." His son said not to worry, for he would contact the manufacturers, explain what had happened, and challenge them to help society by helping rebuild the equipment. In thirty days everything was repaired. Beautiful. He gets teary-eyed telling what God has done. The second experience occurred when prisoners had rioted and burned 27 men alive in one cellblock. The whole place had gone mad. At that time he had a congregation of 1,000 men behind the walls. He went to the warden, saying, "Let me talk to the men over the loudspeaker. God will give the men to me." The warden smiled, "Chaplain, you are crazy and getting crazier by the day! We have the machine guns and are ready to storm the prison." The older man continued to plead until the warden yielded and commanded that the chaplain be taken to the loudspeaker. He did not know what to broadcast, but stood there and finally said, "I want all of the men of my congregation to sing a song," and he led by beginning to sing a Spanish hymn. Soon there was a thundering sound of singing coming from behind the very walls that guards were ready to breach with machine-gun fire. The Christians just kept singing until the unbelievers dropped their weapons and began to join them in singing the Christian hymn. Next he told them to return to their cellblocks. The warden just shook his head at this very different man of God placed in the world to minister to so many. He has a very strong emphasis on hearing God and does not hold on to knowledge but goes empty, waiting for revelation, for God will never fail us.

The elderly man has access to the floor housing the hardest of the hard criminals. He was there recently when some of the men began to tell him that he was a foolish old man. One of the inmates spoke up: "Our chaplain will leave here tonight, go home, and his wife will ask, 'How was your day? Do you need some tea? Are you tired?' She will give him a little kiss; he will read and go to bed. But we, on the other hand, will stay right in this place. Is this man foolish, or are we? I think we should listen to him." That day many came to Christ on that floor. He told me that every year he makes a list to organize his workload. "I will only visit four prisons a day, speak at two meetings a day, and visit with the administration one day a week." However, by the end of the first week he has broken every one of his rules and is working flat out. "Why not, since the Lord is giving me the strength?"

I spent some time with another ministry that has a strong emphasis on prison work; in fact, to my surprise, some of the inmates are allowed out to go to church, sing, and minister. I met the single, older woman who is the motivator for the prison ministry. She told me her story. "One day in my prayers I had a vision of looking over a hill; all I saw was black mud, but in the middle were many beautiful flowers. I heard the voice of the Lord say, 'I am sending you into the mud to get the flowers, and you will not have any of the mud stick to you.' I went into the mud, picked the flowers, and nothing stuck to me. I was not defiled in any way." After that dream the door opened to the prison ministry, and God revealed to her that those were the flowers that she would pick. "I have never had any of the mud stick to me, and many have come to Jesus."

I met a fellow with a boat ministry. He was interested in seeing my teaching reach the jungle interior, and I was interested in his ministry. This led to an invitation to visit his boat, so after the meeting he drove us to the docks. It is great to see such huge boats on a river; these are oceangoing vessels, and the Amazon River can handle them easily. Each boat is tied to another, so to get to his boat we have to walk through and over several other boats. We saw Amazonians in winter parkas throwing frozen fish into the back of a truck; the river fish here are huge. Arriving at the three-story, flat-bottomed boat, we see that the first floor is dedicated to medical services. There is an office apiece for a dentist, a pediatrician, and a general practitioner, plus a room for admittance and a pharmacy. The top floor is dedicated to helpers, preachers, and interpreters. This is a steel-bottomed boat, because the large trees hidden under the river's surface will rip through a wooden hull. The boat goes out each month to remote areas to minister to the Indians. The days are dedicated to medical treatment and the evenings to evangelistic meetings. Doctors volunteer to go, help secure medications, and pay the fuel bill for this upstream, floating clinic. The ministry is not without unique drawbacks. Once he was warned that pirates were going to seize his ship, so he told everyone in the community that the ship would sail at a certain time, though he got up ten hours earlier, in the wee hours of the morning, and sailed without incident.

One pastor is a genuine fellow I am very, very happy to have met. He grew up in the mountains as an ignorant village boy who could not read. At age sixteen he wandered into a church and gave his life to Jesus. At that moment God spoke to him that he must put Jesus first and then others, that he must not waste time, and that he must have a goal. He is very wise and embodies the spirit of Jesus. His approach was to establish schools and begin to work with the students at the very young age of five, so that by age ten, the students would cast off voodoo and embrace Jesus. His approach has been proven, and at present there are over

2,000 students attending. He does all of this with miracle funds. It seems that one day God said, "Build the school!" Someone sent a few thousand dollars, then another person and another. He was able to build the foundation and quit when he ran out of money. A man that he had met in the U.S. and knew over the years came to see him, but he showed up quite thin and obviously very ill. He told the pastor that he had seven cancers and only nine months to live, at best. He had come to see his friend before he died. The pastor looked at him and said, "You did not come to my country to die but to live!" He took the man to the church, called the elders and all the people, and they prayed. The man went back to the U.S. and, upon examination and even a second opinion, was declared cancer free. The end result was that the man gave $50,000 for the completion of the school. The pastor points to the surrounding mountains and says, "I know God made those mountains to keep the sea and storms from this place. I was raised in those mountains. Most never come out of that hopeless situation, just planting a few beans and existing. God brought me out, and that is why I know how each of my students feel." The amazing thing is that 49 of his students went to sit for the government exams, and 44 of them passed. A typical school here averages only 50% of pupils making the grade. The pastor's daily saying is that goodness and mercy will follow us.

There was a church in the very heart of the voodoo center of the country. A girl was demon possessed. The police had tried to deal with her and could do nothing. Therefore, they called the voodoo witchdoctor, but he could do nothing. In the end the Catholic priest was summoned, and he could do nothing. Up to this time, the pastor had been persecuted, but when the police did not know anything else to do, they sent for him. He assembled the elders, and together—in a row and singing hymns—they all went to the police. The girl, who was difficult to restrain, stopped screaming and simply shrank to the corner, shaking and chanting, "My enemies are coming; my enemies are coming; my enemies are coming." The pastor entered the room and had to persuade the police to leave, since they were afraid that the woman would again be violent. The pastor shared Jesus with her, she asked Jesus into her life, and the demon fled! I liked the story, for it is my experience that when Jesus comes, the demons leave without being told. Today she is married to the pastor's brother-in-law. They all know of a voodoo priest who gave his life to Jesus, quite a shock to the people. The priest even went so far as to burn all of the idols, tools of incantation, ancestral garb, and more. The most interesting thing burnt was the list of people that he had killed or made sick over the years through his demonic practices. If this roster had not been destroyed and had been discovered, the man would have been killed by the relatives of the people listed.

Please do remember that I am just the reporter. It is said that in one village a voodoo priest became obsessed with one of the single women in the church and kept pursuing her. One night, through voodoo ritual, the man turned himself into a pig. As the lady was walking home after dark from the church, the big pig stopped her and would not let her pass. There was something strange about the pig. The girl then prayed to Jesus and spoke to the pig. "If you are a pig, go your way. But if you are the voodoo priest,

369

may you remain a pig!" The next day there was uproar in the village; the voodoo priest was missing and his brothers were looking for him everywhere. After a day the lady went to the village and related what had happened, and there at his house was the pig. She then prayed for the pig and it became a man. Many people were persuaded that Jesus was stronger, and this story went throughout the country.

After hearing of so many miracles, I remember a miracle that is greater than any so far. My miracle tops theirs. I witnessed God's turning a man's heart back to his wife and his wife's to him! The heart is much more difficult to turn than a man into a pig! Is that not great?

On one occasion the voodoo priest had mounted an attack against the pastor who is called of God to dig a hole and bury voodoo in this very place. The pastor was driving and became very sleepy. He awoke to find his truck hitting a man on a bridge and then careening into the river. Underwater he felt the breath go completely out of him. Sometime later, people from the village came. They found the dead pedestrian and, looking over the bridge, noticed the truck upside down in the water with a dead man's head sticking out the window. The people did not hurry, since the man in the truck was dead. Eventually they turned the truck over and pulled the pastor out by his feet, then dispatched messengers to his home to report his death to his family. Lying on the ground, the pastor felt the breath of God enter him, and he became conscious after all of that time in the water. The people, amazed, turned him upside down, and yet there was no water or dirt in his nose. A small boy who knew the man was a pastor observed the situation and said, "This is what Jesus meant that He would give life!" Normally if someone from the village were killed, the person that caused the accident would immediately be put to death. However, all of the people had witnessed the breath of life coming back into a dead man, and they released the pastor, acknowledging it as a miracle of God. Another time this pastor was driving his motor scooter. The voodoo priest sent a truck to hit and kill him. He was knocked off the scooter and it was completely destroyed, but he left without a scratch. The pastor organized a crusade in a very popular place important to voodoo. After the crusade the voodoos held a festival and were not able to call forth even one spirit. Since that day, no spirit has been called up in that place, prompting the voodoo priests to meet. The most powerful priest told the others, "Stay away from that pastor, for he has the most powerful devil watching him, more powerful than our devils. He cannot be conquered."

I am told of a voodoo priest whose son came to faith in Jesus, and then the spirits departed the house, rendering inoperative the priest's practice of magic. Of course, people quit coming to him and paying for his services. At length he determined to kill his own son. He had his wife put poison in his son's food. In the morning the son got up, came to the table, grabbed the plate of food, and held it toward heaven, asking God's blessing upon it. Then he ate. Nothing happened to him. The next morning the father went angrily to the mother, accusing her of lying and not putting the poison in the food. This time the father did it himself. Again the son entered the room, held the food to heaven, and prayed for it to be blessed. He ate and nothing happened. This perplexed the man, who repeated

371

the procedure the next day with the same results. However, the third time, the miracle broke him; he confessed Jesus as God, and there was a great stir when the man destroyed the voodoo poles, flags, and other implements outside his house.

One delightful man I met told how he was near death when he was three years old. His father kept taking him to the hospital and at last just gave up. Friends said, "Your son will soon die; you must take him to the hospital." However, the father responded, "I will take him no more. The hospital and doctors cannot help. Only God can help. I will put my trust in God." He took the boy away, privately prayed, and the boy was healed.

You would love one interpreter, who has a smile and a twinkle in his eyes like Santa, but with a slight build. At the breaks he tells us more of the Lord's workings in his life. He and his wife decided some years ago that they would never tell anyone but God of their needs. He then related one financial miracle after another and would conclude each story with a huge grin, saying, "And we worshipped the Lord!" Beautiful! Wonderful! I can see clearly that we are cheated when we never have suffering or want. Men of faith can be intimidating until a person looks beyond them and sees Jesus; and where Jesus is seen, love and acceptance are also present. The intimidation drifts away. I was asking myself, "Why tell anyone your needs when God knows?" But then the thought went deeper to, "Do I really have any needs? I have God dwelling in me!"

During the seminar, for no apparent reason, I started talking about couples that have experienced an extramarital affair. The message is positive, because it is my conviction that marital oneness is not broken by an affair, and there are grounds for rebuilding the marriage. I camped at the topic for some time, leading the interpreter to look a little puzzled, and why not? The message did not fit the context. Afterward, as I was leaving, a man of about thirty came up weeping and held me. He told me his story via the interpreter. He was abandoned at age three after his mother and father died. He did not know how to have a marriage. He and his wife both have had multiple affairs and had just decided tonight that they would divorce. They were walking by the church having the discussion. They heard me speaking and came in to hear the foreigner. The next thing they knew, I was talking about them. They had both come under conviction and decided that they would stay together and learn how to have a marriage. I instantly introduced him to the pastor for follow-up. To me this type of miracle is greater than the deaf hearing. After the man went away, the interpreter told me that she had wondered why I had strayed so far from the message but now understood. Was this chance, or just JESUS, like a Shepherd, leading?

I spoke at a pastors' gathering, after which an old man came to me and said, "The place where you are standing at the pulpit has an interesting story. Over fifty years ago, I passed through this city and asked people if they would like to see a church here. They all said they did not want the Christian plague in their city. I went to my room to kneel down and ask God to bring His Church here. Where you are standing is the exact place I knelt. We bought the hotel, made it a church, and now there are over 200 churches in this city."

The first woman evangelist came to this jungle settlement in the 1930's and had her first convert in the 1950's. When she arrived, the townsfolk believed her to be a goddess, and to prove that she was (though of course she never promoted herself as a goddess), they secretly poisoned her (the shamans are experts with such destructive substances) and waited. At meal's end, she arose and threw up. The dogs and chickens immediately ate the vomit and quickly died; she was fine. At that, they believed her witness to Jesus. However, one day they called on her to pray for a man that was dying. She did, and he died. Then a debate arose, "Is she the goddess that we can trust her words?" She appealed to them, "I am not a goddess but a human that points to the true God. The man who died had believed in Jesus, and my God has received him." At that they agreed that she was not a goddess but had a God, and the man did go to the place called heaven. She was able to stay, and again, the good news of Jesus Christ spread.

Standing outside the church, I hear many stories from missionaries to the interior telling of their experiences. One was working in a tribe whose custom was for the other tribesmen to attempt to extract a tooth from someone who had a vision. If the tooth came out, someone in the village was going to die; if it broke off, someone would get sick. To make sure that he was not the one dying or becoming sick, a tribesman would paint red dots all over his skin. The missionary observed the practice and read them the Passover story. The people could see how, with the mark of blood, the angel of death would pass. It was the beginning of the tribe's conversion. There was a native going downriver when he had a vision in which Christ was as big as a mountain ahead of him, and following him were all of the people of his village in smaller canoes. He asked the missionary what that meant. "You will be the first to believe in Christ, and all of your people will follow you." The man agreed that must be the reason for the vision. He believed, the tribe followed him, and today he is their pastor. One missionary in the meeting is covering the expense of his missionary work through employment as an anthropologist. It takes four full days by boat to reach the tribe with which he works.

The first thing I notice about the pastor is his countenance; the second is that he is missing one eye and cannot be bothered by that fact. He is racing around so fast that I wonder if he could be tolerated with two eyes! He tells me his story while drifting between broken English, fairly good English, and Spanish. At age ten he lost his eye in an accident. From that event until age sixteen, whenever he looked in the mirror, he could only see a monster. His mother often took him to faith healing meetings, where he was marched to the stage for a "healer" to run his finger in the empty socket and proclaim to the audience that the appearance of a new eye was imminent. He never got the promised eye. He quit school and refused to make eye contact with anyone when he went out. One day he decided to kill himself and began to cut his wrists. As he was cutting, the Lord spoke to tell him, "You are not a monster; the monster is between your ears, in your mind!" At that point he had a conversion, an awakening. He could see the truth in what God had said. He gave his life to Jesus and has never looked back. This is one man who is a great blessing to his country and to the Church. I am so grateful that God foiled his plans to end his life. He is a gifted evangelist as well as a wonderful musician and songwriter. He has made a Christian tango album that is really quite nice. On the coast we stopped at a statue of the goddess of the sea. Once each year the witches of various sorts gather on the beach for one week to make sacrifices, worship Satan, and indulge in other cult rituals. The television stations cover the event with great interest. This pastor gathered over fifty pastors and went to the "festival." They formed a circle and started praying the witches into the circle. He has a video of it, and it is apparent that for no reason (of course, we know the reason) a witch would walk up, the pastors would part and allow entry within the circle, close ranks, and keep praying. Soon the witch would fall to the ground and the demon would exit. Then the witch would be taken to a tent where other pastors would tell him (or her) about Jesus, pray with him, give him a Bible, and get him connected with a church. In fact, one of the leading pastors in town is the son of the most famous witch; he also was demon possessed and delivered.

Africa

A vivid example of the Living Word's activity is how He spoke to a widowed, illiterate woman at the end of her rope after the death of her husband and child; she was depressed for years. In 1943 a woman evangelist came to her and prayed for her, and she was healed of her depression. For the next few years she followed the woman evangelist, preaching to and healing the poor, the sick, the stranger, and the lonely. She would walk with God and He would speak to her. One day He said, "Matthew 10." She went to the evangelist who had led her to Christ and said, "What is Matthew 10?" The lady read the passage to the widow and then told her that she was to go and begin her own ministry; this occurred in 1947. Since then the believers from the church she started have planted 700 churches. She died in 1995, and over 60,000 people came to the funeral, which in the end closed the city because of the traffic. She was a renowned saint in her country, and yet few outside of there have ever heard of her. There are many such people in Africa. I am told, "One man was called the African Elijah. He walked from city to city carrying a bamboo cross. He only told the people three things: repent, destroy your idols, and join a church. Millions, and I mean millions, came to Christ." In the West we have heard far more about the great Western evangelists that came to Africa. Did you know, for example, that Saint Augustine was African? At any rate, the woman founder's grandson grew up with his grandmother, and when she died, it was prophesied that he was to become the leader of the church. The fellow is a fragrant aroma of humility and very soft. I asked him, "What did your grandmother teach you all the years you were with her?" "She said that the Christian must not be proud but humble, that we can do nothing apart from Him, and that we were to remember the poor." I asked what to me is an important question. How did the founder act when people disagreed with her? "She would not say anything; instead, she would wait for God to give them the revelation." His mother had nine children, all of whom died at birth except for three. Another died at age nine, one died at age three, and only this man survived. There were many prophecies that he would minister. His father would not bother him with those; he just wanted his son to grow up to be hardworking. His mother tried to overprotect, as you can imagine, but the father, an only child himself, refused to let him be pampered. He took the fellow at a young age to minister on the field and taught him to work without water or food. At age 25 he wanted to finish graduate school. His grandmother told him it was time that he entered the ministry, but the young man disagreed, so she told him to pray about it. He did, the Lord spoke to him to follow, and he immediately began ministering. I have seen churches built on many foundational truths, but never before on humility, waiting on God, and hearing His voice.

One day the director of a large organization of churches had a dream in which there was a piece of land with a wall around it; he was to buy the land. Once he was awake, he called a man in the city, described the land, and said, "Do you know of such a piece of land?" The man did, so the director went there and found it just as it had appeared in the vision. There is now a church on that piece of land.

As we headed for the airport, I witnessed a true miracle. Around one corner we saw just ahead a police roadblock searching cars. The pastor and the driver agreed, "This is not good; they will search everything." Since they were traveling with a white man with three suitcases, we would be detained, items would be confiscated, and payment of bribes would be expected. They had one man out of his car whipping him. We were all praying silently that God would do something. Just as it came time for our car to be searched, the policeman yelled at another car and ran over to it, leaving his post. All of the other officers watched him to see what it was about. For that instant there were no police around. The pastor ordered, "Drive!" We did just that and slipped away completely unnoticed. It was great.

The final day of my foray into a village to do a seminar, the pastor's wife stood in front of the crowd to give a testimony, which was translated for me. This was the first I had heard of this story. She explained that when she and two pastors had dropped me off at the bank the first day I arrived, three men had followed me and waited outside. Because of that, one pastor had come into the bank to see how I was doing. When we came out, the three men followed on foot, then stopped a taxi and followed by car. When we stopped to rent a minivan, my companions wanted me to stay in the car. Once transferred to the minivan, we drove for nearly two hours before stopping for something to eat. The taxi had continued to follow and came behind us to the restaurant, where the three men were let out to enter and sit watching us. At that point in the story, I remembered the three men, but the fact that they had been following us for any length of time was unbeknownst to me. After our meal, when we got in the minivan and took off, the men tried in vain to hail a taxi. The pastor's wife instructed the driver to speed ahead. I remembered that, also. Apparently by the time the men got a taxi to stop for them, we were too far ahead to continue trailing. She expressed much gratitude for God's protection.

A man was giving his testimony that sounded like something out of the Old Testament. His name was Hezekiah, and he had three wives. The first wife had a vision; they were to leave the city because of the approaching fighting. He followed her advice. They went to another city in the interior. In this city the rebel leader was looking for another man with the same name, Hezekiah. The rebel leader had given orders to his soldiers, "I want the head of Hezekiah before me tonight. Not his body, only his head." The soldiers did not know what Hezekiah looked like. This is where the second wife entered in. She had a vision that they must leave this city, or when the soldiers came looking for the second Hezekiah and began to torture the people to find him, the people would give up her husband as the other man just to get the soldiers to stop. It was Hezekiah's story of victory and deliverance, the story of two different wives' visions, and the greatness of the Lord. He is now a pastor and has only one wife.

We arrive at one of the multitude of churches in this homegrown denomination and find the large congregation in the midst of great celebration. The pastor rises to speak and begins his message by saying, "Whoever wishes to be great among you must be a servant of all. If you come to our pastors' school, we will beat you down. Your position, degrees, or money will mean nothing. We are here to serve, not to be served. Are you listening to me? If you want to be somebody, you must be nobody." He continues the message along this vein, though the topic of weakness is a difficult one here. Some of the chiefs of tribes do not even bathe themselves; others do it for them. In some places the people can only meet the pastor if they lay prostrate; in most places they must bow to one knee. To tell a pastor to be weak, to be the servant of all, and to walk across the room and kiss his wife when offended is completely foreign, but it is the Truth. He said to me later, "God will come for my words. That is a very difficult sermon to preach, for Jesus will require that from me." Yes, I know the feeling of preaching one's own funeral. Next I am asked to speak. I am wearing my African clothes, which makes the most sense in this heat. I told the people a story. "Last year these clothes were given to me. I liked them very much, but I wondered if I should keep wearing them after I left you. I went to the next country and still had them on. A very nice lady at the airline looked at me in my African clothes and said, "Too fine!" [That is an African expression for looking very handsome.] I said I decided not to take them off. The whole place erupted in laughter. The women were yelling, "Too fine!" Well, amen! I told them about all the needs that God had met in my life, from health, to money, to travel. Then I shared the greatest thing He had done recently; He had provided me with a toilet every time I needed one during the course of traveling and suffering with salmonella poisoning! There was great laughter; everyone knew what I meant. Then I shared how in always finding a toilet, I began to remember to recognize that God was in my sickness. I talked of all the times that He meets us. If He knows something as insignificant as providing a toilet when I need it, how many greater things does He care about and supply? I also talked about wanting to see their church as a miracle church; the place again erupted, and then I explained what a miracle church was: filled with people who can love an enemy, accept an offense, and pray for those who persecute them. A miracle church is filled with men who love their wives even when offended and fathers who apologize to their children when they are angry. I told them of my travels of the last year and the fact that everywhere I go I tell other churches about their church. At that singing broke out for quite a while. The pastor stopped me and explained. "Many years ago we received a prophecy that others would hear of our church, first in other African countries, and then in the whole world. The prophecy was put to song and is often sung, but especially today, when we hear the fulfillment of that prophecy." They see me as a part of that. Next my travel companion from the U.S. spoke; it was a good testimony about two men, one righteous and the other wicked. The righteous man listened to God. One day my companion, Joe, was in the gym working out, and a man of God came and asked, "What kind of gym is this? Is it anything spiritual?" Joe assured him it was not and asked what he wanted. The man said, "I was in the other building, and God spoke to my heart to go to that gym and pray for a man who has a broken heart." Joe was that man, and that was the beginning of his walk with God. He then encouraged the people: "Do you see that because one man was abiding in Christ, I was saved? If you abide, what would God do with you?" The people so received it. At the end of the service the dancing started; every person came by and placed an offering in a large bowl for us! They are poor, but the founder has taught them to rest, wait, abide, and give joyfully. They just wanted to bless us. Joe was moved to tears, as was I the first trip, and as any believer, also, would be. We left in the midst of shouts and joy.

We drive to our evening meeting for over an hour to reach a church in the lowly part of town. In the midst of the shacks are a concrete slab, four walls, and a tin roof. We enter, sing music for a half-hour, and still there are only three people sitting in the audience. I say to my friend, "The pastor is embarrassed that more have not come, and he is waiting and hoping. Go to him and explain that I never count numbers; I do not care if there is one or 1,000. It means nothing. We let God bring whom He wants. Tell him to start the meeting with the three." The meeting started. I had only spoken for about twenty minutes when the room had become full. I know we are to step out on the water before we see the miracle; it will never be seen from the boat. The next day I got to return to this church to speak, though the drive took nearly two hours because of the traffic. The place was packed and so alive. The pastor got up and said, "We think that we are a small church that does not matter, but tonight, God has proven that we are special to Him and that He remembers us." It was so nice. I talked about idols and coming to the end of our idols, and that suffering was used of God to open our ears. It was wonderful. One thing I did not like was that I had to leave early; I was already late for another meeting. So many came outside to hug me. It is the family of God. Several Africans have told me that Africa is cursed. I do not believe it. In fact, I would not be the least bit surprised to discover that there were more Christians from the continent of Africa in heaven than from any other place. The pastor said to his congregation, "So many are here tonight because you believe God will meet you and your need. He will! But would you be here if you had no need?" Amen.

During the church service a lady shares how her husband was in another city on business. He had a vision that something terrible was going to happen in his home. He fasted for two days and yet the vision would not depart.

He then went to the church and prayed to the Lord, "You promised my grandmother that her generation would know you. I renew my vow to you and I remind you of your faithfulness. For though we are not faithful, You will remain faithful." Still the vision of something terrible would not leave him. He called his wife and told her to stop everything, go to church, and ask the pastors for prayer. She did, yet the vision of a terrible thing would not depart. That night, he received a call. "Has anyone talked to you about what happened at your home?" His heart sank. "There was a fire from a short circuit in the upper room. Your wife found the fire before it spread, called the firemen, and the fire was put out. Everyone is safe. It was a miracle that she got up in the night and for some reason decided to check upstairs. Only one room is destroyed." He and she rejoiced greatly. Another woman told of a terrible bus accident in which she lost the sight in her eye. The doctors told her never to expect to see out of that eye again. Yet after the prayers of the saints, her sight has returned. She is a widow and needed her two eyes.

As I packed to leave for the next country, a young fellow that I met here last year brought in my laundry and wanted to say hello. I reached in my pocket to give him 5,000 local currency, but the Lord spoke to me, "Give him 50,000," and I did. Later he returned and asked, "Was that money for your laundry?" "No, brother, the money is for you!" Later I was down using the phone and he spoke to me. "My mother is sick to the point of dying, and I did not have the money to go and see her. It was 40,000 local currency for the bus ticket, and then I needed some extra travel expense money. I had just given up, prayed, and left it in the hand of Jesus. Then you gave me the exact amount. I would have never guessed where the money was coming from." Well, amen! The Lord knows; He has every hair of our heads numbered.

A Bible school professor was telling me today that he had witnessed firsthand a fellow from Europe that had the gift of interpretation. The fellow came to visit the villages, and though he could not speak the language when he came or when he left, he could understand the languages of the people perfectly. The professor said that he was amazed at how someone would tell a long story of trouble in his own tongue, and the man would turn and tell the professor what to say without being told what was said. That is the biggest twist that I have ever heard on the gift of interpretation, but it makes sense and was so useful.

After the mission started by A. G. Murray was expelled in 1922, this lady's father started the mission anew; he came in 1986 and kicked off the mission work. The lady got married to a real Doer in '87, and they decided to come during the war in 1991 and start the church that is now based at the present mission. They show us photo albums of the place before and after. It had been nothing but an empty field with a few trees; they literally started with nothing. Once he got a small room built in which the family could sleep, he had to park his truck in front of the house every night, because the snipers would shoot into the house, and the thin walls could not stop a bullet. It was very dangerous work, but they had the call and the provision. No one used the paved road because of the ambushes and the land mines. Instead they had to go on poorly built back roads for hours and cover a distance of

250 kilometers rather than 45. He said two things had made him think about the necessity of really listening to God. The first one was when he had ordered the steel to build the church building. A couple of unbelieving, rough, and worldly truck drivers had agreed to deliver the steel to the mission through this war-torn country. One wonders what those men were thinking, since no one else could be found who dared do such a thing. However, the men finally arrived at the mission, having survived the ambushes and land mines of the shorter route, not knowing that road, for all practical purposes, was unusable. The first truck driver came tumbling out of the truck, chain smoking and with sweat running down his forehead, obviously quite shaken. He just looked at my friend and said, "I will tell you, Pastor, if you want to work here, you'd better *#&^@* pray!" Here was an unbeliever telling the pastor the only way to survive was to pray; it was like the ship captain telling Jonah to pray! Oh, we laughed and laughed. The second thing that impressed upon the pastor the necessity of listening to God was the time he had decided to forget the long road (you can imagine the trouble with the long road for a Doer) and take the paved road. However, all day long he was hindered from departing. Finally, God spoke to him: "You must learn to listen to Me. I am telling you not to go on that road." Well, amen, Jesus is alive. The pastor said he had peace and did not go. That day eighteen people were killed on the "easier" paved road. He said that when he started traveling the road after the war, the locals would say, "It is now safe!" He would invite them to ride up front with him, because then instead of saying it was safe, they would say, "You ought to turn wide by that tree." This method of

maneuvering the road by having them with him worked quite well. He also said that he had to gain peace in the midst of the suffering. One day he saw a woman and her baby dying from AIDS. He shared with her, was honest about her condition, but encouraged her about Jesus. She gave her life to Christ and immediately had peace and knew where her next stop would be. Then she asked, "But what about my baby?" He explained that the baby was hers, God had accepted her in Jesus, and Jesus accepts children. Again, she was at peace. She died the next week, and he had peace; he was comfortable with the death around him if Jesus could be introduced. A time came in the life of the church when the size and quality of the youth group increased dramatically. They actually wanted a truck to facilitate their ministry, and so the young people, on their own, decided that they would pray and fast until God gave them one. Someone then sent a new truck from another country in Africa. The father-in-law brought a truckload of Bibles, and every day the people were coming and buying them. However, he discovered that the purchasers were Jehovah's Witnesses, who were paying very little for them, taking them across the border, and selling them for a profit. He cut that off immediately. From this humble beginning, in just a few years, has sprung a really nice mission station with a variety of ministries operating out of it, such as the school, medical care, humanitarian aid of all kinds, and more, a veritable beehive of activity. This fellow, the husband of the founder's daughter, never leaves a stone unturned and is never at a loss for ideas. He invited several men from his home country to come and build. In eighteen hours they put up a roof. When finished, they were really happy. But he asked them, "What did the congregation learn from you? You could have trained them." The next day he called the men of the congregation together. "These men built a roof in eighteen hours; tomorrow we will do better than that!" In the morning he set the men up, showed them how to make the cuts, build the trusses, and more. They actually did beat the other men's time! God has provided so much for them. When a builder was needed, they prayed, and a local fellow came; they did not believe the fellow really knew how to do things, so they gave him a few jobs, but as it turned out, he was the best in the area. This pastor really works outside the box, and the wisdom of God is apparent, since it is just what is needed for this place. The branch that bears the most fruit is pruned back each year; if not, the branch will take more sap and give less fruit. God really wants to prune away what we trusted last year. This brother is really open to whatever God wants to do, and today the total membership is 2,000. He also mentioned how happy the people were with the church; they liked other people seeing that they had a place to worship, and one old man said, "Now we have a face!" After rebuking a border guard—and the guard's replying, "Pastor, this is not like you!"—the Doer decided that because he had really pushed hard for five years, it was time for a break. He left to establish another mission elsewhere, but the church, contrary to the popular opinion that a pastor must be indigenous, called him and his family back. Upon their return, they found the people in the midst of famine. The heavy rains had taken a toll on the crops, which rotted in the fields. On top of that, the people had turned to a cash crop and planted tobacco, something not easily digested if eaten in the absence of proper food. Beyond that, the price for grain was up, so the people had sold their grain from the last year. Altogether this resulted in rice price's skyrocketing eight times over, which resulted in mass starvation that the government refused to acknowledge. Outside their house was a continuous line of people needing handouts. The pastor devised a plan: If people wanted to eat, if people wanted free rice, then they must work. On Monday, twenty people came to work for their one kilogram of rice. By the following Monday 3,000 people were there to work. Some people, having heard of the free rice, had walked up to forty miles to get there, and they reported that many others had died along the way. What the pastor did next was genius. He divided the 3,000 into groups of fifty, each group being supervised by one of his students; after work each student would sit in front of a bag of rice big enough for his crowd and preach the Gospel before the distribution of the rice. The pastor had the people working, and he said they moved like locusts, even filling the potholes that had developed in the main road. To get the rice he had to go to all the businessmen and just say, "Give it, and I promise we will pay it back." They also made appeals in their home country, and grain was sent. It angered the government that the home country had been contacted, because they still would not acknowledge that anything was wrong; the government accused the missionaries of lying. After the famine the president visited the village. Our missionary friend was the only white man at the meeting of 13,000. He gave the president a Bible and then sat down. The president gave his speech, "This is a great day for our country, for we are free from the white capitalists." Well, amen, nothing wrong with being free from the white capitalists, but I do not think it is a beneficial option to live under the control of a corrupt government. The pastor said the members of his church really enjoyed seeing him sitting in the front and taking the disparagement for whites, and they all laughed about it.

We are off and running, for the evening service will fast be upon us. My friend tells me of being lost in Jerusalem. He was exhausted, and a man said, "Let me carry your bags and take you to your hotel." They talked and walked. He got to the counter, turned around, and no one was there, only his bags. "I think it was an angel!" He also told me of missionaries that were to be killed because there was no rain and the tribes had blamed them. Upon being given the word of their impending death, the pastor met with the congregation, prayed publicly, and it rained for all to see. This was a great breakthrough for the people in evangelism in all of the surrounding areas.

The morning service centered on communion and brought about beautiful fellowship. When the service was over, a couple in their 40's came up wanting to talk to me. The wife was weeping and said, "Only three minutes of your time, please." She explained, "I have filed for divorce and am to finalize it tomorrow. Everything is done. I have come to the meetings every night with my husband. I told him this morning, as we entered the church, that I would continue with the divorce. But when I sat there this morning, it was just as though Jesus, not you, were speaking to me. I want to call the divorce off and follow Jesus. I have no emotions of renewed love, I cannot see how it would work, but I want to abandon myself to Him. If He is my focus, I have been convinced that there is nothing His nearness will not fix." I still travel for the one. Her heart was so beautiful. I explained that she was picking the greater truth, but that if we did not look at the things that brought the marriage to the point of ruin, and then they were willing to deny self and make the marriage new, they would find themselves in the same place in just a few years. They could see what I was saying, and we set an appointment for the evening. At that time, we went through their histories. She is a Thinker-Doer with high standards that have yet to be met. She has not entered into the joy of the Lord. I have four words for her, "YOU ARE GOOD ENOUGH!" Perfectionists never believe they have arrived. We looked at their histories, and I was surprised when she said, "I can see things that I did to mess up this marriage." They both understood their part in making the marriage miserable; he was just as open and honest. They want Jesus and a good marriage. She said, "I do not feel like it, but if this is what Jesus is using, I am calling the divorce off." He is still in a bit of shock, since the whole relationship was over until that morning. I suggested that they get a new marriage with two people that were willing to deny the past, focus on the Christ of today, and begin to walk in the spirit rather than the flesh. I had spoken this morning in the service on the natural miracles that we could expect because of Pentecost, miracles that are not imposed but are a more natural part of existence and yet change the direction of our lives. I was witnessing it, and it made all the difference because Christ had spoken already into their hearts.

An Irishman had been called to Africa to assist a doctor. However, the doctor never turned up, so the Irishman had to treat the people for five years, never knowing for sure what he was doing. He was a thinker by temperament, so despite the stress that the unknown caused him, he treated hundreds of people a day, meaning that he had moved out of his own resources and into gifting. He had been put in prison, arrested, accused, and more, and yet he stood fast. There is a story about when a witchcraft village refused to grant him entrance, so he went to the edge of the village and shook the dust off of his feet. Many saw that as a curse, which worked to the favor of the missionaries who followed.

We are off to the orphanage that was established two years ago. My host pastor tells of how he was picking up a load of shoes to sell when the police seized him and the shoes. He was in jail for a week, and there the Lord called him to be a church planter. So far he has planted 319 churches, something only possible where the Lord's Spirit is moving. But with the call comes the provision! A man is only responsible to answer the call, and God does the rest. The pastor kept encountering street children and two years ago decided to start the orphanage. He had no money for such an undertaking, but an elderly woman told him that if he found a building, she would buy it for him. He found a little compound with mud, plaster, and thatched buildings used for storing the corn after harvest. He bought it, converted it, and has brought 100 orphans from around the country to live there. A bamboo fence was built around the compound; there is a small bamboo-walled room that is the toilet. This area is barren from all of the little feet that scurry around the place. I enter the orphanage to the sounds of children singing to welcome me. Many of the children are HIV positive or have AIDS and are taken to the hospital once a month, given medication, and put on a modified diet. Some read poems to me, others sing, and many dance. I tour the school and see the dirt floors on which they sleep and the pieces of wood out of which they have tried to make chalkboards. Most of their clothes are torn, yet they are happy to be there and off of the streets.

When last I was here, one young man listened the whole time. Since then, he has completed four years of Bible School. One day he got to a telephone and called me. The rebels were going from house to house killing people. I could hear the gunfire in the background. He said, "You must do something!" I said, "Brother, what can I do from the United States? Get your family, go to one room, get on your knees, and ask Jesus to protect you." He did, and no harm came to any of them, though neighbors on both sides were massacred.

Epilogue

Since you have been reading the very human story of believers I have encountered far and wide in my travels, perhaps you would indulge me as I recount a few anecdotes of my own human story. Traveling in countries where language, customs, attitudes, availability of supplies—well, you name it—are so very different from those encountered in one's native land on a daily basis; one tends to find himself in situations that may be uncomfortable, uproarious . . . well, again, you name it! This chapter is not intended to have a spiritual application; I am merely sharing some of the thoughts and experiences I had when I was so far away from home, often in developing countries.

Food

Just as a side note, as I reread the trip reports, I realized that ninety percent of the time I had beans and rice for lunch! This is a staple around the world, and it truly is delicious.

Some years when I first started visiting former Soviet Bloc countries, food and mealtimes would simply not be mentioned, because there was so little food available. Then I would be there in a year when beets were prevalent and every meal had beets, or when it was potato season and every meal consisted of potatoes. One lady who had survived Siberia as a child had a real talent for making a meal out of practically nothing. One morning she announced, "Who is brave enough to eat my soup?" I jumped up and grabbed my bowl. The soup consisted of lamb's-quarters picked in a field, a little smoked meat, and one cup of oats, all boiled and then poured over a chopped, hardboiled egg and a tablespoon of cream. It was the best meal of that trip! Incidentally, a few years later, when food was once again available and delicious, our hostesses played a great trick on us to remind us of the scant selection of before. They set the table with only a piece of bread, half a cabbage, and a tomato, and said, "This is dinner!" Then they brought out sausage, mashed potatoes, squash, beans, and a wonderful brandy cake.

There is a fruit the size of a soccer ball grown only in Southeast Asia, the Dorian. Due to the problem of its stench, it is not allowed in public transport, hotel rooms, or cabs, and is restricted to one small area of town. Despite being sternly warned to steer clear of eating it, curiosity got the best of us, so after our meetings, my brother and I found and paid a sum to a vendor, who took us to an open area and split open the pod. Inside were seeds the size of avocado seeds with about three-eighths an inch of brown goo around them. The rest of the pod was a white substance like styrofoam. The idea was to suck the fruit off the seed. It tasted somewhat like garlic and mud. We ate some before giving the rest to a beggar woman. When we returned to the hotel, we went to the room of our friend, Sam Jones. As soon as he opened his door, he jumped back and said, "I am smelling something." Our secret trip was now in the open.

On the way back I saw an eel and some of the "spiny fish," which if stepped on will immediately emit a poison. After being boiled they are delectable, our hosts say. That night my favorite, coconut scones (biscuits), were served. Also, a banana that was about eight inches long and as big around as a bat was boiled in coconut milk until it was the consistency of pudding. One bowlful of that was not enough. The same type of banana was peeled and cooked like a potato, then smashed and biscuits made from it. It was also boiled in water and eaten with its natural juices.

A huge meal had been prepared for us: cassava, rice and beans, fish stew, and goat. I explained that I simply could not continue to eat like this. It is something for me to deal with. In the past, so as not to offend, I would eat everything. However, the blood test I had a few years ago confirmed what I always knew: I am being killed with kindness.

A wild game restaurant had a very nice open-pit grill with a huge ten-feet wide mound of coals under which the meats were cooked. Out of everything served—crocodile, waterbuck, beef, lamb, chicken, and more—I would have to say that I enjoyed the zebra meat the best. The interesting thing was that cats were roaming all around us, because people would throw their scraps. I threw down a little piece and cats came from everywhere to fight over it right next to our table. I said, "That probably was not smart," to which the host and hostess readily agreed.

One out-of-the-way village had beautiful mud huts; the communal grain bin was round, about five-feet through, made of sticks that were woven in a circle. It looked like a giant beehive. I peeked in, but there was no food. My hosts asked, "Did you see the vendors along the road selling food in the city? We starve in the villages."

I have a boat to catch to the interior, my favorite place in this country; I will travel a good part of the day on the boat. We are headed to a new plantation carved out of the uninhabited jungle. They have everything I like: jungle, bats, lions, orangutans, snakes, tribal people, and poor laborers brought over from neighboring countries (people in that situation so often have humble hearts for the Lord). It is a long ride, but there are not enough o's in smooth to describe the glassy surface of the water; the sky reflects perfectly well on it. We see the eagles fishing, and periodically we run through a school of fish. The motor's wake churns the fish up, and the eagles get busy. We spot a lone fisherman and pull alongside his boat. His catch is shrimp, so we buy a couple of pounds of the largest shrimp I have ever seen. There were other things that looked like centipedes, but they were clear, as big around as large cigars, and twelve inches long. We buy the three of those he has, and I am hoping that when served to me, they will be covered in curry and well out of sight, for they do not look appetizing or even edible. I am assured that they are tasty and, therefore, assured of having to eat them. Well, amen!

The food is good, but there is too much MSG, way too much. We begin to talk about it. "Oh, yes, this has too much MSG; in the kitchens of our country's restaurants it is added to dishes by the handful. Notice how your head feels tight. Tonight you will become very thirsty. Many of us lose our hair because of it." Do people really need that much MSG? Anyway, for me it is a migraine trigger, so I eat very little.

One pastor was saying that when he was doing mission work farther north, he was handed a plate of reindeer eyes to eat cold. It is considered a delicacy given to honor guests, but he kept talking and holding the plate low enough that the children could run by and sneak one, until finally the children had taken them all.

We arrive at an airport and have to wait for the ticket counter to open, so in the meantime, we stop in a little diner to eat. I got a plate with smothered steak and my brother got two pieces of pork, at which point our interpreter yelled, "Stop!" He had noticed the posting of the prices: $70 for two pieces of meat. We already had the full plates in hand and had to buy them. We just split the meat between the three of us. Man! Everything here is just that expensive. The country needs hard currency and gets it any way possible.

At one point the sky is nearly black with huge bats, a particular bat that flies in the daylight and roosts at night. Coming in hoards from the south of Africa, they are one of the few bats that can be eaten and are said to be quite good. I would like to try one, since they are fruit eaters.

A jungle publisher and evangelist from a remote area in India visited us in the U.S. He wanted chapati; I took him to the breakfast restaurant and ordered some pancakes, which look a little like the chapati he is accustomed to eating back home. When they came, I held up the pitcher of syrup and said in Hindi, "Hot and sweet." Then, while holding the container, I made the movements indicating a pouring action on the pancakes. When I put it back down on the table, he picked it up, looked at it, and said in broken English, "Yes, thank you!" He put the pouring spout to his mouth and drank the syrup right down. I just watched in amazement. My broken Hindi and his broken English had produced a sugar high that he would not soon forget!

A friend was telling me that he could eat a complete restaurant meal for nine rupees (twenty cents) by ordering all the rice he could eat, fish gravy (with a small hint of fish flesh), two vegetables, and two vegetarian dishes. The others asked me what twenty cents would buy someone in a restaurant in the U.S. I said, "A kick in the pants and a toss out the door." They had a good laugh.

One of the servant girls brought two fresh, tender, immature coconuts! They were opened and the nearly carbonated-tasting juice poured into two glasses. Inside the coconut shells was the fine film of the forming coconut that is the consistency of pudding. The coconut was so young that when scraped clean there were only about two tablespoonfuls to eat. Delicious!

In a village we are shown the huge Brazil nut tree; the pod is the size of a coconut and must be cut in two with a saw. Inside are the nuts clustered in sections, shaped somewhat like an orange. We also find a cashew tree. The fruit looks like a pear, and the nut is hanging on the outside of the fruit in a hard case that is shaped the same as the cashew, one nut for each fruit. The fruit does not have any seeds inside and can be eaten; it is somewhat bitter but nice.

The meals on the boat are magic, usually a new variety of fish with beans and rice. We noticed early in the day that there was a burlap sack next to the kitchen that was moving. In the evening we see that it is a huge turtle; its back is two-feet long. One of the sailors cuts off the head and works feverishly to remove the turtle's shell, no easy task. However, upon completion it is obvious that this turtle yields much meat. I am assuming that it will show up in soup in the next day or so.

The evening meal is beef, of which my father noted, "There is absolutely no way to cut this, but if you put the whole thing in your mouth, it is quite nice to chew." We have had great beef and fish in one day in a place that usually feeds people meat once a week. I am told of a prayer recently offered by one of the students: "Father, please bless this food, forgive the hands that prepared it, and thank you for the spared lives." I laughed.

At certain times of the year the cornstalks are burned in the fields, and the village people line up with the fire blowing toward them. As the fire comes, the mice run ahead to escape the flames. Using sticks, rocks, and dogs, people catch the many mice, their favorite taste treat. The mice are either boiled or deep fried, without being cleaned first, and eaten from head to tail. While eating the fried ones there is a constant crunch, crunch, crunch. I think I am getting an idea for an activity for our next men's retreat! A missionary tells of visiting a village and watching the nice tender pieces of young goat meat being given to the elders. Since he was the guest speaker, he received preferential treatment by being given the guts to eat. On another occasion a woman was cooking for him and tending to her son with cholera. She would wipe off his vomit and then go right back to cooking. He warned her that cholera could be spread in just such a manner. She prepared and brought him some fish; the other missionaries did not want to eat it, but he did not want to offend, so he took a piece of fried fish. However, upon picking it up he noticed that there was a large white worm under it. When no one was looking, he threw the fish to the sand and covered it with his feet. This created another problem: The rest of the night he could not keep the dogs away from his feet!

In a couple of our favorite European countries, dining equals entertainment, and great care is put into picking everything as though one were choosing clothing for a night out. The olives, the cheese, the tortilla (a big round that looks like a flat piece of bread but is actually potatoes and cheese), the salad, the tuna, and the various dried meats must all complement one another in a taste delight. As we are driven to our hotel at nearly 1:00 a.m., I am feeling sorry for my friend, for our hotel is an hour away from his house, and he must drive back home for a short sleep before again driving back the hour for work early in the morning. However, he is happy, as are we, to see and share in what Jesus has been doing. As Alex, my Indian teacher, says, "I am taking 'beautiful' out of my vocabulary and simply going to say 'Jesus' every time I want to say beautiful." Well, Jesus.

Breakfast consists of fried potatoes, eggs, and some water buffalo through which I never was able to successfully cut.

For the driver we purchase some beetle nut; the size of a marble, it is cut in fourths for men to suck on, though it has no flavor and is hard as a rock. I do not get the point. One piece should last a lifetime. We buy yak cheese, which is a different story. It, too, is the size of a marble and just as hard, so it will take up to two hours of a person's sucking and moving it around in the mouth before it grows soft enough to eat. It takes one cup of condensed yak milk to make this small bit of cheese that has the flavor of smoked cheddar and is the perfect energy sustainer for hiking.

The Portuguese love cod and travel the world over for that delicacy. Therefore, we wisely decide we are in the mood for cod. We find a sidewalk oceanfront restaurant and order up. At the beginning of the meal cheese, ham, and bread are served. These appetizers are standard fare, served as part of the meal, and diners are charged for them despite the fact that they were not ordered. But who could refuse? Then cod, swordfish, shrimp, and more come. I have been told for years that Portuguese food was some of the best in the world. I am believing it! It is not expensive but is very nicely done. At the end of the dinner we head to the pastry shop; about this our host is insistent. He mentions that the pastry shops are also the place to get coffees, which are dark, rich, tasty, and nearly of a drug-like consistency. The pastry of choice is a small "pie" with custard in it served six at a time and sprinkled with powdered sugar and cinnamon. An odd feeling comes over me as I sit here. Just hours ago I was hearing of starvation, seeing people in want, sleeping in a tin shed, and now, "Oh my! These luxurious tidbits are lovely!" Strange.

My host does what most any man here does very well: he starts a barbeque. Charcoal, locally made, is purchased along the side of the road. To make the charcoal, a fire is started in a pit, and once it is going full force, it is covered with dirt and left for several days. Then the dirt is carefully dug away, for within the pit are now poisonous gases, and there lying in the pit will be the very good charcoal that, when lit, will burn for hours. The meat and sausage being broiled are really nice and quite a treat, because very few people here would be eating anything other than beans and cornmeal.

Before we leave the market, we stop to buy small, new potatoes, about twice the size of a marble, that have been fried in an oil-filled wok over a wood fire. A three-year-old who is covered in mud has his gaze fixed firmly on us, and all the while he is mindlessly peeling the little potatoes in his hands without looking. We can see that this is an activity that he has repeated thousands of times in his short life, and one that will be duplicated for some time to come. We break up the child's boredom by giving him something to stare at. For him there is no getting up and wondering what he will do today; like every day, he will peel potatoes, until one day he will be old enough to put them in the oil, and finally, with maturity, he will be able to serve them. His whole existence will be lived out with raw, cooked, or served potatoes. Then I remember Madame Guyon's saying that the factory worker who discovered Christ living within could go home from hours of mundane work refreshed. Christ and the deeper life that He offers are available to a potato peeler and cannot be hindered by circumstances. I am encouraged again. The next day for lunch we decided to walk the couple of kilometers to the market again. We wanted to get back to the little fried new potatoes. The "restaurant" has an interesting cooking stove; rocks are laid in a circle about two feet across and held together by clay and mud. The mound rises above the ground about thirty inches, and then a four-foot by eight-foot piece of tin is placed on the top. In the center of the tin piece a wok is hammered out that dips into the space in the mound. A hole is made in the side of the mound for placing the sticks inside and building a fire. We got something special: cabbage chopped up with a little bit of tomato and hot oil sprinkled on top; the potatoes are then mixed in. A little salt is added, our utensils (our hands) are wiped clean on our trousers, and we begin to feast. The food tastes very nice and costs about twenty cents. It is surely better than the fried rats that are sold to those who take the "buses" from city to city.

My companions have purchased some sugarcane. I break off a piece and then notice a monkey tied to a pole by a tree mill. I ask if I can give the piece to the monkey, and when I throw it, the monkey goes nuts, especially when the owner tries to take it from him. It was quite a sight. We have purchased some of the local bread for the evening meal and decide to partake as we walk along. It tastes good, but if I were to keep eating it, my teeth would be completely worn down, for it is full of rocks.

Arriving in the "city" we come to a crude roundabout that leads us to the "bakery." Shops in the outback are not much to look at, and this one is no exception. I went into the first shop and noticed some rolls, but the missionaries' children accompanying us screamed, "That is not the bread shop!" That made sense, because there was so little to eat in there. I proceeded to the next shop; it, too, had rolls, but again the children screamed, "That is not the bread shop!" Finally, I got in the bakery, and all it offered was the same pile of rolls that the other shops had and nothing else except a selection of two types of soda pop, which is what the children were really after. Later, as we drove along, I spied a banana flower, which one of the kids picked for me. It is a huge, purple, tulip-looking flower, probably ten inches long and closed. As the petals of the flower are gently pulled apart, along the base of each one I can see the small yellow flowers, all in a line, that will one day be a complete row of bananas. I wanted the flower because these little pre-banana buds are wonderful to eat. They are not eaten here, and I do not blame them, for in the eating, a banana stalk is taken away. However, I have eaten them several times in India, and the Indians do a wonderful job of preparing them.

The next morning I venture down for an omelet. I would guess that I have seen hundreds of kitchens like this one in my travels, a restaurant run with only one electric hot plate. There are at least forty items to choose from on the menu, all of which would be prepared by one person in this one-person kitchen on this one-pot grill. The omelet tastes exactly like others I have had in these places; it is difficult to distinguish the taste of the egg from the taste of the seldom-changed grease. It fills me up, though, and I am on my way.

In the distance I see a black plume of smoke and learn that it is raw sugar being cooked. This I want to see, so a man escorts me and we have a nice talk that alternates between computers and Jesus. We are walking as we balance on the long, narrow dams that separate the lush green rice fields. We also find ourselves picking the flowers from the pepper plants. Arriving at the source of the smoke, we see the slaves hard at work. They have dug a hole in the ground that has a six-foot wide wok sitting at ground level. There are three other holes at ground level, one through which to feed the fire with the husks of the sugarcane, one for air intake, and the other for the exhaust. The small four-cycle engine is started and is connected to a cane crusher. One man feeds the hungry monster with cane as the giant gears crush the cane and release the sweet liquid. It does not take long to fill several five-gallon buckets. I have been given a glass of it, and it tastes quite nice, with the exception of floating pieces of cane fiber that make it seem like drinking something with fish bones in it. The liquid is poured into the wok and stirred with a large wooden paddle. Another man has a strainer to take out the fiber. In time the boiling liquid begins to solidify and become a deep brown color; the smell makes me want to dive into the middle of it. Soda is added and the mixture is ready to be poured into what appears to be a wooden box, four feet by four feet and about six inches deep. The mixture is quickly becoming hard and is leveled out in the box. It will finish hardening and then will be cut in one-kilogram chunks to be sold as raw sugar. I am given a little piece the size of my thumb, and its flavor is magic. The master sees my delight in it and has a bowlful brought to me. I know I could eat my weight in this stuff. As I am summoned back to the meeting, my host catches me and wants to know what I am doing with the bowl of raw sugar. Joyfully I exclaim, "Eating it!" He admonishes, "No, Brother, even we do not eat that. Only the local people have developed a stomach that can handle raw sugar. Eat just a little bit and you will never leave the toilet!" That prophecy came true, except "never" was actually twelve hours!

We are in a city that is famous for its cooked sparrows. People travel from all around just to sample these spicy little birds. I place my order for the critters as soon as we arrive.

Coming from dense jungle is truck after truck carrying kava trees pulled from the ground for their prized roots that are crushed, put in a burlap bag, and dipped in water until the precious commodity is extracted for drinking. Our cab driver is addicted to beetlenut, a seed that is broken open and filled with salt, a fourth of a cigarette, spices, or anything that looks interesting, then wrapped in a leaf and chewed. This fellow has been at it for years, because his teeth—those few that have not already rotted away from the habit—are all red. He is constantly spitting, and the cab smells of the concoction. This driver has really warmed to us after spending the better part of the day taking us to a tourist site, and he has a special surprise. He stops for us to visit some women sitting by stones under thatched roofs; they have been hammering out the kava root. We purchase a liter jar of condensed kava root juice mixed with the local water. The stuff is nearly as thick as cream, nothing like that to which I am accustomed from other islands. Kava does not have much effect on a Westerner; for that to happen takes a few years of daily drinking to saturate the body. I have never felt anything after partaking, but I have witnessed some of the locals stumbling around. Back in the cab, the driver says to me, "I drink and you drink." I offered, "Just let me put a little bit in my jug." He insisted, "I drink and you drink," which is obviously part of the camaraderie of the kava experience. He tips up the jug and shoves it into his oral cavity—devoid of teeth and dyed red—takes a swig of it, and pulls it away from his mouth with a string of red spit still hanging on the side of the carafe. He handed me the jug and said, "Drink." I just looked at him, and in my heart—rather than letting it sink—I looked up to the Lord for a blessing, said, "Cheers," and took what would be the first of many gulps.

My friend's visiting mother emerges with the biggest cake I have ever seen. I have not even seen a wedding cake this big. It looks like it is made of pancakes three feet in diameter with jellies and creams between each layer, then covered in grapes and oranges and elaborately decorated. She slices a wedge for me that must weigh close to a kilogram. What an enjoyable scene!

The church looks interesting, so we nip in and find ourselves on a guided tour. Having toured so many, a cathedral is pretty much a cathedral at this point in my life; it is a large, dark monument. Then the guide takes us to the damp basement where thousands have had their bones placed in these famous catacombs. We move along through rooms piled several feet high with bones and then see pits with bones on both sides of the walkway. I have never seen that many human bones. I am at the end of the line, so when the guide turns the corner, I pick up a skull and femur, which to my surprise are quite heavy, perhaps because of the humidity. I am reminded of the Greek Orthodox priest that "honored" me by giving me a tea made out of the mold scraped from the bones of a saint.

Frolic

I have often said that I am not a brave man but a protected man, and once the Lord is done with me, I will pass from this world to be with Him. Perhaps I do appear braver than many, only because my wife, Betty, has a very low scream threshold, and after not too many years in our marriage, I learned not to let the adrenalin pump when I hear a scream. Once on a plane I was constantly running to the restroom and trusting I could get in immediately; I had encountered a near-fatal dose of salmonella poison that would not easily or readily let go of its hold on me. It is easy to say I see God in all things when there are only blessings, but I do see Him in situations such as this. He has protected me in what He permits and prevents. It all has been permitted, and I am remembering that one "Praise God" before I understand something is worth 1,000 times of saying "Praise God" after the revelation of what He has permitted. Therefore, "Praise God!" that He causes all things to work together for good!

I was among the first wave of tourists allowed into a dictator's country after a bloody revolt. A government agent was assigned to go with me everywhere. I had to sneak out at night to preach. One night as I stood at the front of the church speaking, a man in a suit threw open the church door, strode down the aisle until he was right before me, and took a photo of me! My father had accompanied me on this trip and was visibly perturbed. It was midnight and we were not supposed to be there! We assumed a government agent was turning us in! However, the man in the suit turned out to be the church's photographer who was getting a photo to be used in the church newsletter!

One morning we started out through one of the most beautiful places in all of Africa. We stopped at a rain forest and walked on the most shocking series of bridges that stretched from treetop to treetop one to two hundred feet above the ground. Only one person at a time could walk on each bridge, the width of which was ten inches. In the end I felt like Peter looking down when he was just about to sink after walking on water.

One of the brothers told me a great story. It seems that they were having a church meeting when one of the older men fell asleep. While he was sleeping, the electricity went off. He woke up to pitch-black darkness and started shouting out, "Brothers, pray for me! Something has happened to my eyes and I have gone blind." It was just about then that the lights came back on, and everyone had a good laugh.

A young boy had done something to merit being chased by a policeman. The boy shot past me, then the policeman flung a bullwhip at the boy's legs. It caught him soundly; the boy was letting out loud yells as he continued to run. He never let the man catch him, though.

The car to fetch me from a village and take me back to town had not arrived by 7:00 p.m. I decided to walk toward the road, quite a few miles away; villagers were happy to walk with me. The sun was setting very beautifully. Ahead of the adults I walked hand-in-hand with two children, and many others surrounded us. The child on my right carried a chicken in her other hand; the boy on my left had a little box to play with. These children did not even have a ball. (I asked that some balls be purchased and distributed for the following day.) We walked for well over a mile before men from the church came on bicycles to take us the rest of the way. I sat on a bookrack being pedaled by loving brothers down a footpath to the road. It was quite an adventure. Eventually the car met us and I got a ride to town. As we drove, the monkeys were running all over the road. It was not dark, but soon the electricity would shut off, so in the hotel I would be back to candlelight.

My son and I were stopped by a very pleasant young man who wanted some U.S. currency. He was given a dollar and was quite happy. Later he found us to give his pen as a gift; not wanting to offend, my son agreed to it. I then gave him a book, which excited him quite a bit. We had him work out a deal for us to go to one of the large temples outside of town; the price had nearly doubled for us when we tried to do it ourselves. Our taxi honked and bounced in and around ruts, past beast and man, all the way to the temple. We saw an elephant working next to the road. Two men had cut and split bamboo, which was passed to the fellow on top of the elephant. He would take a large piece and break it over the elephant's back. It did not seem to bother the elephant; he just continued to work. The temple turned out to be the nicest, cleanest one that we have seen on this trip. It is some special day, for many are standing in line in front of the idols to be blessed by the priests. One priest notices me and comes out. We begin to talk; he knows people from the U.S. I give him a book. He is very interested and begins to question me, "Are you a Christian?" "Yes." "What kind of propaganda do you believe?" I was in the center of a Hindu temple on a holy day, not a good idea. I said, "I do not believe in propaganda, only truth." The crowd was gathering. Next he said, "Tell me, what do you think of me?" "How can I tell you what I think of you? I do not know you." "But you must think something; tell me." He was baiting me, for if I said I believed he was a false teacher, he could incite the crowd against us. I said, "If you will spend time with me privately, I will get to know you and tell you what I think of you." He smiled and walked away. We went back to town. On the way we passed a man sitting in a chair next to the street; he was letting another man pull his tooth with a pair of pliers.

We walked through the downtown on the way back from the embassy; on the street a huge disturbance broke out. A man had been caught pick-pocketing. I actually thought that the crowd was going to beat him to death as they viciously hit and kicked him. Then several police came and tore the crowd away from him. I thought that the man would get some relief, but as soon as the crowd was peeled off, the police went to beating him with nightsticks. In the end, he was just dragged away. My friend told me, "Pick-pocketing has a lot of risk!" Every kid on that street saw it, and he or she now knows the severity of the risk involved. The man knew exactly what would happen if he were caught, and the crowd considers it his choice.

At night we took a little walk to the town center and I thought we could just sit in the city square and talk. However, a fellow with no teeth and a growth the size of a basketball came up, kissed me on both cheeks, hugged me, and then tried to put his hands in my pockets. Well, amen. We just walked on. We got home and sat on the roof. It was a bit cooler there and we had a nice talk about missions.

Presently I am on the roof attempting to find a breeze. The children in the field are yelling, "Give me a dollar!" They do not even know what they are asking; it is just a phrase to them. They go running off if I say, "No, you give me a dollar!" If one were shortsighted enough to give a dollar, he would be trampled by the mob.

In the evening my son, my brother, and I decided to take a walk. The problem with these valleys is that the cold air from the mountains around us holds the heat, smoke, and dust in the city, so there is a constant haze. What we see is so outside of the box from what we would observe walking in a U.S. community. There is activity everywhere, heaps of street vendors, pigs, dirt, filth, and yet it is a comfortable place. The people here are very friendly, and the little English they know is immediately used cordially. "Hi!" "How are you?" "Where are you going?" It is very nice. However, what happened next was startling. We did not realize that about 1,000 people die in acts of violence from the insurgent soldiers (who in reality have become a crime organization) every year. Therefore, the people close their doors, lock them, and get off the streets by 8:00 p.m. We were walking along, and all of a sudden the streets were empty, lights went out, and only dogs were heard barking. Literally within minutes the street that was active before became what felt like a ghost town. That was not as bad as realizing that we could not find our room; every shop looked the same with a big garage door closed over the identifying painted sign on the window. We walked back and forth until finally we determined which one had to be the door. We banged on it, and soon the houseboy came and opened up the door. Amen!

I have just come from a nation in which I was on a short rope due to unrest and anti-American sentiment, and it does not look to be any better in the country I am presently visiting. My host explains that the rebels are fighting with the government, the five different political parties are fighting with one another, and some involved in protests have been killed. Taken as a whole, this has caused several different problems to arise, the first one being that the rebel party is calling for general strikes, and when that happens, it is with hardly any prior warning, and all shops are to be closed; noncompliance results in the building's being burned down. No means of transportation other than bicycles are allowed, and all roads are closed. Second, the government has imposed an 8:00 p.m. curfew. Next, the rebels are recruiting the men in the villages to fight for them, and this is done by force; men who refuse will be killed. This has caused an influx of people fleeing from the villages to the city, but there is nowhere to house or feed them. One church elder returned to his village to check on his house and was captured and killed. As I am being apprised of all of these developments, we notice that the roadway to my hotel has been closed. We backtrack and go down a nearly empty street that is covered in glass, and bricks fly by, seeming to come from nowhere. Several passing vehicles have obviously been hit. Welcome to the unrest! The situation is adding to the stress of my host, who has told me before during my trips here, "Michael, you give me birth pains the way you move about so freely!" The very next year, when my host had us in the far west of his country, four bombs went off in the surrounding area, and the insurgents robbed a bank in a larger city. There were gun emplacements in nearly every city, though these rebels actually robbed the army of its own weapons. There were several roadblocks, and at some checkpoints entire busloads had to be emptied in order for the passengers to walk across the screening area before being allowed to board again. War is always an interruption for the workingman. At any rate, as my traveling companion and I headed toward our hut late one night, the host, still wanting to be reassured that we would be safe, asked, "Are you going directly to your hut?" At the time, I thought we were and assured him there was nothing to be concerned about. However, as my companion and I walked and talked about the possibility of seeing things at night, we thought we should set off on our own excursion. We walked a good distance, getting farther and farther from the village. Finally, we were walking down a small road in the middle of a cane field. The wind was strong and in our faces. It was then that we happened on to what appeared to be some kind of guards' lookout tower up on stilts, and we could hear the men inside. My companion sagely suggested that perhaps we were in the wrong place. He is not the type to shy away from much, so I heartily received his suggestion that we return to our huts.

The airport was made of a sand-colored stone in what appeared to be the middle of nowhere. The land is semi-arid with few trees, yet it has the quite nice feel of a cool, dry climate. As I depart the secure area I identify my hosts, a man and his son holding a sign high in the air. I am ushered outside and into a taxi. They take care of the bags, obviously wanting to get me away as quickly as possible. Something I have learned over the years is that the danger level of a place is directly proportional to the anxiety level in my hosts. These two men are anxious, saying, "Many people would want to kill an American, though others believe that because we have been helpful to the U.S., prosperity is coming. Still, it is good that you not be seen."

We leave for a five-hour trip back, and ahead of us, blocking the road, is what appears to be a hot-air balloon on the back of a small trailer being pulled by a tractor. This massive ball appears to be made of canvas, is some 25 feet high, and is weaving back and forth on the trailer. We discover that it is filled with rice hulls and is being taken to a dairy for cattle feed. The cities that we pass through consist of small concrete buildings, ten feet by ten feet, each with one door, one window, no paint, and a handful of items for sale, nothing worth stopping for. Thirty minutes into the trip we come upon an overturned bus; buses here are the size of our Greyhound buses except they also are fitted with a rack on the top that gets filled with people riding on the roof. The bus has hit a large hole in the road and tipped over. Many people are hurt, and the traffic is quickly backing up. I ask the driver how long the delay will last. "At least eight hours." I ask if there is another way. "Yes, but it is not safe. There are many robbers who might push a cart in front of us, stop us, and rob us all." I asked how long that way would take, and he assured me that we would not lose any time if we went that way. I said, "Quickly, let us pray, turn around, and take the dangerous route." No one was that happy with the idea, but all agreed. There were twelve of us in the bus. As we prayed and turned around, we were instructed to take off our watches and jewelry and give them to one woman to hide in the floor of the bus, and we went on our way, completing our journey without incident.

We have received the news that the political parties have called another strike day, meaning that no one can drive to the conference or get alternate transportation. Everyone will have to walk. Some have come from several miles away. The pastor informs me, "There will be quite a few people missing tomorrow." It is a cool night, and we are ready to return for some sleep. We arrive at the hall in the morning to find that only one couple is missing from the day before. The people had left early in the morning and walked the whole way. The only couple missing tried coming on their motorcycle and had a crash. Gratefully, they are okay but could not get here. They sent word that they would arrive tomorrow. I lecture straight through to 1:00 p.m. We begin the afternoon sessions and finish to have some more news from the East, where we are planning to go when this seminar is finished. The people are already walking toward the location of the next seminar. However, the rebel soldiers have rigged with bombs the main bridge to the city. Hopefully, the army will have the bridge disarmed before the day is out. The next problem is that the rebels have called for a strike in that region. That means that we can fly to the airport, but we cannot get transportation to the site of the seminar, three hours away by car. The new plan is to find a room and get up early enough to arrive at the seminar by 9:00 a.m. the next day. Amen. We finish the current seminar a half-hour early so that the people can get an early start walking home. The next morning we leave in the darkness that 5:00 a.m. presents. There will be twenty pastors from the remote areas waiting for a seminar. We are stopped by the military and asked to exit the vehicle, but once we complied, the commander yelled at the soldier, "Can you not see that they are foreigners?" Immediately we are sent on our way into the heart of rebel territory. We pass several villagers carrying their usual loads of wood, wool, coal, and more upon their heads. As we wrap around a hairpin corner passing a bus, we see the city in the distance. Again we are stopped by the military, and then again at the bridge that the military found wired with explosives this week. These towns located on terraces have buildings constructed of rock, brick, and concrete; the streets are narrow. There are no tourists here. We arrive at the hotel and get the news that the army attacked a rebel camp just over the hill from the city, killing six of them. (The revolutionaries hold the remote areas and the military holes up in the bigger cities.) The rebels returned fire, killing twenty-seven of the government's military and taking another forty hostage. This was the reason for the roadblocks. In fact, we were the only ones allowed to pass into the city; several of the people heading to the conference were turned back. This village is quiet and subdued with this news. I see now that this country is not headed toward civil war but is already in one. The military, consisting of village people, does not seem to have the heart for this battle. We rush off and make our way down a path that is heavily rocked to keep it from washing away, ending up at a recently-constructed Baptist church. Some have walked for days for this conference and are now seated on the cold concrete floor, men on one side and women and children on the other. The smell of an open fire and the lunch to come drifts in the windows. Shoes must be removed to enter the church, so I feel the brutal cold in my feet. I get started speaking but notice large blue quilts are being brought in, so I stop the service while the men cover the entire floor with them. It really helps the people get comfortable and warm. We do four sessions and break for lunch. Here it is customary for the pastor to eat last. All of the people are fed, then the guests, and finally the pastor. In fact, the pastor will sit with us but will not eat until we finish. In the morning there is no hot water, so I take the water that has been in the hot-water bottle all night and use it for a bath. It is no longer even warm, but at least it is not freezing. We have a full day ahead of us and must make up lost time for the first evening of the conference we missed because of the strike. Some of the pastors will have to leave tonight and start walking up to ninety kilometers home. Saturday is once again church day to get around the strike, so we will finish the conference and then preach in different churches on Saturday. I have gotten a little wiser and am wearing three pairs of socks. This is the very first conference these people have attended, which is another reason why I am called to this work in the more remote areas. In the capital city, the people have one conference after another. The smiles on the faces reflect the joy of hearing the witness of what the Lord is doing and create an expectation in me for the future. After we arrive at the room, the pastor's wife calls to tell us that the insurgents have called for a nationwide three-day strike for Sunday, Monday, and Tuesday. Immediately we call for a car to come pick us up on Saturday and take us close to the airport; Sunday's strike would at least allow us to take a bicycle rickshaw to the airport. We will not be preaching here tomorrow after all, but we praise the Lord for His miraculous provision, because all things considered, even though the pastor planned the conferences a year ago, each one successfully occurred right between three nationwide strikes. We arrived in this town less than twelve hours after the battle; we did the conference, and though we had to leave a day early because of another upcoming strike, we later learned that we missed the rebel soldiers, who were right behind us chopping down the huge trees and rigging them with bombs to block the road in and out of this village. Had we waited to leave, we would have been trapped here for at least a few weeks. The pastor is really excited that we went in and out in the middle of a war.

We seize the opportunity to take a tour on bicycle rickshaw and notice a camp of "freed" slaves. I determine to buy a badminton set to take to the youth, that they might have a diversion from the tedious lifestyle of living in a tent "camp" on a subsistence diet. There would be no outlet for them, no place to go. We purchase the badminton set, and I ask my travel partner to stay in the rickshaw and "watch my back" as I walk into the middle of the camp. I was greeted without a single smile as they sorted out the implications of the presence of a white man. I take out the birdies and rackets and start playing. They begin to smile, and we had a good time, but when I got ready to leave, money was demanded. Amen! I just looked bewildered and gave nothing. Unfortunately, as I was leaving, the men were headed off to sell the birdies and rackets. Amid poverty, there is no use for frivolous games. I understand, but I did have a good time playing and wished the young people could have continued in that activity. We went over a bridge and entered a settlement that is in the neighboring country. We stop at the "booth" for immigration. The officer is very rude, but I speak to him in Hindi, and he lightens up a bit. I explain that we want to visit the city for one day, but he is indignant that we have somehow bypassed immigration and ended up in his country. The message is clear: "Get out now before I have to do something regrettable." We read him loudly and clearly, since we can envision this illegal entry into the land as causing much more trouble than we are willing to endure, so we happily leave.

Frontier Work

My ride arrived and we were all in a big rush to leave the city and head for the interior. We went to get the four-wheel-drive that we had rented. We got it all checked out and spent the next four hours driving around town to pick up people. In the end there were five people in the backseat, two of us sitting on the front bucket seat, and the backend was completely loaded. I looked in the back and could only see colorful clothing and heads poking out; it was a ridiculous situation. Then, to my chagrin, I was informed that it was a forty-two hour drive, a bit of information that would have been useful earlier; the plan was to drive night and day to get there. At that I had the driver call the office and rent another truck for five days. This took a couple of more hours to sort out, which pushed our departure back to late afternoon. The women kept thanking me, saying, "This would have been very difficult." No, it would have been impossible! I am discovering that these are a very hardy people that can make do, but eight people riding in a car for so long is not workable. It is an interesting group traveling, and they are all from the village to which we are attempting to drive, though due to the great distance and the civil war, they have not been there for many years; they simply lacked opportunity, finances, and—as I am about to find out the hard way—a decently passable road. Among our travel group we have a young man, an elderly pastor, and a not-so-old pastor who brought his two sisters. One has a wonderful story about raising seven children amid the war; during the rainy season she had to cross a river with four of the children as the rebels chased them. Another man in our group is sixty but has the eye twinkle and innocence of a child; I put him in charge of taking photos, and he is thrilled with that job. Finally, the head driver reminds me so much of my grandfather, approaching everything in "full steam ahead" mode. He is the proverbial bull in a china closet and is always yelling and screaming, perhaps like a wagon-train boss. Between his fits of yelling he stops to pray and then continues shouting. He has taken the duty upon himself to see that I arrive in the village to tell people about Jesus. This is not just a job for him but a mission. It is fascinating to watch him. He tells me, "I am thirty-five; I have bought my own land and built my own house. I am sending my children to school, and I am going to complete university myself. My name, in my local language, means, 'What do I fear?'" Not long after we got on the road, we were weaving around potholes and driving through rain. I asked the Lord, "Will I get there?" He spoke, "I will take you there, and I will bring you back." I hid it with confidence in my heart. On this journey it is abundantly clear that He wants to teach me at least as much as I am teaching others. We are making many stops in local villages. The road built in the dirt is actually an expanded ancient path that goes from village to village, all seeming the same with a "Main Street" type of path running amidst their mud-brick huts with thatched roofs. There are always naked children playing, women hauling a variety of things on their heads, and men working the fields. Often I see boys aged six or so carrying long bamboo poles on their heads. When we stop I move openly among the people. Whenever I turn around, my traveling companions are following. When they can take it no more, they say to me, "Brother, why do you move so freely and fearlessly among the people?" I explained, "They are God's people and I am from Him, so why would I not move without inhibition?" They cautioned, "You must quit letting people hold your camera and teaching them how to take pictures; they will steal it from you." I explained, "Brothers, if I am in the street taking pictures, a thief may steal my camera; but if I give the camera to a thief, show him how to use it, and trust him, he will never steal the camera. You must learn to hold a crown above the people's heads and let them grow into it." At that they withdrew, and I was free to move without being shadowed. Back on the road it has grown dark, and the potholes are impossible to navigate; we long ago moved off the "paved" road; now it is only dirt and mud, which makes for rough going. At 2:00 a.m. I spoke to my driver: "I, too, am a driver, and it is not right that you drive for forty hours! I will now take over." He was not happy with that and protested. When dealing with a Doer, it is often necessary to ratchet the intensity to the next level. "I have hired this car, and I am the boss of this trip.

Pull over and give me the car." At that he yielded. I took over and he slept for two hours. When he awakened and asked for the wheel, I went to the driver of the other vehicle and took over for him. The road surface now was mud and cavernous holes that could stop eight jeeps and swallow them up; no one would be the wiser. Everyone is quiet as the trucks move forward in the dark of a moonless African night. We move along hour after hour, dip after dip, hole after hole, and many times we believe that our teeth will shake right out of our heads. Amen. We arrive at a "city" that is the final bit of civilization for some time to come. Actually, it looks like all others to me. We are told that the roads ahead are impassable. The driver speaks to me privately, "Do we need something in case we get stuck?" I responded, "Of course! I want a shovel and tow rope." He nodded with a smile and said, "Yes, we think alike." I gave him the money and instructed him to get the needed supplies, to fill the trucks with petrol, and to make ready. He was off like a rocket. Because we had been driving already for 28 hours without a break, and I cannot sleep in the dip-and-bounce world of an outback "highway," I realized as I stood there that a previous exhaustion symptom had recurred, so I would need a toilet. I made a friend after being in the city for a few minutes, so I ask him where to go for help. He is genuine "country folk" and leads me to an Arab shopkeeper, who calls for a nephew that knows English. They take me upstairs to use the facilities, consisting of a room with a mound of concrete with a hole in it. There could not have been a more welcomed sight. I emerged to meet the Muslim owner's nephew, who said, "They tell me you are a Christian. I had to abandon

425

education and am self-taught. I have wanted for many years to know about Christianity. Do you have any books that I might read?" I smiled at the "coincidence" and that his uncle spoke only Arabic and French and would have no idea what I gave the boy, so he would not be able to lodge a complaint. I told the young fellow to follow me and I would give him one of each of my books. I had to make another trip to the toilet and discovered him already engrossed in the books. "Lord, you told me long ago that I would go many places for the one person. Amen! I do praise You for this one." I am happy when the caravan is ready to move forward. I have been harassed at the checkpoints since we began this journey. If I am driving, they wave me through, assuming that I have been in the country too long to be a tourist or visitor. However, when I am not driving, they stop and press for the bribe. At one point they refused to let me move forward until I presented a passport, which is not even logical, because once in this country, I had to take my passport to the police station and leave it in order to apply for an exit visa that costs a cool $125 and takes nearly a week to process! How, then, do I travel with the passport in my possession? The bottom line is that the past government officials did not want foreigners here poking around and discovering the evil that abounded within this country. They never said so, but they made policies with rules so difficult and frightening that people would stay away. When stopped, I would simply want to give the officer a dollar or two so as to avoid the thirty-minute delay and the game of extracting money from us. Not so my pastor host! He gets out of the truck and in their faces, countering, "I have with me a man of God; how can you stop him? We are ministers of the Gospel to bring hope to your villages; how can you stop us? How dare you stand in the way of God's business?" Indeed, all but one time they yielded! We are told from reports of other drivers that we are on a journey of two weeks due the road conditions' being so bad. Our driver, being so determined, only says, "It is the devil's attempt to hinder, and it is God's will that we speak to the people. We move forward!" Amen, for I bear in mind the words of Jesus, "I will take you, and I will bring you back." Before long we see what the locals are talking about. We must drive down into the mud until the walls of the road rise far above the roofline of the truck. We see that one large truck is already stuck. We do not go far before we, too, are stuck, but our driver is able to creep the car along and make it out, but barely. The operator of our other vehicle is a city driver with no clue about four-wheeling. Everyone is complaining about him, and my Doer driver is quick to join in and verbally cut him to pieces. "He is the wrong man for the job! He is stuck because he did not even put the truck into four-wheel-drive!" This scenario will be repeated more times than I can count in the next twelve hours. Amen. Now, allow me to boast a bit about the citizens here. I have been to many countries where I was offered help in a jam; however, at the end of the situation, the hand would be held out for some money. Not so, not so, and not so in this country. The people seemingly come from nowhere, take directions from my driver, plunge themselves into the mud, and work. I mean they REALLY work to move us out of the pit, and afterward they ask for nothing. This is impressive and something of which these countrymen can be proud.

This anomaly only exists in the village areas and is testimony to the big difference between country folk and city dwellers. The villages are communes, so no one does anything by him- or herself. The men farm together, the women cook together, and they all pitch in to build a new house. The benefit of the constant awareness of their need for each other extends to travelers such as me. We push on from one stuck situation to the next. Sometimes we can go a full kilometer, and other times it is only a block or two. The other vehicle should never have been rented to us, not only because of ill use by the city driver, but because the vehicle does not stand high enough above the ground. So far we have torn off two bumpers and tied them to the roof; another bumper is dragging, a fender is ready to fall off, and the automobile continues to stop. The battery has begun to melt, the lead is running out of the top, and there is no tool to be found anywhere. Fortunately, I have brought a couple of "Leatherman" tools to give away, and these prove to be lifesavers as we travel along. Eventually the second vehicle dies. It is boiling over, the sides are scraped, and the battery and alternator are finished. I look at the situation, and a still small voice within whispers, "I will take you, and you will return." Amen, I rest. We decide that we are about two hours from the village of our destination. A plan is hatched. The younger pastor, his two sisters, and I will go on to the village, since the meetings are to start at sunset. Our driver will then return for the rest of the folks, and in the next few days the two drivers will decide what to do about fixing the broken-down vehicle. The path narrows, and narrows, and narrows until it finally becomes nothing more than a footpath, but onward continues our driver, saying, "See, what do I fear? We must take you to the village to share Jesus." Amen, at this point in time I would do anything to get out of the car. Oh, I forgot to mention one important detail about my driver: He owns only one CD! It blares out this country's version of rap, which has the same theme as ours: sex. It is amazing that there are signs warning about the AIDS virus absolutely everywhere, and then rap with sexual innuendo is played constantly on the radio. I can close my eyes and still here the incessant reverberation in my ears. I am spent, and after forty hours on the road, accompanied by the repeated rendition of the rap, I would confess to anything! The CIA could learn a tactic or two from this driver. I had fantasies about rolling my hair and fingernails up in the car's window and then pulling them out just to get my mind off of the music. All right, I have digressed. Back to the footpath on which our car is traveling; it has ended, so we are now making our own path. Then, like a scene from "Jurassic Park," we top the mountain and view the village below. The children and the people come running, shouting and rejoicing. A white man has not visited their village in sixty years. Many were skeptical and kept saying, "The white Christian will never come! It is too difficult, and we must not expect him." I was a mere shadow of myself, but I was there! The village is large and beautifully positioned in rolling hills; the soothing, lapping water at the oceanfront is heard in the background. A continuous gentle breeze is comforting. The coconut palms are scattered in manicured fields of rice and taro. There are many thatched roofs on mud huts with handmade plaster covering them. Children are swimming in the stream as we cross it. We wind through the huts, making our way to the meetinghouse, and our driver is quite pleased with the Lord and with himself. He is a destination man, and he has brought us to the people. After forty hours of no rest or sleep, we are awake in response to the fact that the place has come alive. The people have begun to realize that among our baggage they can see faces long forgotten, older and yet memorable. With this realization, there are more cries. We are stopped amid a sea of people. The children at first stand back, for I appear to them as a ghost. Finally, one by one they approach to touch my pale skin. Immediately the truck is unloaded into the cooking house, and we walk in the quest of our intended goal of greeting the village elder. I am whisked along as though in a dream. It is reaching the magical hour of 6:00 p.m. The sun bows its head, yielding relief from the scorching heat. The elder is the younger pastor's uncle. Often, as here, in village culture there is no distinction between one's father and uncle; both are called father. The pastor's father died in an accident when he was seven, and the lighthearted uncle immediately assumed paternal responsibilities. I enter the house to great excitement as immediately a cola nut is brought to me. On the way here I had been forewarned: "Brother, if the cola nut is not offered, leave immediately, because you are not welcome, and you must go." The cola tree has a giant pod that looks like a green bean but is about ten inches long and four to five inches wide. The boys are sent to the very tops of the trees to cut the golf-ball-sized nuts out of the pods. Any uneaten nuts are buried until a special occasion. Just such an occasion has arisen. The nut is sliced into half-inch pieces and left in water. The head of the house takes the first piece, dips it in a very, very, very hot sauce, and eats it. All attention turns to me. Fortunately, I have long lived in proximity to Hispanic communities and their cuisine (something I like very much) and have grown accustomed to hot food. They were surprised when I took the nut, dipped it in the sauce, ate it, raved about its being so tasty, and took another one. They were expecting me to spit it out. There were several comments on that before everyone took some. The nut, by the way, is hot enough by itself. I am back at the meetinghouse where they unpacked my clothes. They asked me to enter and indicated that this is the place where I will be staying. I was distressed to see that they are cooking in this enclosed area, and the only exit for the smoke is the doorway. I enter my room and can barely breathe or see. The wheels in my brain begin to turn. How will I do this? I must wet a towel and put it over my face. Maybe I can sleep outside. That is a miserable thought! However, before any resolution occurs to me, I am whisked off for another meeting and more cola nut. The children follow me everywhere I go, and I like that. I stop and talk to them, hold them, and do magic tricks. The tricks have them all abuzz, and they run off to get their grandparents to come and see me. Once we are done with all of the visiting, I am told to go to the pastor's house where I will be staying! Can it be? Have I been liberated from being cured in the smokehouse? Yes! I enter the pastor's thatch-roofed mud hut. The floors are made of dirt and clay tamped with a piece of ebony wood. I ask if I might be shown to the toilet, which turned out to be of an absolutely clever design. It was in a dedicated bamboo shed, and there was no odor. Inside was a concrete mound with two raised footsteps and a piece of rebar coming out of the middle of the two steps. When the bar was raised, a hole was revealed. As I was being shown that, water was being brought from the river for my bath, but I stopped them and said, "No hot water!" In the first place, I do not need them going to all of that trouble, and secondly, after a hard two-days' journey in tropical heat, I do not relish anything hot touching my body! The "shower" is a bucket and a cup in an enclosure of thatching woven between vertical bamboo rods. I went in, took off my clothes, turned on my flashlight, and waited for the crowd to appear to see the spectacle of a white man undressed. It sounds shocking, I know, but after forty hours with no sleep, I could not care less. Back in my room, the flashlight's beam reveals the three-inch cockroaches running across the bed and my baggage. Amen. The bed is made of bamboo and is a few inches off the ground; it has a "cushion" but is very hard. I carry with me a silk sleeping bag, which when packed is about twice the size of a hand, but when spread across a mattress keeps the imbedded bugs from working their way up to bite me. I slather myself with mosquito repellant and lie down. Oh, yes! I am so ready to get horizontal after the long car trip; it is raining, and though the lightning brightens the room enough to see them on my bed, there are no further thoughts about the cockroaches, the lizards, or the mosquitoes as I fade into drowsiness. However, I hear the men enter to try out the generator that we purchased. I cannot believe it! I am lying there exhausted, and soon there are more people than I can count stringing light bulbs around the room. I stopped them and implored, "Brothers, string the light bulbs outside and let me sleep, because I am an old man." I know that it may sound odd, but in the developing countries, fifty-four is considered old when most people only live to be forty, and therefore I can use my age to good advantage. For the next hour they work on the generator, but I drift off in a sound sleep. I awaken in the morning to the sounds of villagers outside the hut waiting for me to appear. I found crushed cockroaches all over the bed; they had climbed all over me last night, so whenever I rolled over, I would crush them. The lizard living on the bed must be growing accustomed to how quickly I make available his cockroach snacks when I am sleeping. I pull myself together by pouring a little water over my head and combing my hair. I come out to find a roomful of people waiting. I am served rice and some kind of corned beef that looks and acts like gelatin. I have not eaten a meal in three days, so it does taste rather nice. I eat half of it, and we head off to the first of many meetings. We reach the assembly place for the church, and it is packed. The generator is running, so I hook up the computer and the projector. The man I appointed as photographer has been taking pictures along the way, so I begin with a slide show of our journey to come to them. The congregation is thrilled to see this; none of them have viewed photos before. The place begins to fill, and soon there are at least a couple of hundred folks gathered. After the ceremonies, the singing choir that enters and sings, the introduction, and more, I am asked to speak (only the pastor and a very few others can read). "Brothers and Sisters, God ordained that He might become a man and dwell among us. It was His heart that everyone could understand the message that Jesus would bring. To that end, He has spoken in all things

433

created to witness to His Son. You need not know how to read to know your Creator. Look around you; what does nature teach you?" I went on, and the Lord was speaking to them to reveal the mysteries of Christ through the things created and evident to all. The Lord did move, and the people were surprised and encouraged at the same time. We talked of many things, such as suffering, His coming, revelation, and the peace of God. Not a sound was heard during this Spiritual connection. I told them of my son who does not read much and yet was a better preacher than am I. At this they marveled, and yet it is true. We spent the whole day together, and it slipped by as though it were a minute. This is one big reason why the worst of conditions for me as a Westerner do not bother me; they all pass. Therefore, I have learned to enjoy the moment, because there are many things I do not wish to go by so quickly. At the end, I said to the people, "I have a surprise. Take a break, stand up, and return." I was away for fifteen minutes and returned to find not 200 people but 400. They had heard there was a surprise, which is a copy of the movie "The Passion of the Christ" on my computer. It was dark, and I knew the projector would show the movie on an 84-inch screen. Try to imagine that you have never before seen a movie, and the first movie that you see is "The Passion of the Christ"! I loved watching the response. These people had never seen electronic media, and they were watching the crucifixion of Christ. By the end of the night nearly 800 people were stacked outside the openings of the building, and the children were all over the floor and in every empty space. The pastor stood in front of the audience to translate the subtitles. It was interesting that at the scene of Judas being driven outside the city to hang himself, the crowd laughed, jeered, and applauded his death. When it came to the crucifixion of Christ, the people yelled, "No, no, no," and wept. We ended the meeting by saying, "Come tomorrow and we will tell you about the crucifixion." Wonderful! That night I slept very well with no further testing of the generators. In the morning, I was awakened by the sound of the men in the adjoining room. Clearly, something was happening. I entered to find a pastor holding a white chicken. I sat down, and the pastor spoke in the company of many people. "I could not sleep last night. The Lord was trying to say something to me. Finally, I heard. 'You are to give the white preacher a white chicken.' I have come, and here is my chicken." I took the chicken and spoke: "You have heard the Lord rightly, for a white chicken comes to me swhen He is going to bless me. It has happened in the past, and it has happened today." At this the man looked greatly relieved. "I will take the chicken as a sign from the Lord." I reached down and took one feather from the chicken; all looked on as I put the feather in my bag. "This feather will remind me of your faithfulness to the Lord. Now go and give this chicken to the oldest woman in the village." The directive was heard and obeyed. I did not know the blessing that was to come, but I believed that a blessing would come. Next I was ushered off to walk among many mud homes. As in ancient days, the houses were built close together to provide a defense against an invasion. In this remote area there are nearly 5,000 people to protect and so many houses that I cannot pass in front of all of them. Children and old men and women increase in numbers by my side as we move along. Finally, I enter

435

through the low doorway of the mud-constructed hut of the chief, who speaks. "Many, many years ago our own witchdoctors told us that a white man, a plain man, would be coming. When he appeared, he would speak of the God we were to follow." Mind you, he is shouting at me the whole time, the elders and old women are chanting, "Hum . . . hum . . . hum," and the crowd has gathered outside. He looked me square in the eyes to say, "And we were instructed to give you all of the lands. I give you all of my lands. Together we will own the land." He spit and blew into his open palms, and then blew a blessing on to me. All agreed, and the deal was finalized by a shot of sugarcane grain alcohol. One elder followed with the bottle and kept the glass filled. When the glass came to me, my young pastor friend said, "It is alcohol." I turned to him and said, "Should I deny the village their privilege to give to me all the lands?" He looked down. I said, "Brother, the Lord will keep me." I took the glass and prayed aloud, "Father, You are faithful and true! You promised that if I would leave my family, you would give me families, brothers, sisters, and land. You have kept Your word. You have given me a new land, and now I ask, in the name of Jesus, that my land be blessed and protected, that the sun would shine on the days needed and the rain would fall on those days necessary. I pray for the people of my land, that they might be blessed and be fruitful and multiply. I pray for those that will oversee my land until my return. Amen." The people rejoiced over not my prayer, but the prayer of the One Who leads me. Amen! I exited the chief's house and remembered the white chicken. We weaved our way between the mud huts in the glare of the equatorial sun.

We were headed back to the village for another session. Upon arriving, I could tell something was afoot. We started with singing, and then I was asked by the chief to come forward. By this time I was drenched in sweat. The people assembled were told of the meeting in the village, and then the chief said, "We must name you and dress you as a chief." I came forward, and the chief proclaimed my name. "From this day forward, when you enter the village, you will be called Gbannie, the name of our founding chief. You are the mountain that stands above and the one who mends the broken! Now I must clothe you." They put on me the robe of a chief. Now, backtrack a moment to think of this boy, Mike, raised around a farm in Kansas and working in a filling station with his grandfather. I was being made a chief of this people of whom I had never before heard. I know the African dance, and as they proclaimed me chief, I began to dance a dance of joy. It took only moments for the people to see me, and thus the whole gathering erupted in an hour of dancing and shouting. Finally, I proclaimed, "I am Gbannie, a chief among my people!" At that the place appeared to be frozen in time, and again I prayed and the people rejoiced. What a journey! I went on to speak. "I will tell you stories, and he who has ears to hear will understand and change, and those that do not understand will not hear." I only told them stories and ended with saying, "Discuss this story while I am gone, and when I return, tell me what it means." It was a dynamic time. We ended and headed off to pack, though I could barely move, because the crowd was so thick. The children encompassed me and asked that I teach them a little magic trick. When all was said and done, we packed ten people into one truck and headed off. I was not happy with that, but my driver kept insisting that we could reach the broken vehicle, fix it, and offload the passengers. We exited the winding paths and roads just as we had entered them. The children were still playing in the streams, and the people still followed us. We entered the open area and headed toward the broken vehicle. Upon arriving, my driver was determined to fix both trucks. With his resolute nature, it does no good to talk to him, so I withdrew for a time before returning to try to explain the mechanical problem. I tell him that I grew up in a mechanic's shop and that what he is attempting will not work. He disagrees and tells me that he can sew. I explain that I also can sew, but it does not fix an alternator that is bad. We go around and around and around. At last I walk off again and let him work. He is taking the battery from the good vehicle and placing it in the bad vehicle that has a short. The truck does start but begins to melt the good battery and then stops. At last he is persuaded to stop the madness and park the disabled vehicle. All ten people pile into the one good truck; again we are completely enveloped with colorful clothes and heads. It is stupid to me, and I press him to leave half of the people in the village. We can send someone to fix the broken truck, and then they can move on toward their homes in comfort; after all, I am the only person on this journey with a schedule and a plane to catch. No, no, the driver counters, we can get everyone in the truck. We do and press on. When we arrive in the village in which I previously met the Muslim boy, I ask for my friend, and instantly he appears. I tell him that I have a problem, and he is up to the challenge of lending a hand. The pastor calls a cousin, and we all gather at the mechanic's shop. I purchase a battery and give the cousin $50. I ask if he and his coworkers would go to the broken truck in the morning, replace the battery, check the electrical problem, and bring the truck to town. All involved agree. We let the women eat and then proceeded onward. Around 1:00 a.m. the headlights begin to fail, indicating either alternator or battery problems. Since we have not so long ago left the "city" where I purchased a battery and organized a group of mechanics to go after the stranded truck, I say to my driver, "Turn around!" He protested. I asked how far it was to the next city, and he said it was eight hours. At that I said, "Turn around." He paused, looked at both the ground and the heavens, and said, "God is telling me to go forward." I said, "God is telling me to go back." He yielded but was not happy. The amazing thing is that we were both right, both listening to the Lord! We turned around and traveled for nearly one-half hour. By now we had lost our lights, and navigating on this pitted dirt road was even more shocking. We encountered a young fellow on a motorcycle; he asked where we were going. We explained that we did not have a battery or an alternator and had decided to return to the main village we had left. The boy nearly scolded us and said, "Turn right around! I will go ahead of you, and you can follow my light. I know a man in my very small village that can fix the truck." We had to go ahead to find the village, but had we not turned back, we never would have found the young man to lead us to the village! Once there we awakened the man, and naturally he was initially upset at such an intrusion. However, after viewing the problem, the mechanic within him awakened. He had his friends hold flashlights as he took the alternator off and began to work on it. He told me the repairs would take four hours. The village was pitch black. I took my bag and looked for a place to lie down. I found a hut with no lights on inside and lay down on their table under the porch roof. Since there was a very large hole in that roof, I could see the African night sky with a multitude of stars, and I felt blessed to be there. I watched that view until sleep overcame me, and the next sound I heard was an engine starting. Yes! In what had seemed an impossible situation, we were once again going to make progress forward. "I will take you there, and I will bring you back." Jesus was enjoying all of this, and so was I. I asked the mechanic the cost, and he tells me that it is nothing, but that if I want to give something, I can. I want to give him $100, but the pastor and his sisters tell me no, that I should give only $20. I give him $30, and everyone is happy. We set off at 3:00 a.m. and go not thirty minutes when I notice the driver nodding off, so I demand to take the wheel. The headlights actually hide the potholes ahead, and often there is nothing to choose from when it comes to a path. I must stop repeatedly to put the thing in four-wheel-drive. It is a labor, and I have not slept for 24 hours. I drove from 3:30 a.m. to 6:00 a.m., and I cannot honestly tell you that I was awake; I could not hear sounds and did not know up from down. I so wanted to stop, and yet the driver was spent and could not have taken over. It was like a dream from which I could not awaken. At 6:00 a.m. the sun rose and gave me some relief, especially since it also awakened my driver, so he resumed duties at the wheel. The time between 6 and 8 a.m. is magic; the monkeys begin to move along the road, the giant rat (much bigger than a cat) appears on the road, and I begin to come out of my trance. We stopped in a village where the trappers have caught two of the giant rats; one is cleaned and the other is just hanging. All of my traveling companions want one, because the price of rats in the city is four times greater than here. So now we have these in the back of the truck. The smell of fresh flesh mixed with the music and chickens is nearly more than I can take. Amen, the giant rat is treasured with its soft bones, and I am supposed to get excited at the "treat" ahead, because we can boil one, and, as honored guest, I get to eat the skull. I cannot wait! Later I drove again and traversed the worst stretch of road in my life. There was no good option as I drove along, whether going right and bouncing people through the roof, or going left and bouncing people through the roof. I was sick of it and stopped so we could take a break. The old man came forward and said that he wanted out of the vehicle; he was done with the trip. I understood why! He was riding over the axle, had bumped his head, and was dizzy. We would discover only in time that the extensive length of rough terrain had also triggered a diabetic episode. At any rate, I was not happy with how things were turning out. I was in the front seat with the driver and trading off driving. Behind me were the women and the younger pastors. The back held the luggage and four old men. When we stopped, I asked the young pastors, "How can it be right for the old men to ride in the back and the young men to sit in the middle?" Things got shuffled around, and the next thing I knew, there was a group of young pastors in the back of the truck. The driver took over and led us for the next three hours. We were stopped by another roadblock; this time the "officer" was not going to let me pass. I questioned his decision, since I had passed by there a few days earlier. Everything we said or did was predestined to make him angry. I got on the phone and called my brother in the U.S. to tell him that if I gave him the officer's phone number, he was to call him and tell him to release me. However, by the time that plan was worked out, the pastor had paid the "officer" a "fee" to let us proceed. Well, not so fast. After a good bit more driving, the back tire went flat, and we put on the spare tire that is nearly flat. After running for an hour or so, the driver has a plan. We will take the back tire off and put it on the front, since the bulk of the load is in the back; this should allow us to keep going. It works, and we manage to arrive in the next city to have two tires patched. I just keep paying and paying and paying. I took over driving for the next three hours, and at sunset, I backed out of the command seat, for we were nearing the huge city these people call home. This metropolis, of course, does not have electricity, so think of it without lights. The blacktop seems to absorb our headlights with no other light around. My driver does a great job of passing, honking, and maneuvering around the potholes. I am to be the first one let off in the city. Well, that is, after we take care of the older pastors. Then we must stop for the other pastors, until, as might be expected, I end up in the worst neighborhood, late at night, the last passenger in the truck, asking my driver to please take me to my hotel. As he drives, he tells me more of the war, escaping to the jungles, living naked, and the rebels that went from house to house killing people. He drops me off at the front door of the hotel, holds me, and says, "I will miss you!" I will miss him, also; we have not shared in a journey but an amazing adventure, and I am at my hotel in spite of every obstacle. Sleep. I need sleep. I have told everyone that I am not to be bothered in the morning so that I can sleep and get to the airport. At 7:00 a.m. a pastor who did not make the trip calls from the front desk and wants to meet me for breakfast. During the meal I explain to him how I operate. I might receive e-mails for years from someone in a foreign country; these all say the same thing: "We love your ministry and want to partner with you." I hide it in my heart until one day when the Lord might say, "Go." I go, present Christ as life, and wait to see what the pastors say. If they begin to request funds for their projects, their hearts are revealed, and I know the motives behind their invitations. On the other hand, if they want more teaching and training in the message, then their hearts are revealed. I explain that in this way my message will both bless and curse. To those who only wanted money, one day the Lord will speak to them and say, "I came to you and offered the deeper revelation, and you only wanted money." They will say, "When did You come?" He will remind them of the day I brought the message. This pastor hung his head and looked at the floor, for his constant entreaties for funds during and after my last trip here had kept me away from this country for seven years. Amen. He worked at the airport and has many contacts, so when next he tells me that my flight has been postponed from 11:10 a.m. to 6:30 p.m., I go back to the room after breakfast to rest. At 3:00 p.m. I head to the airport with two pastor friends. They have all the security guards on alert, so I am able to move quickly to the checkout desk accompanied by one of the airline personnel. At the desk I get the news, "Your airplane left at 11:10 a.m., on schedule." The perfectionist pastor had gotten the whole thing wrong. There I was, stuck, for flights do not leave every day for my next destination. I was immediately frustrated and turned to the airline person and said, "This will be expensive!" I went outside and moved past the errant pastor to the ticket office. My main objective at this point was to find a way to the next place, even though I had been told that replacement flights would cost over $6,000! The Lord graciously reminded me that the fruit of the Spirit is for others, not so that I will feel better, so when I left the ticket office, I stopped the pastors, who up to this point had refused to look at me. "Brothers, this is God's doing, and I do not blame you. Anyone can make what appears to be either a mistake or a brilliant move; we must see the Lord in it. If we surrender our peace to a situation, we will not have merely the one problem of missing the flight, but many problems. Do not feel guilty, and do not mention this again." They looked dumbstruck, as they should have, for they are constantly rebuking each other harshly for every shortcoming, mistake, and failure. "Let us move on." I called my travel agent, who got on the problem immediately and said, "I will get you out of there in two days; it will cost you nothing, and you will not miss your meetings in the next place." As I was driving away toward the hotel, I remembered the words of the Lord, "I will take you there, and I will bring you back."

Festivals

Our first two nights in one place coincided with Devali, a Hindu celebration with fireworks like our Independence Day, only with much, much larger explosions. It was difficult to sleep with the constant bombardment of noise throughout the night. My brother and I went for a walk; as we passed a mansion and noticed the lighting of candles (part of this celebration of light), the owner (a High Court Judge) noticed us and invited us in. Soon we were sitting in a stranger's house with his wife and servants bringing us all manner of sweets. We thanked him, and he responded, "No, you must not thank me. Every grain of corn is born with a name on it and a time at which it will be eaten; this corn was yours from the beginning. I thank you for coming and partaking." I am not annoyed by the individual Hindus I meet; many of them are genuinely helpful. Their religion is ancient and based in ignorance; my approach is to keep presenting Jesus, not as a competing religion or teaching, but as the only life. Hinduism has brought the world the caste system; child labor; child prostitution (the World Bank has already built over 2,300 centers just for the "child-woman"); and the neglect, suppression, and disrespect for women, yet it is embraced by the West in the form of New Age. I find that baffling.

We went to the Church of South India's annual conference with over 100,000 people in one place. We arrive to a carnival-like atmosphere wherein a variety of vendors have set up along the path to the meeting place. Offered is everything from a viewing of the world's smallest Bible, to ice cream, to bamboo flute salesmen. It is truly unique to see it all. I am stopped and ushered through the

Bible exhibit; for the first time in over 100 years there is a new translation of the Bible, and everyone is excited about it. I meet up with my friend, an old-style Indian teacher who looks as though he belongs in the movie "Lord of Rings" and should be living in a hobbit cave somewhere. He walks slowly due to age. His white hair flows nearly to the shoulders, the beard is just as long, and he walks with a book bag. "You must slow down, Michael!" There is a pause as the computer between his ears grinds and the appropriate saying comes to mind. "Remember, hurry, worry, and bury!" He stares deep into my eyes until there is the recognition that I have processed what he has said. Then he turns and walks away. We work our way through the crowd down the dusty road to the river. The rainy season is yet to come, and the meeting of 100,000 is being held on the flat part of the dried-up riverbed. I followed my old friend, who had more advice: "It is not good to only have input; we must have output. Life is input and output." There in the field stands a fence of bamboo that is six feet high with a 12' X 12' square opening, which we enter. I do not know what I was expecting to see, but what I do see is genius. At the base of the fence a small trench had been dug. Clorox and lime were sprinkled in the ditch and on the walls. This was the urinal. It did not smell in the least bit. We then move closer to the main facility, passing by 75 to 100 booths various ministries have set up in the field. Time after time I am lost in the curving procession of humanity. Now to the riverbed and another amazing sight. The local villagers make thatch from easily grown materials and bring it with them to place on poles stuck in the ground; this allows for a makeshift roof around nine feet tall that results in shade for 100,000 people. People work their way under the thatch and sit on the ground. The speaker is so far away, at the other end on a platform, that he cannot be seen, for there is no rise in the ground. The shelter is not built for viewing but for listening and avoiding the intense heat of the midday sun. The music begins and one hundred thousand people begin singing at once. Malayalam is a beautiful-sounding language. When the preaching begins and the text for the sermon is John 15, I am initially excited, but then the preacher begins to describe how we can work to bear fruit, with no mention of the work of Jesus in our lives; it is just another sermon aimed at motivating the flesh. He is getting worked up and the passion is building. If only he could see the people on the outer fringes of the crowd trying to cope with the heat. Well, amen. India is a place that I call home.

We are traveling by van through the steep canyon walls, and it is beautiful. Terracing goes all the way to the top of the mountain, with a huge green river flowing below. Goats, water buffalo, and other animals are everywhere. The dogs amaze me in that they sleep on the highway and the traffic goes around them. In the rainy season this road is dangerous; the water running down off the steep cliffs will push a truck right into the sea. Today, however, there is a special problem: the festival of Shiva, who is always portrayed with the trident piercing a child. Though not an amiable god, in celebration of his singular deification the children hold a rope across the road, stopping every bus, car, bike, and truck. All drivers must pay a fee in order to proceed along their way. It will add a few hours to our trip, because we have already passed over fifty such checkpoints.

447

One time the driver drove through, breaking the rope. That did not make the children happy! At another roadblock the girls were dressed in colorful saris and threw spice on the car; they were not happy that the driver gave only one rupee. Tonight the core festival will begin, and there will be much smoking of hashish by the celebrants.

We stumble into a Hindu temple, and though one man tells us to leave, we move past him to watch the celebration. In the entrance of the temple is a priest lying in a coffin-shaped hole in the ground. A mirror stands upright at the end of the hole, giving a mystical effect to the image of the priest, who then appears to be standing on his head in front of the worshippers. He is waving a feather back and forth to create an even better illusion. This is quite the high-tech magic. We are asked to leave, and as we do, the ceremonial elephant is brought back from the streets, because the celebration is over. He gets stripped of his fancy attire and has his back foot tied to a tree and the front to a stake. Elephants mostly sleep standing up, and he is not permitted to run wild. The trainer is not at all gentle with the young elephant—he is perhaps five years old—and every time the animal is poked with the spear, he cries like a yelping dog. The elephant is very attuned to verbal commands and can move inches in any direction in response to a single shout.

I ask why so many people are walking with no shoes and carrying what appear to be altars on their heads. Our Christian brother explains that a great temple to the nephew of Shiva, the false god, sits upon a rock mountain. The people will walk up to 500 kilometers to reach the "sacred" place, and as part of their vow, they must wear no shoes. It

448

is obvious that this is torture, for many people have begun to limp and have wrapped their feet in bandages that are formed suspiciously to resemble a shoe! At the temple will be an idol on which has been put sandalwood paste. As the paste dries and cakes up, it drops off. This powder, when given to the worshippers to mix in water and drink, is presumed to heal or give the desire of their hearts. Many have made a vow to shave their heads to receive the favor of the false god. The hair is sold in Europe to make wigs and a very strong cloth. The power ascribed to religion is so prevalent. Imagine having a rebellious child on drugs, and you could either walk for 500 kilometers to receive the favor of a god, or you could wait on God. Walking is something to do, and religion gives confidence in what we do; it busies the flesh in doing something. Actually, all religions have in common the giving of confidence in what man can do. Religion offers the opposite of faith. Different religions may say that they "believe" different things, but that is not the truth. They actually offer different things to do, but they all believe the same thing: that success, on some level, rests in what a person does. Christianity is the only faith-based "religion," assuring the devotee that he can rest and trust, while the activity rests with God. This is a huge difference. There are 500,000 people that make this barefooted journey. It is sad, and yet incredible in light of globalization, which has not daunted this procession one bit. Can one really believe that Shiva's nephew lost his head, so the head of an elephant was cut off and put on a human's body? Well, there are at least 500,000 people that do believe that.

Some distance ahead is the temple to the false god, Krishna. As we approach, the drumming and the sounds from the priests' horns begin to intensify. There is a large arch with the Krishna in a full-sized chariot. On each side is a statue of Krishna; in one hand he holds a snake (his friend). It is like a scene out of the movie "Indiana Jones and the Temple of Doom." Six priests are shirtless, wearing a white skirt and necklaces of flowers, their faces painted with the mark of Krishna. They are playing a kind of trumpet that is very long, and there are bongos. We pass through the middle and move forward. Now there are two rows of priests, all facing each other and all dressed in the same manner, shirtless and a white skirt. One row has only the bongos; the other has what first appear to be rather large bows, with a stretched string from one tip to the other. The drums are deafening. The rhythm is consistent and reverberates in my chest. Then the other row raises what I thought were the bows, puts one tip in their mouths, and begin to blow a long and deliberate note. They all take turns so the sound never ceases. In the darkness, beyond the grand arch and a pole (similar to the one at the Orthodox church), we notice movement, and then the great monster appears. First, I see a faceplate of gold the size of a man's shield. As the creature moves forward, the white tusks of the elephant are evident. Two men have long staffs with five torches on the end that branch out like a tree; a servant quickly pours oil on the torches, they are lit, and the music intensifies. The beast is now in full view, and what makes him loom even more ominously is the fact that the first person on the elephant's neck is holding an eight-foot pole with an elaborate umbrella on the top.

The beast stops, and then elephants on either side of him move forward. It is quite a sight. The music never stops. I notice that one of the drummers extracts a small brass vial hidden in his skirt. A white powder is poured into his hand; he puts a little under each eye and snorts the rest. Then, wiping the substance from under his eyes with a cloth, he takes deep breaths through the cloth in order to inhale the last bit. From then on, his skills at the bongos diminish by the minute until his eyes are half shut and he is lashing at the drum. At this point, the noise and the feeling that we have overstayed our welcome drive us out of the temple. Hindus complain about foreigners defiling their holy places.

Four-legged or Other Critters

Dogs in this Hindu country act quite differently from dogs in countries where they are used as human companions. It is not that their nature is different, but dogs elsewhere are happy, friendly, and considered to be man's best friend. Here dogs are despised; they roam the streets in packs, are malnourished, and wait for one of their own to die, for that is the only time that they have a feast. I finally saw the meaning of the saying, "It's a dog-eat-dog world." These dogs continually bite and devour each other. The whole scene gives new meaning to Paul's use of the word "carnal." While traveling to a church, our driver inadvertently hit a dog, breaking both of its back legs. We could not stop, because the Hindu crowd would have been angry over our hurting an animal, yet they would not help the dog because it is despised. I wanted to stop and

451

mercifully kill it, but that was too dangerous for our driver, so we drove on and took another way home.

I saw an old guard dog that chased me and kept trying to bite me. I thought about how the dog is just about exhausted from years of chasing people. Satan is also exhausted from years of fighting God. How much energy would it take to fight God? Satan's end is near, but like every dying creature on its last day, he will rally.

At one place I stayed I had an ongoing battle with several mice, three-inch long cockroaches, and several geckos. They could not seem to understand the concept of my suitcase, my bed, and my briefcase. One night they gained a recruit in the form of a frog.

Before the evening meeting I had about two hours, just long enough to snorkel to "Bat Island," which is totally inhabited by the fruit bat, also called the flying fox. These bats have a length of fifteen inches and a wingspan of nearly five feet. When we step on the island they begin to panic, dropping from the trees and circling before they land again. It is quite a sight.

We bounce along the jungle road, weaving in and around bamboo. This area floods every year, and huge ponds of water are left behind. The locals go to great effort to drain the water with a series of buckets and hoses. They were just finishing the project and were now in the process of picking up the fish. Soon the rains will come again and the process will be repeated. Occasionally the pastor observes a person carrying elephant meat. Poaching laws are not enforced, and in fact, most of the locals would not even be aware of any such laws; they are just hungry.

Driving from the jungle back to town, little did I know that it was going to be a six-elephant day. We passed the first two and turned around to get a better look; they have been hired for use in a Hindu festival. During this particular festival, one day is chosen in which people can go to anyone they know and call that one any rude name they like. (Denver drivers must have declared that day to be every day of the year!) At one point we stopped to let elephants pass and noticed that all of them were shackled; one is the largest Indian elephant that I have ever seen. Servants are there to lay down the branches of palm and banana for the elephants to eat whenever they stop. These animals will eat over a hundred kilograms of palm branches in a day. It is interesting to see an elephant strip the leaves and eat the stalk; this must be the favorite part, because the leaves are eaten later. Elephants have such a soft nature and only attach themselves to one person; yet every year they kill men—even their trainers—if provoked. One thing that makes an elephant angry is when the trainer is overly drunk and yells and hits at the elephant. The animal may well grab the offensive man with his trunk, smash the man to the ground, and run a tusk through him. It is true that the elephants have a long memory and are not fond of the spears used to poke them or the hooks inserted into their ears to turn them. My teacher was telling me of his brother's once showing off around an elephant that soon had him in his trunk. He was blessed in that the elephant merely threw him across the road and broke a few of his ribs. Male elephants have a hormonal gland behind the eye; at certain times of the season, this gland will burst and fill their eyes with, basically, lust, so they become unreasonable and dangerous. At that time they are given tranquilizers. Elephants are expensive to keep and, with the increasing use of machinery, becoming less and less cost effective to use for labor.

In the newspaper I read of a scene where a baby elephant was caught between two trees. The herd of wild elephants will protect the baby at all cost, which makes rescue attempts quite dangerous. The elephants had wrapped their trunks around the trees and tried to uproot them, but since the trees were too large, all they accomplished was spreading the trees apart like a wishbone, which allowed the one-month-old baby to become wedged deeper down between the trees. The forest rangers have a plan, but implementing it among the wild elephants will be a challenge.

It is nice to be in an area this remote. There are the odd wolves, which do not always provide a positive encounter, because the last two were rabid wolves that bit people, and one child would have died had a dog not fought and killed the wolf; but now the dog must be put to death. There are a few wild boars and even signs of bears that have come in from Russia. In the countries of former Soviet occupation, nature has suffered greatly, and it is sad.

We pass through more water buffalo and arrive at the jungle guesthouse. It is very nice and even has a pool. The bungalows are made of grass walls and wooden plank floors. There is nearly no one there; six years of wars have kept the tourists away. We are asked if we would like to take an elephant ride, which proves to be an adventure. There is a "small" platform on the elephant onto which we must all wedge ourselves. Note to self: wear shoes. I did not, and the jungle hitting my feet and the elephant hitting trees took a toll on me, being very uncomfortable. However, the elephant is a pleasant creature, very humble, and, according to our guide, it is true the elephants are afraid of mice and will keep their trunks covered when one is around. The elephant is also reportedly a reflection of the owner; if the owner is nice, so is the elephant. All elephants here belong to the royal family. On this journey into the jungle we are looking for two things: one, the leopard, and two, the rhino that looks much different than an African rhino, for it is somewhat armored, like a huge armadillo. There were perhaps seventy in the area until poachers and floods—with their ensuing landslides—killed all but twelve. Just three days ago poachers killed two for their horns that are sent as aphrodisiacs to China. Perhaps, then, the one thing that is helping the world rhino population the most is the development of Viagra. This elephant we are riding has a mind of its own and likes to snack. We see monkeys, peacocks, what appears to be an elk but with straight horns, and some spotted deer, but no rhino. We even see a crocodile. We cross the streams and come to a small patch of grassland, where there are two rhinos, both females, one three years old and the other four years old. A bird is jealously guarding one of the rhinos, because it is enjoying the bugs that land on it. They are amazing to watch from the top of the elephant, and we forget our aching bodies; the rhino could not perceive our presence atop and so allowed the elephant to get very close, and we watched for fifteen minutes. In the villages, large platforms are built high in the air and mounds of hay are placed on top of them. This saves for the livestock the precious food that would otherwise be eaten by the roaming rhinos that like to come into the village for a quick meal.

The beautiful birds here appear in so many varieties that there are too many for me to count. We are organized to spend a night at the third largest lake in Africa. It has more varieties of freshwater fish than any other lake in the world; they look like reef fish because so many are brightly colored. The lake is beautiful; the water is crystal clear, and the banks have black, red, and white sand, which must be of different weights, because when the waves take the grains of sand out and then bring them back, they are always separated into colors. The younger fellows all decide to take a dip in the lake and do a little diving off the rocks. Just as my friends' son is preparing to jump in, a hippopotamus surfaces! It is a large male traveling alone, the most dangerous creature in all of Africa, for it accounts for more human deaths than any other animal. The boy's mother is quick to caution her son not to jump in. We watch this amazing creature that is rarely seen in the deep waters of such a huge lake; it moves along under the water, coming up every fifty feet or so to breathe. Hippos can sometimes find their way to the village gardens, and if there is enough destruction to the plants, the forest rangers are called in to kill just one hippo. This frightens the other hippos sufficiently to send them on their way.

In the night we hear in the distance the roars of a male lion; then we awaken to an amazing morning! We discover that zebras have surrounded the place. They even begin to roll like the horses on a farm; one zebra rolls three times. The fellow that built this place was very wise to make a small watering hole to attract animals. Soon the wild boars come and have quite a time playing at the water's edge. There are three babies that come so close it is as though we do not exist.

In the morning I am allowed to release the pigeons, a beautiful sight with over 200 birds circling. These are homing pigeons; other pigeons are there for breeding and can never be let out; they were not born here, and after all these years they would still return home if they had a chance. Some birds are taken 500 miles away, and on their journey home they will get hurt, lost, hungry, and more. They will even stop and stay with other pigeons until they are well enough to leave. In weeks or months, they will arrive home. Home for us is abiding in Christ, with all of the freedom that comes in Him. On occasion we get trapped, hurt, tired, and more. However, let us out of the cage and we will go home once again.

We have gone to visit a beautiful cheetah park that has one royal cheetah. For years it was thought to be a subspecies of the cheetah, but now they know that it is a recessive gene. The royal cat has blobs besides just spots. It is interesting to drive among the cheetahs and the wild dogs. The cheetah can go from zero to sixty faster than a formula-one racing car but can only maintain that speed for about 500 yards; if it does not stop, the blood vessels will begin bursting. This park is typical of many game preserves, where the directors have gone beyond believing "the creation longs for the revelation of the sons of God" to "worshipping and serving the creature rather than the Creator." It is part expanded information and part indoctrination. We are all told to do our part and demand that every park or game preserve have wild dogs within their spreads. We are to tell the owners

457

that we are not going to spend our money where there are not wild dogs. We are also to tell the game preserves to take down their fences and become one big, happy family. There is the constant emphasis on what "man" has done to mess things up, or, more specifically, how farmers mess things up. I watched the wild dogs eat, and I know I would not have them on my farm the way they slaughter. We stop at a cage to view a pair of Egyptian vultures (only forty are known to exist in the wild). This type of vulture picks up rocks in order to break ostrich eggs. Next the guide tells us, "The man who built this vulture cage lives with vultures and has a vulture café, wherein meat is put on a platform and the wild vultures come and mix with the tame ones that need to be released. He is so passionate about vultures that he has stated in his will that upon his death, his body is to be placed on the platform in the vulture café, and the vultures are to eat him. Now that is passion!" I watch my friend as they are saying this; the wheels are turning in his head. There is a pause before he blurts out, "No, that is insane!" I started laughing and had to turn away, for the guide did not know what to say when the mini sermon did not have its intended effect of stirring a like passion in us. It seems that vultures are endangered because of witchdoctors. Vultures will fly at around 21,000 feet. They see a sick animal and wait, so that when it dies they are the first ones there. This has led to the belief that the vulture can see the future, for the natives on the ground just see the vulture appear instantly upon death and did not notice the bird out of their eyesight but watching nonetheless. Therefore, the witchdoctor will cut the head off the vulture, make a necklace of the skull, make a soup with the eyes and brain, and give it to the paying customer to drink. This allegedly allows the client to see into the future and pick the right lottery numbers.

We stopped at an outdoor toilet. Inside it was really dark, and the door was nearly impossible to shut. I went in first, got the door shut, and sat there in the dark. Next, my pastor friend went in, and we waited for him for quite some time. Once he did emerge, he was shaken and pale. While he was sitting on the toilet, he had noticed a coiled cobra behind the door. He moved slowly, taking no small amount of time leaving the room in order to keep from getting bitten. We all went to the park rangers, but they refused to do anything until they got a gun. They said that has happened before, but they were not going to take the chance of getting bitten.

Fitful

In many of the places I have been, the basics are all that matter. Each time I take a drink of water, I think how precious it is. When I hear the hum of a generator, I rush to plug in my computer. When it is dark and hot, I hope to be able to sleep. Simple things matter to the extent that sometimes I get back to Colorado and am in awe just to turn on a light, stand under a hot shower, or open the refrigerator. I am not saying that I am suffering; I do not think about it much, because I enjoy the call of God. It is all just different and odd.

With a water shortage came an electrical shortage. The second night of a seminar was begun with no lights; the topic involved how all progress in Christ will come at the expense of the self-life. The meeting was to start at eight, but the leader came at nine; the notebooks were forgotten; the room with the books for distribution was locked and the key never found; the meeting place had been changed, though the people had not been informed; the new room opened to a city filled with noise; people came and went to the extent that I thought I was preaching to a parade; and the overhead projector with my presentation was not working. Amazingly, though the meeting started with only a few teachers, Sunday-school leaders, counselors, and deacons, eventually the room was crowded with attentive listeners. After I had suffered sauna-type conditions in this place for a week, I was overjoyed later to find that the air conditioner in my room had been fixed. I lay in front of the cooler, hoping to undo the previous week's torment, only to be interrupted by the need to go off to do counseling. When I finally arrived back to my room late at night to pack for a 2 a.m. departure, I threw my suitcase on the bed and . . . the lights and air conditioning went out. In came the hot gas lantern, and I finished packing with sweat running off the end of my nose! I always remind myself that I only endure for a short time what many believers undergo every day of their lives.

By the time I arrived in one developing country, it was 2:30 a.m. I had to clear customs and get some money. My contact host did not know where I was, because of a day's delay from a broken plane in the last country. He had come to the airport the night before, and I was not there. I did not have access to a phone in the war-torn country from which I had last departed, and therefore, in his mind, I was missing. When I left the airport at 3:00 a.m. I had to find my own taxi and a room. One fellow was very helpful, and by 3:30 I was in a decent room immediately calling Betty, because she had not heard from me since before I entered the last country; I asked her to send an e-mail to my host telling him where I was but asking him not to call before noon, because I really needed some sleep. At 4:00 a.m. I was ready for bed. At 8:00 a.m. he called to say, "I will be there shortly to pick you up. The conference started yesterday, so the pastors sat all day waiting for you. It is starting today at 9:00 a.m. and you must come." I suppose if I had been awake, I would have argued. Next thing I knew I was standing in front of the pastors, writing on a chalkboard, and speaking for hours. The pastors were so open and hungry for the Bread of Life. That evening when I finally got to a guesthouse, it cost $15 per night and looked a lot like the hotel in the last country that cost $100. I drug myself over to the sink and turned it on; oddly, no water ran out. I flushed the toilet, but did not hear the tank filling. In the shower, I grabbed the phone-shaped showerhead and turned on the water. Nothing. I look out and find there is a 30-gallon trashcan containing a bucket and the water used for bathing. Later I am told that the water will come on; it just goes off for a day or two each week.

I had an interesting night of non-sleep. Directly behind my window was the village water pump that clanked along at all hours as people came to get their water. In this remote village, it is the only well from which to draw water. So much activity is around a well, and so much is happening. Many believers have said that upon visiting Israel, the Bible came alive for them. This is my experience in faraway villages; they have everything the New Testament had:

idols, lepers, the sick, wells, donkeys, people walking long distances, culture, farmers, strange happenings, the poor, the rich man, shelter for strangers, and more. In these isolated places very little has changed.

We rented a generator and "sound system" for my presentation. The buzz from the speaker was so loud I could not even hear myself. It started to grate on my nerves, like fingernails on a chalkboard. Finally, I stopped speaking and instructed them to shut the thing off. I would rather shout. Everyone looked relieved. An hour of that would be torture; no wonder tribal wars break out if they are using those loudspeakers to incite the people!

Ushers come to take me to the platform up steps made of stacked cinder blocks. The platform, made of poles and a few 1X12's, bounces under the weight of the ministry staff. The music continues for nearly one hour while everyone is dancing and singing. I, too, am enjoying dancing! The Africans cannot sing without dancing. It is great fun. The crowd grows from 100, to 200, to nearly 300. We sit on chairs balanced on the platform, and the bugs discover that there is something new on the menu tonight: Mike. I begin to speak at the makeshift podium, first telling the children a story. Then the electricity goes out. There is a pause, and finally the microphone is working again, but no light. I cannot see any of my notes. One time in India the lights went out and we put candles around the chalkboard. Tonight there will be no need for me to attempt to follow the notes.

At the end of a long and busy day, I arrive at the hotel, jump in the tub, squirt shampoo in my hair, and soap up my sponge. At that point I realize the water to this part of the city has been turned off. Next I see a bucket of water and go for it, but then I am standing in the pitch dark. The electricity has gone off. Nothing new! I work out a bath before trying to pick up e-mail on my laptop, but in the end I give up and go to bed. I have a very busy day tomorrow, but I like to stop myself, slow down, not think of home, and really enjoy where I am.

The air conditioning broke down and we had to open the windows. There was one main window through which the greatest breeze blew. It must have been really nice, for a fellow immediately got up, stood in front of it, and blocked the breeze for the rest of us. Legalists are that way; they never allow the cool breeze of the Holy Spirit to wash across the people. In their greed to have some sort of a kingdom, they block the work of God. They find a little comfort at the expense of everyone else.

I took a walk down the road to a lonely corner one morning and found a phone booth placed next to a few old beat-up huts. It was difficult to make a phone call; the buses came by and blew dust and dirt. I was standing by a donkey and being eaten alive by fleas as I called Betty. It was Thanksgiving Day back home, my first Thanksgiving away from home, but I cannot really comprehend it in these surroundings. I would like to snap my fingers and be there, standing in front of the turkey, knife in hand; I would like to see the family, hear the laughter, and see the decorated table. I am lonely, and yet not lonely; I am with the family of God here in this country; it is where I am to be, and I must find His peace in the situation, peace not as the world gives!

I have objected to staying in the hotel where we were paying "special" American prices of $200 per night, and it was not that nice. I was told that we could move over to a church-owned apartment and stay there. It was a two-room apartment; there were two beds in one room for my brother and me and a couch in the other room for the interpreter. The bathroom had a faucet to turn either toward the sink for water there or back toward the tub for taking a shower. The tub had been painted, but with time the paint was peeling away. Something keeps dropping on my head while I dry, and I discover that it is the flakes of paint from above. All in all, though, it is quite nice to have a hot shower and a bed. I have brought some water-purifying drops, but the tap water always has a brown color. I tried filtering it on a previous trip and discovered that my camping filter, designed to allow 75 gallons to run through it, was plugged up with sediment after just one liter.

It is difficult to drive along in the black, sooty fog of the diesel exhaust. Sometimes a bus will roll alongside the car, and when the bus driver floors it to pull away, the car fills with the smoke. In fact, this night I noticed that my shirt was actually slick with the film. My lungs cannot be much better. We get to the guesthouse and discover that the fuse is blown. That means no air conditioning through the evening and night, but my travel partner has agreed that I can sleep on his floor, since the fuse did not affect his room. It was not a bad night on the floor except for the fact that the bugs found me just after midnight. I felt my face, hands, and feet, and all were swollen. That required getting up, fumbling down the hall, getting into my luggage, smearing myself with bug cream, and working my way back. There is no hot water, the electricity is sporadic, and there are at least fifty one-liter jugs of water crowding the bathroom for when there are times of no piped-in water at all.

We leave the main road and begin our ascent up the winding, washed-out road to the mission. It is nice to be out of the cities and their accompanying pollution. Everywhere people are walking; even after all these years my host is not sure where everyone is going. The plains, the lightning storms, and the smell of fresh rain are intoxicating after hours in an airport. Arriving at the guesthouse we find ourselves in pitch darkness. It seems they have just discovered that there will be an electricity crisis for the next five to six months, necessitating the rolling blackouts typical in the Third World. The electricity is basically turned off and on according to a schedule unknown to the general population. Blackouts are generally a result of poor management or a scam. Well, amen. The reason given in this case is that the floodwaters brought trees that have blocked the turbines at the dam, and it will take up to six months to clean them out. The burden of keeping a business alive with rolling blackouts is stressful. When the electricity goes, the employees are left idle. There is not much of an economy here, just basic subsistence farming, so business needs to be encouraged. We are greeted so warmly by some people who have never before seen us; they are missionaries, immediately embracing us as though we were relatives (which in actuality we are, with our kinship in Christ). Candles are lit, there is a rush to the kitchen, places are set, a neighbor hurries off and returns with freshly baked bread; and soon we are sitting, fellowshipping, laughing, and dining. What is left to say?

Jesus came, lived, died, and lives again so we can experience such things. Thank You, Jesus. This is all Your doing. You do all of the work, and You get all of the glory.

It is morning at the guesthouse, and I pop downstairs for a hot shower. Amen, the water is cold, stone cold. The owner says he bought the place in disrepair and hopes to first get a steady supply of water before getting hot water. Of course, none of that seems to him to be a deterrent to renting the room, but to me the information has come a bit late. We have a full breakfast. As I have often pointed out, in developing countries a kitchen in which meals are prepared—even restaurant meals—usually has just a one-burner stove, so a table of six is served one person at a time.

We get home and the family decides that it is time for me to relax with a massage. The daughter has me lie down and begins to walk on my back. Actually, it did not feel bad to have a ninety-pound girl walk on my back. They asked if I enjoyed it. I made the mistake of saying, "Yes," for then they said, "We have another surprise." They brought in the fellow who lays bricks at the school; he, too, had me lay down so he could walk up and down my back, but he weighed double what the girl did. His toes were like fingers that were used to grab the back of my neck to "massage" it. Then he would stomp up and down on my back. Finally, he took my leg, straddled it on his body, and bent forward until my foot was touching the back of my head. I heard things cracking and noises coming from places that I did not think could make a noise. In the end, I was little more than an alphabet soup noodle. While he was walking on me I was tensing every muscle in my body so as not to let his feet go all of the way through me to the mattress. It all finished with his saying, "Now let me go get the oil." Gasping, I got up, thanked him, and said I was going to be a little too busy to accept the rest of the massage. By that point it hurt so badly that I would have confessed to killing Lincoln.

The airport outside of the small town in the jungle is very small, with only one room. Outside awaits an old bus that will seem to say, "I think I can, I think I can," at each little incline on the way to the frontier outpost. Ninety percent of the population is Ingin (local word for Indian). Surrounding the town are jungles housing numerous tribes, so naturally missionaries abound; it is the only supply base for thousands of square miles. There are freshwater dolphins, small wooden river vessels, and tribal peoples everywhere. Looking downriver to the left of the bank are high mountains covered with mist, reminiscent of those in the movie "King Kong." Looking at the foreboding jungle, my imagination can run wild with what lies ahead. Looking to the right are the rapids that only appear in the dry season. Children learn how to swim in the rapids and navigate the various undercurrents. Last year an eighteen-year-old Italian, an athletic swimmer visiting his uncle, drowned in the river. Previously, three teenagers were swimming, and the missionary who tried to save them died with them. It is a treacherous river at this point. We are checked into our "hotel" room and told we can rest. The plans will change by the hour, something to which I am accustomed and actually do not mind. We are told that we have a room with air conditioning. Not so fast. We see in our room concrete walls, paint flaking, two beds with moldy pillows and mattresses, and an air conditioner that is barely working and putting off more smells than cool air. We are told to keep the door to the toilet closed, and the reason for that becomes obvious. My coworker and I slip off to get something to eat. In a very small market, not being able to discern the markings on the cans, we purchase something that looks edible. Well, when opened, it is not; it smells like canned spew. In fact, we cannot get this additional smell out of the room. Amen.

After a light meal we are informed that we have a 5:30 a.m. prayer meeting at the Bible school. This means that we will need to be up at 4:30 a.m. I am hoping I can sleep just as well at the prayer meeting as in bed, for it has been several days since we slept. I wish someone were here to send in my place. I am still sick, have new sickness, and more. The Lord meets me in it. We arise at 4:30 a.m. and wait for the bus. I daresay not one person on the bus was ready for a two-hour prayer meeting. Amen. We get there, the students are already singing, and we make our way to the front and sit down along the wall. The director then comes and says something to the interpreter, who turns to me and says, "He would like for you to speak." It was the last thing I had in mind. I turned to my accompanying pastor in hopes of enlisting him for the task. To describe how out of it he was, let us just say that had Jesus returned at that moment, his best hope would be that the dead in Christ rise first! I went to the front and started. One hour later, the students now alive and alert, I sat down. The director asked me to continue longer. Afterward, I again sat down. A third time he asked me to return. By then it was 7:00 a.m., and I was happy that I had come to this prayer meeting so blest by God. My pastor friend was invited by the director to sing. Everyone here thinks that he must certainly be a television star of some kind. He finishes one song to the applause of the students only to be asked to play another by the director, who beams as he sings. The prayer meeting ends, and we are invited for breakfast. The director asks that I sit by him. He leans over and says, "It is all about the discovery of Christ in us!"

Form and Function

Society in one village I visited is very structured. Women have certain jobs and so do men. Men are never to cook or serve themselves. If a man serves himself, his wife will climb to the top of one of the huge termite mounds and yell, "My husband is a glutton!" Women are to go to the well for water. Little girls as young as seven can carry the large jugs of water on their heads; a five-gallon container weighs almost fifty pounds. Men, on the other hand, are to dig, cut weeds, plant, build the hut, make the grass roofs, and more. Women are never to wear men's clothes, and pants are a definite no-no. However, Westerners, pushing their agendas, come to these areas wearing pants. It does not bother the locals; they simply see those persons as prostitutes and write off anything they have to say. We have a discussion about pants. I explain that one behavior can have different motives; I can hit someone because he is choking or because I am angry. Someone passing by may not know my motive. If I am doing something offensive without a motive to do so, he is obliged to stop me and inform me. After that, common consideration would dictate that I change my behavior. Actually, the villagers

469

admitted they have not seen any Westerners here in pants; they have only heard about it. We also talked a good bit about moving beyond one's culture to the spiritual culture, the one that is absolute, where love, patience, kindness, etc. are displayed.

A fellow is wearing his left sandal on his right foot and right sandal on his left foot. Like the people of Nineveh, he does not seem to know his right from his left. Then he explains, "My sandals were wearing out on the inside of the sole; I did not have money for new sandals, so I just switched feet. At first it hurt, but now I rather like it." I love this country!

I travel far from tourist sites, so my experiences are a bit out of the ordinary; I spend all of my time off the beaten path. The varying levels of society—the poverty-stricken, the middle class, and the extremely wealthy—are evident everywhere. In each class there are similarities, such as that independent business thrives in each. Doers are Doers in whatever situation they live. On the same street are wall-lined mansions, apartments, and shacks, though "shack" is probably too generous a term for cement that goes up only about two or three feet, then has a roof made of thatch, paper, cardboard, or whatever soaked in oil. People must nearly get on their knees to enter. There is no water, electricity, or sewer. Cows wander the streets, rummaging through the garbage. Dogs move quickly, never making eye contact. Diesel fumes are thick in the air, burning eyes and lungs. The streets are crowded. This country's drivers must be the best in the world, for to me, any intersection approached looks impossible to get through. There are thousands of mini traffic jams a minute. Everyone goes head on into a sea of pedestrians, bicycles, motorbikes, cars, and trucks. I am convinced that our vehicle will kill, cause us to be killed, or just wreck. If our lane is stopped, we just head into the traffic in the oncoming lane. Horns constantly blare. Against all apparent odds, the cars jam, then budge, and suddenly move forward. Garbage is nearly everywhere, and in the bigger cities the early morning still yields miles of people defecating on the streets. All kinds of businesses exist everywhere. This place is buzzing with businesses, and yet is filled with paradoxes. Two shoeless, lonely men are bent over, scraping up the human feces from the day before; they look at the ground as I pass. I stop and give each of them 100 rupees, which to them is a fortune ($2.50). They just stare in bewilderment. I say, "Jesus," in Hindi. The younger man nods his head with a huge smile, as if to say he would expect Jesus to do just that. I walk past several women and small children who have the job of cleaning the gutters; for hours they squat each day. The odd Mercedes Benz passes by them. It is generally hot. The middle class in India is actually living at a better standard than most of us. $300-$500 per month can yield a large home, inexpensive vehicle, and house servants. However, these people work hard and do not have a victim mentality. They make the best out of what they have. There is no social welfare system, which results in a people that stay busy from cradle to grave.

I call the AT&T access number for this poor country, which registers as a local call for a small charge. Yet the hotel clerks know I am talking to America. They do not know what to do; the concept of a calling card's paying for a call to America is not familiar to them and does not compute. They think that I have a card that is able to trick their machine, resulting in their having to pay for the overseas call themselves.

Once I heard a man boasting that in his life he had talked face to face with more people than anyone in the history of the human race. He was doing meetings of up to one million people, so he said. The scene before me is one that has been replayed over and over again for me, and it involves a small, out-of-the-way church up an old, potholed road in a remote place with a few parishioners. That is my call. I will not be speaking to one million, not to one thousand, or even to one hundred. It is a typical small group of village people, who, I am often told, cannot understand such a deep message, but I have never found that to be true. What I am about to write is very important to me. The call to be a missionary was exactly that, a call. In the beginning I was told to get on a plane and go. I questioned the Lord as to why. The first answer that came was that He had called me. I know that does not sound like much of an explanation for all my travels, but it is actually all that is needed. For a missionary, the call supersedes the way, the means, or the method. What I am doing, the why of what I am doing, and the means of what I am doing were all settled in the call. This is in sharp contrast to many in ministry who are waiting for the way, the means, and the successful method to prove that they are called. What drives them is what might happen in the future. What drives me is what has happened in the past. I know it sounds funny, but I do not care if anyone comes to the meetings, if the "ministry" does not get bigger, or if I cannot prove my faith by great wealth and miracles. All of that means nothing in view of the call of God to have the revelation of Jesus and to share it in my daily life. Success in the present has absolutely nothing to do with the fact of the past: that Jesus called me. For many, what happens today will dictate their feelings of success. My success was determined long ago. Would I sell all, pick up with nothing, and go, knowing not but heeding the call? I did, and it is all settled. A group of one means the same to me as a group of 1,000,000.

We are going to visit the home village of the founder of a denomination with 750 churches and 600,000 members. It is a long journey by car. We leave the paved road and travel for many hours on what is little more than a sand path through the jungle. Visible on both sides of the van are sugarcane, banana trees, and palm oil trees. The villages have houses made of four-inch poles running horizontally and vertically that are tied together with six-inch square gaps between the poles. These gaps are then filled with mud. All roofs are thatched. The children wave wildly at the sight of a white man. They have all kinds of things to say. Some act brave, waving their wooden swords and spears. Others just smile. Still others excitedly run to touch our passing hands. We reach a ferry that takes us across the river. In about another bouncy hour we reach the village in which the founder was born, from which she departed for nearly forty years, and to which she returned in her later years to retire. There are four churches here, her grave, the grave of her son, a type of museum, and finally, a cathedral, which seems a bit out of place in a village, but which was the vision of the founder and will seat 2,500 people. We move from the main building to the king's house. This king was born in 1909 and is really quite fit. Before we can see him, he must don the regalia, so we wait in a room; in the corner is a large elephant tusk. There are two thrones; at the base of one lay the city elders' ancient idols, looking like a series of dog jawbones with a wooden ball and stick in the middle. The walls are lined with pictures of the king with accompanying dignitaries. He emerges robed in royal garb that is quite spectacular. I assume that I must speak to him through the pastor, but I am informed that the king knows English and it is proper to speak directly to him. I ask what is the greatest need in this country. The answer, "Every person has a different need!" There is wisdom in that. The king knew the founder personally and speaks fondly of her.

Despite seemingly boiling heat in the church, the people are listening intently as I speak, and I am flowing with a gifted interpreter who just flies along with me. There are a couple of accepted practices here. If someone falls asleep in the service, the interpreter simply yells and takes his Bible and throws it at the person. I suggested that we have more breaks, because the lectures are taking us right through the day. However, at that suggestion the interpreter instead stationed a couple of men to walk back and forth and throw Bibles at the people. It is a method of "giving people the word" that I had not previously witnessed! I asked if it were okay if I threw my Bible at the people. He assured me that it was, and I took mine over to one of the sentinels and traded him my Bible for his small one. "This is bigger and will hurt a little more." He seemed quite pleased.

All roads in this place are dirt, so presently they are muddy. We have fun walking along and talking to the people, practicing our smiling ministry; we do not understand the locals, and vice versa, so we just keep smiling at one another. I stop to help a fellow cut some grass with a machete that has a nine-inch bend at the bottom. It works rather well, and we all get a good laugh. Most of the buildings house government administration, and most are whitewashed, plastered brick. There is one shop with only bags of rice in it. The children are out of school, and we are talking and having fun with them. My dad enjoys taking a video of them. A group of seven-year-old girls stop and sing for us. Upon viewing the replaying of the videotape, they laugh, scream, point, and are delighted to see themselves for the first time on camera. All of this commotion attracts quite a crowd. A young fellow stops us to teach us a little Portuguese. We somewhat imitate his words. He is so full of energy, life, and hope. However, without Christ, this government, like so many others, will beat that out of him, until one day hope will give way to despair. In this way governments and their greed drive people to Jesus. He will not fight them; He will use them. In one way it is so delightful to be in places where Jesus is the only hope. The aid agencies like to believe they are the only hope. The anthropologists hate to admit that Jesus is any type of hope, but He is the only hope.

We learned that one place has a very matriarchal society. After marrying a woman, the young man must move into his wife's house and work under the mother-in-law for a minimum of two years to prove that he is worthy. No mother-in-law jokes are allowed here.

In the national museum are several pairs of wooden sandals. My friend explained that as a child, he was never allowed to touch the sandals of his father; they were

475

considered sacred. When the father dies, the sandals would be given to the son. Also, he could tell if a teacher were home by looking at the front door; if the sandals were there, the teacher was not to be disturbed. In fact, a king might leave the country, but if he left his sandals on the throne, this meant that he was still, in effect, on the throne. The sandals remained in place until he returned. Another interesting custom was that after the death of the head of the house, his feet were dipped in stain to make an imprint on a piece of cloth, which was then hung on the wall and worshipped.

First stop is the harbor and its park, where inlaid in the marble is a map of the world denoting the many discoveries of this country's explorers of old. Next to the map are large statues of those who were responsible for the discoveries, with the figures lined up, each one supported by and built upon the previous one. First is the King that could see the need for exploration, next the captains, then the Jewish astronomers that invented a way to navigate by the stars, then the common man that had to go with the ships, and finally, the explorer. It reminds me of how I always stand on the backs of others in the work that I do; I am indebted to so many. There is a phrase in Portuguese that goes something like, "It takes many men to carry the piano for one man to play it." I do not forget that around me are many who are carrying the piano. I think that I get tired, but so do they. They have labored for months to make a conference come together.

We are traveling through what I call "true Africa." There are small mountains in the distance as we move through bush that has only the occasional tree. It is the dry season, and yet it is very cool. We pass by the mud villages, most composed of round, one-room houses with thatched roofs, exactly what we have all become accustomed to seeing in magazines or documentary shows. There are brick ovens where the newly made bricks are stacked in such a way that there is a hole in the center of the pile where the fire is started, and mud is placed over the outside of the pile. This is a cheap and effective way of firing the bricks, not to mention that when it is all done, the bricks are already stacked. We occasionally pass by markets, which, because this is Saturday, are packed with shoppers and brightly colored goods, with clothes hung on lines and a rainbow assortment of fruits for sale. One big business here is selling old clothes from faraway countries, where a bundle of shirts, pants, dresses, or baby clothes can be purchased for very little, then sorted and put up for sale here. Fashion tends to recycle, so some things are actually coming back into style. However, there are still the polyester leisure suits of the 70's, which must have the half-life of uranium. The colors, as you may recall, are shocking: burnt orange, brown, yellow, and green. They should be burned, but I suppose they probably would not incinerate. One fellow is still wearing the suits that his father found in a bundle and wore his whole life.

We see, as we are driving, that today is camel-market day, and camels will be traded or sold for food and transportation. Camel meat does not taste bad. As we travel through a city that looks very typically Eastern, it is hard to miss the wide variety of forms of transportation used here. People are crawling, walking, and bicycling; carts are drawn by men, donkeys, horses, or three-wheeled tillers.

Then there are (my personal favorite) three-wheeled trucks, auto rickshaws, trucks with one big, rough wheel in the front, forklifts (families ride them through the city in order to find stalled cars to pick up and take to a repair shop), small trucks, large trucks, buses of every configuration and size, and, finally, automobiles. For a mechanic, it is pure eye-candy.

A non-indigenous person who has the misfortune of hitting someone with a car becomes the "relative" of the one run into. That translates into being the guardian for life of the one struck. One lady hit another lady, who was not hurt, but after paying for all damages, the driver was told by the local woman, "Well, now you are my mother." Whenever the native woman had a need she would go to the foreign woman and demand that she help her. "Mother" was even summoned to the woman's funeral. She did not go, but then the local's brother came to visit and said, "Now you are my sister," and started making requests. Hitting someone with your car is like getting hold of an octopus.

The banks say that the two requests for funds that they most often get are for funerals and automobiles. The funerals cost fortunes. The people live in bamboo shelters with reed roofs and platforms on which to sleep. However, a grave is placed next to the house, flowers are kept around it, and food is left to keep the wandering spirit happy. It is nice that our spirits have not wandered since finding Jesus.

Moving upstairs we see the stark contrast to the newly remodeled church area below. Wallpaper is falling off, and everything is painted in the standard colors of green or blue. This was a church, then a kindergarten, and it has now returned to being used as a church. It looks as though everything was an afterthought. The waterlines run on the outside of the walls, as. do the electric lines and the radiators. The first ever earthquake recently occurred, shaking the building; the rats squealed in the attic as they began to run from one end of the building to the other. There are so many little tricks to getting things to work. The hot water must be turned on in the sink and then left trickling to get it to the tub, and the showerhead must be held down by my knees to get the warm water to come out. Amen. At least there is a shower, toilet, and a great ambiance in this place.

Finding Out About Friends

After the service we had lunch at the Salvation Army. One elderly lady played a trick on me by entering with two plates, one on which was dog food and the other holding a typical dish from this country. "Which will you pick?" The dish for humans was interesting; two eggs were mixed with grated cheese and spread on a slice of white bread, which was fried face down (mixture down) first. One of the ladies took me back to show me the "Swedish" room, so named because years ago, the King and Queen of Sweden spent the night in the room. It was decorated with Swedish furnishings. I said, "I grew up around a Swedish community." The woman thought for a minute, her countenance fell, and she said, "I grew up in Siberia. My parents were forced to work in the swamps." Then she paused again, "I think I will talk about things more pleasant." I said, "Well, the Swedish community was not all that bad." She really laughed.

I was sitting among a Chinese group that had a reputation for making money and eating strange food. They asked me, "How do we know that Adam was not Chinese? If he were Chinese, he would have eaten the snake and sold the fruit!"

During the break in the seminar, the interpreter shares something of interest about village life. He is well traveled in the remote areas. "When the people walk several hours to your meetings, they are expecting you to talk for more than forty-five minutes. The people have come so far and sacrificed so much that you must spend the whole evening with them." This bit of information will come in handy in the future. I normally do give breaks after forty-five minutes, because I say the head cannot take in more than the seat can bear.

I am walking in a downtown area talking about the interpreter's temperament. I tell him that he is a doer and a thinker, so he would be the first to act in an accident. No sooner had I said it than an old man in front of us either tripped or had a stroke and fell over. Immediately the interpreter ran up to grab the man and started shouting orders. He picked up the man and, with the help of a missionary friend, was able to carry the man to the bus stop. The older man kept weeping and saying, "I did not know there were still goodhearted people in the world." We got him settled, which took a good bit of time, and then reassessed our priorities. This made the next stop a coffee shop, where we found traditional cheese bread the size of tennis balls that called for two apiece.

A young man tells me of his life before he knew Christ, growing up in one of the favelas, the Portuguese word for slums. There are many of them in the bigger cities, and some favelas have populations of two-and-one-half million. There are no police in a favela; instead, a group of elders rule the slum. It would be unthinkable to report any transgression to the outside police; no one wants the police in the slum. A wife who has been beaten by her husband simply takes her complaint to the elders, and if her case is successfully made, the elders will ask, "What do you want us to do? Do you want your husband beaten? Killed?" She will tell them what she wishes, and the men will handle the whole thing. The streets in the favelas are ever changing, literally, for a lane starting off in one direction may end up with someone's having built a cardboard or tin house right in its path, which causes a new diverted dirt road to be made. When houses burn down, the path changes again. This fellow's father is a bit of a legend in their favela, for he is known as a counselor. However, he never says anything, because he uses more of a Freudian technique. The people tell their woes and he just listens. Sometimes he will nod, and other times not. At the end of the session the people thank him and go off singing his praises. One day this fellow's father started a fire, put a 55-gallon drum of water on it, and let it begin to boil. The first person passed and asked what he was doing. He replied, "Oh, I am preparing a feast, but I have no beans!" The person ran off and came back with five kilograms of beans, which immediately went in the pot. Soon another passed and asked, "What are you doing?" The reply was, "I am making a feast, but I have no meat." This person scurried off, returning with two chickens that also found their way into the pot. This went on until all the ingredients were there and a feast, which was in no small way anticipated, took place. It nearly sounds like a fairytale, but such is life in the favela. Not just anyone can enter these places. This fellow, a university graduate and one of the best graphic designers, made it out of the favela. The last time he went in for a visit, he was stopped at the entrance by a gang and told not to go any further. He just looked at them with his big smile and called them all by name. They stared at him until one by one they recognized him and received him in with great joy like a prodigal son returning.

I will miss these people. I like the look on the missionary wives' faces, which is somewhat between strain, strength, and a countenance that only comes from Jesus in such a place. My friend is taking the bus for eight hours tomorrow and says, "You know, we missionaries have it much better than the people."

I see an old friend at the leper colony and ask him, "Why is there less of you this year than last year?" He explained that, though cured of leprosy, he was still given to infection, and therefore every few years he would get some kind of infection in his extremities that called for a trip to the hospital, where the infected finger, toe, nose, or ear would be removed. It seems that the hospital staff does not like seeing leprosy patients, who they know will return every few years. So when he was in the hospital with an infection in his finger, they just went ahead and took off all his fingers and toes. That is why this year he only had palms with which to eat and heels on which to walk. I have decided to speak only in about forty-minute segments before letting the people stand or move about, because the meeting will be going all day. However, every time I announce a break, everyone just continues to sit there. Finally, I ask my interpreter, "Why do the people not take a break when I give them one?" He just smiled, "Brother, it hurts too much for the lepers to get up."

As regards the attitudes Christians have toward the drinking of alcoholic beverages, there is quite a variation to experience when moving from country to country. Some profess to abstain from drink altogether; others insist on partaking copiously even before preaching. One friend was telling me of a farmer who had a visit from the pastor and offered him a taste of cherry brandy. The reverend liked the brandy very much. The parishioner, seeing how pleased the pastor was, offered to give him a complete case of the cherry brandy on the one condition that the farmer be thanked publicly from the pulpit. The pastor reflected for a moment and said, "Agreed!" He went off with his case of cherry brandy. That Sunday, at the end of the service, the pastor said, "Oh yes! I would like to give a special thanks to Brother Andrew for the gift of the cherries and the spirit in which they came."

Funding

The sun is 865,000 miles across, but the smallest coin can block out the sun if you hold it close enough to your eye!

I admire a driver taking pastors through Africa; he is very good, and not just anyone can drive a car here. The diesel fumes are stifling. Large buses pull alongside and rev their engines, filling our lungs with fumes. As we pass through the cities we see markets or the city centers, but not what you would think. Few are what we would consider proper buildings. We see small booth after booth constructed of wood and filled with every imaginable thing from bananas to luggage. As we travel along the road, we reach a place that has three speed bumps about one hundred yards apart, so every vehicle must go slowly. The windows are down and I hear howling from people that sounds like they are dying. I opened my eyes and looked out the window to see both sides of the road lined with lepers holding out their stubby hands, leaning on canes or lying on the road, and crying out for donations. The pastor motions, and the driver tosses some money out the window.

Often when in countries where I look quite different from the normal citizen, I do not walk long before attracting beggars. I walked past a man that I felt should be begging, since he was missing everything from the rib cage down. He only smiled and welcomed me. As I walked away, the Lord said, "Give something to him." I continued examining the city before eventually finding myself back on the street on which I had seen the pleasant man. I leaned over and gave him the money. He was surprised and said, "Thank you." I have learned that even though beggars wear me out, I must not harden my heart to ALL beggars. I have to listen, because it is never coincidental that I walk by at that exact time. In these places it is so important to keep in mind the possibility of ministering to just one. All of the aid in the world would not make a difference to the average person; it would be stolen by the corrupt powers that be. Again, such leaders have exactly the country they want. It is hopeless to send aid to such countries, as do many of the governments;

it is stolen, sold, and put in foreign bank accounts. At least if I am here and led to do so, I can place something directly in the hands of the needy. Later, another man sidled up to me and started talking; it is so difficult to walk when this constantly happens. I said to the man, "No hablo Ingles." He replied, "That is an old trick! I know you are an American." He kept talking, I would not respond, and finally he dropped away. God spoke to me, "You did not need to lie." Well, amen. I repented. Tomorrow I will go back to being honest with the beggars.

To drive to a village, we had to stop and get petrol; naturally, I thought we would be stopping at a gas station, but we were in an area of town where there were many bicycles on which were hanging five, five-gallon containers filled with petrol. We purchased a few liters, and they were poured into one-liter jars and then poured into the car. The driver explained, "The men take the bicycles a few miles into the next country, purchase the petrol, and smuggle it back. A liter here costs 1,500 shillings, they sell theirs for 1,100, and, since they purchased it for 1,000, they can make 100 shillings per liter. For much pedaling and the danger of smuggling, they make about six cents U.S. per liter."

On an afternoon in which I was still on the mend from salmonella poisoning, we took a brief ride in a human-powered rickshaw. It was not any fun for the fellow pedaling two big American males, but he had already doubled his price from five rupees to ten (25 cents). He still bit off more than he could chew, since the slightest incline dictated that I get off and walk. We finally arrived at the destination. He was just getting ready to argue for more money when

485

I handed him fifty rupees. I do not imagine he worked the rest of the day! We walked over the bridge that spans the railroad tracks to enter the area where the poorest of the poor live. Next to the track are houses constructed from bits of plastic, paper, cardboard, and metal, usually six feet by ten. The area is very dirty, and yet the children play and laugh, calling up to us. We walk past a man with a skin disease that has eaten away the flesh on his legs a half-inch deep. He is a mess, not bathed and barely clothed. He looks at me and puts his hands in the air to display an attitude of resignation. The really sad thing is that some antibiotics and antiseptic cream would probably heal the condition. The drugs are cheap and readily available, but he would not have the money. I stop, return, and give him fifty rupees. He begins to weep, not knowing what to say. I speak in Hindi, "It is from Jesus; Jesus is true life!" He looked quite surprised, stopped weeping for a minute, and then continued on. I walked on looking for a drugstore, but none were open.

The Jewish lady that cleans our room is really perky and helpful. On the first day she confides in me—for no apparent reason—about how things are not working out with her boyfriend. I tell her that tomorrow I will have a talk with her. The next morning I pulled her aside, explained how relationships work, and then took her history. She was crying all the way through. Her father had died; she had grown up having him read her the Torah. Next, her boyfriend from youth died, and now her brother was dying of cancer. Her mother was very dominant, and I showed her how she created in her boyfriend the very thing that she hated. We spent a lot of time together going over the

Old Testament temple and understanding why God would need to talk through a Messiah and not a temple. She got it all. Next I showed her all that the Messiah would have to do. She got it. Then I showed her how the Messiah must come into our lives to live out His victory. This, too, she understood. Then I said, to her surprise, the Messiah has already come, and His name was Jesus. His life was described in detail in Isaiah 53. She was still weeping and taking in all that I said. I told her that I would get a set of CD's to her. Now here is the amazing thing: In the end, when the tears were wiped away, she said, "I will still get an extra tip for cleaning your room, won't I?" I just stood there in disbelief. I was entering into the sufferings of Jesus. A woman with so many problems, learning of Jesus' being the answer, still asked if she would get a tip. A tip was more important than getting out of her daily hell. I could just see Jesus teaching the people and having them ask if they were going to get bread. It all vexed me. I just said, "Yes, if a tip is what you want, a tip you will get."

We pass a river where there are many, many women doing laundry. The sheets and shirts are draped on bushes, trees, rocks, and the ground. The children are constantly screaming out to us the equivalent in their native tongue of yelling, "Whitie, Whitie, Whitie!" My travel companion and I think we know a bit how the Pope must feel as we sit in the back waving to those on the right and the left of the road. Next stop is a mission school. As we head down the path I see some young men playing an interesting card game. The loser must attach a clothespin to his face by pinching a bit of skin. It is obvious that one fellow should never play this game again! His face looks like a pincushion with brightly colored clothespins sticking out of every conceivable place. His chin, jaw, and ears are covered, and even his nose. It is very comical to see, especially since all of the players are so deadly serious! The school is made of pieces of bamboo split in two and tied to bits and pieces of lumber. It is really quite nice, because the gap between the bamboo slats is equal to their width and allows for the air to move freely through. There is a dirt floor and heaps of benches. In this one small room are five teachers and over two hundred students. The school bell is half of a differential box from a car hung in a tree; nearby is a piece of angle iron with which to beat on it. Our tour here is given genuinely to allow us to see how God works in the midst of such poverty. It is also done to solicit funds for the projects. I do not mind it; I have to ask for funds once a year at Abiding Life Ministries. People have to know what the needs are. They are not pressing us at all, just informing us, which is so much different from the endless requests I get in some countries.

I wish you could see this beautiful place with the surrounding mountains, cool evenings, and busy city. I found a barbershop in a small room with a sheet hanging over the opening to act as a door. The inside is nothing more than a shed. The chairs are handmade with what look like crutches sliding down the back of the chair to make a "headrest." There is little paint on the walls and no running water, but two light bulbs shine. Three barbers are waiting for the next customer. The equipment is simple: a pair of scissors, a comb, a straight razor, and a piece of rock salt. I sit down and two of the fellows drag the chair closer to the light. The cutting begins—cut, snip, poke, cut, snip, and poke—and then a spray of water from what looks like a huge perfume bottle. Next comes the shave, a very meticulous project. When that is completed the purpose of the block of salt is revealed. One side is very smooth from rubbing it all over the customers' faces to avoid infection from the cuts. Next comes the massage, fists flying up and down my head. My arms are extended and every finger pulled. I lean forward on the towel and rest my head on a board as every muscle is pulled, stretched, and poked; even the eyelids are pulled in and out and facial skin pinched and stretched. The whole process takes over an hour. Periodically someone runs down to a local well for water. When all is done I must admit that I am feeling capital. The cost of this entire treatment for a local is fifty rupees, or seventy-five cents. I asked what the price was and was told that it was 175 rupees, more than triple for a foreigner. I gave the fellow 350 rupees, or $5. Well, bless those that curse you. If someone wants you to go one mile, go two.

Something happened at the end of the seminar. I had exactly $500 with me for expense money for the whole trip to two countries. I was praying at night, and the Lord spoke to me to give $500 to the interpreter who had worked so hard. There was, as the Lord knew, one problem: that was all the money I had with me. However, in the morning I went up to the interpreter and tapped him on the shoulder. He turned around and saw me, and simultaneously we went into our pockets. I handed him an envelope and he handed one to me. We both laughed. I said, "The Lord spoke to me to give this to you." He replied, "And the Lord spoke to me to give this to you." In the envelope was $300! I am only telling you this story because we are friends together who can rejoice at how God multiplies money. Supporters give to me, I give to someone else, and they purchase what they need from a believer. The vendor then goes to another Christian and purchases from him, and on and on it goes. A hundred dollars may become a thousand in God's economy.

When on the road, I am often stripping my equipment or suitcase of accessories and supplies. It is too difficult for people in many countries to find parts for their computers, memory cards for cameras, batteries, and more. I always think of what my Indian teacher says: "Greed is keeping something of which another person has more need." I have gotten wiser over the years and not applied that maxim to every single thing, because there are times when I think, "Lord, I am using this and needing it myself!"

Frightening

At one village when I arrived, all the children came to see the white man. One little boy could not look at me; I was much too frightening. He hid behind the other children and cried. When I walked by, he would close his eyes tightly so as to see nothing. The rest of us had a good laugh about that.

At another village, I started the session telling stories to the many children who had filed in and sat on the floor in front of me; this was the first time they had seen a white man. There was no video or TV in the whole area. The children just stared; most of them were frightened. They liked the stories, but not the person narrating it. Many of the children wanted to touch me, but many more were still afraid. I tried to shake hands with a little boy, and he went running away, shouting in his native tongue, "The white man wants to eat me!" One little boy just fell apart in tears and could not be consoled, but this would change by day's end after spending more time and showing all of them some magic tricks. Those who got up the courage to come touch me would often stare at my skin and rub my hand. I cannot say how many times I have been so immersed in village life that my own skin color started looking odd to me!

A college student confided, "I like airplanes, everything about them. However, I keep obsessing on dying in an airplane crash or a plane's crashing on me." I responded, "We are born with two fears, the fear of height and the fear of movement; all other fears we invite into our lives. Fear is the highest form of worship; what we fear, we worship. We are to fear God and nothing else. We invite fear in, and we can invite it out. The enemy works by attaching a fear to something that happens daily, so that we often think of the fear and it can become an obsession." I did not know how much significance was attached to the fact that the student asked me this question just one day before the following occurred. First, I must digress. As we stood waiting the next day at the airport, we met an American couple holding a baby they had just adopted from an orphanage at a cost of $36,000! That angers me. Everyone takes a cut, and the only ones who really care about the baby are the adoptive parents. Many more children remain in the orphanage, for who can pay that exorbitant price? This baby never cries, because she so enjoys the attention and being held. The couple has settled on another baby but must return home first to organize more payoffs and paperwork. They are followed by an entourage of "concerned" people; that is, concerned that they will not get paid. The plane onto which we all board is a 1960's vintage plane that needs to be retired. It is old, old, old and has flown many, many miles. It is very noisy and appears to have a little trouble pressurizing. My seat is twisted and really does a number on my back for the next eight hours as we fly through seven time zones. At one point I look up and there is the fellow who adopted the baby. He is pallid and reaches down, hugs me, and just holds on, saying, "Are we going to crash?" He is having a full-blown panic attack. I take him to the back of the plane and work him through it. He keeps asking if the plane is safe. I explain that answering such questions will only feed his fear, since speaking of planes crashing or planes being safe makes his focus remain on the plane. I take his history and discover the root issue: He cannot handle being out of control. He is a control freak who does not have a God. He has nothing in which to put his trust during this time of being out of control and under the control of the pilot and the wornout plane. We spend a lot of time together; I take him aside three different times on the flight. It is odd to see the entrepreneur acting this way. In his own element he is a mover and a shaker, but on this flight he is a broken man.

Next stop is a village made up of church members. The homes are first made of bamboo stuck in the ground. Next, pieces of coconut palm are woven between the bamboo poles. Finally, a pile of dirt is mixed by hand to make mud, which is applied by hand to the pieces of coconut palm, and it looks as though the building is plastered. The whole thing is painted and the floors are dirt. Doors are made from palm leaves. It works well until the rainy season. Too much water and the walls begin to crumble. There are people standing everywhere doing nothing, and there is very little food. On one spot of ground is a bit of wheat to be sifted. One small boy has bleeding sores around his ears. I smear on a little cream to keep the bugs off, and he screams. I do not think he will be happy to see a "Whitie" again. The people are surprised if I wave to them. Many just look ahead intently in the manner I hate, which is the stare of hopelessness.

We decide to take a quick snorkel and go toward a cut in the reef where fishing boats go in and out; this will be the best place to see a large variety of reef fish. We wade toward the cut and put on our gear. The embrace of the skin-temperature water is a delight, but further surprises await us under the water: schools of brightly colored fish, striped, blue, orange, white, spotted, odd shaped, regular, and irregular. It is a real eye feast. However, we notice that we are struggling to stay in one place. We surface, look around, and go back to fish watching. Again we struggle, so my buddy taps me and signals that we go upright. He says, "We are being dragged into the open sea, and we are losing ground fast." Sure enough, we were dangerously close to open sea, and the rip tide was surprising us, for the waves come in but the tide takes us out. We begin the attempt to swim to the shallow water, but we both realize just how quickly we had gotten in trouble; we are still going out. Both of us cup our hands and begin to swim with all our might along the surface of the water. Going full force we can see the coral moving in the right direction beneath us. There is no stopping, for to pause is to lose ground. Finally, we reach shallow water and can stand up. A long stretch of water has been covered by two who are not strong swimmers! I just go out because I have a mask and snorkel and figure that I can splash around and keep breathing, but this time I was very happy to be out of the water and headed back to land.

We are driving through the largest game preserve in the world, a huge bit of frontier where nothing is done to interfere with the animals. We are rewarded very soon with the sight of three lionesses feeding on an impala! The brothers point out the power lines that run through the park and tell me, "The people fleeing the neighboring country will follow these lines to find their way through the park. It is very dangerous, but they see it as the only escape from a life of poverty and squalor. Often they are eaten by lions." One of the fellows said that he met a girl trying to follow the power lines and warned her of the dangers. She said that in her country she only had feathers to eat and was hoping for something more. He gave her all his food and turned her around, because she was in danger.

Frigid

In one of the coldest places I have ever been, men constantly remove snow using shovels handmade from plywood with the odd piece of metal covering the wood. Cars slip and slide everywhere. From the hotel room I can look out the window and see the frozen river boundary that separates two nations. The women are all wearing full-length fur coats with very attractive round fur hats; I watch a mother and her three-year-old daughter plow through the snow in their furs headed for the swing set.

The men have on a variety of lambskin coats; I must need one of those coats, for as we exit the building, the damp cold—forty below zero Fahrenheit—cuts right through our clothes and flesh to the very bone. I just cannot stay out that long. At this temperature one could quickly die. I cannot really explain what it feels like. As a child I would go to the icehouse with my grandfather and freeze while in there; this reminds me of that. I was told about a man who had gone outside without a hat and froze the top of his head; he now suffers with migraine headaches. People also told me of schoolchildren who had died without hats. That would explain why the men I am with kept pressing me to get a hat. I decided it was a very good idea and purchased a hat common in this area made of the pelt of sea otter. It is really nice and very, very warm. In the evening everyone only goes outside for a brief trip to the car or the corner market, moving quickly in the cold that goes directly through the teeth. I do not see how people survive this cold. The next day we take a brief walk among the houses that have not had any maintenance for probably close to eighty years. I do not see how people stay warm inside them. We walk past some magnificent ice sculptures to get a closer view. There we find carvings of such things as a huge castle, trees, various Arctic animals, Santa, reindeer, and more. These will remain intact until the end of April. Police are stationed at night so young boys will not push them over. I am told that gangs often stop a person and ask for his hat or coat. I thought to myself, *In your dreams would they get my coat and hat.* However, each person then told me of his own experience of being asked, which presented the opportunity of witnessing to the gang

495

members and asking them to accompany him to church. This made the gang leave him alone. I think theirs had been a more spiritual response than my initial reaction! I love the flesh; again, it is the great equalizer. Abiding, too, is always a great equalizer. A person abiding is as spiritual as he will ever get; the same person in the flesh is as carnal as he will ever get. We move from one extreme to the other simply through focus. Everyone in between these two extremes is a hypocrite and legalist.

We are taken to our huts. The forest rangers are also having a meeting here. It has been some time since a tourist has ventured this way, due to rebel soldiers, so the businesses are suffering. It is said of the soldiers that they are the most honorable of thieves. One fellow was hiking, and the rebels stopped him and took his camera at gunpoint. The fellow considered himself quite lucky to escape with his life. Later, the soldiers found him again, and this time he was sure that he was going to be killed; however, they only wanted to give him a receipt for his camera. They constantly practice extortion but always want to give a receipt. The pastor here refused a receipt when he paid money to save his life a couple of years ago. I can see my breath in my hut, and I notice there is no hot water or heat, so I decide that the logical thing to do would be to close the window. Good idea, but then I discovered there were not any glass panes in the window. I have two beds in my hut, so I took both blankets, put them on my bed, and determined to keep my coat on all night as I slept. The marriage seminar starts tomorrow, so we are invited to the main "lodge" for some soup and bread before we turn in. In the morning, there is a knock at the door. One of the workers has brought hot water, and I mean hot. It was just short of boiling, smelled like fire, and was barely usable. Also, the air surrounding me is so cold that I do not feel like taking a cup bath today. I must say, however, that I am going to like this place. Looking out the back window is a delight, even though chilly.

Fuming

I was a bit optimistic in assuming that the price I was quoted when I checked into a hotel in Africa, $45, would be the same as when I checked out, but I discovered that it was actually $90. I get tired of arguing and have learned something from my last encounter with deceiving clerks: I see God in it and yield. I said, "Fine, I will pay the $90, but I will not stay here again." For some unknown reason it really upset them that I would refuse to stay there again. I guess they wanted me to say, "Thank you for ripping me off! I cannot wait to return!" A lot of yakking ensued among the people coming and going, until finally I was charged the original rate. Everyone wanted to make sure that I would return. Actually, if I knew what was going to happen next, I would have savored that brief moment of being charged the proper price. When I arrived at the airport, I paused for just a minute before I got out of the taxi . . . just long enough for my bags to be whisked off without me. It is a long story, but in the end I had to pay a $100 bribe to get the bags on the plane. It gets very wearing when everyone from the police, to the cabbies, to the airline personnel do not want to just come out and admit they are thieves. They would rather just keep talking and talking and talking about who took what and what really happened and what really needs to happen. The only thing that ever really needs to happen is money being paid, and it is never that much, anywhere from $5 to $100. Losing money is not as annoying as the constant grabbing of a bag, my hand, or even my tickets and passport, anything that is not directly attached to my body. But I have to consider that if I were living there, would I behave any differently? After that I had to clear through customs, where I was taken behind the famous "African curtain," a small, three-man room made of material in the middle of the customs area. It is the last place a person is taken before he leaves the country; he is searched for accessories that the guards might find useful: pens, pocketknife, cash, etc. I was not that accommodating, and they knew from the fellow beside me that I had already been ripped off for the bags. In many ways it was just a typical boarding experience. One really cannot overly emphasize the difference a Christian foundation makes to a society. Of course, opportunistic airport workers are not necessarily a good representation of a country's populace. It is nice to get that behind me. However, I encountered five more such boarding experiences on this trip. This all reminds me of a point. When God became a man, He would dwell no longer just in the temple, but in flesh. Not only was He committing to dwell in the flesh of Jesus, but in our flesh, with all of our accompanying imperfections. He knew what I would be at my worst, and yet He still decided to dwell in me. I have two options: to dwell in the state of my flesh, or to dwell in the One who in spite of it decided to dwell in it.

For miles, as we drive from one village to the other, there is not a single light. It is very lonely here and too far from the political center to be of concern to the powers that be. The farmers suffer because the produce can be purchased more cheaply elsewhere, so the government does not support its own farmers. When the price comes down low enough to compete, it is cheaper for the farmers to pour the milk on the ground. The last agricultural minister made a contract with the farmers to grow wheat (the topsoil here is rich). When it came time to deliver it, the grain elevators were filled with foreign wheat, and the farmers were sent away. Typically, one small town of 800 at one time had a population of 10,000 until a few purges by the Soviets and a declining economy caused it to shrink.

Sometimes I wonder if some Western "worship" music does not border on absolute fantasy. I just cannot sing all the things that a song might claim I will do, for I know that I am weak and can leave the worship service and do the exact opposite of what I was singing. It is interesting that rarely is the theology of Christian counseling or Christian music questioned.

I was told of an Indian evangelist I had heard about before. The man's claim to fame is that he declares that he is greater than Billy Graham. At his "crusade" he begins by saying very humbly that he has accepted Jesus and then tells how great a man he is. He refuses to talk to less than 100,000 people. His "sermons" are filled with talks about his alleged visits with then U.S. President George Bush. He came to this country to hold a huge crusade; however, the government said no. He kept telling them that he represented the U.S. In fact, his literature has his name on it with a comma and then U.S.A. He could not do an open meeting, so he had to settle for a small meeting in one of the churches. The pastors requested that he not come because he would stir things up and leave them with the mess, but of course he did not listen. At the meeting he actually told the people that since he knew the U.S. President, he could get U.S. visas for the people, and that he had vacancies in his office he did not want to fill with Americans but with those from this country. If anyone wanted a visa he needed to put his name on the piece of paper the evangelist would circulate. Of course, everyone wanted one. This list became his latest record of so-called "new converts." He could not stay long, he said, because he needed to meet with the President. My pastor friend noted how scary it was that the man was physically humble, but spiritually dead and full of self. The man talks of hundreds of thousands of converts in India, though no one believes that these people, if they ever did exist, were baptized. The pastor just shook his head with the final conclusion, "It is sad." I agreed, but said that those of us in ministry need men like that to make us fearful, for anyone who wants to increase may do so on the back of Jesus, but at what price?

I have said before that I firmly believe that some Muslims would leave the faith if not for the threat of death. We tour a mosque that is a fantastic structure but is just as empty as Islam itself. Huge pillars adorn the place, and many are coming and going. Oddly, to me, male witches are sitting outside the front of the mosque and looking like homeless men or Hindu sadhus. I am told, "Nothing ever comes of prayers in the Muslim religion, and so people turn to witches to get what they want." What a testimony to the power of the god of Islam! Well, amen. A woman standing near the entrance has a small cage with hundreds of sparrows in it. The idea is to buy one, make a wish, and release it. I just wanted the joy of liberating it, so I purchased one. The woman was a magician; she put the bird in my hand in such a way that only the head was sticking out between my fingers. I then released my grip to free the bird and discovered that she had actually placed two in my hand. As the two flew off, she was making her case for getting paid for two birds and not one. We paid. Attached to this mosque by a wall shared in common is a Hindu temple, the birthplace of the founder of the Sikh religion. I am assuming that the Muslims do not want the war that would erupt if they tore it down. I asked if we could go in and was told that only a Sikh on a pilgrimage could enter. Just then a Sikh was entering, and I spoke to him in Hindi. We began to dialogue; he is an elderly man now living in Canada. He said, "Come, I will take you with me." However, the guard stopped us and made it clear that those in authority would have his head if I were allowed in. The Sikh man apologized profusely. I like the Sikhs; they have aided me on more than one occasion in more than one country.

I made it out of one African country having determined to maintain my attitude with the people in the city there, but honestly, if I am nice to anyone, say hello, or just say, "Excuse me," that is the high sign for that one to ask me for money; it never ends. Airport security workers organized by the pastor to assist me actually did want to help get me through the customs and security lines quickly, but it was definitely not done out of Christian love or charity, because I was asked for money when they finally saw me safely to

501

the other side! Amen. In order to catch a connecting flight, I must land in another city that is dark due to corruption, the lack of electricity, and being a welcoming home to the father of darkness. This is a rich country, but to find its wealth one would have to look at bank accounts in Europe and America. I am the only passenger in transit. I have no visa for this country, and they try to make me clear customs. The airport clerks from the last place said they did not know how to check my bags through to the destination country, so I have to pick them up and recheck them just to catch the connecting flight. Everyone in authority in this country yells and screams. Therefore, they send me from one shouting person to the next, until one mean female officer gets it through her head that I am only trying to get to the next international gate and shouts at me to sit down in a room. I ask, "Should I get my bags?" She screams, "Sit in the room!" Of course, as she walked off she realized that I had to have my bags, so she turned around and shouted, "Go get your bags!" At that point I can determine either to live like they live and start screaming and rebuking or continue the course of walking in the Spirit. I choose the latter and go get my bags, only to return for more rebuking. They know I will generally take it, just as did the previous travelers, for these airport workers, too, would all get out of this country if they had the opportunity; and since we travelers do plan to get out, the workers pretend that they hold the key to our departure and derive a sick pleasure by dangling that in front of people like me. However, at this point the words of the Lord I received in the last country are burned into my spirit: "I will take you, and I will return you." I am watching the minutes and wondering how I will get checked in and make the flight to my destination. At last, another officer comes along, shouting at me to follow him. We glide past security outside, where I am met by a hodgepodge of thieves and moneychangers wanting me to buy something or exchange some money, all of which is illegal. I just say, "Follow me." This they quickly do, feeling certain there is profit to be made from me. Once they notice the officer walking ahead of me, they get me stopped. The officer turns around and stares. I just said, "My friends want to talk to you about changing some money!" At that they scattered at a dead run. Once in the airport, the officer rebukes everyone in authority, pushes past the clerks at the ticket counter, demands my ticket, bypasses security, and takes me to my gate. What I had thought was a curse turned out to be something quite nice.

I was happy to be going to a certain African country; it had been in my spirit to go for three years. My last trip a few years previously had burnt me out on attempting to work with the local pastors. The mass meeting and small meetings had been great, since I had observed the Lord's witnessing to the people, but I had seen no such movement among the pastors. They were too busy plotting how to extract one more dollar, pen, or material possession out of me to hear the message. I felt like a cut cow in the Amazon River surrounded by piranha. Even in the middle of the night some pastor would get past security at the hotel, knock on the door, and ask for money. ALMI had sent funds for a chainsaw needed to rebuild the churches destroyed by war, but the secretary for the main office of the largest denomination misappropriated the money and flew out of the country!

Fantastic, but not False

I was told about the driving policy in the Ivory Coast. It seems that if a driver's vehicle hits a pedestrian, the pedestrian is responsible for the damage that his body does to the car. Can you imagine? Actually, I have often considered how I should stop telling any stories. Each day of my travels is filled with new information, ministry, and events; but often after I have told some story, someone says, "I do not believe that." Well, amen. In the Ivory Coast, a person on foot that gets hit pays for the car damage, believe it or not.

When we do not know enough of the language to do anything, there always seems to be chaos. My brother is attempting to check us in at the airline counter while I go to the restroom. I return to discover that the ticket agent thinks David is the only one traveling and is upset over his extra baggage. So many times in life God sends an "angel." The woman behind us steps up and says, "Where are you from?" We say, "America." She smiles, explains the whole thing in her language to the agent, helps us pick our seats, and gets us on our way. Later, we talked to her. Her family was not able to buy the basics, and she had made the difficult decision to go to the U.S. to work and not see her family, rather than stay in the condition that they were in. She said that it is difficult for a man to go to the U.S. and make enough money to survive and send money home. Men would get minimum wage and could not find places to live, while women come and illegally get jobs as house nurses for the elderly parents of rich people. As a woman, she could get a job, eat and live with the family that employed her, and send most of the money home. She had already worked for three-and-a-half years in the U.S. In that time she was able to buy apartments for both of her daughters; one place cost $7,000 and the other, purchased after September 11, 2001, cost $17,000. She was also able to send her son through technical school and the daughters through university. She was so nervous about seeing her husband and family after nearly four years. Her son was fourteen the last time she saw him and now is eighteen. She is applying for a green card in the U.S. and is therefore not able to stay more than one week with her family. Desperate times and desperate measures are happening all around us.

In the morning, while talking to a pastor, the topic arose about the workmanship of Russian-made products, nearly all of which we agree are junk. I mentioned that on the positive side, I really do like the Moscow subway. He looked a bit surprised and said, "What do you like about it?" I explained that I liked the size, the marble, the beauty, and the extreme depth of the subway system. He then said, "Oh, yes, its appearance is very nice, but you must consider the cost, and then you will see that it is not so nice. Building the subway cost the lives of nearly 2,000,000 prison workers, and much of the earth was moved with bare hands!" Well, I will no longer say that I really like the subway system in Moscow.

We visited one of the most famous Hindu temples of Shiva; many Hindus from India come there. It is just depressing. The marriage fee there is only 500 rupees, so many choose to get married in this temple; however, there are only six months of the year that a Hindu can get married. In the temple is the "teacher," or sadhu, an attainment sought by many for its privileges, such as breaking many laws without getting in trouble. For example, with the status of sadhu comes the right to smoke hashish. A sadhu will do the oddest things. At this temple one sadhu is taking money, placing the red dot on people's foreheads, and reading or reciting a little drivel. It is disappointing, but not surprising, that they have so little to say that makes any sense. This morning in the paper was a photo of a Krishna sadhu who for six years has stood on one foot with arms outstretched to Krishna in worship. The man has not moved in six years. We also visited the "holy" river; many sadhus are here, as are many monkeys. In reality, it is difficult to distinguish the wisdom of one from the other. The sadhus, though, have a variety of gimmicks to make them look distinct for the purpose of being sought out by others. One has his face painted completely orange, another has not cut his hair for years and has it piled up over one foot high, and yet another has been sitting in a meditative position for years. There are short sadhus and tall, filthy sadhus and filthier, plain sadhus and brightly colored painted ones. Deep down it is all so shallow, reflecting this ancient religion based in fear, which means that it is based in Satan. We ascend the steps to see more and then go toward the river, where there are many rock huts of the sadhus built into the cliff walls. Below we see the sadhus appearing to be drinking the "holy" river water, but actually, they are not; they pour it past their mouths, proving again that religion is filled with hypocrisy.

Once at the hotel, I ask the brothers to take a walk with me, for this ancient city seems like something out of the *Chronicles of Narnia* by C.S. Lewis. Just step around a corner, through a doorway, and one finds himself in another world of ancient temples, open wells, pools, statues, wooden buildings, and animals of every sort. Go down what at first appears to be a boring little alley and find the temple of Kali, the god of blood. See the posts placed in the ground where once each year the animals are tied and sacrificed. Observe the stone that sharpens the hidden and sacred sword. Take in the magnificent temple with a golden rope leading from the ground to the peak and representing the pathway to heaven, and look at the windows, which are always left open because a king that once ruled is returning on the wind! There are the Buddhist prayer wheels; a lengthy prayer is inscribed on each wheel, and every revolution of a spinning wheel thus is said to result in the offering of the whole prayer. Then down another winding wall is always something new and different to discover. It is magical, mystical, and a little edgy! The very next morning we must walk through another ancient town. The sun is only rising, but plenty is happening. Heads of oxen are lying in the street. The people of this town are known for butchering meat early and taking it to sell in the city. Dogs are barking and roosters crowing; women are bathing at the well while still wearing dresses fashioned of long pieces of cloth. The children are preparing for the school day while toddlers play on this rough stone road that leads to the chasm separating this town from the next. Leaving the town and walking along the path, I am stopped by children who ask in broken English, "You know where you go?" This is a polite question, for few people would be descending along this path on purpose; it leads directly to the leper colony. Through the dense fog, at times I can only see a few feet ahead, and then something colorful comes toward me and I hear, "Namastay!" I have a few pencils and small gifts that I give to the passing children, whose looks of shock are followed by big smiles of joy. They usually go running off, yelling something to someone ahead of them.

In the morning we are to drive west, a trip that will take all day, so we leave early in the morning in a rented van. The roads are opened for a day between strikes, and we can make our escape. The mountains at the lower elevation are all made of huge stones, each the size of a house and held together with soil. When it rains, landslides are inevitable, and one landslide can take out a whole village, not to mention the repeated eroding of the roadbed. Trips are not easy but are predictable: they will incessantly be stop-and-go affairs. The scenery makes up for it; every turn reveals a new wonderland. The poor are in the riverbeds breaking up stones the size of shoeboxes into gravel that will be sold. Once a worker's basket is filled, he balances it on his back and then ties a cloth band to the basket and around his forehead. The men have necks the size of tree stumps! All roads follow a river, and again, all roads are constantly being repaired.

We visited an ancient fort; the place was amazing. Inside was the entrance to a tunnel that ran 300 miles. It was built hundreds of years ago as an undetected means of moving troops and supplies between the Mogul kings. It is now closed off. The stairs and the tops of the fortress walls were all made in such a way that elephants could walk four-abreast on them. There was a courtyard where the commoner could make his case and a courtyard for the wealthy. This empire could not survive for three main reasons. There was the constant fight with the Hindus, there was the fight with the British, and the system of kingdoms working together was so complex that no son was trained to manage it all.

We stop for directions, turning this way and that through the jungle until we reach an ancient site. We must walk on an elevated path made from volcanic stone and filled with crushed seashells. We walk through the jungle for several minutes and emerge at the seacoast, where over fifty islands have been built of the stone from the quarry on the opposite end of the island. The ruins are similar in scope to the pyramids. It is staggering what can be done when the labor is free. The whole complex looks like it is built out of stone logs that have five sides, but the wall is always as deep as it is long. Some believe that the stones were cut and then put on wood and floated to this side of the island, though no one knows for certain. One very beautiful structure looks like a castle surrounded by a great wall; each of the corners rises like the bow of a ship. The tide is down so we can cross the lagoon to the entrance of the castle; our feeling seems akin to someone portrayed in an "Indiana Jones" movie. Our taxi driver believes that the stones were laid up by magic, because even many men would not be able to lift a single stone log, and the walls are up to twenty feet tall. There is a roof designed in such a way that all must bow to enter into the throne room . . . not a bad idea. The chief sat in the middle with an escape route through the back of the main hall. Outside the entrance is a stone that was used to crush the kava root hundreds of years earlier. The stones for crushing are there, and so is the indentation in the slab where the roots were laid and crushed. The lagoons are genius by design; the tide comes in over the walls, and when it recedes, it leaves behind the fish in the pools for easy picking. We are walking where men and women many hundreds of years ago walked. One cannot help but wonder how much blood was spilled for this forgotten kingdom.

Foiled

In a meeting I experienced a real oppression and was not able to communicate even simple words to the interpreter. I wanted to talk about who Jesus was, what He did, where He came from, and what it means that He is in us. I could never get a flow going because of the miscommunication. I finally just stopped and had everyone stand up. I tried again and again, but nothing seemed to work. I paused again and just moved into talking about Thinkers, Feelers, and Doers. The place came alive, and the interpreter understood everything. When the meeting was over he said to me, "You should have started with the personalities! Everyone got what you were saying. What you started out talking about, no one comprehended." I then explained that we were under attack, that what I had wanted to say about Jesus was the most important thing, and the only reason the people came alive is that personality information often only ministers to the flesh. I said, "We were attacked and defeated. Jesus is all that matters!" I explained that I did not have a ministry of explaining personalities; I only use it because it breaks up the seminars with something light, lets people laugh, and does help them in relationships. But our message is Jesus. I learned something today, and I trust I will be more aware in the future.

There were so many flight delays during a return from an international trip that I arrived in Miami about an hour after my flight for home took off. I could not be rebooked until the next day. Tam Airways, true to form, took excellent care of me, putting me up in the airport hotel and giving me meal vouchers. I really wanted to get home, but amen. I went to the restaurant with my meal voucher for fifteen dollars. I was looking forward to a nice meal, until I discovered that water was nearly $14.99! I sat there eating by myself, and three flight attendants came and sat across from me to drink and talk. I listened to their banter about being remarried to older men; they joked about the fact that they did not love their men at all but had hoped for some kind of security. One said that she hoped her current husband did not die before he got the will changed. It was odd and unpleasing to hear after spending time with Christians for the past month, and it was sad; their lives seemed so shallow and wasted. It renewed my desire to share Jesus with more and more unbelievers. Life on earth is the womb in which the believer is formed. The earth will either bring a person into full judgment or perfection. I just do not want to waste my life, and by saying that I do not mean that I want to do something spectacular with my life. Wasting my life would be going day by day not being perfected by everything that God, in His perfect love, has permitted. I want the revelation of Christ. I want to know the power of the resurrection, the fellowship of His sufferings, and to be like Him in his death. Anything else is a wasted life. The beautiful thing about having the proper goal is that it can be accomplished in any place, under any circumstances, in any job, and with any person.

One young fellow that interprets is really good. I teasingly told him to interpret to the crowd something that I had said about him, and he would not. I grabbed him and made him say it, and the people really laughed. Then while I was speaking I said something in Chinese, which just left him standing there with a blank face. We are having a great time.

I am back at the room and working on my computer. Wherever I am, I always let youngsters play with my computer. Once in Africa, my father said to me, "Do you know what you are doing letting others play with your computer?" Just after he said that, it locked up while children were playing with it, and it was not until the next week in Europe that I got it fixed. Here a young man wanted to look at my computer while I was talking to his sisters. I turned and asked what he was doing. "Making it faster!" It was then that my father's words echoed through my mind, until they were interrupted by the young man's outcry, "Oh, no!" The hard disk was wiped out, completely wiped out. All work was lost, including a trip report and three chapters of a book I was finishing.

The trip is typically long, eleven hours, but being exhausted works for me, and I do get a bit of sleep. When I arrive, I discover the approaching winter. For once, I am the first one off the plane, down the ramp, and through immigration. All I have to do is pick up the bag and be off for two weeks. Not so fast, Mike! Your bag has not arrived. After filling out the report, the fellow asks for my credit card number so it can be credited for $130, which

I can use to get some basic supplies until my bag arrives on tomorrow's plane (actually, they never got around to crediting my account). I woke up in the morning with one of my customary lung infections. Not a concern, for I know when the bag comes, I have antibiotics that should help. The bag never arrives! Amen, I have a sermon to prepare. The host pastor has given me a shirt and the only suit coat that he owns. He asks, "Do you want deodorant?" I just laughed and said, "Why would I need it? It is not my shirt!" It is another fitful night. Jesus, as He has done on so many occasions, will meet me in my illness. In the morning we arrive at the church founded by Andrew Murray, the devotional writer that has had the most impact in my life. I am very happy to be there. I sit down and then spill my notes everywhere. I never could seem to get them organized again, because I had just scratched them out the night before. It was like one of the nightmares of sitting in class with a term paper to present but having no clothes on. The problem here was that there was no waking up from this. Well, amen. Again, the Lord met me. The topics kind of got bounced around, and yet there was a consistency. The glue that held the sermon together was Jesus. I talk of revelation, the love of God, and this one thing that I appreciate more and more, the discovery that the weight of my relationship with Christ has always been on His shoulders. I may think I make time for prayer, but actually, He puts me in a situation where I need to talk to Him. I listen, because He made a date with me and put me in a place where I had to listen. I have only learned because He has taken the time to teach me. The weight of the whole relationship has always been and will always be on His shoulders. He has persuaded me, He has wooed me, and He will keep me. His life, His life, His life is the theme. It was one branch witnessing to another, for an old man held me with tears in his eyes, saying, "Thank you for that word." I am still down for the count with the illness, so I spend the afternoon resting, full of hope that my bag will arrive. No one from the airport calls. I call and am assured they will give a return call in twenty minutes. The call never comes. The problem is quite simple according to them: "We do not have the bag and no one in Amsterdam will answer us." Period. No recourse, just the same explanation and a promise to check and call in twenty minutes. It has been three days. I had to laugh when I was put on hold and transferred to another couple that was looking for their bags and on hold. I kept asking if this was baggage claim, and they kept telling me they were happy to be talking to baggage claim. It was good, laughable chaos, but still no bag for me or for them! Amen. I am sick and just want to return to bed. We are up very early the next day for a car trip. By afternoon I have to stop and do a bit of clothes shopping. I do not have a single thing, and we are in a bit of a rush to find the basics, which turn out to be pricey. We stop at the pharmacy to get some of the items. When the woman discovers that my bag has been stolen, she does everything within her power to help me. We go through a list of everything that would be needed, and she is right there helping and appearing to have fun. She is thinking of things I would not, and that is a blessing. After five days of phoning the airline, no return call about my luggage has been forthcoming. When finally I am back in the city into which I flew, I went to the airport. By now, everyone on staff at the airline has spoken with me and knows who I am, so each one quickly shuffles me off to the next person. Finally, I come to Mohammed, the one in charge; he hangs his head like a disappointed relative. "I did not call because I was too embarrassed. Someone from the ranks of our own employees has stolen your bag. I have never had this happen. They even erased its tracking information from the computers. If you did not have a baggage check tag there would be no proof that the bag existed. We will pay $400 to replace it." The bag alone cost $300, and I have spent years collecting the necessary travel accessories it held. Amen. Now I must change gears and believe, once again, what He has revealed to me about how He permits what could be prevented. He is ultimately in charge and in control. As soon as Mohammed said, "In ten years I have never seen anything like this," I yielded and broke. This thing has the thumbprint of God all over it. I may never know why, but God is in this, and I am ready to stop fighting it. Peace floods me, and I am finished with all of the effort. Time to find a suit for the Sunday service. We head over to the church basement where the giveaway bin is, and I am able to find a couple of articles of clothing.

It is late again when we leave the church. We arrive at the hotel past midnight and have yet to eat. I have to laugh in that each night we go to the hotel restaurant, the waiter comes running with menus, returns to take the order, and then tells us that the kitchen is closed. Go figure. We just laugh and really have a go at the fellow for leading us on.

Fellowship

We are off to a friend's house for a private churrascaria. When we arrive, the women go off to a room to talk, and the men head out to the room dedicated to cooking. The churrascaria is cooked by the men, with each one having his own little specialty; it is a time of real Christian male bonding. This fellow is an excellent cook and has a little of this and a little of that cooked up for us to try. We snack, tell stories, and laugh. It is something that I wish were done more in America, where once married, the fellows often do not spend much time together as men. Well, fair enough, it is likewise true that there are many men who need to have their priorities changed and spend more time at work or with their families, but generally speaking, we tend to miss the positive aspects of male bonding and fellowship. The Brazilian churrascaria reminds me of the Kava ceremonies in Fiji, which are important traditions in the lives of the men. Eventually we get around to cooking all the meat and preparing it for serving. Great fun. The whole family comes together for the final meal. I just sit there and thank God that He does give us houses, brothers, and more in this life. After dinner, the daughter of our host comes to me and says, "I know you are tired and you should lie down, but before you do, would you tell me something about Jesus?" Beautiful! I sat down with her and soon the room was full, and we talked about Jesus for nearly an hour. This group adamantly believes in the invisible Church that takes place not in a building, but together with people. Though none of them attend a church building, the hunger and thirst for God among them is deep. The father of this house is in the top tier of the business/academic world. He had to leave the next day for a court hearing in one of the major cities. He said, "I love my job, for tomorrow I will get to share Christ with someone whom others cannot reach." He does, and he did!

I recognize my new friend as a man of vision, love, and a true missionary heart. He loves and cares for the people, and he is willing to give his life to them. Beautiful. He speaks several languages and moved here some ten years ago, helped pioneer an accredited Bible school, and has four wonderful sons and a wife that never stops smiling. At dinner we were joined by several more missionaries and pastors who have traveled great distances to get here. One pastor has made me a map showing me the different churches that he visits. Some are two hundred fifty kilometers (150 miles) away, and he travels on bicycle. Amazing.

At 8:00 p.m. the barbecue was being prepared. I found the men sitting outside around the fire. Malaria is a real problem here, and so we have to keep on the repellent. We sit on rocks with blankets on them and tell stories. It is great fun. Though they prefer their own language, they are polite and speak in English. One tells an interesting story. Certain religious officials were aligned with the government and were unhindered in persecuting the Christians. One Christian had the gift of healing and was performing many healings in and around the mission station. The more the healings occurred, the more confident the man became in himself; instead of seeing the power of Jesus, he was shifting and seeing the power as in himself. One day the man actually killed a young girl by throwing her onto a fire. He had the people stand back; he was going to prove that he could raise the girl from the dead. In the end the girl remained dead. This event in the 1950's allowed the officials to make a major offensive and accuse the Church until it was expelled from the country. One of the host's sons told an interesting story of being in a meeting where everyone raised hands and spoke in gibberish. The whole thing made him uncomfortable, but he passed one boy who was crying out to God in the son's own language. He stopped the boy to speak to him, but the boy did not know the language. In the midst of all the confusion, he had found something genuine. Other stories of the weird and unnatural were also told, events and experiences that ended up being mere waves that took people from the shore of Jesus. Our barbequed meat is finished and it is tasty, really nice pieces of beef, chicken, and sausage. They have really taken care of us. Around the dinner table the conversation is lively. I want to revisit a theme you may remember my discussing before. If two men are thrown into prison, one has the Bible and the other does not, who will grow the most? Obviously, the apparent answer is the man with the Bible. Now, that presents a problem, for a lesser gives way to a greater. If God cannot move without the Bible, then the Bible is greater than Him. Also, there is the truth of the matter. How is it that our seminaries and pastorates are filled with people who have the same defeats as those in the congregation, and yet they are known to have a greater understanding of the Bible? What is the missing dynamic? These men I am with never react but take time to think, and all of us so enjoy the input and the conversation. There is another issue we discuss that is a difficult one. God is not a God of partiality; only wicked men show partiality. Therefore, it is hard to swallow, but some people are so strong in their flesh that it takes a war, it takes starvation, it takes sickness, or it takes fleeing to a refugee camp to get them to listen and yield to the message of Jesus. God does not show partiality in the things that matter to Him. He is working the perfect situation into each life to draw it to Himself. He has every hair of our head numbered. Dinner is over, and it has been a long but refreshing day.

We are ushered off to the pastor's house. On the way I stop at the toilet, a real surprise. A hole has been dug, clay and manure mounded up to make a bowl, and a seat placed on top of it. It works. At the house we are greeted with incredible warmth, offered soda pop, and given the best seats. The pastor tells us about his work, welcomes us, and then has his wife come out. She bows to each of us and is delighted that we are there. She has been cooking a meal consisting of rice, some chicken in red sauce, and vegetables. It is really quite nice, and we all enjoy it. The elders wait for us to eat, because we are the guests. The pastor asks for nothing except this: "When you think of us, pray for us!"

I am supposed to be resting at the lake, but my tickets were changed the last two weeks before the trip so that I lost the opportunity to go. Therefore, I am in a hot little room waiting to leave. However, "Jesus, like a shepherd, lead me." He knows the reason that the tickets got changed, that I cannot go to the lake, and that I am waiting here. The Lord has brought a pastor that I met last night; I was able to explain the ministry of ALMI and its focus on Jesus. God touched his heart, and he is so excited about it, not with the enthusiasm that comes from potential gain (I have seen

519

that so often, and it is easily recognized), but exhilaration in his spirit. I explain unbelieving believers, marriage, and the need for a focus on Jesus. "This is what we need; this is what we are looking for," he says. "Please, Brother, come again. I have 140 pastors under me. We will organize everything. Just come!" It was a wonderful meeting that continued on as we drove to the airport. I laid down several principles, and though some were difficult, he could see them all. He could see that God used suffering, Satan, and our failures. He could see that apart from Jesus, we could do nothing. We had an instant oneness. Beautiful. I felt as though I had known the man for many years. It was just great. I got out at the airport praising the great Shepherd for leading.

In the morning a lawyer drives by to pick us up. I cannot believe that he has come or is willing to take the time off. The poor fellow works incredibly long hours, and I see firsthand, as I have all over the world, people ministering for the sake of the Jesus in me. It is done for Jesus, and I am riding on His coattails. Christians are as hard to come by as hen's teeth in this country. There are around 25 churches; the largest has about 1,200 members, but the others are considerably smaller. As is the case in many places where Christians represent only a minority of the general population, believers tend to move past doctrinal differences to form loose alliances. The young people have the difficulty of finding a believer to date.

Well, back to the van for another trip. However, when I climb in, there is something different; the driver that has been indifferent to me for days wants to talk about the message all the way home. This morning I handed him a pocket tool, which he genuinely seemed to like. I did not know that he had snuck into the meetings and listened to them all. The Lord had touched him, and I could see we had gone from stranger and preacher to fellowship and friends. Wonderful!

At the conference break, I see the elderly women of the ministry to the poor and disenfranchised. What a beautiful group; it is great fun to see them again. One has flowers for me; she is so soft because every hard edge she might have ever had was knocked off by years in Siberia. We have a good laugh when we see each other. I walk away and a word keeps coming into my mind, but I do not even know what language it is in. I ask my coworker if there is such a word in his language. He immediately responds, "It means tasty." I laugh again, because I associate the elderly woman with the delicious food that she always cooked for us, and the word came back into my mind upon seeing her. What a family God has given us!

Our pastor host wants to take us to a new restaurant. When we arrive, the "doormen" ask for our coats. This frustrates the pastor, and he wants to leave, but another coworker and I see its purpose is that the restaurant is having some trouble with the Mafia, and these are not normal "doormen"; they do not want anyone coming in there with a concealed weapon. I am happy with that, and the pastor reconciles himself to it and goes on in with us. We sit and talk about different aspects of Jesus and the false guilt with which so many in ministry live, where one is never meeting his own expectations. From my own experience, I know that if I finish writing one book, there is little joy, because I reflect on the ten I have left undone. If I talk all day on the phone, I stare at the stack of messages to which I did not reply. I can finish fifty e-mails only to discover that another one hundred and fifty are poised at the threshold. I joke with the pastor, "Have you heard of Michael's wine?" He says, "No," and in a whining voice I start saying, "I have too much to do; I never get things completed! I am too tired. Someone does not like me." I explained it was Michael's whine, not wine! This pastor, like many in ministry, enjoys being with those who have a similar workload. His questions are heartfelt, and there is not a contentious bone in his body. He genuinely wants to know.

The Life, Times, and Ministry of Abiding Life Ministries International

I always like sharing the structure that Abiding Life Ministries International uses to expand, because often we are invited to benefit from the services of a believer. I like to use the picture of the vine. Initially a branch may need some support and becomes attached to another branch, albeit both receive sustenance through the vine. The ministry of ALMI works to support the like calling and ministry of others, to see men or women come into their own call, own organization, own ministry, and their own expression of Christ in them as they abide in Christ. The nature and intent of this support is to enable them to make the shift from reliance on ALMI to be attached directly to the Vine. In such an approach no one branch becomes too big and bears the burdens of the other branches. No branch becomes a kingdom but recognizes the Kingdom of Jesus that already exists. Each ministry will be supported through Him and not through ALMI. Each person will live out of the Lord's resources and not the resources of ALMI. It allows the founder of the ministry to be free to minister and not raise funds to support a huge organization. It keeps all of us focused on Jesus. The

523

purpose of ALMI is not to promote ALMI but to promote Jesus and others' unique expression of Him. This is how we expand. There are practical matters to which to attend, but each ministry, though we work WITH each other, must operate in the unique manner in which God leads. In the end, ALMI is not responsible for the success of a ministry or its failure. Each man or woman stands before God. This is the approach that God has given me, and it is effective. It is initially hard for some to grasp, because it is outside the box of usual kingdom building. First, we want to minister. Then, as we minister, we recognize those with a like call. We support them with training and materials. However, the day comes when they must move out on their own and into their call of God. A call will keep someone when nothing else will.

One day I was sitting in a Bible school as a famous old man was lecturing. He was allotted one hour to talk but spoke for two-and-a-half hours, and the meeting was as dead as Washington. I watched as the students fell numb and vacant, until the moment they could finally rush out of the building. Yet later, I observed a young professor relating the same old man's principles in a manner that was timely and fresh, and the students were wild with excitement. I thought how one day I would be that old man, and therefore, I needed to give this message to as many in the following generations as I could, so they would keep the message freshened up. I have tried to do that, and it has proven to be a difficult task. I do not want people to imitate but to participate in Him and the message He gives, then rework it in a way that makes it become theirs. They may use some of the same illustrations or terms that I use, but those now belong to them through revelation. A man once came to me after a seminar to tell me, "You said a couple of things that an old man I know also says. Do you know him, and if so, why do you not give him the credit?" I said, "Oh, yes! I know him, and he has had an impact in my life. I do not remember what I said that he previously told me, but I will give you his phone number and you can call him. Tell him that Mike Wells said something he says and did not give him the credit. Then come back to me with his response." The man most certainly did know my old friend, for he refused the offer to make the call. The old man would have chewed him out, for he takes the same position that if something ministers to a person, it is because the Holy Spirit is moving. We know there is no spiritual power in the mere words of any man. Therefore, if we boast, we must boast in the Lord. Everyone has a unique expression of the truth that must be processed through his particular filter and then expounded.

I have seen many, many people move out into a ministry with their unique expression, and ALMI can take no credit for what they are doing. The bravest man I personally know has been given by God the privilege of witnessing the work the Lord is doing in others. I say the man is brave because when he witnesses to the work God is doing in people's lives, this fellow takes the credit and glory for it. It is sad that the man cannot see God's hand in others' lives before, during, or after he met them. Everyone, he claims, owes him because he did the work. I fear for such a one. Well, amen, we can all watch and learn. His ministry is much greater than even he thinks it is, for God is using him to show others what not to do.

Other books by Michael Wells are available through Abiding Life Press

Abiding Life Ministries International
www.abidinglife.com
P.O. Box 620998
Littleton, CO 80162-0998

Find samples of Michael Wells' teaching at
www.mikewellsdownload.com

Sidetracked in the Wilderness
First printed 1991
Find the way back to a victorious, abundant life.

Problems, God's Presence, & Prayer
First printed 1993
Experience the joy of a closer walk with God.

The Gardener's Love
First printed 1997
Illustrated by Karen Malzeke-McDonald
Storybook of our position on the Vine

Abiding Stories
First printed 2005
Illustrated by Bob Fuller
Collection of stories from around the world

Heavenly Discipleship
First printed 2006
Witnessing to the indwelling fullness of Christ
in every believer